Re-Visioning Romantic

Re-Visioning Romanticism

British Women Writers, 1776–1837

edited by Carol Shiner Wilson and Joel Haefner

University of Pennsylvania Press

Philadelphia

Jerome McGann's essay in this volume, "Literary History, Romanticism, and Felicia Hemans," appeared in an earlier form in *Modern Language Quarterly* 54, 2 (June 1993), 215–35. It is reprinted here with the permission of the University of Washington.

Portraits of Charlotte Smith, Mary Robinson, Anna Barbauld, and Felicia Hemans, from frontispieces of books in the Carl H. Pforzheimer Collection of Shelley & His Circle, New York Public Library, Astor, Lenox, and Tilden Foundations, are reproduced by permission.

Copyright © 1994 by the University of Pennsylvania Press
Printed in the United States of America

Library of Congress Cataloging-in-Publication Data

Re-visioning romanticism : British women writers, 1776–1837 / edited by Carol Shiner Wilson and Joel Haefner.
    p.   cm.
    Includes bibliographical references (p.) and index.
    ISBN 0-8122-1421-8
    1. English literature — Women authors — History and criticism.   2. English literature — 19th century — History and criticism.   3. English literature — 18th century — History and criticism.   4. Women and literature — Great Britain — History.   5. Romanticism — Great Britain.   I. Wilson, Carol Shiner, 1946–   .   II. Haefner, Joel.
PR457.R4556   1994
820.9'9287'09034 — dc20   94-27188
                                                            CIP

Cover: George Romney (1743–1802), *Lady Seated at a Table*. Pen, brush, and sepia. Metropolitan Museum of Art, Rogers Fund, 1911 (11.66.3a). Reproduced by permission.

For Daniel J. Wilson
For Cynthia, Alyssa, and Leigh Huff

For in thy heart there is a holy spot . . .
   — Felicia Hemans, "The Image in the Heart"

Contents

viii   Contents

Illustrations

Acknowledgments

Any text is a collaboration in the broadest sense, a patchwork of vision and voices. This collection is no exception. In fact, given our objective — to suggest ways in which women's texts force us to rethink British Romanticism — this collection had to be a collage of viewpoints. Hence we owe thanks to many people who have contributed in different but always significant ways to this volume.

Stuart Curran has been the guiding spirit of this collection. In 1990, he directed the NEH Summer Seminar on Women and Men Poets in British Romanticism, during which the plan for this book was hatched. Stuart encouraged our efforts, gave us invaluable advice about negotiating the waters of publishing and editing, wrote recommendations for grants and jobs, buoyed us up when we were discouraged, served as a keen reader, and contributed an important article. This collection would not exist without his mentorship.

The members of that 1990 seminar also played an important role in this book through their spirited seminar discussions, suggestions and sincere interest in the project, good will, and, in two instances, fine essays.

Susan Wolfson, a contributor to this volume, also served as a mentor and counselor for this collection and for the editors. We appreciate her guidance and support. We also wish to thank Mary Lynn Johnson at the University of Iowa, Stephen Behrendt at the University of Nebraska, and John Shields at Illinois State University for serving as readers for several of the contributions. June Schlueter, Lafayette College, assisted us as essay reader and, early on, advisor on building a collection of essays. We also appreciate the enthusiasm and contribution made by Julie Shaffer, an expert on the Corvey collection of works by women and a fellow traveler.

In addition to supporting the 1990 Summer Seminar, the National Endowment for the Humanities awarded a Summer Study Grant to Joel, which broadened his reading in the field and contributed extensively to his piece and editing tasks. We should mention as well the superb work done by the Women Writers Project at Brown University, without which the broad Romantic recovery project now underway would be impossible.

We would also like to thank colleagues at our institutions. Reference and Interlibrary Loan librarians Richard Everett and Betsey Moore at Lafayette College, Scherelene Schatz at Muhlenberg College, and Carol Ruyle and Sharon Wetzel at Illinois State University worked tirelessly to locate and obtain hard-to-get materials.

At Muhlenberg College, Tom Cartelli, Head of the English Department, and Nelvin Vos, Dean of the College and former Head of the English Department, lent their encouragement to Carol in this project. She also values the moral support of friends and colleagues at Lafayette College and Muhlenberg College. Special thanks are due her Feminist Research Group for their helpful critiques, encouragement, and friendship in this endeavor and others over the years. Susan Basow and Lynn Van Dyke, members of the Feminist Research Group and Coordinators of Women's Studies at Lafayette, merit particular thanks as does Galen Godbey, Executive Director of the Lehigh Valley Association of Independent Colleges. Carol also appreciates the support of family members Larry Shiner, Kay Klausmeier, Richard Klausmeier, and friend for over twenty years, Louise Kempka.

Joel would like to acknowledge the encouragement rendered by Charles Harris and Ron Fortune, past and present chairs of the English Department at Illinois State, and its Professional Growth Committee, as well as other colleagues at that campus. Shawn Staley, a student at Illinois State University, performed important bibliographic and biographic services during an Honors research project as a senior English major.

Jerome Singerman, Acquisitions Editor, has been an encouraging guide at the University of Pennsylvania Press. We also thank editors Ridley Hammer and Alison Anderson, who worked patiently with us through the production stage at the Press. Ethel Symolon at the Yale Center for British Art, Stephen Wagner and Lisa Browar at the New York Public Library, and Mary Doherty at the Metropolitan Museum of Art have been especially helpful in locating appropriate artwork for this volume.

Finally, we would like to thank our families, who have tripped over stacks of books and boxes of typescripts, listened to the whine of printers, and waited patiently through long evening telephone conversations. To Cynthia, Alyssa, and Leigh Huff, and to Daniel J. Wilson, our deepest appreciation and love.

Carol Shiner Wilson and Joel Haefner

Introduction

> Re-vision—the act of looking back, of seeing with fresh eyes, of enter-
> ing an old text from a new critical direction—is for us more than a
> chapter in cultural history: it is an act of survival.
> —Adrienne Rich, "When We Dead Awaken: Writing as Re-Vision"

When we hold the mirror up to current Romantic studies, what is reflected
there? Some might see a traditional, canonical Romanticism; others, a poststructuralist corpus; others, a confused collage of splintered images. What
we see, and what this volume addresses, is a dynamic vision of Romanticism, one that is shaped by the recovery of long-neglected women writers.
"Feminist and cultural materialist criticisms," writes David Simpson in a
recent article, "with their attentions to hitherto ignored or excluded components of literature, . . . are proving as formative of a new 'Romanticism' as
they are of other objects of study" ("Romanticism, Criticism, and Theory"
19). This collection of essays, then, is a radical re-vision, in Adrienne Rich's
sense, not only of the Romantic period, but also of what we call canonical
literature, how we view the artistic process, who and what the artist is. We
do not claim to have the only accurate reflection of Romantic literature. But
we do believe that this volume will help us understand the images already
present and see others that have long been veiled.

Romanticism has always been a tantalizingly slippery term, open to
interpretation, reinterpretation, and debate by scholars and critics. Typically, critical perspectives reflect the concerns of the specific historical times
out of which they grow. Meyer Abrams, for example, in years of crisis and
promise after World War II, felt compelled to rescue the English Romantic
poets from New Critical accusations of intellectual flabbiness, and to argue
that they internalized and transformed the crises of the French Revolution
into high art. Today, with society and the academy more aware of the
historical exclusion of women and minorities from the dominant discourse,
scholars are reexamining the late eighteenth and early nineteenth centuries
to find what is missing from traditional literary histories: modes of literary

production and consumption, the role of radical dissent, diversity of genres, women writers and their works.

We may roughly identify the twentieth-century chronology of interpretive paradigms as New Critical, mythological, poststructuralist, and, most recently, new historicist, cultural, and feminist. Each critical perspective has been elastic and dynamic, constantly interacting with previous perspectives and containing within it the makings of the next paradigm. Yet, until new historicist, cultural, and feminist perspectives, the dominant voices to study have been four, then five, then six male poets: Wordsworth, Coleridge, Shelley, and Keats, with Byron and Blake eventually admitted to the canonical club. Blake, in fact, appears in only the most recent edition (4th, 1985) of Jordan's authoritative MLA research guide, *The English Romantic Poets*. Appearing the same year, J. R. Watson's survey of English Romantic poetry for Longman included a discussion of Blake on over forty pages, as much space as devoted to the other canonical males, with a mention of Anna Barbauld on one and no mention at all of Mary Robinson, Charlotte Smith, Felicia Hemans, or Jane Taylor. Critical assumptions about what is high Romantic art have long privileged poetry over fiction. We are hard pressed to think of a novel as Romantic literature, and most discussions of the novels of Jane Austen, which appeared the same years as poems by Shelley, Coleridge, and Byron, ignore that she, like the male poets, inhabited a world of martial conflict and political repression.

The six canonical male poets are included in almost any anthology of British literature designed for undergraduate teachers: the *Norton Anthology of English Literature* includes roughly a hundred pages on each of these six writers, but (except for Burns) no other poet gets more than four pages, and no women poets are included at all. These are the six poets who dominate our critical discussions. Between 1981 and 1992, the MLA Bibliography records 951 books and articles published on William Wordsworth, 610 on Coleridge, 427 on Percy Shelley; 410 on Byron, and 387 on Keats. The tally for women related to well-known male writers drops significantly: Dorothy Wordsworth, 32 articles and books; Mary Shelley, 126; Elizabeth Barrett Browning, 101. And, finally, women poets who stood on their own during the Romantic period tallied single-digit totals: Anna Laetitia Barbauld, 4; Charlotte Smith, 8; Hannah More, 9; Mary Robinson, 3; Letitia Landon, 3; and, most incredible of all, Felicia Hemans, zero. And most of these few articles, such as those on Mary Robinson, discuss the women writers only in relation to male writers, not on their own merit. New historicist, cultural, and feminist scholarship, with a different set of questions, concerns, and areas of study, although indebted to New Critical, mythological, and poststructuralist perspectives, can never look at a survey like Longman's, an anthology like David Perkins's *English Romantic Writers* (1967), a collection of essays like Kenneth Johnston's and Gene Ruoff's *The Age of Wordsworth* (1987), or even our own syllabi of a decade ago in the same innocent way.

Although Arthur O. Lovejoy did not include women writers in his influential essay, "On the Discrimination of Romanticisms" (1924), his argument was an early one that anticipated the inclusion of women's literary productions. The historian of ideas argued that "differing versions of the age and lineage of Romanticism are matched by a corresponding diversity in the descriptions offered by those of our time who have given special care to the observation of it" (228). By meaning so many things, he continued, the word "romantic" by itself meant virtually nothing; only "Romanticisms" could assist us in discussing works, times, and authors intelligently (235). Susan Hardy Aiken, writing in 1986, recognized a similar multiplicity of contexts, urging that the male canonical tradition be in "ongoing dialogue — or, more accurately, polylogue" with the emerging female tradition ("Women and the Question of Canonicity" 298).

From the 1920s to 1950s, Anglo-American critics like Irving Babbitt, T. S. Eliot, Cleanth Brooks, I. A. Richards, and T. E. Hulme considered English Romantic poetry confused, excessive, and self-absorbed. New Critic Cleanth Brooks, in *Modern Poetry and the Tradition* (1939), charged the Romantics with being, in essence, unmanly, with a lack of irony and wit, a suspicion of the intellect, sloppy imagery, and a lack of verve. By the 1970s, when the New Critics seemed tiresomely monolithic, the very Romanticism they condemned was valued as anticipating modern sensibility.

René Wellek, writing in 1949, rebutted Lovejoy, claiming to find a "unity of theories, philosophies, and style" in Romanticism across national borders ("The Concept of Romanticism" 129). Finding the English Romantics consistent with the French and German, Wellek identified three shared criteria: "imagination for the view of poetry, nature for the view of the world, and symbol and myth for poetic style" (161). The only woman writer he considered was Mme de Staël, whom he found important for her "intermediary role" in bringing the romantic theories of Schlegel to readers through her *De l'Allemagne* (138–39). Wellek's scheme excluded Byron. Morse Peckham, in a 1951 essay in *PMLA,* sought "to reconcile Lovejoy and Wellek, and Lovejoy with himself" through what he called a "dynamic organicism," whose values included change, growth, imperfection, diversity, and the creative imagination ("Toward a Theory of Romanticism" 235, 241). Wellek was distressed to see Byron newly accommodated under the rubric "negative romanticism" ("Romanticism Re-examined" 199–221). Although grappling with the complexity of voices in Romanticism(s), none of these male critics looked at the works of Charlotte Smith, Mary Robinson, or Jane Taylor to extract or test questions of the centrality of the imagination, dynamic organicism, negative romanticism, or irony.

Abrams, in his impressive *The Mirror and the Lamp* (1953) and *Natural Supernaturalism* (1971), argued that Romantic poetry and poetics are expressive rather than mimetic, a dramatic break from the eighteenth-century tradition of Pope or Johnson. In *Natural Supernaturalism,* strongly echoing Wordsworth and Shelley, Abrams claimed that true poets are philosophical. That philosophical role is, implicitly, public and male. Romantic writers, he argued, sought to secularize significant themes and values of Christianity in a post-Enlightenment age. Harold Bloom's *The Visionary Company* (1961; rpt. 1971) argued for the brilliance of Blake's secularized Christianity. Discussions of religion in Abrams, Bloom, and others overlooked the dissenting tradition of Anna Barbauld, Lucy Aikin, or Hannah More.

In the 1970s and early 1980s, critics including Paul de Man, Geoffrey Hartman, Anne K. Mellor, Tilottama Rajan, David Simpson, and Jerome J. McGann identified indeterminacy, or Romantic irony, as fundamental to Romantic poetry, reflecting a world that is dynamic, open-ended, fraught with dangers and possibilities.[1] Within this context, Michael G. Cooke, in *Acts of Inclusion* (1979), claimed that Romanticism, resisting the male-vs-female orthodoxy, attempts the "interpenetration and interpresence" of the masculine and feminine (xix). The title of a pivotal chapter in his book is "The Feminine as the Crux of Value."

In *The Romantic Ideology* (1983), a touchstone of new historicist writing, McGann argued that theories of Romanticism have been constructed by critics who, seduced by "Romanticism's own self-representations," have become "priests and clerics" perpetuating rather than analyzing the absorbed premises of Romantic art (1). In this framework, the Romantic poet manifests the self-fictions of the canonical six: disillusioned by political, social, and religious upheavals; apart from society because of his disillusionment and poetic genius; visionary; and, although never explicitly stated, male. Although McGann does not discuss women writers, Paul Cantor has rightly argued that, once "the Romantic idea of the artistic genius is discredited, we are free to reevaluate all the so-called lesser figures of the early nineteenth century, especially long-neglected female authors, often stigmatized as mere popular authors . . . and thus forced to live in the shadow of the so-called High Romantics" ("Stoning the Romance" 715).

The paradigm is shifting yet again. Virtually no scholarly publication in the 1990s dealing in a serious way with British Romanticism can ignore the contributions of women writers, and virtually no survey of British Romanticism can leave out Charlotte Smith, Mary Robinson, or Joanna Baillie as part of the literary and cultural conversation. The major impetus for restoring and examining women's writing has come from feminist studies. Scholars like Sandra Gilbert and Susan Gubar, Mary Poovey, Margaret Homans, Mary Jacobus, Susan Wolfson, Anne K. Mellor, Susan Levin, Jane Aaron, and others have written about authors, including Mary Shelley, Dorothy Wordsworth, and Mary Lamb, who have been marginally canonized primarily because of their association with husband or brother.[2] Some scholars pursue new examinations of the fictions of Jane Austen or Maria Edgeworth. Others, like Mitzi Myers, explore previously devalued works, such as the children's stories of Maria Edgeworth, for literary, cultural, and ideological significance.

A whole corpus of ignored work remains to be mapped. Curran, Wolfson, Ross, Ellison, and others in this collection are examining the literary works of women who were celebrated in their own time but whose works are virtually unknown to modern readers and who might be, at best, relegated to a dismissive footnote in Perkins, as is Felicia Hemans. Curran, in "Romantic Poetry: The 'I' Altered," his remarkable essay in Mellor's *Romanticism and Feminism* (1988), examines the publishing landscape of the 1790s and 1830s to find women writing outstanding poetry, dominating as well the world of prose fiction, essay, and theatre. Curran asks us, rightly so, to rethink, in light of the women's literary works, our assumptions about gender and genre, the gendered meaning of visionary, the value of the quotidian, romantic sensibility, and Romantic irony (186–98). He pursues these lines of thinking in his essays, "Women Readers, Women Writers" and "Romantic Poetry: Why and Wherefore?" in the *Cambridge Companion to British Romanticism* (1993). The table of contents and chronology reveal women and their literary production as a vital dimension of the Romantic conversation.

Marlon Ross, in his *Contours of Masculine Desire* (1989), scrutinizes the socio-historical context of the period to craft the nature of conversation and influence in writers that include the canonical Wordsworth, Coleridge, Keats, and Shelley, and women poets, famous in their time: Barbauld,

More, Hemans, Landon, Lady Mary Wortley, Montagu, Mary Tighe. Ross argues that the Romantics' "anxiety of influence" was in truth the male poets' anxiety about the new flood of women's voices on the literary scene. In her *Romanticism and Gender* (1993), Anne K. Mellor examines what she terms "masculine romanticism" and "feminine romanticism" (209), the latter based on a fluid and responsive subjectivity grounded in the theories of Hélène Cixous.[3]

Texts by women writers from the Romantic period are now making small inroads into the standard undergraduate Romanticism class, but the underrepresentation of women writers persists. Harriet Kramer Linkin's recent survey ("The Current Canon") of Romanticism syllabi indicates that, while the Big Six are still taught in over 90 percent of courses, there are some inroads by women writers. Mary Shelley is taught in 56 percent of the courses, Dorothy Wordsworth in 49 percent. As Linkin points out, Mary Shelley and Dorothy Wordsworth are "safe" additions because of their connection with already canonized figures. Maria Edgeworth, Anna Barbauld, Felicia Hemans, and Charlotte Brontë are read in only 4 percent of the courses; Jane Taylor, Anna Seward, Mary Hays, and Mary Robinson at least have been taught in a few courses. These are small numbers. But the fact that these women are being read at all is a sign of hope.

For many teachers, the sticking point for including women writers is often the availability of texts. There are two major anthologies on the market, David Perkins's hardbound volume and the paperback anthology edited by Harold Bloom and Lionel Trilling. Both are dated, and both include very few women. Fortunately a number of recovery projects are underway. Oxford has published an anthology of eighteenth-century women's poetry, edited by Roger Lonsdale. Everyman has published a slim paperback, edited by Jennifer Breen, devoted to women poets, 1785–1832. Garland and AMS are both reprinting some volumes; Pandora is issuing a Mothers of the Novel series. Moreover, the Women Writers Project at Brown University is putting on-line many texts by women published before 1830, and an Internet archive that will include women's and men's poetry published between 1790 and 1900 is being mounted at the University of Virginia. Several proposed anthologies focusing on or including women writers are expected to appear within two years of the publication of this collection. Perkins will add the poetry of several women to his text; Anne K. Mellor and Richard Matlack are preparing a complementary text of women's writing, including novellas and letters, from a new historicist perspective. Oxford University Press has recently committed itself to publishing six texts by women Romantic writers, based on the Women Writers Project. *The Poems of Charlotte Smith* (1993), the first in the Oxford series, was edited by Stuart Curran. Anthologies are currently available that provide resources and models for restructuring Romanticism: *The Meridian Anthology of Early Women Writers,* edited by Katharine M. Rogers and William McCarthy; *The Female Spectator,* edited by Mary R. Mahl and Helene Koon; *The Other Eighteenth Century,* edited by Robert W. Uphaus and Gretchen M. Foster; and *British Romantic Poetry by Women,* edited by Paula Feldman.[4]

Taking into consideration the claims and counterclaims about Romanticism and Romantic writers since the publication of Lovejoy's essay, we find ourselves engaged in an enterprise that not only includes a discussion of women's voices unheard in the critical discourse but fundamentally challenges us to rethink—indeed to *re-vision*—Romanticism. While the contours of this emerging perspective on Romanticism are open to interpretation and are dynamic, we find several recurring issues in this new project.

Since the publication of Jerome McGann's *Romantic Ideology* in 1983, it has become increasingly difficult to conceive of Romantic studies as static, as a settled field, as progressing steadily toward some final truth. In fact, we are now very aware that Romantic studies (like literature itself) is historically conditioned. Many Romanticists may not agree with McGann's view that critics have adopted the "self-representations" of the Romantic writers, that a Romantic ideology has been assimilated by generations of scholars. But McGann's argument, in conjunction with the rhetorical/textual analyses of Hayden White and others, have made it clear that we have fictionalized the history of Romantic criticism. Even the narrative we have provided here—with its underlying strategies of dominance/repression and "periods" of Romantic studies—is a reconstruction and fictionalization of the instabilities of critical viewpoints on Romanticism. The once-certain boundaries of our field of study—1798 to 1832—now blur, expand, become problematic.

McGann's emphasis on the self-representations of the Romantic writers themselves and the subsequent adoption of those self-representations by critics, coupled with recent feminist psychological theory, has led to radical challenges to and reinventions of the idea of the Romantic self. Informed by the feminist psychology of Nancy Chodorow and Carol Gilligan, both Anne Mellor and Susan Levin have posited a Romantic self, constructed by women writers, which is, in Levin's words, "an equipoise of self and the phenomenal world that challenges the inwardness projected on to the world and the notion of assertive self advanced by so many male writers of the romantic world" ("Romantic Prose and Feminine Romanticism" 183). We have not really seen, in Romantic studies, the impact of class and race on questions of subjectivity; but once we admit new definitions of how the self is constructed in Romantic texts, questions of narration, perception, aesthetics, and poetic form are suddenly changed. And, at the same time, the Shelleyan notion of the poet as the unacknowledged legislator or Wordsworth's self-endorsement as a Prophet of Nature must be read as one alternative vision of the role of the poet among many.

Along with revisions in our ideas of the Romantic self and the Romantic writer, we must now reinvestigate our conceptions of who read "Romantic" texts during the Georgian period and how we are to read Romantic texts today. When critics question the delineation of the growth of a poet's mind and the quest for the mythopoetic codes of the High Romantics, our strategies for reading Romantic texts — and those of our students — change drastically. In her important critique of the New Historicist Romanticists, principally McGann, Susan Wolfson notes that New Criticism advocated a radically new kind of reading that parallels, in mirror image, the project of McGann and others. "In the interests of locating and critiquing the text in a certain ideological constellation," Wolfson writes, "these readers tend to neglect textual nuance, ambiguity of import, and ambivalence of tone" ("Questioning" 430–31). In contrast, Jon Klancher argues in "English Romanticism and Cultural Production" that the reading of Romantic texts and the meaning of Romanticism "is inseparable from its institutional history and thus its cultural emplotments" (83). Implicit in Klancher's article, and generally in the New Historicist and feminist rereading of Romantic texts, is that the actual reception of Romantic texts, as well as our later critical evaluation of them, is open for examination. What are we to do, after all, with the fact that Charlotte Smith's *Elegiac Stanzas* went through numerous editions? Whatever perspective one takes, the problem of how we are to read is just as crucial as which texts we choose to read and teach.

This juxtaposition of Wolfson's and Klancher's essays suggests a fourth issue now dominating Romantic studies. How necessary is contextualization, what are the dangers and virtues of broadening our focus from the text itself? Lest it seem that the question of cultural contextualization grew only out of New Historicist readings, it is important to remember that contextualization has always been at the center of feminist literary study, and that feminist critics in eighteenth-century and Victorian literature have been engaged in such cultural reconstruction for many years now. The work of Janet Todd, Dale Spender, Katharine Rogers, and others comes to mind. Reflecting these two directions — feminist contextualization and the examination of cultural production — Stephen Copley and John Whale, the editors of the recent collection *Beyond Romanticism,* argue that there are two "oppositional strands" in recent Romantic studies, one (represented by Marilyn Butler) scholarly and pragmatic, and a second (represented by E. P. Thompson and Raymond Williams) with "explicitly political ends" (2). The debate over the exigency of contextualization, and its cultural/political direction, now dominates critical thinking.

As contextualization unearths more texts, especially those by women, that have been ignored by modern readers, as contextualization shifts our attention away from lyrical expression of the poetic self, the assumptions which have governed the form and content of Romantic poetry and other genres becomes shaky. Is our privileging of the lyric, for example, or the long blank verse epic, really accurate for the era? Does our neglect of Romantic drama or hymns reflect the popularity of these forms during our period? Curran points out in "The 'I' Altered" that "some of the genres we associate most closely with British Romanticism, notably the revival of the sonnet and the creation of the metrical tale, were themselves strongly impelled by women poets," and that "quotidian values," the stuff of much women's poetry, "has been largely submerged in our comprehension of Romanticism" (189). Questions of genre and content, as much as questions of gender and culture, are in the air.

Behind all these issues — contextualization, new strategies of reading, new constructions of aesthetics, new narratives of critical histories and the canon — lies the conundrum of binarism. Poststructuralism, of course, highlighted the cultural/theoretical imperative of dichotomous thinking, but Romanticists are now experiencing this dilemma in critical writing, in reading, in the classroom. Did a counter tradition, largely female, thrive in opposition to the canonized male tradition? Are we now at the stage of institutionalizing a new paradigm for Romantic studies in the way that Thomas Kuhn outlines in *The Structure of Scientific Revolutions*? Is text-based reading giving way to context-based reading? Our discussions seem often to veer towards the dichotomous, our own version of what Mary Poovey calls "binary logic" during the Victorian period. Yet even as such oppositions are delineated, the articulation of those oppositions unfolds. In her influential article "Treason Our Text," Lillian Robinson cautions that "while not abandoning our newfound female tradition, we have to return to confrontation with 'the' canon, examining it as a source of ideas, themes, motifs, and myths about the two sexes" (118). The essays in this volume engage just such an articulation, even as they explore a new world of women's texts from the Romantic era, a "terra incognita," as Stuart Curran writes, "beneath our very feet."

Given the issues we see catalyzing current Romantic studies, we have divided the essays here into three categories: "Reading Women's Texts" (essays by Stuart Curran, Linda H. Peterson, Susan Allen Ford, and Katharine M. Rogers); "Gender and the Cultural Matrix" (Marlon B. Ross, Jane Aaron, Susan J. Wolfson, and Carol Shiner Wilson); and "Re-Visioning Romantic Aesthetics" (Judith Pascoe, Jerome J. McGann, Julie Ellison, Joel Haefner, and Catherine B. Burroughs). We have chosen somewhat arbitrary cultural dates for our period, stretching from the American Revolution to Victoria's coronation, because we wanted to encompass the Bluestocking tradition as well as the later phenomenon of the Poetess and the writers who fall between; our expansion of the conventional dates for the Romantic period purposefully challenges the androcentric limits of the traditional era, questions setting period limits based on literary rather than cultural events, and finally, we hope, provokes a reexamination of the primacy of periodization.

The essays in "Reading Women's Texts" contextualize specific literary productions within conversations about power, authority and female authorship. Stuart Curran argues that Mary Robinson's *Lyrical Tales,* conscious of Wordsworth's *Lyrical Ballads* and Southey's "English Eclogues," goes beyond the male competitors in range of tone and exposure of social injustice. Linda H. Peterson examines the role of genius and domesticity in Robinson's *Memoirs,* a pivotal work in the tradition of autobiography and the female artist. Susan Allen Ford relates the father-daughter incest motif in novels by Robinson, Elizabeth Inchbald, and Mary Wollstonecraft Shelley to questions of power, society, and the self. Katharine M. Rogers investigates heroines' frustrated desire for sexual and imaginative expression in key novels by Charlotte Smith.

"Gender and the Cultural Matrix" examines women writers' responses to culturally defined expectations of female sentiments and behavior. Marlon B. Ross discusses selected works by Hannah More, Anna Barbauld, and Lucy Aikin within the dissenting tradition in England, and Jane Aaron examines the Welsh hymn-writer Ann Griffiths and the Anglo-Welsh poets Felicia Hemans and Jane Cave within the Methodist and evangelical tradition in Wales. Susan J. Wolfson analyzes modes of accommodation and resistance to the feminine ideal in Felicia Hemans. Carol Shiner Wilson explores needlework as complex trope and lived experience in poetry and children's stories by Barbauld, Maria Edgeworth, Jane Taylor, and Mary Lamb.

The pieces in "Re-Visioning Romantic Aesthetics" interrogate the concepts of genre, the quotidian, space, sensibility, and genius. Judith Pascoe analyzes Charlotte Smith's *Beachy Head* within the context of women's botanical writings to argue a female earth-bound aesthetic of minute detail. Jerome J. McGann suggests that close readings of texts like the Della Cruscan *The Florence Miscellany* or Felicia Hemans's "The Homes of England" can enable critics to construct alternative readings that revise received notions of periodicity, stylistic taste, and cultural ideologies. Julie Ellison argues that sensibility is a dynamic, ambivalent discourse of emotional action in Anna Barbauld, Phillis Wheatley, and Hannah More. Joel Haefner examines the isolated spaces dominant in male Romantic writing and the contrasting communal spaces in many women's texts. Finally, Catherine B. Burroughs discusses prefaces by playwright and critic Joanna Baillie to articulate a theory of theatre that illuminates Romantic presentations of women's lives and anticipates contemporary gay and lesbian drama theory.

To return to our initial image, what reflections will we see in the mirror of Romantic studies in the next decade? Current criticism, including the essays in this collection, suggest to us that several images will accompany our thought into the twenty-first century.

Late Georgian, Regency, and early Victorian culture will be reinvented and critiqued through the agency of old texts reread and new texts found. In particular, the untold stories of British culture — its social history and its marginalized subjects — will affect the way we look at canonized and un-canonized texts. A book like Catherine Hall's and Leonore Davidoff's *Family Fortunes,* for example, which focuses on the Taylor family as part of a broad social canvas, may shape the way we think about Romantic literature.

The ideology of the critic, his or her subject position in the context of culture, will continue to be problematic. We believe that, given the work of McGann, Marjorie Levinson, Marilyn Butler, and others, Romanticists must be aware of their own ideologies and must inscribe those ideologies clearly into the essays they write. The texts we discuss will become part of this process, and the act of rereading familiar texts may become a way of fixing our interpretive stance in a shifting critical universe.

Moreover, Lovejoy will prevail, to some extent, in his dispute with

Wellek. That is, Romanticism as a monolithic field of study, as a constant set of universal concepts, will be increasingly challenged, and we will be engaged in a discrimination of Romanticisms. Ironically, we may find ourselves following the example of Romantic-era reviewers by attempting to identify "schools" of Romanticism — groups of writers who, to a greater or lesser extent, produced their texts collectively. And race, class, and gender will be important social factors figuring into our examination of these writing groups. In particular, race and class, linked as they are in cultural representations of the Georgian and Regency period, afford interpretive strategies that have yet to be fully realized.

Following an important thread in both feminism and postmodern cultural studies, psycho-social interpretations of texts, particularly those by women and working-class and ethnically diverse writers, will have an impact on Romantic studies. Mellor's recent *Romanticism and Gender* shows how such a strategy might be applied to both canonized and marginalized texts. But this will differ significantly from earlier psychological interpretations, chiefly because the text, the self, and culture at large will be dynamically balanced: the text as a reflection of a unique psyche has become less relevant in contemporary criticism.

We will continue to engage the conventional definitions and conceptions of Romanticism that have been generated since World War II in a dialectic, perhaps a polylogue, with counter-definitions. The work of Wellek, Abrams, Hartman, de Man, Bloom, and others will continue to be important as each detail of their picture of Romanticism is scrutinized and challenged. The whole notion of the self, for example, is now being reinvented; the Romantic sublime, organicism, the primacy of the fragment, the importance of the past, associationism, Miltonic influence — in short, the nuances of Romanticism as we have known it — will no longer be assumed but open for discussion. A kind of theoretical dialectic may preoccupy us for a while, as we engage the traditions of Romantic scholarship; yet the problem of falsely dichotomizing the literary, theoretical, and cultural issues of our period will need to be addressed.

Finally, these new strategies will be possible partly through the continuing recovery and republication of texts that have been excised from the Romantic canon. As noted above, a number of anthologies and new editions have been or will soon be published, including novels by Mary Robinson and Leticia Landon (L. E. L.), collections of women's poetry, volumes by Joanna Baillie and Felicia Hemans. While some of these new publications are reprints, authoritative critical editions are appearing or are in the works; more are sure to follow, and the need for such scholarly editions goes without saying. The availability of these new texts, critical discussion about marginalized writings, and the marketing of inexpensive anthologies will have a tremendous impact on upper-division and graduate-level Romantic literature courses. The conceptual framework as well as the content of those courses will likely change dramatically as we hear new voices.

In 1798, Mary Robinson published "Thoughts on the Condition of Women, and on the Injustice of Mental Subordination." Robinson ends her letter with an assertion of a female literary tradition: "There are men who affect, to think light of the literary productions of women; and yet no works of the present day are so universally read as theirs." The last sentences of her piece become almost prophetic:

> I am well assured that it will meet with little serious attention from the MALE disciples of MODERN PHILOSOPHY. The critics, though they have liber-ally patronized the works of British women, will perhaps condemn that doc-trine which inculcates mental equality; lest, by the intellectual labours of the sex, they should claim an equal portion of power in the TRIBUNAL of BRITISH LITERATURE. (*Complete Poetry* 39)

This volume is a new appeal, on behalf of a whole class of writers, to the tribunal of Romantic criticism.

Notes

1. See, for example, Paul de Man, *The Rhetoric of Romanticism*; Geoffrey Hartman, *Criticism in the Wilderness*; Anne K. Mellor, *English Romantic Irony*; Tilottama Rajan, *Dark Interpreter: The Discourse of Romanticism*; Jerome J. McGann, *The Romantic Ideology*.

2. See Sandra M. Gilbert and Susan Gubar, *Madwoman in the Attic: The Woman Writer and the Nineteenth-Century Literary Imagination*; Mary Poovey, *The Proper Lady and the Woman Writer: Ideology as Style in the Works of Mary Wollstone-craft, Mary Shelley, and Jane Austen*; Margaret Homans, *Bearing the Word: Language and Female Experience in Nineteenth-Century Women's Writing*; Mary Jacobus, *Ro-manticism, Writing and Sexual Difference: Essays on the Prelude*; Susan Wolfson, "Individual in Community: Dorothy Wordsworth in Conversation with William"; Anne K. Mellor, *Mary Shelley: Her Life, Her Fiction, Her Monsters*; Susan M. Levin, *Dorothy Wordsworth and Romanticism*; Jane Aaron, *A Double Singleness: Gender and the Writings of Charles and Mary Lamb*.

3. See Hélène Cixous, "The Laugh of the Medusa," and "Castration or De-capitation?"

4. Some of the current anthologies available are Jennifer Breen, ed., *Women Romantic Poets, 1785–1832*; Katharine M. Rogers and William McCarthy, eds., *The Meridian Anthology of Early Women Writers: British Literary Women from Aphra Behn to Maria Edgeworth, 1660–1800*; Robert W. Uphaus and Gretchen M. Foster, eds., *The Other Eighteenth Century: English Women of Letters, 1660–1800*; Roger Lonsdale, ed., *Eighteenth-Century Women Poets: An Oxford Anthology*; Mary R. Mahl and Helene Koon, *The Female Spectator: English Women Writers Before 1800*; Harold Bloom and Lionel Trilling, eds., *Romantic Poetry and Prose*; David Perkins, ed., *English Romantic Writers*; and Paula Feldman, ed., *British Romantic Poetry by Women: 1770–1840*, forthcoming.

Reading Women's Texts

Mary Robinson's *Lyrical Tales* in Context

Joseph Cottle concludes the first volume of his *Early Recollections* with the departure of Wordsworth and Coleridge for the continent following his publication of the first volume of their *Lyrical Ballads,* an event by which he marked his own retirement from an uncertain vocation:

> I for ever quitted the business of a bookseller, with the earnest hope that the time might never arrive when Bristol possessed not a bookseller, prompt to extend a friendly hand to every man of genius, home-born, or exotic, that might be found within its borders. (*Recollections* 1: 324–25)

In 1798 Cottle was justifiably proud of his achievement in "becoming the publisher of the first volumes of three such Poets, as Southey, Coleridge, and Wordsworth," which he later rightly claimed was "a distinction that might never again occur to a Provincial bookseller" (1: 309). By 1800, secure himself from the necessities of competing in the marketplace from so distant a vantage as Bristol, Cottle through the printing firm of Biggs and Cottle, as the accompanying advertisement sheet indicates, still retained an active entrepreneurial interest in fostering a new school of poetry (one that would, he hoped, also include himself and his brother Amos among its noted members).

One month before the second edition of *Lyrical Ballads, with Other Poems* appeared in London, Longman published Mary Robinson's *Lyrical Tales,* which had also issued from the press of Biggs and Cottle. Robinson, like the others in Cottle's "school," had a close association with Bristol, where she was raised and educated at the Miss Mores's celebrated academy. In 1797 she had enrolled herself among Longman's increasing list of popular novelists, and with the poetic command of *Lyrical Tales* she was once again demonstrating her literary versatility. In recent years, however, if her volume enters the critical literature on Romanticism at all, it has generally been in a footnote, where it is registered as a minor irritant to the success of Wordsworth's groundbreaking collection of 1800. Apprised that she had boldly usurped his title, Wordsworth that autumn attempted without suc-

BOOKS

Printed for T.N. Longman *and* O. Rees, *No. 39, Paternoster-Row, London*

---

1. The NATURAL DAUGHTER, a Novel, by *Mrs. Robinson,* 2 Vols. price 7s. Boards

2. The FALSE FRIEND, A Novel [by Mrs. Robinson], 4 Vols. price 16. Sewed

3. JOAN of ARC, An Epic Poem, by *Robert Southey,* 2 Vols. small 8vo. the second edition, price 12s. in boards— A few copies of the Quarto edition may be had, price 1l.1s.

4. POEMS, by *Robert Southey,* 2 Vols. price 10s. in boards

5. LETTERS, written during a short residence in Spain and Portugal, by *Robert Southey,* 8 vo. price 7s. in boards

6. ANNUAL ANTHOLOGY [ed. Southey], 2 vols. small 8vo. price 12s. in boards

7. ALFRED, an Epic Poem, in Twenty-Four Books, by *Joseph Cottle* Quarto, price 1l. 1s. in boards.

8. POEMS, by *Joseph Cottle,* second edition, price 4s. in boards

9. MALVERN HILLS, a Poem, by *Joseph Cottle,* price 2s. 6d

10. ICELANDIC POETRY, or the EDDA OF SAEMUND, translated into English verse, by *A.S. Cottle,* price 6s. in boards.

11. LYRICAL BALLADS, in 2 vols. by *W. Wordsworth.*

12. POEMS, by *S.T. Coleridge.* To which are added, POEMS, by *C. Lamb,* and *C. Lloyd.* The second edition, price 6s. in boards.

13. POEMS and PLAYS, by *Mrs. West.* 2 Vols. elegantly printed in Fool's-cap 8vo and hot-pressed, price 10s in boards.

14. A TALE of the TIMES, by *Mrs. West.* 2 Vols. 3 Vols. price 12s. sewed.

15. A GOSSIP's STORY, and LEGENDARY TALE, by *Mrs. West* 2 Vols. price 7s. in boards.

16. An ELEGY on the DEATH of the Right Honourable EDMUND BURKE by *Mrs. West,* price 1s.

17. The PLEASURES of HOPE; a Poem, in Two Parts, by *Thomas Campbell,* embellished with Four elegant Engravings.

18. POEMS, by *Anne Bannerman,* price 5s. boards

19. POEMS of ACHMED ARDEBEILI, a Persian Exile, with Notes, by *Charles Fox,* 8vo. price 8s. in boards

Advertisement sheet for Mary Robinson, *Lyrical Tales* (1800).

cess to have it changed simply to *Poems in Two Volumes,* the rubric he resurrected for his next collection in 1807.[1]

But it is clear that neither Joseph Cottle nor Thomas Longman saw Robinson's title as a usurpation of Wordsworth's rights; indeed, from the refusal of Longman to accede to Wordsworth's request we may conjecture that this highly successful firm had its eye shrewdly on the marketplace. Longman and Rees obviously had high expectations of Robinson's volume, playing her £63 for a press run of 1,250 copies, which in both categories signifies very respectable numbers.[2] The collusion of printer and publisher in enlisting titles so nearly identical and in printing them in sizable quantities within a month of each other suggests an effort at public relations and at maximizing the visibility and thus the profitability of what would be construed as poetic collections with similar features. And, indeed, when we place these publishing ventures within the perspective of Cottle's justified pride of two years before in nurturing not just Wordsworth, but Coleridge and Southey too, we should see Mary Robinson's entry into these lists as a determined effort to establish herself firmly in the public mind as one of these associated voices that would carry English verse into a new century. Her earnestness was sustained by the rapid failure of her health and her attendant recognition that *Lyrical Tales* would be the main conduit for her poetic reputation.[3] Between the publication of *Lyrical Tales* and *Lyrical Ballads, with Other Poems,* on 26 December 1800, Mary Robinson, just twelve years Wordsworth's senior and by far the best known of these four poets, died.

To establish the dynamics of the interrelationship of the four poets is to recontextualize the poetry each was writing in this remarkable period of creative rivalry and must by its very nature change the perspective by which Robinson has all but disappeared from view. The interrelationship, it must be stressed, was for Robinson almost wholly literary. Wordsworth never met her, nor, it appears, did Southey, though she succeeded him as Daniel Stuart's chief correspondent to the "Poetical Department" of the *Morning Post* when he left for Portugal at the end of 1799. Coleridge seems not actually himself to have made Robinson's personal acquaintance until January 1800.[4] Yet all three of the poets later to be identified as comprising the Lake School had been, through their contributions to the *Morning Post,* associated with Robinson as early as November 1797, when Robinson and Coleridge were both given contracts by Stuart. By December of that year Tabitha Bramble (Robinson), Albert (Coleridge), and Mortimer (Wordsworth) had all published in Stuart's columns, and in the next month

Southey, who favored anonymity in his newspaper publications, joined the group and quickly became its principal member, contributing, as Kenneth Curry has so valuably documented, in the range of two hundred poems before he resigned his position to return to Portugal.[5] Thereafter Robinson took on this demanding role, producing some ninety poems, among them major components of *Lyrical Tales,* over the next ten months, when her physical collapse abruptly halted a creative surge that, however necessitated it was by penury, was by any standard remarkable.[6]

This literary record, accented as it has been by presuppositions of value in later scholarly reconstructions, bears scrutiny from a rigorously objective historical perspective. Even before Coleridge entered the London literary world he crossed Mary Robinson's path, at least figuratively. The ninth of his early "Sonnets on Eminent Characters," a tribute to William Godwin, was published in the *Morning Chronicle* on 10 January 1795, the same day that its rival for the liberal readership of the metropolis, the *Morning Post and Fashionable World,* first introduced to its pages the verse of Mary Robinson, writing a sonnet "To Liberty" under the nom de plume of Portia. Another three poems from Portia's pen followed during that month. Well before this time, Robinson had figured in occasional reports of the newspaper — the lead item in the "Fashionable World" column for 4 September 1794 was the information that "Mrs. ROBINSON is with the MUSES in Berkshire" — and the political tenor of her work had been warmly applauded and defended against adverse criticism:

> Mrs. ROBINSON's *"Widow"* [*The Widow, or, a Picture of Modern Times,* 1794] is replete with sentiments of Philanthropy for the "Swinish Multitude;" for this reason, it receives the lash of these mercenary stabbers. She, whose writings, two years since, they worshipped even to idolatry, whom *they* named, "the ENGLISH SAPPHO!" to whom they applied the line of Horace, *"ex egi monumentum aere perrenous!* [perennius]" whose Literary Fame would *"outlive the Pencil of a Reynolds!"* is now the subject of abuse, because her Novel breathes the Spirit of *Democracy!!* But the source of such Malice is too glaring to be concealed, by the smooth and shallow artifice of pretended Criticism. We hope to see the labours of Genius triumph over the prejudices of contracted minds, and the *Freedom* of the *Press* unshackled by the destructive fetters of Hirelings and Sycophants. (*Morning Post,* 14 October 1794: 3)

What this passage reveals is how significant a presence Mary Robinson cast in the London literary world of the early 1790s, as poet, novelist, and outspoken liberal. The subtitle of *The Widow* links her novel with the political fiction of Robert Bage (*Man As He Is,* 1792) and William Godwin

(*Things as They Are; or, The Adventures of Caleb Williams,* 1794).[7] Although Robinson certainly capitalized on her public association with Sappho, using the name as a pseudonym in the columns of the *Morning Post* and even writing a sonnet sequence *à clef* on being deserted by Banastre Tarleton, *Sappho and Phaon* (1796), this account explicitly traces the source of her sobriquet to reviews of her 1791 collection of *Poems* in which Reynolds's celebrated portrait served as frontispiece.[8] Robinson was the first of Daniel Stuart's poetical correspondents to be hired, then, because she was the best known. Coleridge and Southey, who had both published their initial original volumes in 1796, were young literary men on the rise, and Wordsworth, though he had made his debut three years before them, was simply not yet a name to conjure with. It may be true that Stuart treated Coleridge with utmost deference to his talent, as David Erdman has argued,[9] but that respect cannot compare with the puffery Mary Robinson could constantly expect in return for adorning his "Poetical Department" with the productions of her pen.

Certainly it was highly flattering for Robinson to find herself linked with this group of young, talented poets. It must have seemed a far cry from the days early in the decade when she played Laura Maria as one of the countless female admirers of Della Crusca (Robert Merry) in *The Oracle* and *The World*. Now it is Wordsworth who writes "Alcaeus to Sappho" and who models "The Solitude of Binnorie" after the metrical effects of Robinson's "Haunted Beach" and allows it to appear in the *Morning Post* on 14 October 1800 (this less than two weeks after his inquiry about altering the title of his collection) with an uncharacteristically gallant tribute, acknowledging "that the invention of a meter has so widely diffused the name of Sappho, and almost constitutes the present celebrity of Alcaeus." Wordsworth came by his model through Coleridge's reading Robinson's poem in the *Morning Post* for 26 February 1800 (a version in which the sixth stanza is wanting) and suggesting that Southey include it in the *Annual Anthology* for 1800: "the Metre—ay! that Woman has an Ear" (*Collected Letters* 2: 576).[10] Although it was doubtless Coleridge, intermittently in London during this period, who was the catalyst for Robinson's sense of being accepted as an equal among the rising school of poets, their deference to her manifests much more than mere gentility. On the one hand, as Coleridge's remark intimates, however critical he could be of the unevenness of Robinson's achievement, he had great respect for her craft. And on the other hand, these rising stars, we tend too often to forget, were as yet unregarded in the heavens. It was not until the publication of the enlarged edition of

Lyrical Ballads and of *Thalaba* early in 1801 that the accomplishment of the three young men could be singled out for a composite review that first identified them as comprising a school. Yet it can never be overemphasized how significant it was that Francis Jeffrey's famous attack in the first number of the *Edinburgh Review* was directed at Robert Southey, for it was he, and not Wordsworth or Coleridge, who by 1802 could be identified as the most prolific and most prominent of the group. Two years before, as a "group" with shared interests, the shared patronage of Daniel Stuart, and a shared printer and publisher, their most prominent member was clearly Mary Robinson.

To recontextualize the actual historical situation out of which came Robinson's *Lyrical Tales,* then, is to recontextualize that of the *Lyrical Ballads* as well. This does not mean that we need once more rehearse the dynamic and somewhat tense relations between Coleridge and Wordsworth, nor to place the second edition of that work within the ambience of Wordsworth's ongoing autobiographical reconstruction of his life. These critical operations have been so well done by others as to have erected preliminary commonplaces that seem to block from view other, and in their time more crucial, matters. First, as Jeffrey implicitly recognized, the poetic kinship and rivalry at issue are not simply those between Wordsworth and Coleridge, but those involving the two of them and Southey. And initially, just to be certain that the obvious pattern is underscored, what drove Robinson in the direction of her own competition with Wordsworth's title was her own rivalry at the *Morning Post* — not with Coleridge, who came to that conduit for his poetry only infrequently, but with Southey. Southey had derisively dismissed his friends' *Lyrical Ballads* in the *Critical Review* of October 1798 shortly after their departure for Germany and in his extensive productions during 1797–99 seemed bent on establishing himself in public as undisputed leader of the new school of simple, unadorned, and vernacular poetry. In the *Morning Post* he largely set the patterns Mary Robinson reconstituted in her twenty-one poetic insertions during 1799 and her ninety or so after taking his place in 1800.[11] Only after Wordsworth and Coleridge returned to England and achieved a reconciliation with Southey was their weight reestablished in the exchange; it was only really at the point when Southey himself was preparing his remove to Portugal in the early months of 1800 that the relationship between Coleridge and Robinson developed its full direction. So, though *Lyrical Tales* may seem in its title to direct its intertextual energies directly at Wordsworth, in subject matter and in style (particularly as seen in the flattened blank verse bordering on

prose in which Robinson is more dextrous than Southey), often her interlocutor is Southey. But since he and Wordsworth are themselves so mark-
edly in competition, which would explain his generally adverse review of
Lyrical Ballads, the threads of influence, extension, and reconception become tangled indeed and require some sorting before we can measure
Robinson's relation to them.

The pertinent texts among Southey's early poems are the six "English
Eclogues" he described in prefatory remarks as bearing "no resemblance to
any poems in our language" — "The Old Mansion House," "The Grandmother's Tale," "The Funeral" ("Hannah"), "The Sailor's Mother," "The
Witch," "The Ruined Cottage" — published as a set in the second volume he
added to his *Poems* in 1799, along with their counterparts in the *Annual
Anthology* of 1799 ("Eclogue. The Last of the Family") and that of 1800
("Eclogue. The Wedding"). Robert Mayo long ago noted the similarity of
subject matter between "Hannah," Southey's blank verse description of the
wasting away of an unwed mother, and "The Thorn" ("Contemporaneity
of the *Lyrical Ballads*" 496–97). Southey's poem was written at Burton in
Hampshire, where he lived from mid-June to early September of 1797, and
first published in the *Monthly Magazine* for 4 October 1797. In the winter
he was in London, where he first met Dorothy Wordsworth and probably
renewed the acquaintance with her brother developed in Bristol in 1795,
then in the spring moved first to Bath and then back to Bristol. Although
Coleridge reports constant conversations with Wordsworth about Southey
(*Letters* 1: 525), there appears to have been no further contact between
them at this point (their actual intimacy was delayed until October 1803).
If Wordsworth was influenced by Southey's poem five months later in
writing "The Thorn" (19 March 1798), we can only speculate that it was
through the interest Coleridge — sometimes against his will — took in the
career of his brother-in-law. In the case of "Hannah," the inference is
inescapable, since Coleridge wrote Southey a glowing tribute to his poem
on 15 September 1797 (*Letters* 1: 345–46), a period when he was in daily
intercourse with Wordsworth. The supposition of Coleridge's mediation is
strengthened by the presence of "The Ruined Cottage" among Southey's
"English Eclogues." Although the plot is different from that of Wordsworth's poem — it concerns a mother's dissolution after the seduction of her
lone daughter — the general theme of female betrayal and decline and a
narrative frame through which the tale is imparted by an older man to an
inexperienced male friend are sufficiently alike that it is scarcely possible to
believe that the two poems were written in total independence one from the

other. There are likewise similarities between Wordsworth's "Old Man Travelling" — to "take a last leave of my son, a mariner / Who from a sea-flight has been brought to Falmouth / And there is dying in an hospital" — and "The Sailor's Mother," where Southey adapts Wordsworth's technique of contradictory perspectives to a similar encounter, and between "Goody Blake and Harry Gill" and Southey's "Grandmother's Tale" of "blear-eyed Moll," murdered by a smuggler whose conscience subsequently torments him to the point that he confesses and is hanged. When Southey's "English Eclogues" arise in the critical literature (an infrequent phenomenon, to be sure), they are by the inner logic of canonical evaluation placed as foils to Wordsworth's greater achievement.[12] But what is diminished or simply ignored in the process is the extent to which Southey is engaged, and (if we credit the influence of "Hannah" on "The Thorn") perhaps Wordsworth too, in a complex revisionary act whose central stake is the nature of the new realism that will impel English poetry into the nineteenth century.[13]

Mary Robinson is as deeply committed to this effort as were the two men who formed the "Lake School." But before we turn to her distinctive viewpoint, the juxtaposition of "English Eclogues" and *Lyrical Ballads* allows us to perceive that Southey has a genuinely different recognition of the exigencies of "real life" in rural England than does Wordsworth. His poems are of a piece in mode and style, genuine slices of quotidian provincial life written in the vernacular of everyday speech. Everywhere he emphasizes deep-rooted social codes that are conservative and constraining. Among his rural folk superstition and bigotry are rife, and scapegoating, as in "The Witch," is openly tolerated, not simply, as in "The Thorn," a subtly implicit process. Economic hardship is ubiquitous and visited disproportionately upon women: the experienced woman observer of "The Wedding" frequently wishes her children in their coffins. Past stabilities are crumbling, whether through the normal process of death, as in "The Old Mansion House" and "The Last of the Family," or through the more sinister brutalities of seduction ("The Ruined Cottage") and war ("The Sailor's Mother"). Southey, who is England's most politically outspoken radical poet throughout the 1790s, represents rural society through a perspective that, however disguised so as to retain its universal appeal, is fundamentally political. He employs the dialogue conventional to the eclogue with a shrewd awareness of its ideological propensities: each of his poems embodies an implicit class conflict in its voices. Indeed, this is Southey's shrewd contribution to the English pastoral and of signal historical importance in its modernization during this decade.[14] And yet, whether from prudence or from the instinctive conservatism that is allied with his kind of populism and that would only be fully manifested some fifteen years later when he became poet laureate, Southey brings each of his eclogues to a liberal closure. The class conflict is contained through compromise or accommodation: all social forces in the "English Eclogues" can unite behind a single, progressive vision of a common nationhood. That such a pretense from a representative of bourgeois privilege has by now in Britain a long history of exacerbating the class conflicts it wishes away is true enough, but such an awareness should not detract from our recognition that Southey's is actually the first collection of modern English verse to center its focus deliberately on the divergent perspectives conditioned by social roles. From the kind of materialist theoretical perspective that has in recent years gained a considerable following, Southey has a much more fully developed sense of cultural conditioning than Wordsworth and is far more willing to look hard reality in the eye without idealizations. And even as one may regret the facile liberalism by which he achieves closure, one recognizes that in large measure it mirrors the actual temper of his times and the practice of his culture.

In general contrast to this conception of cultural formation Wordsworth tends to focus on the values and painful losses experienced through the radical contingency of all mental perspective. With both poets of the original *Lyrical Ballads,* even where the subject is wrapped, at first, in the trappings of the Gothic ("The Rime of the Ancient Mariner") or, at last, in those of the grand style ("Lines written a few miles above Tintern Abbey"), the project is to deflate these issues to a common level of awareness so as to reveal the complex patterns of feeling and mental activity, the lyrical, that are involved in the mundane doings, the ballads, of daily life. With some stretching by the reader, semblances of Southey's cultural awareness can seem to impinge on these explorations of consciousness: there appear to be economic contingencies lurking behind the sorrows of "The Last of the Flock," an awareness of being doomed by gender in "The Complaint of a Forsaken Indian Woman," a sense of the deprivations of the current war with France implicit in "The Female Vagrant." But if the signs of destitution and alienation are everywhere, they are generally controlled: Goody Blake is distanced by being made the subject of a story, as is Martha Ray, the little girl amid the family tombstones, and even, for that matter, the Ancient Mariner. Whether or not the poets are consciously involved in suppressing the public realm in which their characters and their selves move, or simply programmatically choose to accentuate mental phenomena, has been a recent matter of debate, which has been salutary even if confined too closely to the two collaborators themselves. What Southey and after him Robinson provide in their creative rivalry with each other and with the poets of *Lyrical Ballads* is a contemporary repositioning and enlarging of the focus.

Southey narrows his concerns, sacrificing range of subject matter for authenticity of cultural representation. His eclogues are studied in their contemporaneity and their "Englishness": there are no hermits in his harbors or his woods, no emigrés forsaking the old world or natives forsaken in the new. On the other hand, his eye for detail and ear for plain speech allow him a sure reach for comic effect in "The Grandmother's Tale" and "The Witch" that most readers would deny to Wordsworth's "Idiot Boy." His class and generational dialogism allows a superimposition of cultural preconceptions, though, it could be argued, in such a schematic way as to offer little capacity for nuance or true human variety among them. Yet if his realism, like that of George Crabbe, lies mainly on the surface, in a culture that knew remarkably little about what was to become characterized in the ensuing century as the "condition of England," an accurate representation of that surface was surely a value. And a sense that the inner life below that surface had a political and economic component was one that would become increasingly central in nineteenth-century thought. Southey's counter to Wordsworth, then, is one of plain, unmystified, and unapologetic materialism.

Paradoxically, though Robinson is the one of these writers in the throes of poverty and holding herself above destitution by the strength of her pen alone, she eschews Southey's economic realism. (Perhaps, of course, she does so because it is an everyday threat.) Nor does she ever adopt Southey's mode of dialogue. Yet her range of voice and situation seems deliberately broadened beyond that of either *Lyrical Ballads* or the "English Eclogues," and the precariousness of her existence seems to have invested her poems with a more urgent sense than even they convey of the stark contingency of human desire. The larger paradox, and what gives *Lyrical Tales* its claims to a much more serious consideration than was accorded it in its own day or is manifest by its present neglect, is the way in which its abundance of voices, modes of representation, and fertile creativity collide with its sense of a continual thwarting of potentiality to accomplish a thematic tension between means and ends, past and future, consummation and consumption characteristic of the greatest Romantic poetry, and in particular of Wordsworth in a poem like "Tintern Abbey."

Mary Robinson's habits of publication may have encouraged an opening up of perspective beyond that of her younger associates. Unlike Southey, in writing for the *Morning Post* she employed a variety of pseudonyms, some ten alone occurring in the output of her last year.[15] She clearly had elaborated at least some of these into the character of personae. Sappho and Lesbia write amorous verse; Sappho generally the victim of her experiences with men, Lesbia with her illusions of happiness still intact. There are a rakish male voice represented by her Oberon and a witty middle-aged Scottish spinster derived from Smollett who, along with Coleridge, debuted as Tabitha Bramble in the "Poetical Department" of December 1797. This figure is of considerable importance to *Lyrical Tales,* for six of the poems, all humorous and most linked by a sexual thematics, were published under her signature during the first half of 1800.[16] The questions that a few of these poems — "Deborah's Parrot, a Village Tale" and "The Granny Grey, a Love Tale" — raise about the propriety of so pronounced a feminist voice targeting sex-starved old maids and subjecting them to male discipline are obviated when the poems are read in their original position, through the perspective of a gossipy and somewhat malicious spinster who is an inveterate telltale. Needless to say, such a voice — and the rich vein of wit that supports it — is essentially foreign to the poetry of Wordsworth, Coleridge, and Southey, whose grandmother tells the tale of "blear-eyed Moll" without asserting any personality traits of her own.

As Robinson expands the range of voices to be accommodated by a deflated, interiorized poetic, she also opens up its metrical possibilities. Generally eschewing simple ballad meter or the vernacular forms favored by Southey, *Lyrical Tales* is notable for its virtuoso employment of stanzaic and sonic patterns. Coleridge's excitement over the "fascinating Metre" of "The Haunted Beach" (*Letters* 2: 575) and his (or Wordsworth's) public tribute to its invention accentuate how high are Robinson's claims as a practitioner of her craft. The opening stanzas of the poem immediately establish the eerily haunting effects created by a combination of rhyme, meter, and repetition:

> Upon a lonely desart Beach
>   Where the white foam was scatter'd,
> A little shed uprear'd its head
>   Though lofty Barks were shatter'd.
> The Sea-weeds gath'ring near the door,
>   A sombre path display'd;
> And, all around, the deaf'ning roar,

Re-echo'd on the chalky shore,
　By the green billows made.

Above, a jutting cliff was seen
　Where Sea Birds hover'd, craving;
And all around, the craggs were bound
　With weeds — for ever waving.
And here and there, a cavern wide
　Its shad'wy jaws display'd;
And near the sands, at ebb of tide,
A shiver'd mast was seen to ride
　Where the green billows stray'd.

There is not a little here of the pyrotechnic skill of "The Rime of the Ancient Mariner," which is probably what attracted Coleridge in the first place. But the uncanny way in which subject and technical treatment reinforce each other — the liberating effect of the feminine rhymes of lines 2 and 4 being broken by the reiterated rhyme of lines 5, 7, and 8 and bound down by the incantatory repetition of the last line reflects the fisherman's obsession with the man he murdered — surpass the capacity of Coleridge's ballad meter, however brilliantly employed, to assume complementary meaning. A similar precision with contrasting masculine and feminine rhymes informs "The Poor, Singing Dame," while in a different timbre a half-refrain at the end of each stanza reinforces the comic effect of "The Trumpeter, an Old English Tale." A fluid combination of short and long lines is used to similar effect in "Old Barnard, a Monkish Tale," whereas the intrusion of pentameter, then hexameter lines to brake the end of each stanza in "The Negroe Girl" attenuates the agony she experiences in watching the wreck of the slave ship that carries her lover. Against this effortless display of technical facility, Robinson occasionally intrudes the strong measure of her distinctive blank verse. It bears neither the grand tonalities of Wordsworth's "Tintern Abbey," nor the conversational ease of Coleridge's "Nightingale," nor the flat plainness of Southey's "Ruined Cottage." Although closest in style to Southey, its tones are rhetorically compressed, its sonic patterns accentuated, its colors enriched. Thus in "The Widow's Home" we hear a distinctive fourth voice rehearse the familiar integration of child with nature that is a burden of the poems just cited from their collections, as the soldier's son awaits his father's return:

                              On the hills
He watches the wide waste of wavy green
Tissued with orient lustre, till his eyes
Ache with the dazzling splendour, and the main,
Rolling and blazing, seems a second Sun!
And, if a distant whitening sail appears,
Skimming the bright horizon while the mast
Is canopied with clouds of dappled gold,
He homeward hastes rejoicing. An old Tree
Is his lone watch-tow'r; 'tis a blasted Oak
Which, from a vagrant Acorn, ages past,
Sprang up, to triumph like a Savage bold
Braving the Season's warfare. There he sits
Silent and musing the long Evening hour,
Till the short reign of Sunny splendour fades
At the cold touch of twilight. Oft he sings;
Or from his oaten pipe, untiring pours
The tune mellifluous which his father sung.
When HE could only listen.

As unassuming as is Robinson's expansion of metrical possibility in this volume, extraordinary claims could be made for the effects it presages, if not directly impels. Among the thousands of volumes of verse published in the eighteenth century, there are probably no more than a handful like hers. Except for the four pieces in deflated blank verse, all the poems of *Lyrical Tales* are constructed differently; most are unpretentiously masterful in their metrical effect. That this volume appears in the last month of the eighteenth century foreshadows the concern with technical inventiveness that characterizes much nineteenth-century verse in English. Unquestionably, its impetus within the century came from the women writers we group under the rubric of poetesses, figures like Felicia Hemans, Letitia Landon, and Elizabeth Barrett. Their common source, acknowledged or not, is Mary Robinson.

Within the more limited context pursued here, which are the poetic positions being staked out by her younger associates, Robinson tends to be more inclusive, less constrained by conceptual homogeneity, than they are generally considered to be. Perhaps, however, if instead of just the "English Eclogues" we were to read as counterweight Southey's entire second volume of 1799, with its long "Vision of the Maid of Orleans" and its many gothic ballads, we would be less conscious of a determining ideological purpose; or, if we paid as much attention to the four poems Wordsworth earlier styled as Lines (as in "Lines written near Richmond, upon the Thames, at Evening") as we do to "Lines written a few miles above Tintern Abbey," we might see the original *Lyrical Ballads* as more miscellany than monument. Robinson, at any rate, through range of historical period and culture as through metrical variety, exemplifies the heterogeneity we sense in the fact that nine of her poems bear subtitles distinguishing the particular sort of "tale" each purports to be. Although the tale teller and the narrative process never intrude self-reflexively on the text as they do in *Lyrical Ballads*, Robinson shares Wordsworth's attention to the sensibility of the central figures and psychological reverberations within the tale. Less concerned than Southey with specific cultural formations or pressures, she is much more attuned than he to endemic injustice and abuse of power. If Wordsworth sees in marginality an arena forcing into play a range of mental reactions from fear to compassion, and Southey finds it an aberrancy prompting a dialectical counter-movement toward community, Robinson, herself a deeply victimized woman, views it as the normal condition of life, stressing either the anarchic or the existential, depending on the timbre of her tale.

Although the seven years of war with France only intrude on *Lyrical Ballads* in the oblique last lines of Wordsworth's "Old Man Travelling" and on the "English Eclogues" in the anathema against French cruelty of Southey's "Sailor's Mother," Robinson's "Edmund's Wedding" in its multiple ironies is weighted against warfare as a violation of domestic stability. The conscript Edmund returns to his village to find his betrothed Agnes dead from a broken heart; mourning on her grave, he is arrested by his former comrades as a deserter and condemned to be shot. So reduced to the essentials of its plot, the poem may seem simply to reach for any pathos it can grasp; but in its unfolding "Edmund's Wedding" surpasses the raw materials of its construction, revealing beneath patriotic catchwords an essential dehumanization. The agents of cruelty are not the French but the British soldiers who attack the very fabric of English village life. Likewise, in her "Deserted Cottage," though it seems highly unlikely that she could have known Wordsworth's manuscript poem, Robinson reverts to the war as first cause in the decline and disappearance of a family. If Robinson were reacting only to Southey's poem, her replacement of seduction by conscription asserts the common sense of the already seduced, that behind any individual abuse of masculine power lies the political system that authorizes it. Robinson had suffered it straight from the top, in the Prince of Wales and his father George III, who with impunity if with different motives left her life in ruins.

The common theme of Robinson's pathetic poetry is a sudden and total displacement of the stabilities on which existences depend. The revolutionary and counterrevolutionary warfare of Europe stands behind fully seven of these twenty-two poems — in its domestic shatterings ("Edmund's Wedding," "The Deserted Cottage," "The Widow's Home"), in its inescapability ("The Hermit of Mont-Blanc"), in the flotsam of displaced people it leaves in its wake ("The Fugitive," "Poor Marguerite," "The Alien Boy"). It is a metaphor for the grotesque patterns by which society reduces the vulnerable to the status of victims, particularly, as already noted, conscripts to war, persons of color ("The Negroe Girl" and the east Indian "Lascar," a remarkable indictment of imperial racism), children ("The Alien Boy" and the unfathomably other boy in the opening poem, "All Alone"), animals ("The Shepherd's Dog"), the old ("The Deserted Cottage"), and (as exemplified in "The Poor, Singing Dame" and "Poor Marguerite"), of course, women. This is a sad world, one that witnesses constant abuses of power, where armies do no one any good, where class conflict is systemic and cannot be wished away by liberal compromise, and where not perspectivism but insanity and stark alienation seem the logical end of interiorizing social conditions. However constant and pressing the pathos in *Lyrical Tales,* the extremity of the depiction make it seem a just response to the tears of real things.

There are in Robinson's volume two other responses that indicate she is deliberately reacting to the models set before her by Southey and Wordsworth. The opening poem, "All Alone," is an ingenious recombination and redirection of "We Are Seven" and "The Thorn," perhaps with a glance at "The Rime of the Ancient Mariner" as well. A well-intentioned member of the community, presumptively maternal, confronts a boy who, like Martha Ray as the retired captain of "The Thorn" constructs her story, spends his days by a grave, attempting to reintegrate the child within fostering social bonds. The genuine kindness of the adult and the visible presence of other children happily playing at rustic sports set the stage for a sentimental reconciliation. Instead, the boy tells his interlocutor of how one by one all of the beings who connected him to life died until he was left alone, attached only to the dead, fetishizing his mother's grave. "The Alien Boy" toward the end of the volume pictures a similar being who at least has

mental alienation to distance him from the collapse of supporting structures, but the orphan of "All Alone," like Wordsworth's young girl of "We
Are Seven," is soberly rational. In immediate contrast with Robinson's
portrayal, however, Wordsworth's elaboration of the saving continuities of
memory perhaps seems facile. The unaccommodated child who stands at
the gateway to *Lyrical Tales* is a totally existential figure, simply and irre-
mediably cut off. If the society pictured in the later tales of the volume is
generally antipathetic to life, the calm embrace of entropy in "All Alone,"
however it may be thought to figure Robinson's reaction to her own
physical decline,[17] testifies to a strength of will still residing within the
power of every individual. If it can at last only be expressed in refusal, still,
as Byron would later insinuate, refusal is its own mark of value, an assertion
of the self where there is nothing left to gain.

But there is a second and far more positive assertion of self that marks
this volume and Robinson's response to her male associates. These are the
comic tales interspersed with the pathetic poems, often taking similar
themes and resolutely laughing away their pathetic import. They are for the
most part not nice poems; their general theme is to keep your eyes open,
stand up for yourself, and get your just deserts without worrying about the
consequences for those who stand in the way. For a highly talented woman
who, however else she succeeded, spent her adult existence barely able to
manage her equilibrium where men held reins of control, they must have
been tonic to write. In an age when sexuality was driven underground by
evangelical piety and military duty, poems like "The Mistletoe," "The Fortune Teller," and "The Confessor," emit an earthy air that Robinson can
breathe freely and of which there is scarcely a hint in either Southey or
Wordsworth. Even where a modern reader draws back from what appear to
be implicit reaffirmations of male prerogative, the issue to Robinson is
female sexual repression, an internalized male control she refused, to her
social disgrace and dishonor, to accommodate.

Mary Robinson lived on a fringe that neither Southey nor Wordsworth ever experienced. She observes the outcast and the marginal from a
participant's standpoint. Her poverty and her collapsing health in 1800
immerse her in an existential limbo, only exacerbated by the incessant
demands on her pen. For the leisure of Southey's constant relocation to
avoid his law books or Wordsworth's rural vagrancy in search of subjects,
she had her physical paralysis and the wolf at the door. One result is poems
of grotesque, even extreme alienation, as the initially marginalized are cut
away from whatever moorings are still at their disposal. Its complement are

poems of refusal, and principal among them are those that originated in the voice of her sharp-tongued spinster Tabitha Bramble. T. B. in her unreprinted verse in the *Morning Post* of 21 August 1800 called "Domestic Beverage" begins by citing the value of "A little *acid,* now and then." Under the influence of this sobriquet Robinson considerably enlarges the notion of what constitutes the "lyrical," so that sexuality is assimilated to the psychological components from which Southey and Wordsworth (though not Coleridge) have unnaturally severed it and the comic mitigates the insistent claims of pathos. In Robinson's depiction of rural England resides a resilient life-force that refuses to be victimized. Its counterpart in the Windsor cottage in which she spent her last months is the technical accomplishment and forceful creativity by which she staved off the inevitable to the very end. *Lyrical Tales* is a testament to an indomitable spirit who demanded her place in the creation of what we now call English Romanticism.

Notes

1. Dorothy writes to Mrs. John Marshall (10–12 September 1800) that "he intends to give them the title of 'Poems by W. Wordsworth' as Mrs. Robinson has claimed the title and is about publishing a volume of *Lyrical Tales*. This is a great objection to the former title, particularly as they are both printed at the same press and Longman is the publisher of both the works" (*Letters of William and Dorothy Wordsworth: The Early Years, 1787–1805* 297). By early October Wordsworth informed both publisher and printer of his wishes (303–4), but without effect.

2. For this information I am indebted to the meticulous research in publishers' archives conducted by Jan Fergus and Janice Farrar Thaddeus, "Women, Publishers, and Money, 1790–1820." Cottle paid Wordsworth 30 guineas for a run of 500 copies of the original *Lyrical Ballads* (*Recollections* 2: 23); for the 1800 imprint Wordsworth secured £80 for two anticipated editions, consisting of 750 (volume 1) and 1000 (volume 2) for the first and 1000 copies each for the second (*Letters, The Early Years* 310).

3. Robinson's concern for the successful reception of her volume is evident in a letter she wrote to S. J. Pratt on 31 August 1800: see Kenneth Neill Cameron, ed., *Shelley and His Circle* 1: 232.

4. Martin J. Levy supplies the relevant biographical documentation in "Coleridge, Mary Robinson, and *Kubla Khan.*" For further information on the relations of the two poets, see David V. Erdman, "Lost Poem Found: The Cooperative Pursuit and Recapture of an Escaped Coleridge Sonnet of 72 Lines."

5. See *The Contributions of Robert Southey to the Morning Post,* ed. Kenneth Curry. For the record of Coleridge and Wordsworth's contributions to this and other newspapers, consult Appendix D (3: 285–311) to Coleridge, *Essays on His Times,* ed. David V. Erdman.

6. In her letter to Pratt of 31 August 1800, Robinson acknowledged, "I continue my daily labours in the Post; all the Oberons. Tabithas. M R's and indeed most of the Poetry, you see there is mine" (Cameron, ed., *Shelley and His Circle* 1: 232).

7. Kenneth Neill Cameron attributes Godwin's interest in Mary Robinson not just to her being beautiful and "celebrated," but, as evidenced by her long poem "The Progress of Liberty," "also because her social philosophy was similar to his own" (*Shelley and His Circle* 1: 235). Robinson was intimately acquainted with Mary Wollstonecraft and Mary Hays as well. Godwin and John Wolcot (Peter Pindar) were the only associates to attend her funeral in Windsor on 31 December 1800.

8. This portrait is now in the Wallace Collection, Manchester Square, London, which has published a monograph by John Ingamells, *Mrs Robinson and Her Portraits* (1978), concluding with a checklist of twenty-three portraits of her.

9. See *Essays on His Times* I: lxxii–lxxiv, where Erdman marginalizes Robinson's significance in his effort to underscore that of Coleridge.

10. Erdman suggests that Coleridge rather than Wordsworth wrote the commendation that prefaced "Alcaeus to Sappho" as a component of this later "newspaper flirtation" (*Essays on His Times* 3: 291).

11. To pursue this subject fully would require a comparative treatment of Southey's reconstituted further editions of the two-volume *Poems*, his two volumes of the *Annual Anthology*, and his *Metrical Tales and Other Poems* of 1805, along with the run of Robinson's contributions to the *Morning Post*, which have never been gathered, as well as her last volume. Indeed, it could well be that, even as *Lyrical Tales* refers to Wordsworth's volume, so Southey's *Metrical Tales* is meant to invoke Robinson's. Such an extended analysis, though valuable for sorting out the incremental nature of poetic fashion and influence, is manifestly beyond the scope of the present essay.

12. See, for instance, Steven Maxfield Parrish, *The Art of the Lyrical Ballads* 116–19, a scholarly and critical pillar of our knowledge of these works. In all fairness, it is perhaps only natural to observe Southey's own defensiveness about his originality turned against him.

13. For contexts of this "realism," consult Robert Mayo, "The Contemporaneity of the *Lyrical Ballads*"; Mary Jacobus, *Tradition and Experiment in Wordsworth's Lyrical Ballads (1798)*; and Betty T. Bennett, ed., *British War Poetry in the Age of Romanticism*.

14. To place this within a larger context, consult Chap. 5, "The Pastoral," in Stuart Curran, *Poetic Form and British Romanticism*, 2nd ed. 85–127; also Lore Metzger, *One Foot in Eden: English Pastoral Poetry*.

15. These are Laura, Laura Maria, Lesbia, M. R., Oberon, Sappho, the Sylphid (in prose), T. B., Tabitha Bramble, and Titania.

16. The sequence is "Mistress Gurton's Cat. A Domestic Tale" (No. 9774, 8 January), "Old Barnard. — A Monkish Tale" (No. 9791, 28 January), "The Tell Tale; or, Deborah's Parrot" (No. 9821, 4 March), "The Confessor. A Tale" (No. 9835, 20 March), "The Fortune Teller" (No. 9855, 12 April), "The Granny Grey. — A Tale" (No. 9906, 10 June). Five other poems later revised and included in *Lyrical*

Tales, all serious in tone, were published over the name of Mrs. Robinson. These are "The Poor Singing Dame" (No. 9789, 25 January), "The Haunted Beach" (No. 9816, 26 February), "Agnes" [retitled "Edmund's Wedding"] (No. 9818, 28 February), "The Deserted Cottage" (No. 9829, 13 March), "Poor Marguerite" (No. 9851, 8 April). In all, half the 22 poems of *Lyrical Tales* were published, most in shorter versions, in the *Morning Post.*

17. Stuart published "All Alone" in the *Morning Post* of 18 December 1800 to note Robinson's "just published" volume: it was thus the last poem printed during her lifetime. With it one might compare "The Savage of Aveyron," another portrait of existential childhood and a brilliant technical accomplishment.

Linda H. Peterson

Becoming an Author: Mary Robinson's *Memoirs* and the Origins of the Woman Artist's Autobiography

How does a woman become an author? Romantic mythologies of the male artist, with their emphasis on natural genius and superior literary taste, posit an organic development deriving from innate capacity; recent books by literary historians have, in contrast, stressed more practical nineteenth-century efforts to make authorship a legitimate profession, one equal to medicine and the law.[1] These books, as well as autobiographical studies of authorship, have only coincidentally touched on the Romantic female writer — in part because Romantic myths were specifically gendered to describe male artistry, in part because autobiographical accounts by women writers were few and far between until late in the nineteenth century.[2] Such accounts were few not just because women were socially discouraged from public self-display but also, I believe, because women writers were deeply ambivalent about the myths of authorship their male counterparts had created. Women were able to imagine their lives within the patterns of those myths, yet they were quick also to recognize the deviations in their experience that made the patterns inoperable or irrelevant.

In this regard, Mary Robinson's *Memoirs* is a historically pivotal and generically significant text: it allows us to trace the ambivalences of a Romantic woman writer who chose to author(ize) herself in and through autobiography. Published in 1801, one of the earliest of English artists' memoirs, it illustrates a woman writer's attempt to participate in Romantic myths of authorship and the difficulties of such participation; indeed, in its ambivalences, it contains the seeds of a very different autobiographical tradition that Robinson's Victorian successors chose instead to develop. To state my argument simply, I shall suggest that Mary Robinson tried, in her *Memoirs* and other autobiographical texts, to present herself as an authentic Romantic artist but that her readers, both her contemporaries and, more important, her female literary successors, rejected Robinson as their literary mother and also her autobiographical mode of self-presentation. Instead, most nineteenth-century women autobiographers embraced a version of female authorship that repressed assertions of genius, literary taste, and the poetic production of original knowledge and that accepted the woman writer as a being of lesser imagination and education who transmitted (masculine) knowledge within a private (feminine) sphere.

I. Robinson as Romantic Artist

For Robinson and her contemporaries, genius was a (perhaps *the*) prerequisite to becoming a writer. As Mary Jean Corbett sums it up, "the primary fiction about nineteenth-century authorship [was] that the man of genius is wholly his own product, an individual whose native abilities alone enable him to succeed" (*Representing Femininity* 18). In 1795, for example, in an *Essay on the Manners and Genius of the Literary Character,* Issac D'Israeli described the true literary artist as one who possessed the "faculty of genius," and he posited an international fellowship of writers who, "uninfluenced by the interests or the passions which give an impulse to the other classes of society, are connected by the secret links of congenial pursuits."[3] William Hazlitt put it more succinctly: "Professional Art is a contradiction in terms. Art is genius."[4]

Robinson's *Memoirs* accepts this Romantic fiction and begins with a passage intended both to recall and illustrate her natural genius. The passage, a verbal painting of the Gothic ruins among which she was born (1–2),[5] functions much like the opening section of Joyce's *Portrait of the Artist as a Young Man* with its display of its young hero's facility with words. Robinson links her verbal facility, which tends toward the melancholic, not only to environment but also to physiology and physiognomy: she was born, she notes, with "singularly large" eyes and a face "exhibiting features marked with the most pensive and melancholy cast" (7); as soon as she could read, she took to "learning epitaphs and monumental inscriptions" and to reciting elegies like Pope's "Lines to the Memory of an Unfortunate Lady" and Mason's "Elegy on the Death of the Beautiful Countess of Coventry" (9). Robinson goes on to describe her early capacity for writing poetry while a student at Miss Lorrington's Chelsea academy and later at Oxford House, Marlyebone, and notes that these "juvenile compositions," "written when I was between twelve and thirteen," were eventually published in a "small volume" (23). And, while such personal recollections demonstrate her natural abilities, she is also careful to include more indisputable testimony: the opinion of her governess, Mrs. Hervey, that she possessed "an extraordinary genius for dramatic exhibitions" (30) and the "encomiums" of David Garrick, who, when he first heard her recite dramatic poetry, lavishly praised her "juvenile talents" (32).

What Robinson gives as evidence of youthful genius her daughter Maria, the compiler and editor of the *Memoirs,* amplifies with examples of mature poetic inspiration and production. Maria's examples focus on Mary Robinson as an *improvisatrice* — that is, a maker and reciter of spontaneous verses. The continental tradition of improvisation became known in England during the 1790s, and well known after the 1807 publication of Madame de Staël's *Corinne.*[6] Reproducing both continental and English features of the inspired poet and anticipating de Staël's fiction, Maria Robinson recounts scenes in which her mother "poured forth those poetic effusions which have done so much honor to her genius and decked her tomb with unfading laurels" (204) — poems like "Lines to Him Who Will Understand Them," in which Robinson bids farewell to Britain for Italia's shore; or "The Haunted Beach," inspired by Robinson's discovery of a drowned stranger; or "The Maniac," written, like Coleridge's *Kubla Khan,* in a delirium excited by opium. Such *improvisatore,* in Maria's view, give "no less credit to the genius than to the heart of the author" (214).

For literary critics like Issac D'Israeli, genius was sufficient evidence to prove "literary character": genius "can exist independent of education," he argued, and "whenever this [genius] has been refused by nature, as it is so often, no theory of genius, neither habit nor education, have ever supplied its want" (*Literary Character* 28). But although D'Israeli was willing to minimize the importance of education, not all nineteenth-century theorists concurred; R. L. Edgeworth, father of the novelist Maria, argued in his *Essays on Professional Education* (1809) that theories of "peculiar genius" were too often the result of "the inaccuracy of common biography" and "ignorance of facts" and that the "natural genius" usually turns out to have had an excellent education (4–5).[7] Most Romantic writers, irritated by the proliferation of hacks professing to be authors, similarly emphasized education as essential to the development of literary taste. Wordsworth, in the "Preface" to the second edition of the *Lyrical Ballads* (1800), insists that an "accurate taste in poetry" can be acquired only "by thought and a continued intercourse with the best models of composition," and it is no coincidence that he illustrates a key argument in the "Preface" not only by citing English writers but also by comparing two groups of Latin poets (Catullus,

Terence, and Lucretius versus Statius and Claudian) to demonstrate his own familiarity with the "best models" (Woodring, ed., *Prose of the Romantic Period* 50, 67). It is no coincidence either that his autobiographical poem, *The Prelude,* includes long sections about his educational experiences at Hawkshead and Cambridge. Even if Wordsworth laments his lack of learning at Cambridge, his university experience, as Corbett tellingly points out, allowed him to be "integrated into a body of elites" (*Representing Femininity* 30).

In the early pages of her *Memoirs* Mary Robinson similarly stresses her superior literary education. As a young child, she attended Hannah More's Bristol academy, a fact she mentions for its intellectual cachet but declines to amplify for reasons I shall later suggest. After her family's move to London, she studied under Meribah Lorrington, an "extraordinary woman" whose "masculine education" included both "modern accomplishments" and "classical knowledge." Lorrington knew "the Latin, French, and Italian languages," as well as arithmetic, astronomy, and "the art of painting on silk" (21). Presumably Robinson received instruction in all these areas, for she depicts herself as Lorrington's protégé, claiming "All that I ever learned I acquired from this extraordinary woman" (22). The acquisition of "classical knowledge" (21) was particularly important, given that a lack of Latin and Greek often shut women out from legitimate authorship; as Nigel Cross explains, women's "utterly inadequate education" made them "female drudges" rather than authors (*The Common Writer* 164–68).[8]

Two narrative details in Robinson's account of her education are crucial in her adaptation of Romantic myths of authorship: (1) that she received a "masculine education" at Lorrington's academy; and (2) that, during her stay there, she began to write poetry. For Robinson the "masculine education" — that is, the training in classical languages and modern subjects women so rarely received — fulfills a prerequisite for writing poetry and, indeed, leads to her first literary productions, her "writing verses" and "composing rebuses" (23). This narrative association would seem to confirm the Romantic myth that genius complemented by education makes the poet; it also implies that a woman might, in certain fortunate circumstances, find herself becoming a poet too. Yet Robinson is deeply fearful of the effects of reproducing this masculine myth in real life, and her fear is registered in a biographical sketch of an "other" woman, Meribah Lorrington. After leaving Lorrington's academy, Robinson re-encounters her former governess, now given over to drink and "completely disfigured" (26); she can only shudder at the "horror" that this desexed woman represents. If we read the Lorrington episode as an instance of what Janice Carlisle has called "specular auto-biography," as a piece of self-analysis in which the autobiographer uses an "other" to understand the self, then Lorrington embodies the negative effects of a masculine education, the loss of feminine virtues and even female form (*John Stuart Mill and the Writing of Character* 223–59). Coming to authorship the masculine way may be a dangerous, ultimately self-annihilating course of action.

Given this fear, Robinson's account of her education introduces, consciously or unconsciously, an alternative myth of authorship, one more feminine than masculine in its literary associations. In this myth the special features of Lorrington's academy, not just the "masculine education" but the domestic arrangements, are crucial for producing a female poet. What Robinson describes is an academic institution in which an older, well-educated woman teaches, encourages, and inspires young girls in a life of literature. She notes that Meribah Lorrington "had only five or six pupils," that she "called me her little friend," that teacher and pupil shared "domestic and confidential affairs," and that Lorrington's encouragement "after school hours" led Robinson to try writing poetry (22–23). What she suggests, in other words, is a modern version of Sappho's female academy, and it seems likely that Sappho's life — or, rather, contemporary myths of the great Greek poetess — influenced the shape of Robinson's *Memoirs,* at least in this account of her preparation to write poetry.[9]

In 1796 Robinson had published a volume of poetry, *Sappho and Phaon, in a Series of Legitimate Sonnets, with Thoughts on Poetical Subjects, and Anecdotes of the Grecian Poetess.*[10] The Sappho Robinson imagines, like most eighteenth- and nineteenth-century Sapphos, is a mature woman smitten by (heterosexual) love for a younger Phaon, a distinguished poet whose "lute neglected lies" because of an all-consuming, unrequited passion (Sonnet IV 42). Robinson's sonnet sequence can of course be read as an autobiographical fiction, as a thinly disguised account of her agonies over her loss of the Prince of Wales and fall from power (or, alternatively, over her later loss of Banastre Tarleton).[11] In the "Account of Sappho" that prefaces her sonnets, Robinson gives us a poetess much like herself: a woman of genius who "derived but little consequence from birth or connections" (21), who married and gave birth to a daughter, whose "genius" gave her fame but also "excited the envy of some writers who endeavoured to throw over her private character a shade" (22), but who nonetheless continued to her great poetry "for future ages" (26). Some of the details — of Sappho's marriage, motherhood, and fame — were standard features in eighteenth-century biographies of the Greek poetess, but the conjectures about Sappho's obscure birth and the envy of other poets are pure invention, suggestive of Robinson's desire to draw implicit parallels between Sappho's life and her own. She had been called, after all, "the ENGLISH SAPPHO."[12]

More important for our purposes here, however, is to consider this biographical account as it delineates a pattern for becoming a poet(ess). Robinson, quoting Abbé Barthelemy, emphasizes the educative function of Sappho, the role of her academy in Greek culture and her personal role as an intellectual exemplar for Lesbian women: "Sappho undertook to inspire the Lesbian women with a taste for literature; many of them received instructions from her, and foreign women increased the number of her disciples" (28). Alas, Robinson laments in her "Preface," Britain lacks such high respect for poetry and poetic genius. Not only is it "a national disgrace" that Britain should, "of all enlightened countries [be] the most neglectful of literary merit" (15–16), Robinson adds that Englishwomen of genius have particularly suffered because of lack of institutional support:

> I cannot conclude these opinions without paying tribute to the talents of my illustrious countrywomen; who, unpatronized by courts, and unprotected by the powerful, persevere in the paths of literature, and ennoble themselves by the imperishable lustre of MENTAL PRE-EMINENCE. (16)

These critical comments, taken in conjunction with the biographical account, testify to Robinson's awareness that cultural conditions vary in their nurturing of poetic genius and that contemporary conditions work against Englishwomen who aspire to authorship. More positively, however, they underline a determination to create a viable myth of female artistry for herself and other women.

In this (re)creation, Robinson follows (or anticipates) her continental counterparts who, as Joan DeJean has shown, revivified the Sapphic myth for their own self-authorization.[13] Sappho represents, for Robinson and other women poets, an ancient, original, and originating figure who fulfills the criteria for Romantic artistry yet adds specifically female features to the myths of becoming a poet.[14] Sappho adds the possibility of female community and a female literary tradition. In the *Memoirs,* this possibility is hinted at, though never fully realized, in Lorrington's female academy and later in the literary circle that included Robinson, Lady Yea, and Mrs. Parry. Indeed, if Meribah Lorrington encouraged Mary Robinson to write poetry, it was the Duchess of Devonshire who encouraged her to publish; the "small volume" written "when I was between twelve and thirteen" (23) and published as the *Poems* of 1775 was the "neatly bound volume of my poems" to which the Duchess gave her approval.[15]

II. Robinson as Female Artist

If Sappho provided Robinson with an alternative myth for becoming an author, and if this myth was more enabling than terrifying, it nonetheless pointed to an (auto)biographical perplexity. In most eighteenth- and early nineteenth-century fictions of Sappho, the poet's love for Phaon was added to the biographical facts, and thus the question of love was added to the myth of female artistry.[16] Did love enable and inspire the female poet, or did it silence her voice—"my Lyre neglected lies," in Robinson's phrase?

One Romantic fiction—John Nott's *Sappho: After a Greek Romance* (1803)—associates passionate romantic love with the flowering of poetry.[17] Nott's young Sappho exhibits the skills and inclinations of a poet, but not until she loses Phaon and experiences the despair of love does she produce genuine poetry. Nott calls love "the richest material for versification" (251), and his fictional biography sets the writing of Sappho's two great odes in Sicily, where Sappho has fled to recover Phaon and where she enjoys the company of other poets and philosophers who discuss the poetic tradition. In this myth of female artistry, the poet needs more than genius and education; she needs also to experience the pangs of love (if not the sexual act of love itself, about which Nott is prudishly silent).[18]

Robinson seems less certain about the alignment of romantic love and female artistry, more worried about a negative relation. In her 1796 *Sappho and Phaon* the female poet is already an artist before the sonnet sequence begins, and the loss of Phaon's love results in a loss of poetic voice:

> Why, when I gaze on Phaon's beauteous eyes,
>   Why does each thought in wild disorder stray?
>   Why does each fainting faculty decay,
> And my chill'd breast in throbbing tumults rise?
> Mute, on the ground my Lyre neglected lies,
>   The Muse forgot, and lost the melting lay;
>   My down-cast looks, my faultering lips betray,
> That stung by hopeless passion,—Sappho dies! (Sonnet IV 42)

Robinson's sonnet, in large part a translation of Sappho's second ode, adds to the Sapphic myth what male poets never added: the possibility that erotic love might stifle poetic production. In other nineteenth-century redactions of this ode, most notably Swinburne's "Ode to Anactoria," unrequited love becomes the means and occasion for the triumph of poetry. While Robinson's sonnet may be read (and dismissed) biographically as an inflated tribute to the Prince of Wales and the power of her love for him, it is more interesting as evidence of her uneasiness about assuming this alternative feminine myth of authorship. Love is a sticky wicket for the woman writer. She can imagine occasions, as in Sonnets XIV and XV, in which an "Aeolian harp" or "Grecian lyre" may accompany the joys of love, but love may as readily result, as in Sonnets IV and XXXVI, in a "Lyre neglected" or a "lost Lyre."[19]

In the *Memoirs* Robinson retains this ambivalence about the influence of romantic love, tending to dissociate the plot of her affair with the Prince of Wales from her account of becoming a poet. One plot of the *Memoirs* traces a progress (or regress) in love; in it Robinson appears as a vulnerable woman — left unprotected by her father, unwittingly married to a London rake, exposed to the temptations of the stage, and then fondly charmed (and deceived) by the Prince of Wales. Robinson might have associated this traditional feminine plot with authorship, in that she turned to novel writing and journalism when the Prince abandoned her and refused to pay the £20,000 bond he owed her. (Indeed, one of her contemporaries, Laetitia Hawkins, gives just this explanation; after Robinson was deserted by the Prince and then Colonel Tarleton, Hawkins says: "She then took up a new life in London, became literary, brought up her daughter literary."[20]) Had Robinson made this narrative link, however, she would have aligned her *Memoirs* generically with the *chroniques scandaleuses,* thus suggesting that she was merely a hack writer who wrote for money and negating her claim to genuine artistry.

Instead, Robinson links authorship to a second feminine plot, that of the good mother and daughter who faithfully cares for her family.[21] During her married lifetime, Robinson supported herself, her daughter Maria, her mother Mrs. Darby, sometimes her husband, sometimes a brother — first by acting, later by writing. Yet even though she describes her financial role in the *Memoirs,* she resists making economics the motivating force behind authorship. Well before she discusses economics, Robinson associates maternity with literary production. In an early episode in which an amorous suitor comes upon her unawares, she recalls:

> In a small basket near my chair slept my little Maria; my table was spread with papers, and everything around me presented the mixed confusion of a study and a nursery. (107)

This combination — book and child, study and nursery — gives cultural sanction to Robinson's literary work (even as it defends her against unwanted amours). It aligns biological and literary creation; it makes authorship seem as "natural" a role as motherhood.

Moreover, this passage anticipates what will become a dominant Victorian myth of female authorship, a myth developed in the biographical addendum to the *Memoirs* by Maria Robinson (a Victorian editor before her time if ever there was one). As Maria completes the story of her mother's life, she dates the "commencement of her [mother's] literary career" from 1788, the year they both returned to England from the continent (202).[22] In 1788 Mrs. Robinson began not only to write but to nurse her daughter back to health:

> Maternal solicitude for a beloved and only child now wholly engaged her attention; her assiduities were incessant and exemplary for the restoration of a being to whom she had given life, and to whom she was fondly devoted. (203)

In the daughter's account, maternal devotion pays off in literary production — or perhaps literary production reactivates maternal conscience. As Maria states it, "the silence of the sick-chamber prov[ed] favourable to the muse" (204). Whatever the case, in editing her mother's life, Maria Robinson effects what the *Memoirs* only hint: that a safe, culturally viable myth of female artistry could be created by shifting the narrative focus from romantic to domestic love. Put another way, we might say that Maria foresaw the virtues of linking the artist's autobiography generically with the domestic memoir.

III. Robinson and Her Literary Successors

Robinson's *Memoirs* stands, in the English autobiographical tradition, as one of the first attempts to combine (masculine) myths of the Romantic artist with (feminine) versions of becoming a poet. Some second-generation Romantic poets — most notably Letitia Elizabeth Landon (known by her initials L. E. L.) and Felicia Hemans — continued to represent the female artist as a creature of genius, although they did so by aligning their work with Mme de Staël's illustrious *Corinne* rather than with Robinson's more dubious *Memoirs*.[23] Landon's poem "Sappho," for example, derives its details — the improvisation of verse, the homage of the audience, the public ceremony of presenting Sappho with a laurel crown — from Book II of *Corinne*, not from Robinson's *Sappho and Phaon* or *Memoirs* (1859 *Poetical Works* 367–70). Most of Robinson's autobiographical successors, however, gave up Romantic claims to genius, superior literary production and taste, or the poet as the producer of original knowledge, instead acceding to the Victorian doctrine of separate spheres, with the woman writer occupying the private (and decidedly inferior) realm.

A key figure in this transition was Hannah More, the woman writer whose practical efforts in education first influenced Mary Robinson. As I mentioned earlier, Mary (then Darby) Robinson attended the celebrated Bristol academy run by the Misses More, a fact that she mentions early in the *Memoirs* (10–11). She says no more about Hannah More, however, even though both women came from respected Bristol families, both had close friendships with the actor and stage manager David Garrick, both achieved fame in the London theatre during the 1770s, and both retained ties with Bristol and its nearby summer resort, Clifton.[24] Robinson represses her knowledge of More, I think, because it is so inimical to her own views of female artistry. More's increasingly dominant evangelical tendencies would have set the elder woman against the more worldly Robinson, but it was More's opinions about female authorship that required real repression.[25]

In *Strictures on the Modern System of Female Education,* published in 1799, the year Robinson began writing her *Memoirs,* More chastised parents and teachers who encouraged female scribblers. She argued that young women should be given books that "exercise the reasoning faculties," like Locke's *Essay on the Human Understanding* or Butler's *Analogy of Religion,* rather than light reading like novels. More's intention was not simply to develop the mental faculties of women; she also wanted to stop the proliferation of female novel-writers: "Who are those ever multiplying authors that with unparalleled fecundity are over-stocking the world with their quick succeeding progeny?" (*Works* [Harper and Brothers, 1854] 1: 345). More believed that reading novels resulted in writing novels, that the "easiness" of fictional production was "at once the cause of [its] own fruitfulness," that "every raw girl, while she reads, is tempted to fancy that she can also write" and triumphantly exclaim "And I too am an author!" (345). Robinson certainly was one of those "raw girls" who wanted to write and who, during the 1790s, produced the fictional "progeny" More so dreaded. Small wonder that Robinson acknowledged Meribah Lorrington rather than Hannah More as her literary mentor. More's educational philosophy insisted that women spend their time reading male authors rather than becoming authors themselves.

More important, More's views of women's intellectual and imaginative capacities were inhibiting to female writers like Robinson who aspired to genuine Romantic artistry. More believed in women's natural inferiority; as she states in her comparative summary of "the different capacities of the sexes": "women have equal *parts,* but are inferior in *wholeness* of mind, in the integral understanding" (367). Even when More admits that women may possess genius, she chooses a classical myth to explain it away — not that of Sappho but of Atalanta. "Woman in the career of genius," writes More, "is the Atalanta, who will risk losing the race by running out of her road to pick up the golden apple"; her male competitor "will more certainly attain his object, by direct pursuit, by being less exposed to the seductions of extraneous beauty" (367). The myth to which More alludes depicts Atalanta's loss of virginal freedom and her accession to marriage; it implies that women will, naturally and inevitably, succumb to their role as wives and mothers, thus giving up the possibility of becoming great artists. It is a myth directly in opposition to Robinson's vision of motherhood and authorship as mutually-enriching activities.

Most nineteenth-century autobiographical accounts after the *Memoirs* follow in the tradition of More rather than Robinson — not that they repeat or openly ascribe to the myth of Atalanta, but they accept woman's lesser literary capacities and her role within the domestic realm. As Robin Reed Davis has documented, Hannah More's example, both in life and in the hagiographic biographies published immediately after her death, influenced the self-conceptions of such popular women writers as Mrs. Sherwood, Charlotte Elizabeth Tonna, and Charlotte Brontë ("Anglican Evangelicalism"). In Tonna's *Personal Recollections* (1841), for example, there are no Romantic claims to genius or superior literary taste. Rather, she is content to mark her entrance into authorship as an unforeseen act of providence. While alone on her husband's rural Irish estate, she receives a parcel of religious materials published by the Dublin Tract Society; the tracts inspire her to think, in an appropriate feminine mode, "Since I cannot give them money, may I not write something to be useful in the same way?" (27). And Tonna explicitly accepts her literary production as inferior intellectual work, noting that she subdued her pride to make her style readable by any five-year-old.[26] Like most of her female contemporaries, Tonna makes no claim to producing original knowledge, only to disseminating received wisdom to needy readers: children, the working-classes, and other women.

There was, of course, a compelling reason for assuming this secondary position: it gave women culturally sanctioned access to the literary marketplace. Valerie Sanders and Mary Jean Corbett have argued that nineteenth-century women writers adapted the form of the spiritual autobiography to stress its exemplary and imitative functions and that, in so doing, they legitimated the public work of authorship by treating it as an extension of the good work that women normally performed within the domestic sphere. In Corbett's formulation, "Christian discourse g[ave] the autobiographer authority over that domestic space, which [was] redefined as the new locus for cultural and even literary authority." ("Feminine Authorship and Spiritual Authority" 15).[27] Put more cynically, we might say that Christian humility was a more palatable mode for women writers to adopt than Romantic self-aggrandizement.

The historical, social, and literary pressures that encouraged this new feminine mode of autobiography are too numerous to trace in this essay, but we may certainly point to one problem that most nineteenth-century women writers faced with Romantic myths of the artist: they depended on the artist's selling of himself. In presenting himself as a genius, with special knowledge and superior taste, the Romantic artist was offering himself, not just his books, to his reading public. Underlying Romantic myths of authorship, perhaps contributing to their formation, were the economic and social realities of aspiring to professional status. As Magali Sarfatti Larson explains, there is a difference between the work of a professional and a craftsman or laborer: "unlike craft or industrial labor . . . most professions produce intangible goods: the product, in other words, is only formally alienable and is inextricably bound to the person and personality of the producer" (*The Rise of Professionalism* 14). This association of product and producer was particularly troublesome for the female artist.

Robinson's life and *Memoirs* were far too implicated in the selling of the self to become a model for subsequent women writers, who worried far too much about the possible taint of entering the public sphere. Robinson had not only sold her face and body during her career as an actress, but she had also — more literally and transgressively — sold herself during her years as mistress to the Prince of Wales. Viewed from one perspective, her *Memoirs* were a final act of self-prostitution. In writing her autobiography, she was selling her "life" to make money — "making pennyworths of myself," as Margaret Oliphant would later describe the public autobiographical act (*Autobiography and Letters* 75).

Not that Robinson would have agreed with this assessment. Given her alignment of motherhood and authorship, she would have viewed her *Memoirs* as a legacy to her daughter. Begun on her deathbed in 1799, it was a final literary production to provide financial support for Maria, who edited, completed, and published the text in 1801 after her mother's death. Viewed more broadly, it was a model of the woman artist's autobiography, one showing her (literary) daughter(s) how to become an author. From this maternal perspective, the *Memoirs* is a confirmation of and testimony to Robinson's genuine female artistry, uncompromising in its insistence on genius *and* domestic solicitude.

Notes

1. See, e.g., Victor Bonham-Carter, *Authors by Profession;* Nigel Cross, *The Common Writer: Life in Nineteenth-Century Grub Street;* John Gross, *The Rise and Fall of the Man of Letters;* Patrick Parrinder, *Authors and Authority: A Study of English Literary Criticism and Its Relation to Culture, 1750–1900;* and J. W. Saunders, *The Profession of English Letters.*

2. Cross includes one chapter, "The Female Drudge," on women writers, and in its final chapters Marlon Ross's *The Contours of Masculine Desire* discusses such writers as Hannah More, Anna Laetitia Barbauld, and Felicia Hemans. Mary Jean Corbett's recent *Representing Femininity: Middle-Class Subjectivity in Victorian and Edwardian Women's Autobiography* includes an excellent discussion of Romantic myths of the male artist, to which I am endebted, but her book considers no women's texts published before the 1840s. Neither does Julia Swindells's *Victorian Writing and Working Women,* which also begins with Victorian autobiographies — that is, texts written after the notion of separate spheres was firmly entrenched and thus after a separate tradition of women's autobiography had begun.

3. See also ch. I, "On the Literary Character" and ch. IV, "Of Natural Genius." According to Corbett (*Representing Femininity* 27), D'Israeli's essay was much "read and admired by Scott, Moore, Byron, Rogers, and others."

4. Quoted by David Bromwich in *Hazlitt: The Mind of a Critic* 119.

5. For this essay I have used the Grolier Society edition of the *Memoirs,* which reproduces the text of the original 1801 edition.

6. For a discussion of the continental tradition of improvisation and its use in Madame de Staël's *Corinne* (1807), see Ellen Moers, *Literary Women* 183–87.

7. If biographers knew more about "the early education of the subject of their memoirs," Edgeworth believed, they might attribute less to "natural genius" (*Essays* 4–5).

8. Note that Robinson displays her knowledge of Latin in such volumes as *Sappho and Phaon* (1796), where she cites Ovid as well as his English translators;

note, too, in that volume her emphasis on her writing of "legitimate" sonnets — that is, with Italian rather than English rhyme schemes — to display her literary knowledge and taste.

9. On this subject, see also Joel Haefner's essay in this volume.

10. My quotations come from the 1813 Minerva Press edition of *Sappho and Phaon*.

11. Stuart Curran's essay in this volume suggests that *Sappho and Phaon* was written as "a sonnet sequence *à clef* upon being deserted by Banastre Tarleton" (p. 21), but I think it as likely that Robinson had her greater loss of the Prince of Wales in mind. Although the date of the sequence, 1796, is closer to the end of her long affair with Tarleton, several details in the sonnets suggest the Prince of Wales: the younger age of Phaon (the Prince of Wales was only 17, Robinson over 21, when their affair began), the "smooth cheek" and "golden hair" of sonnet X (the Prince was fair-skinned and fair-haired, Tarleton dark), and the setting of the love scenes in sonnet XV on the banks of a stream or river (Robinson and the Prince had their first rendezvous on the banks of the Thames, on an island near Kew).

12. See the review of 14 October 1794 in the *Morning Post,* quoted by Curran.

13. See Joan De Jean, *Fictions of Sappho, 1546–1937*, especially the "Introduction," 1–28, and Lawrence Lipking, *Abandoned Women and Poetic Tradition,* especially ch. 3, "Sappho Descending," 57–96.

14. Of course, male poets also used Sappho's poetry as an initiatory vehicle. De Jean posits a triangulation of desire in which young male poets compete for recognition and priority by translating Sappho's lyrics and thus taking possession of her voice. Female versions of Sappho tend, in contrast, to trace "the origin of women's poetry to shared female experience" (39). On the differences between "masculine" and "feminine" modes of influence, see Leslie Brisman's "*Maud:* The Feminine as the Crux of Influence," in which "masculine" modes are associated with force, aggression, explosiveness, acquisitiveness, and institution, and "feminine" with balance, responsiveness, perseverance, the accumulative, and community.

15. Robinson lost access to the literary circle surrounding the Duchess of Devonshire after her affair with the Prince of Wales became public.

16. This spurious biographical episode was added largely on the evidence of Ovid's *Heroides,* although writers like John Nott claimed they found evidence for it on the island of Lesbos.

17. Nott was a physician and classical scholar whose publications include medical treatises on thermal hot springs and translations of Greek, Latin, and Italian poetry. It is possible that he knew Mary Robinson, given that he resided and practiced medicine in the Bristol area from 1793 until his death in 1825.

18. Nott suggests that Sappho remains a virgin, neither consummating her love for Phaon nor engaging in any sapphic relations (about which Nott expresses only disgust). On the rumors of sapphic relations, see pp. 256–57.

19. There is also the possibility that Robinson fears openly embracing a Sapphic myth of authorship, given the sapphic implications. Robinson seems to be aware of the linguistic and sexual ambiguities of the second ode, for in her biographical "Account of Sappho," she denies that Sappho would have produced "any composition which might tend to tarnish her reputation" (26).

20. From Laetitia Hawkins, *Memoirs, Anecdotes, Facts, and Opinions* 2: 33–34.

For a fascinating discussion of the financial aspects of Robinson's literary career, see Jan Fergus and Janice Farrar Thaddeus, "Women, Publishers, and Money, 1790–1820."

21. I have written more fully about the conjunction of these feminine plots in "Female Autobiographer, Narrative Duplicity."

22. Maria gives the date as 1787, but the chronological sequence makes it clear that they arrived back in England at the beginning of 1788.

23. See the chapter "Performing Heroinism: The Myth of Corinne" in Moers, *Literary Women* 173–210. For the most widely read English translation of *Corinne* (1833), Letitia Landon translated the improvisations that appear throughout the novel into verse; Felicia Hemans noted that the novel had "a power over me which is quite indescribable; some passages seem to give me back my own thoughts and feelings, my whole inner being, with a mirror more true than ever friend could hold up" (quoted in Moers 177).

24. For details about More's life, see Mary Alden Hopkins, *Hannah More and Her Circle,* and M. G. Jones, *Hannah More.* Jones notes that "the lovely and unfortunate Perdita" attended the Mores' academy and that "her reputation was, later, used as a stick wherewith to beat Miss More" (9, 238, n. 19).

25. An anonymous nineteenth-century retelling of Robinson's life, "Our Old Actors: 'Perdita,'" *Temple Bar* 51 (1877), 536–48, speculates that "even so rigid a moralist as Hannah More could not condemn her," but I think this anonymous journalist fails to recognize how seriously More would have objected to Robinson's *literary* deeds.

26. "If, on reading a manuscript to a child of five years old, I found there was a single sentence or word above his comprehension, it was instantly corrected to suit that lowly standard [of homely simplicity]" (*Personal Recollections* 179).

27. See also Valerie Sanders, "'Absolutely an act of duty': Choice of Profession in Autobiographies by Victorian Women."

Susan Allen Ford

"A name more dear": Daughters, Fathers, and Desire in *A Simple Story*, *The False Friend*, and *Mathilda*

> "Is there not a name more dear than friend or guardian?" interrupted
> Lord Denmore. "Is there no whisperer within your breast, that tells
> you, I have a yet more tender claim upon your feelings?"
> — *The False Friend*, II 56

> "[T]he holy name of father was become a curse to me."
> —*Mathilda* 239

In a world where the family and family relationships constitute the most
legible signs of identity, language that signifies relationship — most especially the word "father" — can take on an almost mysterious power. This
power informs the plots of three novels, all published or written between
1791 and 1819: Elizabeth Inchbald's *A Simple Story*, (1791) Mary Darby
Robinson's *The False Friend*, (1799) and Mary Wollstonecraft Shelley's
Mathilda (written 1819–20). These novels participate in a Romantic fascination with the myth of the fall from innocence into the dark world of
experience and with the consequent motif of exile. They also share a
concern with the relationship between language and perception that informs Romantic fiction — an investigation of the problematic nature of
articulation. Moreover, like other novels of the period, they focus on the
dynamics of family relationships. But even more remarkable than those
features which clearly align these novels with the rich mythic and verbal
traditions all around them are certain qualities that truly *distinguish* these
works, that test and finally transform those traditions. These fictions of
father-daughter incest all share a plot powered by forbidden desire, a
characteristic definition — and then redefinition — of both daughter and
father, a significantly absent mother, and a rhetoric of incest that develops
through spatialization as well as through the suppression of speech. And in
all these novels, the involuted matrix of family relationships charts the

disruptive connections between sexuality and power, figuring this forbidden desire as threat to the family, to the society, and to the very self.[1]

Each of these novels explores different aspects of incestuous desire. *A Simple Story* tells the recursive tale of the daughter's attraction to and rebellion against patriarchal authority through two generations. At Miss Milner's father's death, he appoints his long-time friend Dorriforth, a Roman Catholic priest, as her guardian. Miss Milner falls in love with Dorriforth, a passion that seems hopeless until he unexpectedly inherits the title of Lord Elmwood and the church releases him from his priestly vows so that the power of his title might be perpetuated in a Catholic family.[2] For a while, after their relationship has improved from that of guardian-ward to the comparative equality of lovers, she gets a chance to display *her* power. That display of power, however, effectively ends her relationship with Dorriforth until Mr. Sandford, Dorriforth's Jesuit mentor and Miss Milner's harshest judge, joins them with an almost divine authority. They marry, but the novel's second half opens with the account of the disintegration of the marriage: Lord Elmwood's extended absence in the West Indies so disrupts the domestic ideal that Lady Elmwood is unfaithful. Fleeing Lord Elmwood's house in shame and repentance of her disobedience to her marriage vows, she buries herself in the seclusion of the country, where, after lingering for ten years, she dies.

Inchbald's account of the second generation replicates and intensifies this tyranny of the patriarchy. Lord Elmwood transfers his anger at his ward/wife to his daughter, the six-year-old Matilda, casting her out while keeping with him their adopted son, his nephew Harry Rushbrook. Matilda's obedient filial love struggles with her resentment of his commands. She eventually crosses accidentally into Lord Elmwood's path: he punishes her transgression by again expelling her from his house, making her vulnerable to the attentions of and eventual abduction by a cruder and less intelligent version of her mother's seducer. Only this challenge to Lord Elmwood's legal possession of his daughter can energize his interest in emotionally reclaiming her. The novel's conclusion reconciles father and daughter and cements that bond through the marriage of Lady Matilda and Harry Rushbrook, her father's heir.

In *A Simple Story,* where the incestuous desire is only subtext, the novel can end happily — or at least with the ending of romance: children are reconciled to the father; the marriage of Lady Matilda to her brother/father-substitute strengthens the family bonds that her mother's rebellion has shattered. In the two later novels, however, the incestuous desire is foregrounded: *The False Friend* charts the dynamics of the desire; *Mathilda* explores its consequences.

The False Friend, epistolary in mode, begins as the orphaned Gertrude St. Leger joins the family of her guardian, Lord Denmore. He has "sworn to bestow on her the protection of a father, [while] she now comes to prove that worth which sanctions the distinction" (1: 5). Her arrival strains the weak links that hold together Lord and Lady Denmore, as Lord Denmore's mysterious behavior (his affectionate attentions to Gertrude alternate with his inexplicable avoidance of her) suggests both to the jealous Lady Denmore and to Gertrude herself a relationship beyond that of a guardian for his ward. A pattern of attraction and repulsion, approval and condemnation, candor and suppression, characterizes the relationship between Gertrude and Lord Denmore throughout the novel. Time and again, their relationship hovers mysteriously on the brink of articulation when she manages to offend him and he pushes her away, sending her wandering unprotected across the southern regions of England, liable to kidnapping, imprisonment, and other depredations. Despite her resentment at his treatment of her, she loves him, can think only of him, and when she hears, after Lady Denmore's death, that he plans to remarry, she feels betrayal, jealousy, and the impulse toward revenge. Only after his mortal wounding in a duel (fought over the question of whether he must explain his relationship to her) does he reveal himself as her father. Tied to him in death as in life, she too expires, in the novel's concluding phrase, "A VICTIM OF SENSIBILITY!" (4: 367).

Mary Shelley's *Mathilda* explores the heroine's consciousness of both the nature of her predicament and the form of her own tale.[3] Her tale is a redaction of the banishment from Eden, a fall due to sympathy, to the desire for knowledge, to speech. As narrator, Mathilda in what will be her last act "unveils the mystery" for her friend Woodville of "my solitary life; my tears; and above all of my impenetrable and unkind silence" (176). Because Mathilda's mother died in childbirth, Mathilda herself exists, for her father, only as a living emblem of his loss. He abandons her, but on his reappearance seventeen years later they become close companions. When another man shows an interest in Mathilda, however, her father recognizes his own love for her and retreats to their estate in Scotland. This time, she follows and pries the secret of his despair out of him. In response to Mathilda's horror at his revelation, he runs off again and drowns himself in the North Sea.

Mathilda's guilt — that she is responsible for her father's desire as well as for his death—drives the last half of the novel. She counterfeits her own death, disguises herself as a nun, and goes off to live by herself on a blasted heath, consumed by despair and self-hatred brought on by her guilt: "unlawful and detestable passion had poured its poison into my ears and changed all my blood, so that it was no longer the kindly stream that supports life but a cold fountain of bitterness corrupted in its very source" (229). Ultimately, lost in a reverie of celestial union with her father, she is caught in a midnight rainstorm, which leads her into a rapid consumption. The death she looks forward to will be a marriage: "In truth I am in love with death; no maiden ever took more pleasure in the contemplation of her bridal attire than I in fancying my limbs already enwrapt in their shroud: is it not my marriage dress? Alone it will unite me to my father when in an eternal mental union we shall never part" (244).

In all these novels, the relations between daughter and father power the plot. Although that relationship, as Patricia Meyer Spacks has argued, "seems to have provided for many women a model of emotional satisfaction and safety" ("Ev'ry Woman" 45), in these novels the sheltered security of that relationship masks a dark emotional imprisonment—in which the daughter may sometimes conspire. In the female family romance, as defined by Marianne Hirsch, the plot is driven by the daughter's desire for the power that the father might transfer to her, a "confla[tion of] eros and ambition" (57). The daughter's simultaneous desire for and resistance to the father's power and the father's desire for control enact what Linda Boose has identified as a characteristic pattern of the conflict between retention and separation ("The Father's House" 32–33).[4]

The daughters in these novels are both peculiarly powerless and acutely threatening. They are all orphans: they have no mothers and, if their fathers are not demonstrably dead, these daughters have long been separated from them and from the power that they can confer. While, as Nina Auerbach argues, "the orphan emerg[es] as the primary metaphor for the dispossessed, detached self" ("Incarnations" 395), there is a paradoxical resilience that characterizes him: "the Romantic waif is brimming with a certain equivocal energy that threatens the world he is homeless in. His solitude energizes him as visionary, artist, and silent schemer, his appearance of winsome fragility feeding into his power of survival" (395). But these female orphans are neither sturdy nor dynamic enough to engage in that endless refashioning of the self that characterizes Auerbach's male orphans. In fact, their powers of survival are severely limited by the return of the father with his power to redefine and then nullify his daughter's incipient selfhood. Sandra Gilbert argues that the culture formulates "a 'daughteronomy' preached for the growing girl, [which] says: You must bury your mother; you must give yourself to your father. Since the daughter has inherited an empty pack and cannot *be* a father, she has no choice but to be *for* the father—to be his treasure, his land, his voice" ("Life's Empty Pack" 265). And yet, somehow, the female orphans in these novels do threaten the very structures of their society and do achieve a certain visionary status.

In *A Simple Story,* Miss Milner enacts all the roles available to female characters: the rebellious daughter and the submissive daughter; the woman seeking power over her lover and the woman conscious of her powerlessness; self-denying virgin, haughty coquette, dutiful wife, fallen (and repentant) woman, selfless mother. Though Miss Milner's "quick sensibility," "energy" (15), and "spirit of contradiction" (38) threaten to flame into rebellion, as Dorriforth's ward she recognizes and acts on her duty to submit her desires to his will. Sandford becomes the focus of her rebellion and the agent of her humiliation, as he continually monitors her failure to conform to the pattern of young womanhood represented by the passive Miss Fenton. This treatment has its effect: "She felt an inward nothingness she never knew before, and had been cured of all her pride, had she not possessed a degree of spirit beyond the generality of her sex" (40). Deferring to Dorriforth's priestly status, she submits to voluntary exile, during which "her health [becomes] impaired from the indisposition of her mind" (96), yet another conventional feminine response to the stern controls of the patriarchy. When she transgresses the accepted boundaries of her role in her infidelity to her marriage vows, Lady Elmwood not only loses her identity as Lord Elmwood's wife but as a consequence has no way to define herself: she has "no will" (203). Instead, she represents herself finally in the role of chastened daughter whose complete submission entails an entire loss of self. The letter she leaves Lord Elmwood she asks him to read *"for her father's sake"* (208). She inscribes herself as her father's daughter and Matilda as "the grand-daughter of Mr. Milner" (210), the only terms that will justify either. "It is Miss Milner your ward, to whom you never refused a request, supplicates you" (208).

While Miss Milner's rebellion temporarily liberates her from the plotlessness of total submission (though only to lead her into the plotlessness of loss of self), Matilda, trapped in the role of good daughter, inhabits a plot that is always managed by the more powerful male characters around her—Sandford, Harry Rushbrook, Lord Margrave, and, of course, Lord Elmwood. Matilda's story only clarifies her mother's essential powerlessness.

She both fears Lord Elmwood and adores his awe-inspiring image: "to this picture [of Lord Elmwood] she would sigh and weep; though when it was first pointed out to her, she shrunk back with fear, and it was some time before she dared venture to cast her eyes completely upon it" (220). But even for Matilda submission cannot be total. Her acknowledgment of her father's authority and her desire to win his love (and so to participate in that authority) contend with her real resentment that she is so shut out of his affections, excluded from her true position as his daughter. Matilda's resentment can be expressed safely only as it is deflected onto Harry Rushbrook. Her anger, a violation both of the commandment to honor her father and of the rules of feminine decorum, must be suppressed. That suppression wears her into a "deadly pale[ness]" and "a fixed melancholy" (304); her anger at Rushbrook erupts with increasing force as her confinement endures.

For Robinson's heroine, the very meeting with her guardian/father underscores the isolation of her orphaned condition. Lord Denmore's embarrassment and reserve pain and puzzle her: "Never, till I experienced this agonizing moment, did I know the misery of an orphan's destiny. All the tenderness of parental care seemed to recede from my awakened fancy, and I . . . looked round in vain for an eye to pity, or a bosom to protect me" (1: 9–10). The very self is unstable in the face of his power: "I found that, to please, and to be pleased, I must become a new being" (1: 22). His powerful self is enough to unravel hers: "with all the boasted pride, with all the stern and rigid sense of virtue which guards my heart; when I meet the dark and penetrating eyes of Lord Denmore, I become as it were *nothing*" (1: 296–97). Gertrude is indeed a good daughter—but that is not enough to empower her. She is resistant to (other) male interest but continually offending, her very obedience to her father often apparent rebellion against his dictates. She sees herself "a solitary atom in the vast universe" (2: 336). Moreover, the duplicity of the world of this novel, a world populated by false friends who can misrepresent her to Lord Denmore, intensifies her powerlessness. Like Inchbald's Matilda, she is both attracted to and resentful of her father's authority and power.

More than any of the other heroines, Gertrude is most aware of herself as victim. That victimization comes, however, not only from the corrupt institutions of the society but also from within. The greatest tyranny woman is subject to (she argues) springs from her own heart, her passionate nature. "Woman, created to be [man's] solace and companion, . . . is formed to be his slave! Her vaunted strength is but the shadow of a giant"

(1: 158). She becomes "a timid, trembling, guilty wanderer . . . wishing every moment for complete annihilation" (2: 339).

Mary Shelley, too, emphasizes the isolation of her heroine. Rejected at birth by her father (who "existed from this moment for himself only" [181]), Mathilda is left to the protection of an aunt whose heart "was totally incapable of any affection" (182). Isolated in "a remote part of the house" (182), she is raised by a nurse until her eighth year, when her nurse's departure removes her only friend. Instead, she creates objects for affection out of "memories" of parents she has never seen. "I clung to the memory of my parents; my mother I should never see, she was dead: but the idea of [my] unhappy, wandering father was the idol of my imagination. I bestowed on him all my affections; there was a miniature of him that I gazed on continually; I copied his last letter and read it again and again" (185). Her father's return marks her real birth: "And now I began to live" (187). But as her father recognizes his incestuous feelings, she is returned to a darker isolation: "suddenly I was left on a barren rock; a wide ocean of despair rolled around me: above all was black, and my eyes closed while I still inhabited a universal death" (190). Again transformed, she is "dead to all regret," her heart "changed . . . to stone" (215). She sees her self as "monster" (239), renames herself: "I am Despair" (236).

Ironically, the catalyst of this isolation is Mathilda's impulse for connection, her plea that her father communicate his sorrow to her. "I said to myself, let him receive sympathy and these struggles will cease. Let him confide his misery to another heart and half the weight of it will be lightened" (197). The result of this communication, however, is "that solitude which alone could suit one whom an untold grief seperated [*sic*] from her fellow creatures. . . . There was too deep a horror in my tale for confidence; I was on earth the sole depository of my own secret" (216). Indeed, so radical is this change that Mathilda frames her narrative with a description of Nature's participation in her blighted and friendless condition. The winter sun has set on the solitary heath where "no voice of life reaches" her: "I see the desolate plain covered with white, save a few black patches that the noonday sun has made . . . , a few birds are pecking at the hard ice that covers the pools—for the frost has been of long continuance. . . . I am alone—quite alone—in the world" (175). She begins and ends in isolation, her only power and her only connection the force of the tale she can leave for her friend Woodville.

If these orphaned daughters are defined in terms of a powerlessness and isolation that contribute to their lack of self-love, even of self, the fathers are defined in terms of authority, whether personal or institutional, that manifests itself through both love and the sometimes angry exercise of power.[5] Lord Elmwood in his religious function as well as in his role as guardian represents patriarchal power that is underlined when his inheritance of an earldom provides a motive for releasing him from his vows of celibacy. Dorriforth's "skilful management" (24) of the forms of society keeps Miss Milner within bounds: "his politeness would sometimes appear even like the result of a system he had marked out for himself, as the only means to keep his ward restrained within the same limitations" (23). And instead of the sound of Lord Elmwood's voice Matilda can hear only the sound of his gun, indistinguishable from Rushbrook's, merging his individuality into a generic expression of masculine power. Lord Denmore, like Lord Elmwood, is a peer. He and his friends quite clearly control both the church (and its ability to minister to the powerless) and the local magistracy (in the person of Sir Hector Upas, later Lord Arcot). His power is emphasized as he repeatedly delegates authority over Gertrude to one or another of his male friends. Mathilda's father's power is manifested less in any *political* power he may have (though certainly he possesses both wealth and landed estates); rather it is exerted mainly (and usually benevolently) through the force of his personality: "he was impatient of any censure except that of his own mind" (188). And even after he feels he has forfeited a right to Mathilda's love, he takes for granted his authority over her: "although I have forfeited your filial love, yet regard [my words] I conjure you, as a father's command" (211).

Initially, the formative power of love is most manifest in these novels. The guardian/father takes on the role of education, and books—the word—become a medium of affection and love. Dorriforth tries with Miss Milner to impress the need for "time not always passed in society; of reflection; of reading; of thoughts for a future state; and of virtues acquired to make old age supportable" (18). And even before Lord Elmwood acknowledges Matilda as a daughter, while there is even a ban on speaking her name, he takes care to help Miss Woodley select books for her, "as the most cautious preceptor culls for his pupil, or a fond father for his darling child" (273).

In Robinson's and Shelley's novels, the role of the father as nurturing teacher is even more critical. Gertrude and Lord Denmore, to the consternation of Lady Denmore, spend long hours together in the library, and her education by this "superior master" (1: 148) has made her "a new-created being" (1: 149): "Has he not taught me to analyze the human heart; to separate the dross of folly from the pure and solid ore of truth? Have I not explored the paths of virtue and philosophy, guided by his classic taste, and enlightened by the power of his intellectual pre-eminence?" (1: 148). Lord Denmore's absence and the removal of his bust from the library leave it "like an empty casket, from which a valued jewel has been taken" (1: 165). And finally, Mathilda's time with her father is spent in study and excursion: "I was led by my father to attend to deeper studies than had before occupied me. My improvement was his delight; he was with me during all my studies and assisted or joined with me in every lesson" (190).

But that love is revealed as dangerously unstable. While the daughter submits — or appears to submit — to the father's authority, commands are given with smiles of approval. But with resistance, even apparent resistance, all smiles stop together. Thwarted paternal benevolence hardens into anger and the threat of separation. The austere "obstinacy" (33) that marks Lord Elmwood's character before his marriage — that can allow him, for instance, to separate himself from a sister who marries against his consent — turns, after the breakdown of his marriage, into "implacable rigour and injustice" (195). He becomes, in the words of the narrative, "a hard-hearted tyrant" (195), banishing his own infant daughter for her mother's offense, banishing other dependents for the mere mention of mother or daughter. Even to the stern Sandford, his former mentor, he becomes terrible: "he exalts his voice, and uses harsh expressions upon the least provocation — his eyes flash lightning, and his face is distorted with anger on the slightest motives — he turns away his old servants at a moment's warning, and no concession can make their peace" (223).

To control Gertrude (who is often unaware of the nature of her offense), Lord Denmore resorts to threatening the withdrawal of his love, setting himself up as judge and as regulator of what he sees as dangerous female power.

> "I know all your faults; you are proud and impatient; your sensibility is too acute; your resentment too hasty."
> "I plead guilty, my Lord," said I.
> "And I acquit you," interrupted my guardian. "But have a care how you transgress in future. I shall watch with jealous eyes; I shall not suffer that proud impetuous heart to tyrannise with impunity." (1: 36)

His most constant character as guardian seems not friend or parent or even lover but judge and tribunal. Not only does Lord Denmore withdraw his love from her at each real or imagined offense, but he (like Lord Elmwood) withdraws his protection also. His anger sends her wandering, unprotected, across England in ever more danger of male predation. In Robinson's novel, fatherly love is most definitely conditional. Lord Denmore recalls "how tenderly" he loved Gertrude "till by your conduct you forfeited my fondness" (4: 166). When she denies that she loves Edward Ashgrove, for instance, Lord Denmore warns her that "if you attempt to deceive me, my hatred will be final" (4: 163).

And even the Edenic companionship in *Mathilda* is destroyed as the father attempts to mask his desire with withdrawal and coldness. Mathilda "fall[s] from happiness to misery . . . as the stroke of lightning—sudden and entire" (191). "[H]arshness or a more heart-breaking coldness," "terrible emotions," and "anger" replace "sweet counsel," reducing her to "silence and tears" (191). His passion for her is awakened as he discovers her liability to change, her potential resistance to his control: "But when I saw you become the object of another's love; when I imagined that you might be loved otherwise than as a sacred type and image of loveliness and excellence; or that you might love another with a more ardent affection than that which you bore to me, then the fiend awoke within me" (209). When Mathilda's "presumption" attempts to break his silence, he responds with anger directed at her: "you are the sole, the agonizing cause of all I suffer, of all I must suffer until I die. Now, beware! Be silent! Do not urge me to your destruction" (200).

The currents of desire that energize these plots flow between daughter and father: the mother is absent. When, at the age of sixteen or seventeen, on the threshold of womanhood, these heroines meet their guardian/fathers, all of them—Miss Milner, Lady Matilda, Gertrude, and Mathilda— are revealed as images of their mothers. The image of the mother (in all but Miss Milner's case) reawakens the father's sense of loss and initiates his desire. Lord Elmwood is careful not to see his daughter Matilda lest "another attachment near to his heart . . . might a second time expose him to all the torments of ingratitude" (202). When he does finally (and accidentally) see her, "Her name did not however come to his recollection—nor any name but this—'Miss Milner—Dear Miss Milner'" (274). Both Gertrude St. Leger and Lady Denmore suspect Lord Denmore of a strange passion for Gertrude, having observed him reading a letter containing a lock of hair her color, swooning over what is apparently a miniature portrait of her, and obsessively repeating her name. Mathilda, like her mother's namesake Diana, is described by her father as a "nymph of the woods" (208). He tells himself that "Diana died to give her birth; her mother's spirit was transferred into her frame, and she ought to be as Diana to me" (210). In fact, when father and daughter return to their Yorkshire estate, he points out her mother's rooms in which nothing—workbox, writing desk, the book she was reading—has been changed. But even as he desires her to fill her mother's place, he recognizes the danger: "We walked together in the gardens and in the evening when I would have retired he asked me to stay and read to him; and first said, 'When I was last here your mother read Dante to me; you shall go on where she left off.' And then in a moment he said, 'No, that must not be . . .'" (195).

But maternal absence is significant not just as a space in the fathers' lives for their daughters to fill. It also requires these daughters, whose very physical form resembles their mothers, to re-enact with varying degrees of difference their mothers' histories. As Marianne Hirsch observes about the nineteenth-century novel, "Plot itself demands maternal absence. Ironically, however, that absence, the silence of mothers about their own fate and the details of their lives, insures that those lives, those stories will be repeated by daughters. . . . [F]or female writers, motherlessness means freedom not only from constraint but also from the power that a knowing connection to the past might offer, whether that past is powerful or powerless" (*The Mother/Daughter Plot* 67).

Indeed, *The False Friend* offers a particularly intriguing example not just of maternal absence but of maternal erasure. Lord Denmore's library contains companion busts—one modeled after his own head, the other the head of the poet Sappho, whom Gertrude describes as "the most favoured and the most unhappy of women" (1: 166). These busts are eventually moved to Gertrude's room, where, on a tempestuous night of the soul, unable to sleep, she attempts to remove the bust of Lord Denmore. As she struggles with its weight, her arm "touched the head of Sappho, which fell to the ground, shattered into a thousand pieces" (4: 206). The next morning, her maid Patty tells her of a leather case marked with the initials "G. S." and containing a lock of hair and a portrait of Gertrude. This case Patty has stolen from Lord Denmore and (in a panic) thrown into a brook, effectively erasing the image. Both the bust and the portrait, "as like you as it could stare" (4: 213), Gertrude learns, were images of her mother (also named Gertrude St. Leger). Returning to her chamber, she discovers in the fragments of alabaster "that nearly the whole of the countenance had escaped destruction. . . . I gazed on the precious fragment. I raised it to my lips; kissed it with a mixture of tenderness and awe; talked to it in the language of filial affection; pressed it to my bosom, and on my knees invoked the gentle spirit of my parent to sustain my soul, and soothe it into resignation" (4: 262). Its whiteness, however, "present[s] the paleness of the corpse" (4: 263). There is little such a mother can teach her — but teach her she does. With Gertrude's discovery that she is the perfect image of her mother comes the recognition that the image she has been erasing is not only her mother's, not only the image of the expressive and emotional female self, but also her own.

A Simple Story, The False Friend, and *Mathilda* also develop a rhetoric of incest that incorporates both spatial motifs and the silencing or suppression of speech. Spatially, these novels chart the conflict between retention and separation: daughters are alternately confined in locked rooms and set to wandering through London or across a countryside. Lynda Boose sees this spatialization as a constant feature of father-daughter texts: "The daughter's struggle with her father is one of separation, not displacement. Its psychological dynamics thus locate the conflict inside her inner family space. Father-daughter stories are full of literal houses, castles, or gardens in which fathers . . . lock up their daughters in the futile attempt to prevent some rival male from stealing them" ("The Father's House" 33). These novels, however, because of their pattern of imprisonment and expulsion, move the daughters between house and landscape.

Inchbald, Robinson, and Shelley configure these spaces differently. Inchbald's interiors and exteriors are realistically, if minimalistically, depicted, yet Miss Milner's confinement to the house, her exiles from London to the country, from the country to Bath, from Lord Elmwood's house to the "most dreary" (*A Simple Story* 197) isolation of Northumberland work symbolically to illustrate her changing relationship with Lord Elmwood and indicate her place with respect to the larger society. As Terry Castle points out, "Transgressions take place, for whether by accident or design, the heroine always goes where she is not supposed to" (*Masquerade and Civilization* 295). Lady Elmwood requests in her deathbed letter that Matilda be allowed to live in one of Lord Elmwood's houses as a clear sign that she is under her father's protection. And in fact her distinctly personal reading of Luke's Prodigal Son parable attests to the mythic power her father's house has accrued. Like "the unfortunate child in the scripture" (211), she too will return to her father's house. And as Lady Matilda wanders through the corridors of Elmwood Castle her transgression into her father's field of vision seems necessary, almost psychologically determined. Castle underscores this point: "Matilda tests her father's command in subtle, obsessive ways, haunting his library in his absence, gazing at portraits of him, listening for the sounds of his carriage" (324). Her consequent exile leads to her kidnapping, which leads her back to her father's London house, the habitation of Miss Milner, where she will be cherished as daughter and retained as wife.

Mary Robinson's locked rooms and her landscape track Gertrude's displacement as well as provide her with an exile's opportunity for social and political comment on hypocrisy and vice, on governmental tyranny and true patriotism, on justice, liberty, and the rights of woman. But even as Gertrude crisscrosses southern England, the focus shifts to her internal quest for identity. This "timid, trembling, guilty wanderer" (*The False Friend* 2: 339) understands her life as a journey through a landscape of sorrows: "From my infancy I have struggled along a mysterious and mazy path; I have since wandered in vain through all the changes of my tedious journey, and have found at every turn some new sorrow to encounter" (3: 214–15). The goal of this vain quest, as Lord Denmore tells her, is the secret of her own destiny: "A spell encircles you; a labyrinth of sorrow forms the outline of your fate; the central clue is enveloped in darkness" (2: 50–51). It is not Gertrude, however, but Lord Denmore who holds the key to her own identity, to the labyrinth of self: "He watched the strong emotions of my soul; he traced the torturing thought through all the labyrinths of my brain, and found that it led to his image indelibly impressed upon its fibres" (2:57–58). What lies at her center, the only answer she can make to the riddle of her own identity, is the image of her father.[6]

The landscape through which Mary Shelley's Mathilda wanders seems like a dreamscape, unpeopled, created by the psychic needs of her imagination. The landscape reflects the geography of both her emotional and narrative state. On the day of her father's arrival, Mathilda's excitement is such that she, like Dante's Pilgrim, finds herself in a dark wood where the straight way is lost: "My father was expected at noon but when I wished to return to meet him I found that I had lost my way: it seemed that in every attempt to find it I only became more involved in the intracacies [sic] of the woods, and the trees hid all trace by which I might be guided. I grew impatient, I wept, and wrung my hands but still I could not discover my path" (*Mathilda* 186–87). In contrast to both Inchbald and Robinson, Shelley's natural detail is simultaneously precise and symbolic. The revelation of Mathilda's father's love for her comes at "the end of May" in a wood "which but for strange passions might have been a paradise to us":

> the slim and smooth trunks were many of them wound round by ivy whose shining leaves of the darkest green contrasted with the white bark and the light leaves of the young sprouts of beech that grew from their parent trunks — the short grass was mingled with moss and was partly covered by the dead leaves of the last autumn that driven by the winds had here and there collected in little hillocks — there were a few moss grown stumps. (198)

These lights and shades play on a scene of generation and death, beautiful but sometimes parasitic growth: parent trees nurturing offshoots, phallic beeches wound with ivy, new grass still partly covered by dead leaves, tree stumps harmonized by moss. Ultimately, Mathilda's obsessions attempt to recreate the landscape. After bidding farewell to her friend Woodville, she loses herself in a Dantesque vision of her meeting with her father in Paradise: "I was so entirely wrapt in this reverie that I wandered on, taking no heed of my steps until I actually stooped down to gather a flower for my wreath on that bleak plain where no flower grew" (241).

All these daughters enact the pattern of displacement and quest described by Boose: "the quest of a daughter displaced from the house most often inscribes her disguised search to reenter it" ("The Fathers' House" 34). But in these novels the search to reenter the father's house is only successful in the most limited terms. Inchbald's Matilda, in the ending of romance, is re-established at the novel's point of origin, the house of Lord Elmwood. But the narrative regressiveness suggests a real claustrophobia, a feeling intensified by the implosion of the family structure. Matilda is successful in marrying her father, marrying the power he and through him Rushbrook can offer, but she has no independent viability, no ability to propel herself across the landscape. Although Lord Elmwood apparently endows her with the power to bestow what Rushbrook asks, that power (to bestow herself) can exist only at his pleasure.[7]

More usual in these novels is the failure of the quest. Miss Milner's banishment is permanent: she is buried not, as Elmwood somewhat tardily desires, with her father or with Elmwood's family, but alone. For the other two heroines, union with the father is possible only in death. Gertrude's now "for ever tranquil bosom . . . [is] deposited in the monument of the Denmore family" (*The False Friend* 4: 366), along with her father. All the earthly compensation Shelley's Mathilda can look forward to is an integration with the landscape, new life springing from her blighted self: "the turf will soon be green on my grave; and the violets will bloom on it. *There* is my hope and my expectation" (*Mathilda* 246). Her hope for a celestial reunion with her father, that indeed has come to define her life, is inextricably rooted in a desire for death.

As the epigraphs to this essay suggest, articulation in these novels is problematic. In all these novels, language functions as a tool of power. The fathers in both *A Simple Story* and *A False Friend* exercise dominion as they insist that their "children" (Miss Milner, Mr. Rushbrook, and Gertrude) *name* the person that they love. More benevolently, but more dangerously, in *Mathilda* the daughter insists that her father name his suffering. But in all these novels, power also resides in what is not named. Indeed, articulation is avoided, as if specificity might precipitate too much understanding, might plunge these characters into the dark world of experience. In *A Simple Story*, desire is never directly spoken. Miss Woodley, Mr. Sandford, and finally "a stranger" mediate the articulation of father-daughter desire and effect their union.

In the novels where the incestuous desire is foregrounded, suppression is even more insistent. In *The False Friend*, Denmore holds the secret of Gertrude's identity, and that knowledge is a power that charges his ambiguous communications with a dangerous and unstable force. Denmore's equivocal language leaves perilously unspecified the meaning of that "name more dear," allowing Gertrude and others to fill that blank as desire leads.[8] In a scene that epitomizes the process of this novel, Gertrude finds and reassembles, "with nice and laborious care" (1: 268), the torn pieces of a letter Denmore has written and destroyed. As ever, articulation is incomplete. "The precious morsel which should have terminated the short letter, was not to be found": "I will avow myself, in the face of God and man, thy——" (269). Gertrude's diligent efforts at reconstruction once again recapitulate the novel's riddle. Who is she? The missing fragment will describe Denmore's relation to her, and it is only through that relationship that she can arrive at her identity.

Once the desire has been articulated, once the forbidden hidden meaning has been discovered, the family structure can only implode, and both fathers and daughters, deprived of that support, have no possibility for relationship, no place in the world, no support for the self. Shelley's Mathilda describes her "wretched self" as "the source of guilt that wants a name" (*Mathilda* 239). Indeed, that very namelessness is what she has struggled against. Her father claims "secret thoughts working, and secret tortures which you ought not to seek to discover" (199). She opposes her words to his, which would silence her: "my whole heart is in the words I speak and you must not endeavour to silence me by mere words barren of meaning" (200). He sees articulation as a deadly and powerful temptation: "one word I might speak and then you would be implicated in my destruction; yet that word is hovering on my lips" (200). She sees articulation as an unburdening, an opportunity for connection through love's healing power: "Speak that word; it will bring peace, not death. If there is a chasm our mutual love will give us wings to pass it, and we shall find flowers, and verdure, and delight on the other side" (200). But articulation, of course, separates father from daughter and both from the rest of the world: "I was silent to all around me. I hardly replied to the slightest question, and was uneasy when I saw a human creature near me. I was surrounded by my female relations, but they were all of them nearly strangers to me: I did not listen to their consolations; and so little did they work their designed effect that they seemed to me to be spoken in an unknown tongue" (215).

Naming the desire and telling the story struggle in these novels with the suppression of knowledge and desire as well as the silencing of the female voice. Christine Froula describes this pattern as "the hysterical cultural script: the cultural text that dictates to males and females alike the necessity of silencing woman's speech when it threatens the father's power. This silencing ensures that the cultural daughter remains a daughter, her power suppressed and muted, while the father, his power protected, makes culture and history in his own image" ("The Daughter's Seduction" 112). Female voices are raised in *A Simple Story*. Miss Milner's rebellion against Sandford's attempts to negate her is linguistic, her verbal energy puncturing his sententiousness. And Matilda raises her voice against her father's anger to ask that Rushbrook be forgiven. Indeed, the very ending of the novel enforces a similar linguistic and formal tyranny: this narrative *is* a simple story of the father's law and the daughter's necessary submission to it; its complexities are reduced in its closure to a fable whose moral is the value of "A PROPER EDUCATION" (338).

Because of their form, on the other hand, *A False Friend* and *Mathilda* privilege the daughter's voice. But as the destruction of Sappho suggests, there can be no discovery of a poetic voice that can transcend and give form to Gertrude's suffering or that can give form to a self. Gertrude's letters to Frances have an obsessive, repetitive quality only partly accounted for by Robinson's financial concerns. And once the riddle of her identity is solved, the blank filled, once Denmore reveals himself as her father (significantly he dies because he will not be compelled to explain himself), her voice is silenced. Miss Stanley, the voice of reason and virtue, concludes the narrative, reducing Gertrude by means of an almost comically partial definition to "A VICTIM OF SENSIBILITY."

With more consciousness and more control than Gertrude, Mathilda takes on the telling of her tale, inscribing her father's voice within its bounds. Although the revelation of her father's desire has cut off language and communication for her, she "write[s] her tragic history" (*Mathilda* 175) out of motives she does not understand, "a feeling that I cannot define" (175). Indeed, the parallel to her father's communication is striking. Her "impenetrable and unkind silence" (176) ends as she writes to Woodville. She anticipates the result she had earlier assumed, connection through love: "to you, Woodville, kind affectionate friend, [these pages] will be dear — the precious memorials of a heart-broken girl who, dying, is still warmed by gratitude towards you: your tears will fall on the words that record my misfortunes; I know they will — and while I have life I thank you for your sympathy" (176). By breaking her silence she gives form to her life, restores to language its connection with the heart. And there is another kind of power operating here. Earlier, Mathilda has feared that she will become a text that Woodville might appropriate: "I am, I thought, a tragedy; a character that he comes to see act: now and then he gives me my cue that I may make a speech more to his purpose: perhaps he is already planning a poem in which I am to figure. I am a farce and play to him, but to me this is all dreary reality: he takes all the profit and I bear all the burthen" (233). In constructing this narrative, Mathilda seizes control of her own story. And although she describes herself as monstrous, her tale — through its very telling — undermines that definition — or perhaps elides the barriers between the monstrous and the human. But even so, the telling of her secret seems inimical to life: "While life was strong within me I thought indeed that there was a sacred horror in my tale that rendered it unfit for utterance" (175). Although communication will restore connection, that very utterance still marks her as something different, something other. Once she has finished this story, narrative for her, as for all these heroines, is ended.

The appearance of these novels in the context of other fictions of the family is significant. Romantic writers as various as Edmund Burke and Mary Wollstonecraft, Charlotte Smith and Samuel Taylor Coleridge, figure the revolutionary impulse of their era and its attendant upheavals in domestic terms. And for novelists across the political spectrum (from Robert Bage and Thomas Holcroft to Jane West and Hannah More), the family is the site of change or stasis, the place where the possibilities for reform are tested. The heroes of Robert Bage's *Hermsprong* and Thomas Holcroft's

Anna St. Ives raise questions about the very ties that bind parent to child, brother to sister, and those questions have clear application to the relations between citizen and citizen, king and subject. Jane West's *A Tale of the Times* argues that "filial reverence," "domestic harmony," "*amor patriae*," and the institutions of religion, moral law, and government are threatened by the covert designs of modern writers (3: 388). Hannah More's Mrs. Stanley, in her Utopian *Coelebs in Search of a Wife*, sees in the modern family "a spirit of independence, a revolutionary spirit, a separation from the parent state. IT IS THE CHILDREN'S WORLD" (216). The extent to which the domestic is under siege, the sheer numbers of doomed families in the novels of this period, suggests an anxiety about that most basic social unit.

In these fictions, the pressures that destabilize the patriarchal family, pressures arising from both within the family and without, mirror a similar interaction of internal and external forces that threaten the larger social institutions and even the basic fabric of these communities. Why at this particular time is there a conjunction of novels exploring father-daughter incest as the destructive force? One answer may lie in the fascination the idea of incest held for Romantic writers. At a time when questions about the relations between Nature and the shaping power (in all its effects) of the human mind are being explored, such examination of father-daughter incest as we find in these novels raises questions about the natural, the forbidden, the organization of society, the very relation of the self to its origins, power. In *The Elementary Structures of Kinship,* Claude Lévi-Strauss identifies the incest taboo as a paradox, a universal norm, or a point of "transformation or transition" at which we see the intersection of the two contradictory forces, Nature and Culture. "Before [the prohibition], culture is still non-existent; with it, nature's sovereignty over man is ended. The prohibition of incest is where nature transcends itself. It brings about and is in itself the advent of a new order" (25). Peter Thorslev indicates that parent-child (most usually father-daughter) incest represents not only "the ultimate . . . horror to be visited upon a sensitive and long-suffering young woman" ("Incest as Romantic Symbol" 43) but also "the irruption of the irrational" (44). Unlike other forms of incest, which suggest a rebellion against traditional authority, father-daughter incest, according to Thorslev, is an "object of horror" as it embodies the extent to which the past, figured both by fathers and the institutions they represent, is "parasitic upon the future" (47). James B. Twitchell underscores this point: "Whatever parent-child incest may have represented to romantic artists — oppression, degradation, possibly even reunion — the very irreconcilability of the act made it a touchstone of individual, familial and, by extension, social concerns" (*Forbidden Partners* 111).

Finally, these fictions of father-daughter incest, at a time when the family structure had been transformed by what Lawrence Stone has termed affective individualism, seem peculiarly charged.[9] In these novels, the ideal family, with its emphasis on the bonds of love and filial obedience to the patriarch, is revealed as dangerous — and terrifyingly so — in its very strengths. Although the Victorian sacralization of the home was yet to come, the domestic was certainly inhabited by associations of privacy and shelter and love. In trying to account for the repression of the Apollonius story through the eighteenth and nineteenth centuries, Margie Burns suggests that at this moment a fiction of father-daughter incest might be just too much to bear: "inevitably, the narrative becomes unbearable just at the point when human warmth and mutual protection became the domain of the family almost exclusively, against perceivably inimical external forces which had appropriated the workplace and most public space" ("Oedipus and Apollonius" 11). These novels demonstrate the fragility of the domestic, its liability to disruption and dissolution. And as these family fictions chart the energies that hold in tenuous balance the patriarchy's most and least valued members, father and daughter, they also suggest the fault lines that reveal the instability inherent in the structures of that society.

Notes

1. The resemblances among these novels, other incest texts, and analyses of the pathology of father-daughter incest are striking. Judith Lewis Herman argues that father-daughter incest "represents a paradigm of female sexual victimization" (*Father-Daughter Incest* 4), an "exaggeration of patriarchal family norms, . . . not a departure from them" (110). She identifies as elements of the pattern the father's dominance and concept of his patriarchal "right" to his daughter; the daughter's resultant view of herself as outsider, as "marked"; the mother as absent (either literally or because of her own powerlessness); the consequent isolation of the family from other families.

2. Terry Castle argues that Miss Milner's attachment "violate[s] literary convention. . . . The guardian/ward relationship is typically a sacrosanct one in English fiction of the period — sentimental in form and nonsexual in nature. . . . To imagine an eroticization of the guardian/ward bond, in English literature at least, is to diverge abruptly into the realms of pornography and burlesque" (*Masquerade and Civilization* 299–300). Inchbald's narrative suggests that if Miss Milner had been raised a Catholic, "education would have given such a prohibition to her love, that

she had been precluded from it, as by that barrier which divides a sister from a brother" (Inchbald, *A Simple Story* 74).

3. In *Mary Shelley* (1980) Anne K. Mellor explores the significance of the heroine's name, connecting it with Dante as well as with a tradition of Gothic heroines: "Mathilda thus figures that very female innocence that must be neither lustfully desired nor sexually possessed by a man" (196). Given Godwin's friendship with Inchbald, however, it seems likely that a connection between Inchbald's Matilda and Shelley's Mathilda might exist.

4. Spacks's formulation of a tradition of sentimental novels by women is helpful here as it emphasizes the daughter's confrontation with authority that is simultaneously individual, institutional, and generic. These novels, she argues, "confront directly the problem of power as the originator of event, hence of plot. Focusing on domestic manifestations of force, they express through the development of their plots anger at female subjection to authority" (*Desire and Truth* 134).

5. Paternal power — often paternal tyranny — is part of the paradigm of father-daughter incest. Margie Burns points out that Antiochus, the incestuous father in the Apollonius story, "is also a tyrant — deliberately rather than accidently incestuous" ("Oedipus and Apollonius" 9). In Ovid's *Metamorphoses* (Miller Book X), Cinyras, Myrrha's father, is a king. In Jane Barker's *Exilius,* Turpius, Clarinthia's father, is described as a tyrant. And for Percy Bysshe Shelley's Beatrice Cenci, "tyranny, and impious hate / Stand sheltered by a father's hoary hair" (*The Cenci* I.iii.100–101).

6. Boose sees the retention "motif also occur[ing] through riddles of enclosure . . . , which enclose the daughter in the father's verbal labyrinth and lure her suitors to compete with and lose the preemptive paternal bond" ("The Father's House" 33). Barker's Clarinthia invokes this spatial metaphor as well: "What difficult Paths has Fortune mark'd out for thy Virtue to trace? . . . I am in a Labyrinth so intricate, that even the Line of Reason is not able to conduct me through its wild Mazes" (*Exilius* 1: 35). In *The Cenci* the paternal enclosure seems diabolically determined: Beatrice and her brother become "as scorpions ringed with fire" who can only "strike [them]selves to death" (II.ii.70–71).

7. Castle reads the novel's ending differently: "patriarchal violence is quelled, and feminine delight made paramount" (325).

8. Again, this motif seems to be part of a paradigm. Ovid's narrative points to the confusion of names that will be caused by the consummation of Myrrha's desire: Myrrha's nurse, even as she decides to help Myrrha to sexual intercourse with her father, is unable to say the word "parente" (X.430). Breaking the incest taboo initiates a corruption of language: "forsitan aetatis quoque nomine 'filia' dixit, / dixit et illa 'pater,' sceleri ne nomina desint" ("It chanced, by a name appropriate to her age, he called her 'daughter,' and she called him 'father,' that names might not be lacking in their guilt" (Miller's translation, X.467–68). In Alfieri's 1785 version, Myrrha tries to substitute the word "lord" for "father" (III.ii), and, after her confession of her desire, "She is no more our daughter" (V.iii). And Beatrice Cenci, marking the corruption of "father," cannot find a word to call herself: "Is it my crime / That one . . . / Who tortured me from my forgotten years, / As parents only dare, should call himself / My father, yet should be! — Oh, what am I? / What name, what place, what memory shall be mine?" (III.i.70–75).

9. Lawrence Stone identifies "four key features of the modern family — intensified affective bonding of the nuclear core at the expense of neighbours and kin; a strong sense of individual autonomy and the right to personal freedom in the pursuit of happiness; a weakening of the association of sexual pleasure with sin and guilt; and a growing desire for physical privacy . . . all well established by 1750 in the key middle and upper sectors of English society" (*Family, Sex, and Marriage* 8–9).

Katharine M. Rogers

Romantic Aspirations, Restricted Possibilities: The Novels of Charlotte Smith

Charlotte Smith wrote her novels in the 1790s (from *Emmeline* in 1788 through *The Young Philosopher* in 1798), at the time when Romanticism was just beginning to vitalize English literature. She shared the Romantics' intense relationship with nature and was drawn to their ideals of political and sexual freedom. But she could not pursue these ideals as freely as her younger contemporaries Blake and Wordsworth, partly because the novel is more restricted than poetry by actual circumstance, more because, as a woman writing about women, she could not claim the boundless power of the Romantic imagination.

Even though the novel was in some ways unreceptive to Romanticism, however, its development in the later eighteenth century into feminized sentimental and Gothic forms both prepared the way for and shared characteristics with the new movement. Some of what might be considered Romantic features of Smith's work came from the tradition in which she was writing. From mid-century, these novels had affirmed the value of subjectivity by focusing on the consciousness of their protagonists and consequently setting feeling above institution and law. Sensitivity became an essential attribute of superior people, and it alienated them from the obtuse society around them; sentimental novels typically display sensitive characters suffering in a crass world. This suffering was best displayed in young women, socially powerless and therefore dominated and exploited by unworthy established authorities. From the contemporary Gothic tradition, Smith took exotic adventures, which she used in a mechanical way, and wild natural settings, which she developed to better effect than any of her contemporary novelists.

All her sensitive characters share her own intense responsiveness to nature, which she explicitly identifies as romantic. Mrs. Stafford and Emmeline are "romantic wanderers" because they like to take walks through an unspoiled forest, and vulgar Mrs. Ashwood sneers at Emmeline's "pretty romantic notion of contemplation by moonlight" (*Emmeline* 147, 202). Mrs. Glenmorris looks forward to "wild romantic solitude" in northern Scotland (*Young Philosopher* 2: 77), as does Celestina, whose worldly suitor tries to keep her near him by deriding her plan as "wild, romantic, unpleasant" (2: 236). Enthusiasm for wild scenery and use of natural description to heighten the emotional effect are equally prominent in the novels of Ann Radcliffe (published 1789–97), but Smith's backgrounds are more authentic and more sensitively adapted to her characters' moods.[1] In Radcliffe, natural scenery functions as a self-consciously picturesque backdrop, invariably sublime and intended to elicit generalized religious awe; and it signifies the finer sensibility of those characters who can respond to Nature's grandeur. In Smith at her best, it seems to flow from and amplify the emotions of characters in a particular situation.

Typically, her natural descriptions are called forth by her characters' state of mind. Temporarily cheered by the hope of meeting Marchmont's family, Althea can appreciate the signs of early spring in the desolate manor house she has been banished to: "the faint tinge of fresh green" in the ruined garden, some red buds on the long-neglected fruit trees, a few surviving crocuses (2: 90–94). Celestina goes off by herself to contemplate a sublime sunset in the Hebrides:

> The sun was already declining in an almost cloudless sky, and gave the warmest splendour to the broad expanse of ocean, broken by several islands, whose rocky points and angular cliffs caught the strong lights, in brilliant contrast to the lucid hue of the heath with which their summits were cloathed, and which on the northern and eastern sides threw a dark shadow on the clear and tranquil bosom of the sea. The sea birds, in swarming myriads, were returning to their nests among the ragged precipices beneath her. (3: 28)

She thinks how Willoughby would share her delight and how, with him, she could enjoy spending her life even in so desolate a setting. When her hopes of marrying Willoughby wane, with the waning year, she finds a bleaker solace in Nature.

> The sun, far distant from this northern region, was as faint and languid as the sick thoughts of Celestina: his feeble rays no longer gave any warm colouring to the rugged cliffs that rose above her head, or lent the undulating sea that sparkling brilliance which a few weeks before had given gaiety and cheerfulness even to these scattered masses of almost naked stone, against which the water incessantly broke. Grey, sullen, and cold, the waves now slowly rolled towards

the shore, where Celestina frequently sat whole hours, as if to count them, when she had in reality no idea present to her but Willoughby lost to her for ever. (3: 40)

Geraldine, traveling through a war-torn area of France to meet her unspeakable husband, describes "one of those cold, damp, gloomy mornings, which impresses a dreary idea that the sun has forsaken the world. — The wind sighed hollow among the half stripped trees; and the leaves slowly fell from the boughs, heavy with rain — The road, rough, and hardly passable, seemed leading us to the dark abode of desolation and despair" (*Desmond* 3: 289). The long opening sequence of *The Banished Man* makes even more effective use of natural conditions. Smith's characters are fleeing by night from their castle, which will soon be overrun by the French Revolutionary army; they cannot see their enemies or know their future. The whole scene is drenched with water — torrential rain that makes it impossible to see, marshy ground that they cannot depend on, and a river that they must cross without knowing where the ford is. The amorphous watery confusion both heightens their anxiety and symbolizes the uncertainty of their fate.

Smith and her characters turned to Nature in the manner of the major Romantic poets, to respond to their emotional needs and help them to articulate their feelings. But there is a significant difference: they could not count on finding consolation there. Wordsworth knew that "Nature never did betray / The heart that loved her" (*Tintern Abbey* ll. 122–23); Byron's Childe Harold found an unfailing "pleasure in the pathless woods" and solaced his troubles by mingling "with the Universe" (Canto 4, stanza 178). But Smith's repeated conclusion, in her own person and through her characters, is that Nature cannot cure human misery. Leaving her castle, Emmeline is offered a set piece of sublime landscape — a rushing mountain stream, a ruined monastery and a castle "still frowning in gothic magnificence," a rugged seashore, and a rich autumnal valley set off by "blue and barren hills." But, despite being "ever alive to the beauties of nature," all Emmeline feels is that she is leaving the only home she has ever known (37).

We can approach a definition of Smith's Romanticism by contrasting her with Ann Radcliffe, who wrote at the same time and in the same genre, but who was (despite Byron's admiration) much more conservative. As Smith's use of natural description was more innovative, so her interpretation of the conventions of the sentimental novel approached far closer to

Romantic radicalism. Both women created sensitive heroines who recoil from crudity and resist attempts to coerce them into loveless marriages, but who also consistently exert rational control over their impulses. Radcliffe, however, lays more emphasis on control; well-conducted Emily in her *Mysteries of Udolpho* is constantly exhorted to control her sensibility. Smith's heroines, on the other hand, sometimes luxuriate in theirs. In her first letter, which opens Volume 2 of *Desmond,* Geraldine Verney presents herself as a unique sufferer: "Is it, that I set out in life with too great a share of sensibility? or is my lot to be particularly wretched?" (2: 1). Without any troubles like Geraldine's to justify her conclusion, Rosalie at eighteen had "already . . . acquired that painful experience that had made her fear she should taste of unalloyed happiness no more" (*Montalbert,* 1795, 1: 25).[2]

Sensitivity leads Smith's characters to the alienation from a crass society that marked Romantic heroes. Inability to fit in, a comic or blameworthy trait in Fielding's or Smollett's novels, becomes a distinction in Romantic literature. Although none of her characters are self-conscious rebels and outcasts like Cain or Prometheus, they do not fit smoothly into the established social order, any more than she herself did.[3] Alone in the woods on a still November evening, Orlando contrasts Nature's quietude with man's anxious activity, runs through the various careers open to a young man, and concludes that all are pointless, if not pernicious (160–61). Rosalie, the heroine of *Montalbert,* who is supposed to be the daughter of the local vicar, feels alien from him and his family, who, though presentable enough, are commonplace. She goes off whenever she can to read or draw by herself, for she has long been "conscious, that such sort of people as she was usually thrown among, people who only escape from dullness by flying to defamation, were extremely tiresome to her, though she saw that nobody else thought so, and suspected herself of being fastidious and perverse" (2: 137). Her timid self-doubt is not justified, of course; the Romantic heroine really is superior to the commonplace, conventional people around her.

Smith's heroines (after her first, Emmeline) are also distinguished from Radcliffe's by being more ready to commit themselves to love than was strictly compatible with contemporary standards of feminine prudence and propriety. In *The Old Manor House,* timid, inexperienced Monimia declares, without having consulted any older authority: "I do not know, Orlando, why I should be ashamed to say that I love you better than any body else in the world; for indeed who is there in it that I have to love? If you were gone, it would be all a desert to me" (43). Shortly after meeting Montalbert, Rosalie engages herself to him without any thought of consulting her parents, even though he is a Roman Catholic and her supposed father is a Church of England clergyman. She then agrees to a clandestine marriage by a priest for fear of losing Montalbert; Smith censures her lightly, but does not punish her with remorse as was customary at the time. Althea feels a strong interest in Marchmont shortly after meeting him and before he has made any declaration to her; this soon develops into an "extreme concern" that instigates her to help him even though she knows the world would disapprove (*Montalbert* 2: 148); and she accepts his declaration of love while knowing that there is no hope of marriage or of her family's consent.[4]

Smith often calls her characters "romantic," almost always to show their superiority to commonplace people. The word was used throughout the eighteenth century to mean reaching beyond the bounds of reason and common sense, but in the earlier period it generally suggested fatuous wishful thinking or quixotism. Smith, however, typically applies it to idealistic characters whose principles rise above expediency and whose aims rise above mercenary prudence. FitzEdward, a hardened young rake in *Emmeline,* dismisses Delamere's intention of marrying a penniless girl of uncertain birth, rather than seducing and abandoning her, as "a boyish and romantic plan" (*Emmeline* 52). When Rosalie refuses to marry a crass but rich young clergyman, her supposed father accuses her of "affecting . . . fine romantic airs." Her supposed mother exhorts her "to follow, like a reasonable woman, the advice of those who know better what is fit for you than you do yourself" and ridicules the idea of women's marrying "just according to their own romantic whims" (*Montalbert* 1: 57, 61, 74–75).

The most Romantic lover in Smith's novels is Desmond, who adores the unhappily married Geraldine Verney. He is aware that a love that finds total satisfaction in serving a woman and contemplating her virtue from a distance would be considered "romantic, and even ridiculous" by ordinary people (*Desmond* 2: 241). His hard-headed friend Bethel doubts that an erotic passion can be at once intensely pure and intensely ardent and warns against cultivating one that cannot be lawfully fulfilled.[5] Bethel advises Desmond to distract himself from a passion that can only serve to render him miserable by finding some other woman worthy of his love or, if he has "become, through the influence of this romantic attachment, too fastidious for reasonable happiness," to go abroad and seek relief in a change of scene or a pleasant liaison (1: 188–89).

Even after he seems to have lost Geraldine forever, Desmond insists on the superior value of his love: it "may be very true, and very reasonable" that, "if I could once determine to look out for some other enjoyments than those my romantic fancy had described, I might yet find as reasonable a portion of happiness as any human being has a right to expect" — but he cannot, because he has envisioned a higher degree of felicity: "I know there are a hundred, nay, a thousand other plans and people, with whom other men might sit down contented; but I have made up a *'fair idea,'* and losing that, all is to me a blank." He goes on to marvel that a man of Bethel's fine mind, who knows Geraldine, "cannot comprehend the delight of living only for one beloved object, though hopeless of any other return than what the purest friendship may authorise" (3: 214–16). Smith presents her hero and develops her plot to indicate that Desmond's "unreasonable" attitude, his refusal to settle for what is attainable, is to be accepted as admirable. Desmond's total commitment to his passion and Smith's insistence that it is not quixotic and morally questionable, but, rather, idealistic beyond the reach or even the conception of ordinary people, makes him a Romantic hero, even if not so forceful and exciting a one as Manfred or Heathcliff.[6]

The sentimental novelists consistently affirmed that women should not be forced to violate their feelings in choosing a husband, but they agreed that, once married, a virtuous woman had to repress her feelings as necessary to fulfill her conjugal duty. The sacred institution of marriage took precedence over personal feelings, except for extreme radicals and Romantics. Although Smith never explicitly asserted that it was unjust to keep people bound forever to an unequal bargain or that love should take precedence over legal bonds, she filled her novels with deserving people (of both sexes) permanently chained in marriage to odious spouses. In her time, it was shocking even to hint that some marriages should be dissolved; only Mary Wollstonecraft was bold enough to declare, in *The Wrongs of Woman,* that a woman whose marriage had been destroyed by a vicious husband had the right to find emotional and sexual fulfillment with another man.

Smith did shock her contemporaries by her presentation of Lady Adelina Trelawny in *Emmeline.* Adelina, overpersuaded in early youth to marry a man who abuses and deserts her, yields to a congenial lover and becomes pregnant. Overwhelmed by guilt and fear of the brothers she has supposedly dishonored, she retreats into seclusion, suffers from critical illness and insanity, and longs for death until her child gives her the will to live. All the while, however, she has the unhesitating sympathy and support of the virtuous heroine; and in the end there is a hope that she will marry her lover.[7] This was a liberal position in a world where moralists like

Hannah More defined Christian forgiveness of an adulteress as isolating her from society to spend the remainder of her life meditating on her sin (*Strictures* 1: 47–49). Even Mary Wollstonecraft (in her prudish youth) condemned Smith for making Adelina too attractive and romantic and insufficiently reformed (*Analytical Review* 27). Without explicitly justifying Adelina's sin, Smith's detailed account inevitably suggests the absurd injustice of giving it overwhelming importance, imposing the responsibility for an entire family's honor on a desperate young woman, expecting anyone not to prefer a loving, attentive man to one who broadcasts his total disregard for her.

Although Smith does criticize women who yield to unlicensed love, she often endows them with good qualities that completely overshadow their failure in chastity. Emily Cathcart in *Celestina,* seduced as a girl and now a kept mistress, is noted for her generosity rather than her unchastity, as she supports her destitute sister and strives on her deathbed for the moral salvation of her lover; she is "amiable, unhappy" (4: 80), rather than sinful. Mrs. Vyvian, Rosalie's real mother, is treated with total sympathy even though she gave birth to an illegitimate child: we hear only of her beautiful character and her sufferings at the hands of the hard-hearted husband she was bullied into marrying to cover her supposed disgrace. The fact that Mrs. Vyvian sees her own situation in that of Rosalie, who has been imprudent although not seduced, suggests a more daring sexual message than Smith is prepared to make explicit — that is, that a heroine might violate the law of chastity and still attain a happy ending; in short, that unchastity need not be punished by lifelong remorse and domestic oppression.[8]

In *Desmond,* Smith daringly placed an adulterous passion at the center of her plot. The novel is set in the early stage of the French Revolution, and Smith draws a pointed parallel between despotism in the nation and in the home. The French have thrown off the oppression of king, aristocracy, and church, but Geraldine Verney remains the slave of her worthless husband.[9] When she must obey his order to follow him into war-torn France, she consoles herself with the thought that even "the wildest collection of those people, whose ferocity arises not from their present liberty, but their recent bondage," will not "injure *me,* who am myself a miserable slave, returning with trembling and reluctant steps, to put on the most dreadful of all fetters[.] — Fetters that would even destroy the freedom of my mind" (3: 71). Unfortunately, Geraldine's insight into her oppression does not liberate her — or Smith — sufficiently to nerve her to resist it. Smith goes no further than to hint that there is something unhealthy and mechanical in

Geraldine's rigid obedience, motivated by duty and not at all by love, and presumably fueled by guilt for not loving and a masochistic satisfaction in behaving correctly with no reward in view (3: 72, 271).

Yet the circumstances Smith presents cannot fail to lead to a questioning of English marriage law. How can any law make Verney's atrocious exploitation of Geraldine morally right, or require her to be loyal and loving to a man who insults her even as he exorbitantly demands her services? How can the tie that binds Geraldine to Verney be more sacred than Desmond's idealistic devotion? If the representation "of a man capable of . . . a passion so generous and disinterested as to seek only the good of its object" is the height of morality, as Smith claims in her Preface (ii), marital fidelity is clearly a lesser value. Smith further qualifies Geraldine's orthodox saintliness by supplying two sympathetic female characters who are not so rarified. Madame de Boisbelle, also married to a worthless husband, is allowed to have an affair with impunity; and Fanny Waverly, Geraldine's sister, freely condemns their selfish, stupid mother and her attempts to keep ideas out of her daughters' minds. In her lenient treatment of sexually transgressing women, in her repeated representation of extramarital relationships that are more loving and responsible than the corresponding marriages, Smith implies, in true Romantic fashion, that love is more sacred than law.

Although Smith never explicitly condemns the excessive power that a husband held in marriage, she reiterates the injustice of primogeniture, an almost equally sacrosanct part of the family property system. All of her female and most of her male protagonists are dispossessed in favor of less worthy brothers. Typically, the men are younger brothers whose selfish, irresponsible older brothers squander the inheritance that by rights belongs to the whole family (Orlando in *The Old Manor House*, D'Alonville and Ellesmere in *The Banished Man*, Montalbert, George Delmont in *The Young Philosopher*). Sisters, of course, are routinely sacrificed to the interest of their brothers, a point Smith hammers home in *Desmond*.

Smith's enthusiastic faith that the French Revolution promised universal liberation, personal and sexual as well as political, was shared by all the Romantics. Robert Southey, for example, reminisced that the Revolution had seemed to open up "a visionary world": "Old things seemed passing away, and nothing was dreamt of but the regeneration of the human race" (Abrams, *Norton Anthology*, 5th ed. 2: 14). In its early, idealistic stage, the Revolution seemed to verify the Romantics' hopes for limitless human improvement in a new society cleansed of the old corruptions.

It was daring for a woman, who was not supposed even to express opinions on public affairs, to defend the French Revolution; and Smith went so far as to make her hero attack the great Edmund Burke's "elaborate treatise in favor of despotism," *Reflections on the Revolution in France* (2: 62; cf. 3: 209). The action of *Desmond* runs from June 1790 to February 1792: that is, after the abolition of the special privileges of the church and the aristocracy but before the September Massacres, the trial of the King and Queen, and the Reign of Terror. Smith filled her book with political discussions, in every one of which an enlightened, virtuous character defends the Revolution against opponents who are either unthinking or self-interested and corrupt. The Revolution did more than simply reform abuses in France: in showing what the people could accomplish, it brought light to the world. Desmond declares that its success "involves the freedom, and, of course, the happiness, not merely of this great people, but of the universe" (1: 106–7). English "*soi-disant* great men who love power" had better recognize that "the hour is very rapidly approaching, when usurped power will be tolerated no longer" (1: 178).

Desmond's intelligent but cynical friend Bethel counters his enthusiasm with the traditional eighteenth-century view that it is not so easy to reform human nature. Bethel has not yet noticed any success produced by the new modes of government in France, his personal experience indicates that politicians are inevitably selfish and insincere, and he has not seen enough steadiness and virtue among the Revolutionary leaders to be confident that their admirable principles will be put into practice (1: 197–98). But this reasoning does not puncture Desmond's Romantic optimism; instead, he convinces Bethel that the Revolution is a "great and noble effort for the universal rights of the human race." However, as he sees hostile reactionary forces arising in all the surrounding nations, Bethel cannot agree with Desmond's optimistic hope "that uncemented by blood, the noble and simply majestic temple of liberty will arise on the site of the barbarous structure of gothic despotism" (2: 52–53).

Writing *The Banished Man* after the atrocities of the Revolution had begun, Smith still did not abandon her faith in its ideals (Preface, 1: x). But by the time she wrote her last novel, she had given up hope for a reformed society in Europe, agreeing with Bethel "that liberty having been driven away to the new world, will establish there her glorious empire" (*Desmond* 2: 55). In *The Young Philosopher,* Glenmorris confirms this glowing vision. He had settled in America after arriving there by accident in the middle of the Revolutionary War and admiring the Americans' determination to be free.[10] After returning to England and being overwhelmed by troubles, he cannot wait to bring his family back to America, where nature and cultivation are happily combined, without the corruption, the false values, the mental restrictions, and the exploitation that have marked all previous civilized societies:

> To cultivate the earth of another continent, to carry the arts of civil life, without its misery and its vices, to the wild regions of the globe, had in it a degree of sublimity, which, in Glenmorris's opinion, sunk the petty politics and false views so eagerly pursued in Europe, into something more despicable than childish imbecility. . . . When he reflected on the degradation to which those must submit, who would make what is called a figure in this country; that they must sacrifice their independence, their time, their taste, their liberty, to etiquette, to forms and falsehoods, which would to him be insupportable, he rejoiced that he had made his election where human life was in progressive improvement. (4: 201–2)

In America Glenmorris will not have to "see a frightful contrast between luxury and wretchedness . . . daily witness injustice I cannot repress, and misery I cannot relieve." There he can study "the great book of nature" instead of corrupt European society, "where all greatness of character seems lost" and where it is impossible "to study human nature unadulterated by *inhuman* prejudices" (4: 391–92). It is a grand Romantic vision of human society as it ought to be, and, at the end of the book, Delmont and the Glenmorrises go to America, the only place where free, enlightened characters can be at home.

However, George Delmont, the Young Philosopher, is an idealist who has managed to remain uncorrupted by English society. Educated by an enlightened mother according to the principles of Rousseau's *Emile,* he has been brought up to form his own opinions, "which he never was flogged out of . . . at Eton" (1: 34). Even as a child, he was an individualist who often wandered off by himself, "threw himself down under a tree with some favourite book, then fell into a reverie as he listened to the wind among the branches, or the dashing of the water against the banks, where, among the reeds and willows crowding over the Thames," he avoided both the crude mirth of his schoolfellows and the mechanical pedantry of his lessons (1: 49–51). As he generously relieved needy people, he not only glowed with indignation against those who had oppressed them, but looked beyond the individuals to the systems that made the oppression possible. "From detestation against individuals, such as justices and overseers," this remarkably penetrating young analyst "began to reflect on the laws that put it in their power thus to drive forth to nakedness and famine the wretched beings they were empowered to protect; and he was led to enquire if the complicated misery he every day saw . . . could be the fruits of the very best laws that could be framed in a state of society said to be the most perfect among what are called the civilized nations of the world" (1: 54). In earlier books Smith had occasionally related corrupt lawyers to the corrupt institutions that nourished them; here she has moved to a full-scale radical attack on the legal system itself.[11]

"Early taught to have on every point an opinion of his own," Delmont considered his career options and "determined to yield his freedom to none of those motives which the love of power or of wealth might hold out to him, but to live on his little farm unfettered by the rules he must submit to if he entered into any profession." Aware that this decision will bring ridicule and blame on him, Delmont nevertheless thinks it more valuable to be a farmer than a judge "condemning wretches legally to die on the gallows," or a bishop sitting in Parliament and voting for war, or a general presiding "at these human sacrifices," where men destroy each other without even daring to ask why (1: 92–94). When Orlando reached the same conclusion in *The Old Manor House,* it might be attributed to old-fashioned sentimental retirement from the world; but here it is definitely Romantic defiance of convention.

In contrast to the conventional moralists of his time, who preached that woman's supposedly natural inclination to comply with those around her was an amiable feature of her character, Delmont wishes that his sweet and compliant sister were less pliable, fearing "that her character would not be formed on reason and conviction, but on the sentiments and conduct of those among whom she might be thrown" (1: 95). He deliberately chooses his own company. Having long discovered that associating with his neighbors "was a very great waste of his time, as well as a needless trial of his civility," as soon as he was grown up and his own master, he decided to "recover the portion of his days thus unnecessarily given to persons whom he could not discover were at all the better, while he felt himself a great deal worse." He realized that this decision would make him enemies, but as he had no ambition "to be chairman at a quarter session, or foreman of a grand jury, . . . he quietly submitted to invidious remarks he did not hear." However, though he had freed himself from the constraints of meaningless forms of politeness, he did not impose his exacting standards on his sisters; for he made "it the rule of his life, as well in trivial as on material occasions, never to trench upon the liberty of others, while he guarded against being cheated out of his own" (1: 119–21).

Medora, the heroine of *The Young Philosopher,* is a less satisfactory example of natural reason and rectitude. She is presented as "entirely the child of nature," and she is a more plausible example than such highly socialized children of nature as Frances Burney's Evelina and Camilla. Medora has "not one idea . . . that she blushes to avow," not because she is too "innocent" to have any desires, but because she is free of prudery and unaware of sexual competitiveness. She will later, we are assured, develop a mind and character like that of her enlightened mother, Mrs. Glenmorris (1: 244–45). But Medora fails to display any mental or moral quality that would distinguish her from her contemporary heroines. All Smith's heroines show this discrepancy between aim and achievement. She recognized this problem herself, complaining in *Marchmont* that she had to conform to conventions that dictated that heroines must be very young, and that very young women must not distinguish themselves by independence of mind or freely expressed passion; indeed, *any* strongly marked qualities were considered out of place in a young woman (1: 177–79). Smith was also unable to create a fable that would make real the Romantic attitudes and qualities of her characters, resorting instead to tired Gothic devices: Medora is abducted, and Mrs. Glenmorris goes insane from her anxiety at Medora's disappearance.

Mrs. Glenmorris does, however, voice Smith's most eloquent expression of Romantic values. Most people, she says, condemn as "wildly romantic" anyone who "ventures to feel or to express themselves out of the style of common and every day life. But why is it romantic?" She would not like to see Medora let her imagination outrun her reason and make herself "either useless or ridiculous" by bewildering "herself among ideal beings":

> but if affection for merit, if admiration of talents, if the attachments of friendship are romantic; if it be romantic to dare to have an opinion of one's own, and not to follow one formal tract, wrong or right, pleasant or irksome, because our grandmothers and aunts have followed it before; if not to be romantic one must go through the world with prudery, carefully settling our blinkers at every step, as a cautious coachman hoodwinks his horses heads; if a woman, because she is a woman, must resign all pretensions to being a *reasoning* being, and dares neither look to the right nor to the left, oh! may my Medora still be the child of nature and simplicity, still venture to express all she feels, even at the risk of being called a strange romantic girl. (2: 13–15)

This is a vision of the emotional freedom, intellectual independence, and openness to new ideas that the Romantics insisted was the natural birthright of every human being. We might wish for more bold and full portrayals, but Smith does show young women protesting against mental limitations (Fanny Waverly), celebrating gains in human liberty (Geraldine Verney), and feeling sexual love outside the bonds of strict propriety (most of her heroines). Neither Smith nor anyone else before Charlotte and Emily Brontë created fully realized Romantic female characters.

Mrs. Glenmorris is protesting against the limitations imposed by a narrow conception of reason that equated it with prudence and a common sense acceptance of things as they are. Thus circumscribed, reason directs us to accept the status quo as the only possible reality, to resist any change as risky, and to dismiss hopes for radical improvement as fanciful. Romantic imagination, as its opposite, liberates the mind to conceive of something better than what presently exists, to dare to strive for and possibly achieve radical improvement.[12] Smith's younger contemporary Jane Austen, who had made fun of romantic excesses in her youth, came to see the value of romance, by which she meant much what Mrs. Glenmorris did. Anne Elliot "had been forced into prudence in her youth, she learned romance as she grew older" (*Persuasion* Ch. 4). That is, Anne learned to trust her own feelings and judgment, to venture beyond common sense and prudence, to try for what might be better rather than to settle for what she already knew. Smith's and Austen's claims for the Romantic imagination are comparatively modest, but they point toward the human longing for something better than the life that is reasonable for us to expect — a longing that Emily Brontë was to express with consummate beauty fifty years later: for a world "where life is boundless in its duration, and love in its sympathy, and joy in its fulness" (*Wuthering Heights* Ch. 16).

Yet, of course, Smith was not a fully committed Romantic: she did not find transcendence in Nature, she insisted that passions must be curbed, and she did not believe that imagination led to a more real world than sense. If the Romantic imagination was sublime and spellbinding, it was also self-assured to the point of arrogance. Wordsworth's imagination displaces the evidence of his senses to reveal an invisible world of infinite potentiality that is the proper home of humanity (*The Prelude* 6: 593–609). Blake asserts even more decisively that his imagination creates a world more real than the one around us. Women, socialized to be receptive, compliant, and conventional, could not develop such confidence in their individual judgment. As a woman, Smith could not make the enormous claims of men possessed by the Romantic imagination. She had to work within the social world she knew, with characters bound by mundane circumstance. She questioned conventional thinking and established institutions, but she could not cast them aside altogether.

Smith's form further tied her to the actual life around her, since the novel requires a strong emphasis on things as they are. As Robert Kiely points out, a romantic novel is something of a contradiction in terms, a battleground on which the claims of imagination and the self collide with those of "reason and the public welfare" (25). The battle rages in Smith's novels, where she claims to aim at probability more than at "the wonderful and extraordinary" (Preface to *The Banished Man* 1: x), but has one heroine imprisoned in a tower and two others abducted. She constantly calls up romance in her novels in order to deflate or discredit it, as when ridiculous Clarinthia purposely falls in love so as to be sure of "opposition from her family, and . . . such imaginary miseries as might establish her in her own opinion the 'heroine of a tale of sympathy'" (*Ethelinde* 5: 85). But for five volumes Smith puts Ethelinde herself, the exemplary heroine, through very similar "imaginary miseries."

Often, however, Smith effectively juxtaposed romance and realism in order to bring out the contrast between idealistic aspirations and the limitations of actual life. In *The Old Manor House,* Romantic elements emphasize the disparity between the unworldly, unselfish hero and heroine and the sordid world they must live in. Romantically named Orlando (who, however, was named after his ancestor to curry favor with the ancient cousin who controls the family property) wants to marry Monimia because she is lovely and he loves her, regardless of her social inferiority and their lack of money. Their love is all-important to them, but the financial constrictions that prevent their marriage are worked out in grinding detail. Monimia is a princess locked away in a tower of the old manor house, and her knight Orlando climbs up to her by a concealed staircase; but both exist in the prosaic context of mean-minded, absurdly self-important Mrs. Rayland and the servants who flatter and outsmart her. "Sanguine and romantic" Orlando loves to contemplate "visionary prospects" (138); but for most of the book he is constrained by petty authorities and irksome circumstances.

As a woman novelist focusing on women, Smith was further limited by the conventions of feminine propriety. Romantic abandon was out of the question for heroines if they were not to forfeit readers' sympathy. Moreover, letting her heroines abandon themselves to passion would mean giving up the claim to rationality that feminists had worked so hard to establish throughout the eighteenth century. Nor would it have been realistic to show women liberated as men could be. The Young Philosopher has been educated to think for himself and acts according to his own views of morality. His sisters neither feel his need for independence, since they have

never been encouraged to develop their own ideas, nor would be able to defy convention if they did feel it. They have to listen to their unpleasant great-aunt and sit with boring company, while George blithely goes off to his friends. He claims the right to escape social intercourse that would be disagreeable to himself and not useful to anyone else (1: 257); they have no such option.

Like Radcliffe, who was also concerned with female dignity, Smith never abandoned rational standards of conduct. Byronic heroes who reject all convention and social obligation to pursue their grand, resistless passions may be attractive or, in Smith, sympathetic; but they must be reprehended. Delamere, the original hero of *Emmeline,* makes no attempt to restrain his passions and repeatedly distresses the heroine by heedlessly pursuing her; he forces Emmeline to lock herself in her room to escape his temper tantrums and grandly dismisses her fears of scandalmongers, refusing to see that a young woman's reputation was more vulnerable than a male aristocrat's. Emmeline, in contrast, invariably maintains rational control and judiciously weighs possibilities. Even when she feels most warmly toward him, she is not subject to "that violent love, which carrying every thing before it, leaves the mind no longer at liberty to see any fault in the beloved object, or any impropriety in whatever can secure it's [sic] success, and which, scorning future consequences, risks every thing for it's present indulgence" (149). In the end, he gets himself killed in an unnecessary duel, and she is provided with a suitably self-disciplined young man. Clinging Montague Thorold and overbearing Vavasour, the unwanted suitors who harass Celestina, are closer to the conventional romantic lover than Willoughby, the hero, who seriously considers a prudential marriage for the sake of his family. Smith's ideal heroes show their love by thoughtfulness and consideration, not, like Thorold, by flamboyant offers to die for their beloved. Even Desmond demonstrates infinite consideration more than fiery passion. He is the most Romantic of Smith's major characters, yet, far from pursuing his emotional needs at all costs, he constantly restricts his actions so as to avoid embarrassing or distressing Geraldine.

None of Smith's approved characters recklessly follow their impulses. Orlando is deeply in love with Monimia and dreads a long separation from her, but when Warwick, about to elope with Isabella, tempts Orlando to elope with Monimia at the same time, he resists out of consideration for his parents (*Old Manor House* 333–35). After he has married her, he learns that poverty is miserable even if one shares it with a dearly loved wife: "the romantic theory, of sacrificing every consideration to love, produced, in the practice, only the painful consciousness of having injured its object" (517).

Smith's moral ideal is the person who quietly fulfills his or her obligations. Her admirable characters are mindful of the claims of reason and family responsibilities, although most of them commit themselves to an unalterable romantic attachment. Even George Delmont, the Young Philosopher, embarrasses himself to pay his brother's gambling debts. This insistence on consideration for and responsibility to one's family came from Smith's life circumstances more than convention. As a mature woman with an inadequate husband and a family of children to bring up, she was painfully aware that stable family life was more important than romantic raptures. Perpetually weighed down by family cares, she could not escape to or even maintain faith in an ideal world. In an amusing sequence in *The Banished Man,* her alter ego, Mrs. Denzil, complains that she must devise a tender dialogue between two idealized lovers while worrying about bills and struggling to meet her publisher's deadline in order to pay them, meanwhile fretting about the destruction of her garden by the neighbor's pigs (2: 225–28). In such a setting, a woman could not see herself as a prophet in the manner of Blake and Wordsworth. As a hard-working professional whose works had to meet the bills, she was tied to this world. Romanticism enhanced Charlotte Smith's response to natural beauty, strengthened her feminism, enlarged her interests; but it could not provide her, or most women, with a consistent world view.

Notes

1. There is one embarrassing exception when, in *The Old Manor House,* Smith made injudicious use of a secondary source and placed the St. Lawrence River in a subtropical landscape. It is also true that she sometimes wrote minutely, even pedantically, detailed descriptions more suggestive of James Thomson than of Wordsworth.

2. Other sensitive characters who suffer in an unsympathetic society are transparent alter egos of Smith herself: a succession of irreproachable middle-aged matrons afflicted by irresponsible husbands and dishonest lawyers (Mrs. Stafford in *Emmeline,* Mrs. Elphinstone in *Celestina,* Mrs. Denzil in *The Banished Man,* Leonora in *The Letters of a Solitary Wanderer*).

3. Smith constantly presents herself as excluded from privileged circles, dropped by her prosperous, conventional friends. As Stuart Curran points out, alienation is the prevailing theme of her *Elegiac Sonnets* and *The Emigrants* ("The 'I' Altered" 200–201).

4. Emmeline, Smith's first heroine, is more concerned about propriety than any of her later ones: there is more emphasis on her self-command, and she delays tiresomely in confessing her love for Godolphin. She is pointedly differentiated from "a romantic girl" by her ability to distinguish between true love and the

mixture of liking, gratitude, and pity that she feels for Delamere (*Emmeline* 73). Goethe's *The Sorrows of Werther* is mentioned with disapproval in *Emmeline*, with sympathy in *Celestina* and *Desmond*.

5. Smith herself, remembering that she is writing a realistic novel, concedes that Desmond's feeling is not *quite* so pure as he intends; he would like physical fulfillment.

6. Celestina, the heroine of Smith's preceding novel, anticipates Desmond's unalterable constancy in her refusal to consider loving any man other than Willoughby, even though she believes they can never marry and she has another devoted and eminently acceptable suitor. In contrast to the lesson inculcated by Richardson, Celestina "found it impossible . . . to transfer to another the same attachment" she had formed for Willoughby (*Celestina* 4: 158). Her attitude would be considered (foolishly) romantic by some, but not by anyone who understood her motives (4: 300).

7. In pointed contrast, another woman in the book, Lady Frances Crofts, who commits adultery without the excuse of love, is punished by being immured for life in a convent.

8. Cf. the hero's widowed grandmother in *Ethelinde*, a common law wife who is presented with utmost sympathy. The only person who receives Orlando kindly when he returns, destitute, to his former home is a kept mistress, who is sensible and generous (*Old Manor House*). Smith also presented a series of virtuous men married to unworthy wives who are in love with the admirable heroine (Sir Edward Newenden and Ethelinde, Walsingham and Rosalie in *Montalbert*, and Eversley and Althea in *Marchmont*).

9. This is no hyperbolic metaphor. Geraldine speaks of herself as the "property" of Verney, and soon afterwards Desmond attacks the institution of Negro slavery (3: 148, 161*–64*); husbands and slaveowners shared many of the same powers over their subjects. See Diana Bowstead's analysis ("Charlotte Smith's *Desmond*") of the connection between political and sexual oppression in *Desmond*.

10. In *The Old Manor House*, Smith had argued effectively for the American Revolutionaries. Stupid Mrs. Rayland and corrupt General Tracy scorn and condemn the "rebels." Orlando, though fighting in the British army, comes to realize that the Americans are fighting for their just rights.

11. Marchmont is imprisoned for debt, and the system that imprisons him is an indictment of "a country boasting of its enlarged humanity and perfect freedom" (*Marchmont* 2: 22). He protests that it does little good to punish individual villainous attorneys, when "no radical cure can be administered" to legal abuses, lest it endanger "the sanctity of the laws" (4: 39–40). Appalling Lawyer Vampyre is the more appalling because he is a "*legal* monster" (4: 180, Smith's italics).

12. For a discussion of (Romantic) imagination in some of Smith's contemporaries, see Katharine M. Rogers, *Frances Burney: The World of "Female Difficulties."*

Gender and the Cultural Matrix

Marlon B. Ross

Configurations of Feminine Reform: The Woman Writer and the Tradition of Dissent

During the 1790s, when the controversies of revolution, rights, and reform were on every man's, and every woman's, lips, women writers of every political stripe concurred that, in being cut off from the formal political arena, women possessed a potential moral edge in bringing about reform that could benefit the welfare of all rather than merely advancing the partisan interests of any particular group. Those who advocated women's rights, like Mary Wollstonecraft and Catherine Macaulay, were eager for women to enter into the arena of governance, not as it was constituted but in order that it might be cleansed, in order that women might chasten men's destructive ambitions as much as fulfill their own potential. The problem for radical writers like Wollstonecraft is how women can enter the loop of power without being further contaminated by the consequences of power. Gaining their rights might simply transform women's state, from one of being more victimized by male power than guilty of its abuses, to one of more equally shared corruption and guilt.

At the opposite end of the political spectrum, Hannah More is no less entangled in this dilemma. In writing her treatise on women's education, *Strictures on the Modern System of Female Education,* she must invade that masculine sphere of politics and risk becoming corrupted by it. She chooses the respectable genre of the female conduct book as a way of maneuvering around the mire of politic words which characterize political debate and literary composition, as a way of subordinating her words directly to practical action, to "conduct." According to More's logic, women should happily grant men their natural sphere of formal governance and politics (the orator, the pleader, the debater), for the apparent power inherent to this sphere is also necessarily attended by the corrupting influences of indirection, inaction, and compromise. "That kind of knowledge which is rather fitted for home consumption than foreign exportation, is peculiarly

adapted to women." Women can act more directly and more purely in regulating the moral temperament of a nation and in being "instrumental to the good of others." Whereas the public lives of men call them away to trade and battle in foreign places, women "in the case of our children . . . are responsible for the exercise of acknowledged *power*: a power wide in its extent, indefinite in its effects, and inestimable in its importance" (*Strictures* 374–89).

At every turn, however, the political nature of More's project uncovers itself and reveals its relation to state partisanship, oratory, debate, pleading, and the hyperbole of panegyric. Her literary efforts proved so successful that they brought her to the attention of princes, government ministers, parliamentarians, and bishops, who sought her advice and entangled her in the most controversial political undertakings. In writing her treatises, More had no choice but to enter that formal network of political power not only discursively but also bureaucratically.

During the early Romantic period, women's political discourse — across the ideological spectrum — occupies a position of dissent. Simply to speak about politics is to place oneself *against* the political establishment, where women's role is normatively defined solely by silent obeisance. The woman who speaks out purposefully *not to dissent* but rather to reaffirm her total subordination to the political establishment inevitably finds herself in a problematic position of dissent. The only pure form of feminine action she can take in offering her (non)political support to the status quo is to be silent. The woman who desires to dissent, however, finds herself in an ironically fortuitous position, possessing a political voice without the draw-back of belonging to the corrupt interests of established power. For her, to speak politics is automatically to assault the status quo. Her primary problem is how to speak politics without being contaminated by the moral compromises which characterize mainstream politics.

This is a formal dilemma even more than a question of ideology, morality, or politics. Without bounded forms which can construct the process of reading as a political rather than merely a "literary" phenomenon, ideological, moral, and political meanings will be lost. This is especially the case when a female dissenter borrows a literary form that is explicitly and traditionally cued as political discourse because its formal structure is deeply embedded within status quo politics. Because politicized generic forms are notoriously conventional — requiring author and reader to identify already legitimated political discourses — the female dissenter

may have both an advantage and an impasse in resorting to such forms. Although the conventionality of the form may tie her more closely to the status quo political structure from which the form gains its meaning and authority, the fact that she has no formal authority within that structure may help to unbalance the form's links to established power.

The intrinsic dissenting status of the political woman is further complicated by the fact that most *overtly* politicized women belonged to a long tradition of Nonconformist religious and civil dissent. Deprived of their civil liberties, the nonconforming religious sects of the late eighteenth century were compelled to make the connection between freedom of conscience and political liberty. Taking seriously the project of political "protest" veiled within the religious label "protestant," they understood that the only way to have genuine freedom of conscience was to gain the fundamental civil liberties that were jealously guarded by the established church and government. Freedom of conscience translated easily into the obligation to stand firmly for what is perceived as morally right, even though such a stance risks disobedience to established authority. But the dissenting sects were also responsible middle-class citizens, who wanted nothing more than to be the paragon of *law-abiding* freedom.[1] They desired not just political freedom, but also political power. They wanted the right, not just to participate in government, but to control the concept of what constitutes just government and thus to control government itself.

To be a woman within this movement was to possess equally with men the freedom of conscience valued so highly by the liberal dissenting tradition. Because it was woman's fate to learn how to balance a chaste conscience with faithful submission to the "politic father,"[2] she found that her feminine subordination gave her special knowledge which it became her obligation to spread as a voice of dissent. Her status of double dissent — as a political female and as a female within a nonconforming community deprived of civil liberties — presented obstacles equal to the opportunities it afforded, for it required her to articulate the insight peculiar to her dual position without having any access to sanctioned political forms (academic oratory, parliamentary debate, legal pleading, court and ministerial intrigue, and so forth). More tellingly, her access to formal political participation was limited even within her own nonconforming communities. Among the conventional modes of politics practiced by the dissenters in their fight for civil rights (the petition, the political sermon, the political association, the corresponding society, and so on), the only formal avenue

open to the political female was the periodical, which welcomed her literary contributions, even though these contributions were easy targets for controversy and could be dismissed as the presumptions of a political female.

Unlike political men, women like Hannah More who hoped to influence the "conduct" of the nation had to take an indirect route to political participation through *politic words* (words chosen with an eye to feminine caution and decorous conduct), written as literary composition. At best, a woman writer could attempt to duplicate in her politic words those more "direct" means of active political exchange such as the dissenting sermon and the corresponding society, which their accompanying advantages of direct contact and mutual interchange in an oral or conversational situation. She could compose a sermon, which she could "deliver" only as a written text, or she could compose a political dialogue (a favorite form in the liberal journals), imitating the conversations available to men within their political societies, and hope that it would influence the actual dialogue within these societies despite her banishment from them.

With literary composition being her only avenue to formal political participation, the dissenting female found herself contradicted yet again by the traditions of literary composition itself, for the topical literary modes overtly associated with political discourse were off limits to her, unless she could find ways, ironically, of seeming to depoliticize the topical nature of the modes themselves. It is not that she would be prevented from writing a political tract (some brave women did so), but that in writing it she jeopardized, in the eyes of her readers, the feminine purity of her position and thus the basis for her political advantage — becoming More's "disgusting" and "unnatural" female politician, a licentious or mannish woman (*Strictures* 364). Just as More's status quo political tract is veiled by the form of a female conduct book, so the dissenting women writers had to find ways of exploiting traditional topical forms to suit their double dissension. Because literary composition itself was being increasingly reconceived as a nonpolitical arena, at least partly due to the increasing visibility of women within it, political women had to steer a difficult course, between exploiting overtly politicized literary modes for seemingly nonpolitical ends of general moral conduct and exploiting the depoliticized mantle of "the literary" in general to veil their passion for politics. They could choose to speak politics in nonpolitical modes, and thus risk greatly diminishing the clarity and pointedness of their political passion, or they could choose literary modes that were overtly political while trying to infuse them with a recognizable "feminine" decorum, again risking a softening of their political agenda. The

latter option also risked readers' being blinded to the deeper ideological substance and political stance by their own disgust with the surface indecorousness of a female politician.

One literary mode that was especially inviting and problematic for dissenting women was the occasional poem, a form that during the period stood at the crossroads between overt political satire (the province of political men) and apolitical sentiment (a province women were making increasingly their own).[3] As the Romantic poets were turning away from this highly conventional topical form or turning it into modes (like the "conversation" poem or the "greater romantic lyric") that stressed the unique powers and limits of the poet's utterance as a transcendent dialogue with universal nature and human nature, women poets within the dissenting tradition were seeking to exploit the topical nature of these conventional forms to meet the political challenges of double dissension.[4]

When Anna Barbauld published her poem *Eighteen Hundred and Eleven* in the year 1812, she took the risk of writing an occasional poem, a poem conventionally composed to mark an event of state or national significance. (The poem was published in a volume entitled *Eighteen Hundred and Eleven, a poem* by her publisher J. Johnson in London and immediately pirated in America. I cite the edition from Barbauld's *Works*.) Popular during the seventeenth and eighteenth centuries, the occasional poem was normally written by great men for great men: by poets laureate for royal personages, by the patronized for their patrons, by grateful gentlemen for military officers on the success of a battle. Often combined with the topographical mode, the occasional poem is decidedly topical, stressing the greater national import of a particular event that might otherwise seem merely quotidian, private, or personal — a monarch's birthday, for instance. Because of its topical association with state crisis, ceremony, or celebration, the occasional poem tends to be overtly politicized, but politicized in such a way that political factions within the state may be subsumed by an overriding national interest that affects all good citizens. In its parodic or mock form, the occasional poem tends to veer off either toward hard-hitting topical satire like Dryden's *Absalom and Achitophel* and Swift's "Satirical Elegy on the Death of a Late Famous General," or toward light satire on ephemeral, quotidian, apparently private topics, like Swift's "Stella's Birthday" poems and "Verses on the Death of Dr. Swift."

Toward the end of the eighteenth century, the private events often mocked by light occasional verse were being taken seriously as subjects for topical poeticizing. The topical quotidian subjects of occasional verse had

become closely allied with sentimental modes, such as poems marking a sublime natural occasion like seeing a magnificent twilight, marking the occasion of a pathetic or picturesque sight like a child begging or a wounded bird, or marking the occasion of an intimate, personal revelation like the loss of a close friend. The sentimental overtones of late eighteenth-century occasional verse shifted its emphasis from topical politics to topical morality. With this shift to sentimental didacticism, More's moral conduct (the peculiar province of women of rank and talent) displaces political commentary. Even though the political potential of occasional verse resides always at the edges of its topicality, women poets felt more at ease with the sentimental version of this form, making it their own and popularizing it for an enlarged readership. And even though their sentimental lyrics of occasion focused on little domestic moments, women poets saw these moments of private reflection and feeling as occasions for influencing the moral conduct of the national culture. The moralizing tendencies of the sentimental lyric grew out of the period's fascination with theories and practices of education, especially as this fascination related to women's changing cultural role as guardians of moral conduct.

Like More, who was infamous for her lower-class literacy projects in the moralistic Sunday school movement, Barbauld was heavily involved in education, both as a practitioner and as a theorist. The daughter of a famous dissenting educator, Barbauld taught in her husband's dissenting boys' academy, and was most famous for her children's books, a moralizing literacy project for the middle classes. More, however, aimed her *theory* only at the upper classes, through her *Thoughts on the Importance of the Manners of the Great to General Society* (1788), *An Estimate of the Religion of the Fashionable World* (1791), *Strictures on the Modern System of Female Education* (1799), and *Hints towards Forming the Character of a Young Princess* (1805). Her educational *practice* was aimed solely at the middle and lower ranks (respectively through her *Stories for Persons in the Middle Ranks* and *Tales for the Common People*), revealing the tendentiousness of her conservative project, which ghettoized "conduct" as a province of practical action pertaining to women, the middle, and lower classes. As a dissenter, Barbauld, on the other hand, refuses the distinction between moral theory and practice, and views the conduct of middle-class dissenters as universalizable in its exemplarity. Thus Barbauld sees education as comprehensive, operating totally and in exactly the same way for all ranks and both sexes. Education, she points out, "includes the whole process by which a human being is formed to be what he is, in habits, principles, and cultivation of every kind"

("On Education," *Works* 1: 306). Theories cannot educate, examples occasionally do, but circumstances inevitably must:

> The moment he was able to form an idea his education was already begun; the education of circumstances — insensible education — which, like insensible perspiration, is of more constant and powerful effect, and of infinitely more consequence to the habit, than that which is direct and apparent. This education goes on at every instant of time; it goes on like time; you can neither stop it nor turn its course. . . . Maxims and documents are good precisely till they are tried, and no longer; they will teach him to talk, and nothing more. The *circumstances* in which your son is placed will be even more prevalent than your example; and you have no right to expect him to become what you yourself are, but by the same means. (*Works* 1: 307).

The dissenting woman writer takes seriously the idea that small, daily experiences determine the grandest principles of conduct. Because no line can be drawn between what is preached and what is practiced, only the practice of living itself can be trusted to instill virtue. "If these [manners] are different from what you yourself experienced, you must not be surprised to see him gradually recede from the principles, civil and religious, which you hold. . . . I believe it would be difficult to find an instance of families, who for three generations have kept their carriage and continued Dissenters" (1: 314). Based on the dissenters' unitarian concept of life, a seamless thread runs from practical experience through moral conduct to political action. To cut that thread at any point would be to alter the character of all three spheres. Thus, when Barbauld speaks of the education of the young, she is in the same breath speaking politics. It is not surprising, then, that her essay "On Education" concludes with a political lesson, linking the morality of the state to the political responsibility of the individual citizen:

> States are educated as individuals — by circumstances: the prophet may cry aloud, and spare not; the philosopher may descant on morals; eloquence may exhaust itself in invective against the vices of the age: these vices will certainly follow certain states of poverty or riches, ignorance or high civilisation. But what these gentle alter[n]atives fail of doing, may be accomplished by an unsuccessful war, a loss of trade, or any of those great calamities by which it pleases Providence to speak to a nation in such language as *will* be heard. (1: 320).

Like More, but even more radically, Barbauld here saps the masculine discourses (preacher, philosopher, orator) of overt political power, reducing them to "talk" and subsuming these "gentle alternatives" by the greater

power of circumstance. Just as she has blasted throughout the essay the gentleness of a supposedly natural Rousseauistic education and the upper-class gentility some middle-class families have attempted to imitate in educating their children, she concludes by insinuating that the political forces wielded by the "gentle" classes must yield to the great educator, circumstance. Because the greatest national states are educated in exactly the same way as children in a domestic setting, the circumstantial principles which guide the moral conduct of individuals will determine the conse-quences of the nation. This, in a nutshell, is the substance and stance of Barbauld's most overtly politicized, and thus most controversial, poem, *Eighteen Hundred and Eleven*; it is a moral claim whose political practice is inseparable from the various discursive forms it takes in her verse and prose. Unlike More, who used discursive "theory" for the upper ranks and exem-plary story for the middle and lower ranks, Barbauld did not need to change the form to fit the audience. For Barbauld, the medium always belies the message to a greater or lesser degree, for it always threatens to divert the reader from circumstantial political resistance to inconsequential "talk."

Guided by the principle that experience is both circumstantial and unitarian, Barbauld can maneuver between politics and moral decorum without giving up either, regardless whether she writes in the more moral-izing form of sentimental verse or in a seemingly indecorous polemical mode. Like most women poets of the period, she wrote many sentimental occasional poems, but rather than blunting the edge of her political agenda, the form serves to sharpen the calamitous consequences that must befall the unprincipled conscience, even as the poem skirts the overtly politicized topics that haunt its edges. "The Mouse's Petition" (*Works* 1: 35–38), for instance, a typical sentimental occasional lyric, has obvious political im-plications, but resists becoming a politicizing poem. Barbauld's title refers to the petition, the most radical version of a political letter, which targets the heart of established power by directly addressing the monarch and parliament. The petition ironically is really a demand, a way for disem-powered individuals and groups to demand their rights by asserting the true source of political power in the voices of those who are governed. The language of the poem is suffused with politicizing phrases, seeming to carry through with the radical logic of the petition for rights:

> If e'er thy breast with freedom glowed,
>   And spurned a tyrant's chain,
> Let not thy strong oppressive force
>   A free-born mouse detain! (36)

The petition was a significant site of struggle during this period, as a reactionary establishment wrestled with liberal agitators over the powers and limits of this ancient chartered right. In fact, the petition was often seen and used during the time as the ultimate justification for liberal reform. At first glance, Barbauld appears to be using a mock form, humorous occasional verse, which would seem to undermine her allegiance to the political agenda of petitioning for rights. Indeed, a common tactic of status-quo writers was to ridicule the concept of political rights by reducing it to an absurdity. "It follows, according to the natural progression of human things," Hannah More writes, "that the next influx [after the rights of women] of that irradiation which our enlighteners are pouring in upon us, will illuminate the world with grave descants on the *rights of youth* — the *rights of children* — the *rights of babies!*" (*Strictures* 409).

As Barbauld's "Petition" barrages us with its series of petitions for the mouse's rights, the first half of the poem teeters on the brink of satire, however light, and could go in any direction. Is it a genuine or mock sentimental poem on the occasion of a wounded mouse? Is it a political poem that uses the occasion of an "imprisoned" mouse to satirize the "enlighteners"? Is it a political poem that uses the occasion of a trapped mouse to make a serious petition for the rights of commoners? The specific topical event — a trapped mouse — lends itself to this studied waffling between decorous morality and lightly irreverent satire. This studied indecision seeks resolution midway through the poem:

> The cheerful light, the vital air,
>   Are blessings widely given;
> Let Nature's commoners enjoy
>   The common gifts of Heaven. (36)

The liberal political language is retained ("Nature's commoners"), but subtly transliterated into moralized sentiment and subtly transferred out of the sphere of topical satire and political factionalism. If the poem were to take the expected direction of topical satire, there would have to be both an identifiable object of ridicule and a recognizable political scapegoat as object-lesson; the poem, however, resolutely refuses this opportune, expedient option, which would resonate so harmoniously with the usual mode of talking politics. The last two lines of the stanza, instead of pursuing a factional political agenda of a faction, gives way to "common gifts," which may be seen to have no partisan ideological interest.

Rather than politicizing its own stance by self-consciously dramatizing

its own political objectives to a sympathetic readership, the poem *discourages* readers from viewing themselves as members of any political faction but instead enlists them within the "kindred mind" of humanity:

> The well-taught philosophic mind
>   To all compassion gives;
> Casts round the world an equal eye,
>   And feels for all that lives. (37)

The egalitarian substance and stance of the poem cannot be mistaken, but it is an ideology that promotes itself and implicates its own agenda, or more appropriately *demotes* itself and *sublimates* its own agenda, by embracing all readers with "an equal eye," and likewise by demanding from each reader a response which—even as it is common and "*all*"-inclusive—appeals to every conscience individually and uniquely in the specific experience of particular everyday circumstances. This particular moral instance, then, converts the ideological substance and political stance undergirding the poem into a genuine topic, a *place of diversion*. Barbauld's strategy is to remind us that a topic is a figure (of speech, mere talk) that points us to a place necessarily outside of its own figuration. Her humble topic drives us outside of the poem and into circumstance, away from the diversionary pleasure of reading as a singular politicized moment (the expected occasion) and toward the duty of living as a morally conscientious, ongoing, and outgoing activity. In other words, the more universal and ubiquitous the poem aspires to be through its moralizing sentiment, the more "uncircumstanced" it becomes, threatening to abstract the process of reading from the experience of actual circumstance itself. It is not the inherent talkiness of the poem that will make people take a political stand, but the circumstantial nature of experience itself, which can never be embodied in the formal representations of language. Competing theories of life do not matter here, Barbauld explicitly says. Whether we adhere to an egalitarian political belief based in neoplatonism (that "mind . . . / A never dying flame, / Still shifts through matter's varying forms, / In every form the same") or to a skeptical belief that causes us to stress the differences among creatures and ranks (that "this transient gleam of day / Be *all* of life we share"), the practical circumstance and the moral consequence are the same—demanding a predicated but unpredictable response, one that the reader can enact only under the tutelage of actual circumstance.

Sentimental lyrics tend to construct a generalized audience of poten-

tially benevolent readers by transforming unfortunate occasions, either real or imagined, into reiterated scenes of sentimental instruction.[5] This is why the addressee in such poems tends to be, contrary to topical satire and occasional verse generally, not an individual but the world at large; when it is a named individual, it becomes one with whom every reader can immediately identify. Contrary to occasional verse, which pinpoints a specific nonrepeatable event, sentimental verse chooses topics that are so generalized and repeatable that they tend toward instant cliché. To have read one sentimental poem is to know them all. Barbauld follows this conventional pattern of reiterable cliché and totalized address meticulously. However, while accepting the conventional parameters of sentimental occasional lyric, thus avoiding gender indecorum, Barbauld draws attention to the implicit link between the all-inclusive gesturing of sentimental verse and the political agenda of equal rights for "Nature's commoners." Undergirding this conventional sentimental conclusion, then, the implications of petitioning remain, entirely bifurcated into both a political petition to the individual conscience *and* at the same time a depoliticized appeal to that same conscience. "O hear a pensive prisoner's prayer," the poem begins, and it ends appropriately with a prayerful blessing: "So may thy hospitable board / With health and peace be crowned . . . May some kind angel clear thy path, / And break thy hidden snare" (1: 38). From Barbauld's dissenting perspective, petitioning, rather than tearing apart the political from the moral fabric, is transformed into a weaving gesture that binds the aggressive act of a political demand to the submissive act of prayerful blessing. By ending with petition as *both* demand and prayer, Barbauld points the reader away from the hypothetical, figurative scene of the poem and toward the consequential circumstance of life which no poem can refigure (1: 232–50).

Although *Eighteen Hundred and Eleven* takes the other option, transposing the sentimental occasion of national warfare into pointed political verse, the principles of circumstance, consequence, and conscience play exactly the same unitarian dissenting role. One notorious review (perhaps by John Wilson Croker but also attributed to Robert Southey[6]), printed in the *Quarterly Review* of June 1812, calls attention to the poem's recalcitrant topicality: "The poem, for so out of courtesy we shall call it, is entitled 'Eighteen Hundred and Eleven,' we suppose, because it was written in the year 1811; but this is a mere conjecture. . . . what we do understand we very confidently assert that there is not a topic in 'Eighteen Hundred and Eleven' which is not quite as applicable to 1810 or 1812" (*Quarterly Review* 16: 309–

10). By noting how the poem's actual topics seem to empty themselves of their topicality, the reviewer is pointing out how the poem is both topical and "fatidical" at the same time. This paradoxical status, to seek empowerment while retaining the moral authority of the disempowered, replicates exactly the dissenting female's double dissension. For the male reviewer, however, this self-inflicted split merely confirms the unavoidable embarrassment that must result when a "spinster" presumes to speak politics, and especially dissenting politics. He automatically reads her earnest prophecy as failed satire. "Our old acquaintance Mrs Barbauld turned satirist," he exclaims in the first sentence of the review. "The last thing we should have expected, and, now that we have her satire, the last thing that we could have desired" (309). Being widowed, Barbauld is not a spinster, but she is, according to this reviewer's logic, metonymically a spinster. The moment that she "has wandered from the course in which she was respectable and useful, and miserably mistaken both her powers and her duty," she must embarrass herself, for her appropriate life of spinning or knitting has no direct relation to the momentous events of state she mistakenly takes as the occasion for her poem. The reviewer continues:

> We had hoped, indeed, that the empire might have been saved without the intervention of a lady-author: we even flattered ourselves that the interests of Europe and of humanity would in some degree have swayed our public councils, without the descent of (dea ex machina) Mrs. Anna Letitia Barbauld. . . . Not such, however, is her opinion; an irresistible impulse of public duty—a confident sense of commanding talents—have induced her to dash down her shagreen spectacles and her knitting needles, and to sally forth . . . in the magnanimous resolution of saving a sinking state. (309)

In conclusion, he warns her to "desist from satire, which indeed is satire on herself alone," and he entreats her to refrain from "writing any more party pamphlets in verse" (313). Because the topics that give sustenance to satire remain beyond her sphere, Barbauld cannot write topical poetry, and so her attempt to delineate the "interests" of Europe in order to sway public opinion must automatically become a form of self-embarrassment, unintentional self-satire, according to the male reviewer. In case she cannot sense her own self-dimunition independently—after all, she has proved the weakness of her judgment by writing the poem in the first place—the male reviewer must force her to feel this through the sharpness of his own satire against her, a form of ridicule that merely pointed out the obvious ridicule the lady politician has inflicted on herself by wounding her own feminine virtue.

According to the prevailing ideology, the "spinster" should "resist" politics as she should sex itself, meaning both that it should be beyond her desire and that such resistance should define her desire. Just as the chaste woman may have knowledge of sex, but cannot know the pleasure of its practice, so the political spinster may have knowledge of politics, but cannot know the power of its practice. Innocent of politics even while suffering the consequences of political warfare, the female, in this sense, represents the ultimate innocent, the justifiability of man's often violent political actions. He commits awful deeds in the world to protect her from the savagery of power, and because she represents the site in which life is bred and nurtured, her innocence is necessary not just for the justification of his power but also for the continuance of life itself. Furthermore, her political innocence serves as an inverse gauge for his political prowess. The degree to which her feminine sphere is shielded from state politics indicates the degree to which he has succeeded or failed in sustaining the political establishment of the state. So long as she is not distracted from fashion, or knitting, or the education of children—her genuine areas of influence— then his politics can be seen to be sustaining order, no matter how forcefully disruptive it is to the actual lives of individual men and women.

Barbauld's "intervention," therefore, functions as a double violation for readers like this reviewer. When she dashes down her knitting needles to sally forth into dissident politics, when she is distracted from writing children's tales to pen party pamphlets in verse, Barbauld dashes the myth that women must suffer the consequences of political intrigue while remaining politically chaste themselves and questions the myth that men's political power can be justified by women's innocence while not being interrogated by that innocence.

But it is exactly against this kind of intervention that Hannah More warns. More cautions her readers against satire, considering it the "most deadly weapon in the whole arsenal of impiety, and which becomes an almost unerring shaft when directed by a fair and fashionable hand" (*Strictures* 366). More's linking of satire to warfare represents the logic that views satire as off-limits to ladies: it is the disgust of a female warrior. The link between warfare and political skirmishing implies that the disgust of the female politician is also at stake here. Barbauld is all too aware of the risk she is taking in writing topical poetry; accordingly she carefully avoids satire, despite its traditional alliance with topical verse. In 1811 Napoleon is at the height of his glory and England seems to be bungling the war and losing the continent, and the world, to France; in fact, England's swinging door

ministry seemed to be incapable of forming a government, much less of designing a strategy to deal with Europe's problems or its own labor riots and royal scandal at home. The year 1811, like Shelley's 1819, is a perfect year for politically directed ridicule, for there is so much incompetence and so much anxiety about the lack of political talent that it would have been easy to target enemies, the way Shelley later takes on Sidmouth, Castlereagh, and the Prince Regent. Barbauld's resistance to topical satire is motivated by a desire to practice a different kind of politics, a politics that can discern a crisis without turning that crisis into an opportunity for exploiting one's own power to mutilate an enemy. For dissenting women who are pushed off to the edges of political participation even within their own dissenting communities, resistance to power must be enacted as conscientious dissent (grounded in politic words, not action) at the margins of active power.

That the *Quarterly* reviewer is incapable of distinguishing between satire and nonsatirical occasional verse is not surprising. Satire is the most conventional approach to politicizing verse. It pits one camp against another in the most verbally violent manner. By assaulting any reader who does not succumb to its own political objectives, political satire divides the sheep from the goats and discounts any possibility of alliance based on pure principle because it tends to identify with the political expediency of factions. Another way of saying this is that satire is the other side of the accommodationist coin, the word play of negotiation and panegyric, represented in the epistolary form. If politics is a form of mediation which can be practiced only by those with legitimate power, then satire is the literary obverse of conventional establishment politics. Satire refuses any possibility for mediation, legitimating the "right" side, the writer's (and reader's) side, and ridiculing the "wrong" side.

Although we do not have space to examine the myriad, complex ways in which *Eighteen Hundred and Eleven* preempts the satirical barb even as it adapts the form of occasional verse, with which satire is conventionally allied, we can point to one example. Barbauld has clearly rejected this conventional kind of topical satire in the poem for a topicality that plays out the submission of the individual political will to the higher truth of principled circumstance. There are three interrelated arenas: the conscience of the individual reader, not found *inside* the poem but haunting the margins of it, and shaping its political and moral objective by pointing us away from the poem's figures and toward unfigurable circumstance; the historical-political fate of the nation-state, which the individual will cannot change

but must endure; and the collective fate of those who conscientiously endure the expedient politics of the nation. We can see all three arenas at work in the last four lines of the first stanza:

> Colossal power with overwhelming force
> Bears down each fort of Freedom in its course;
> Prostrate she lies beneath the Despot's sway,
> While the hushed nations curse him — and obey. (*Works* 1: 232)

The dominant image of the poem is one of bearing down. Colossal power bears down on every object in the poem — attempting to level every "fort of Freedom." The irony is that established power is both successful and ineffective. Freedom lies prostrate beneath the force of power; she is always on the defensive but never defeated. This idea is emphasized in the next two stanzas through the relation between Nature and "man": "Bounteous in vain, with frantic man at strife, / Glad Nature pours the means — the joys of life." Nature continuously pours life, no matter how vainly, as "frantic man" strives against Nature's unceasing bounty. A whole series of figures is represented as bearing the weight, without being able to wield the sword, of power: the hills; the helpless peasant; the matron; Beauty; "some soft one" bending over a newspaper "to learn the fate of husband, brothers, friends" gone to war. Though these figures are usually feminine, Barbauld presents men, notably tradesmen, and we can assume *dissenting* tradesmen, in exactly the same position:

> Sad, on the ground thy princely merchants bend
> Their altered looks, and evil days portend,
> And fold their arms, and watch with anxious breast
> The tempest blackening in the distant West. (235)

Even as power (as political expediency) rules the day, it is also always in decline, just as "fairest flowers expand but to decay." "The worm is in thy core, thy glories pass away." Neither individuals nor factions have any way of controlling or altering the ultimate outcome of this historical process. Like Freedom, the righteous remnant has to endure this corrupt and potentially corrupting process. It is not by coincidence that Freedom is a feminine figure. She represents the capacity for a chaste conscience even at the point of rape.

   This position should not be read as permission passively to accept

power's assault. The "fatidical" nature of the poem's forward or downward thrust is a call to action, not in the sense of ad hoc expedient politics — the frontal attack — but rather a call to sustained, principled activity. Such conscientious activity is seemingly invisible, internal, and indeterminate compared to the visibly grand and discrete actions of worldly embattled political men. The nonconformists formed their own schools, associations, and businesses in order to make and keep themselves strong and prosperous in mind and spirit. It is only such intellectual, moral, and material strength that would enable them to withstand political woes directed against them and others. Their strength also prepared them to meet the crisis once they are called to act more directly in the interest of an unerring historical judgment. It is not the point of the poem to give political advice — another error made by the *Quarterly* reviewer. Instead, the poem calls on the conscience of the reader to respond to the gravity of this historical moment, 1811. In other words, the reader is fully burdened with the poem's vision. A refusal to act not only bears out the prophecy but also impugns every individual who does not bear the weight. Like Nature and the nonconformists, readers must commit themselves to unceasing bounty — cultivating storehouses of mental, material, and spiritual prosperity — even in the midst of senseless slaughter. The insistent address of the poem is directed at Britain, but it is "indirected" at the readers, individually and collectively:

> And think'st thou, Britain, still to sit at ease,
> An island queen amidst thy subject seas,
> While the vext billows, in their distant roar,
> But soothe thy slumbers, and but kiss thy shore?
> To sport in wars, while danger keeps aloof,
> Thy grassy turf unbruised by hostile hoof?
> So sing thy flatterers; — but, Britain, know,
> Thou who hast shared the guilt must share the woe. (234)

The success of power is deceptive. It tricks those on top into thinking that they have won the war because they are victorious in battle. It deceives them into thinking that they can enjoy the treasure won in political warfare while remaining "unbruised." The repeated message of the poem is that all must share the woe, but only those who refuse to act conscientiously will be exempt from sharing the guilt.

Finally, conscientious action matters because, even though it cannot alter the natural process of the strife for worldly power which goes on

unabated, it can help to sustain and carry forth the "fort of Freedom," which also endures, though always under duress. Individual and collective action contributes to the "progress" of freedom, even though the ways of this progress are mysterious:

> Ardent, the Genius fans the noble strife,
> And pours through feeble souls a higher life,
> Shouts to the mingled tribes from sea to sea,
> And swears — Thy world, Columbus, shall be free. (250)

It is too late for England and Europe, caught up in their downward descent into the colossus of power, but it is not too late for other tribes in other places, more innocent and thus less weighted with guilt. These final lines of the poem suggest the way in which conscientious activity shapes the objective of the poem at the outer rim, where both the reader and the actuality of unfigurable circumstance await. The new world "shall be free" not only because of its own relative innocence but also because of the labor of those who are working to free that world. The "higher life" is achieved by the endurance of a shared woe, for European power bears down on peoples in the new world perhaps even more than in Europe. Individual readers need not fear, then, that their conscientious action is in vain. Freedom is always blooming elsewhere, and any refusal to share the guilt ultimately contributes to the flowering of "a higher life."

In the end, the female dissenter finds herself in a different position from both the eighteenth-century versifying polemicists, who strengthened the link between occasional verse and establishment politics, and the "romantic" poets, who attempted to implode those links through an individual poetic voice so forcefully shattering in its legislative capacity that it could annihilate conventional forms from within those forms themselves, thus transcending the unpoetic compromises of partisan politics. Nowhere is this better represented than in Lucy Aikin's occasional poem "On Seeing Blenheim Castle" (*Epistles on Women* 144–45). Aikin, Barbauld's niece, takes up the same topic as Swift's "Satirical Elegy on the Death of a Late Famous General." The force of Swift's satire gives Swift himself no room for maneuver, for it reminds us how the satirist's damning words boomerang and retarget Dean Swift himself. One satirical volley begs to be answered with another, as Swift's final lines beg the question of how to determine — in the context of an embattled partisan discourse where one man's ill-got gain is another's well-got praise — the appropriate objects of attack and honor.

Aikin takes the sighting of the Marlborough estate, Blenheim Castle, as an occasion neither to praise nor to blame its lords, but to distance us from the anticipated discourse of political jockeying that normally attends a view of this icon of established political power. Rather than giving us a Swiftian satirical outburst that merely inverts the rituals of praise expected in occasional verse, Aikin diverts our attention away from the place and occasion named in the title:

> O ask not me of Blenheim's marble halls,
> Her towering column and triumphal gate;
> With vacant glance I viewed the trophied walls,
> The wide unsocial haunt of sullen state! (Aikin 144)

She notices the castle, the seat of corrupt political power, without envisioning it, without figuring it for our view. By placing the "not" directly after "ask," Aikin stresses that others who take in this view, but not she, may be asked to represent it for us. Her "glance" is "vacant" (changed to "careless" in the final stanza) despite the hard memorializing "marble halls," "towering column," "triumphal walls," "wooded green domain, / Formed by the labourer's hand, the artist's rule"—all those self-promoting accoutrements of masculine political might. In diverting our sight and attention away from the expected scene, and its topically politicizing occasion, Aikin turns us toward an unexpected sentimental rural scene, isolated, tangential, self-consciously naive in its innocence, and glaringly devoid of exactly the kind of aggrandizing mementos erected to make permanent Marlborough's power, and usually ritually celebrated in occasional verse:

> Be mine the cheerful view of village green
> With ruddy children scattered far and near,
> The babbling brook thro' willow hedgerows seen
> That turns the mill with current cold and clear! (144)

Unlike romantic occasional verse (especially Wordsworth's), which would displace the politicized scene of politic power with a compensatory poetic scene of natural power, Aikin's poem glories in its own dislocation from the political scene as a corrupting source. Rather than offering the "cheerful view" as an alternate way of making a bid for the seat of power, or as compensation for not visibly occupying its center, Aikin's sentimental view remains tangential, fleeting, dislocated, discentering. "At scenes like

these the feeling breast may warm . . . / The poet's mind new dreams of beauty form, / And fancy own the promptings of the heart." The conventional topicality of occasional verse is not imploded or emptied here, as it would aspire to be in a similar romantic poem; instead it is glimpsed vacantly, allowing the walls of encastled power to reveal themselves as erecting the structural walls of the poem's encapsulating form. As the dissenting poet glances away, owned by fancy's promptings of the heart, and thus armed, not with a fierce weapon, but with disarming words, she builds within the castle's ominous shadow a shielding conscience, a tiny "village green," where we can resist the "wide unsocial haunt of sullen state."

Notes

1. On the differences of social rank among the Dissenting sects, see Raymond G. Cowherd's *The Politics of English Dissent* (15–16). The label "dissenter" characterizes a broad segment of nonconforming sects. I am using the term here to refer to the "rational dissenters," who by the 1790s were primarily Unitarian in doctrine and who were the most highly educated, most "liberal" practitioners of dissent. They came from the middle-middle classes, ranging from the professional to the artisan rank. For explanations of the doctrinal differences among dissenting sects, see Ursula Henriques, *Religious Toleration in England, 1787–1833* and Michael R. Watts, *The Dissenters* 1: chapter 5. For a discussion of the usage of the word "liberal," see J. E. Cookson, *The Friends of Peace* (2–4).

2. A phrase used by Lucy Aikin in her Introduction to *Epistles on Women*: "The politic father will not then leave as a 'legacy' to his daughters the injunction to conceal their wit, their learning, and even their good sense, in deference to the 'natural malignity' with which most men regard every woman of a sound understanding and cultivated mind" (vi).

3. Occasional verse is a complex form related to myriad other forms and modes in complicated ways. It is especially close to the verse epistle, also popular among women writers, but also has ties to the tract, and dissenting sermon, the political letter in prose, the polemical novel, the epistolary novel, mock epic, the polemical play, the petition, the parliamentary speech. Ideally, the network among these forms in relation to the political, social, and cultural institutions that nurture and sustain them would be examined in detail. Due to space constraints, I have had to limit discussion here to the isolated example of the occasional poem.

4. I do not intend to suggest that occasional verse, topical satire, and epistle were not written during the "romantic" period, even by the canonized romantic poets; rather I am suggesting that the critical history of romanticism has stressed and still stresses the political and formal transgressivity of the canonized romantic poets. Romanticism has been seen by such diverse critics as E. R. Wasserman, W. K. Wimsatt, Jr., M. H. Abrams, Paul de Man, Geoffrey Hartman, and Harold Bloom as emptying, contesting, and radically transforming the inherited assumptions un-

dergirding conventional generic modes, largely as a result of political crises that the romantics both personalized and universalized. (For an excellent critique of this critical view, see Stuart Curran's *Poetic Form and British Romanticism*.) Ironically, more recent historicist critics like Jerome McGann, James Chandler, Marjorie Levinson, and Alan Liu have further deepened our view that the overt form of romantic poetry is a transgressive depoliticizing mode, not only diminishing the role of those eighteenth-century poetic genres which were most closely associated with political discourse (topical satire, occasional verse, and verse epistle), but also emphasizing the ways in which implicitly political gestures (like the address) borrowed from such genres serve to repress the ideological nature of the poets' apparent political stances. Neither the earlier nor the more recent kinds of criticism apply very well to dissenting women poets, who heavily rely on the conventionality of forms and whose politics and writing practices exploit these forms in ways quite different from the canonized romantic poets. Rather than trying to transgress, explode, or empty the form of its authority, as the romantics are seen to do, the women dissenters are more interested in remotivating the form's conventionality to capitalize on its authority in order to legitimize their voices and views.

5. More recognized benevolence as a philosophy with leveling and politically radical tendencies, and so she warned her readers against it, telling them to trust instead the disciplined life of Christian dogma outlined in the Ten Commandments (see *Strictures* 372–73).

6. It was attributed to Southey by Betsey Rodgers, *Georgian Chronicle* 142–44.

The Way Above the World: Religion and Gender in Welsh and Anglo-Welsh Women's Writing, 1780–1830

I

In 1847, the publication of the *Report of the Commissioners of Inquiry into the State of Education in Wales* aroused considerable shock and outrage in Wales, particularly in response to its findings that sexual impropriety was rife in the principality. The so-called "Blue Books" cited female promiscuity as one of the most distressing consequences of an alleged Welsh backwardness; not only did Welsh women share in the nation's lack of education, but they were also judged to be more licentious than their English sisters. The *Report*'s accusations were angrily refuted by numerous defenders of the virtue of Welsh womanhood. Ieuan Gwynedd in his *Facts, Figures and Statements in Illustrations of the Dissent and Morality of Wales* (1849) alleged that, contrary to the exaggerated and erroneous claims of the Report, "the daughters of Cambria need not blush when their reputation is measured with that of their Anglo-Saxon sisters," and proved his argument by demonstrating that the ratio of illegitimate to legitimate births was no higher in Wales than in other parts of the United Kingdom at that time; on the contrary, it was frequently lower. And yet, for all this, Ieuan Gwynedd also deemed it necessary to edit during the 1850s a periodical aimed at Welsh women, *Y Gymraes,* which, in its emphasis on the need for its readers to adopt more refinement, does by implication acknowledge that, though the actual conduct of Welsh women may have been virtuous enough, their deportment and general demeanor were not sufficiently restrained: they needed to *appear* more modest, as well as to be in fact chaste, if they were to avoid censure. *Y Gymraes* and its successor *Y Frythones* are periodicals which in effect introduce into Welsh culture in the second half of the nineteenth century the bourgeois English ideal of the "Angel in the House"; their advice to women resembles that of the numerous conduct books, which,

from the late eighteenth century on, had instructed English women on how to shape themselves into the required model of feminine propriety. Hannah More, for example, in her influential *Strictures on the Modern System of Female Education* (1799), exhorted mothers to instill in their daughters a strict decorum:

> An early and habitual restraint is peculiarly important to the future character and happiness of women. . . . They should be led to distrust their own judgement; they should learn not to murmur at expostulation . . . It is of the last importance to their happiness even in this life that they should early acquire a submissive temper and a forbearing spirit. (1: 142–43)

In 1879 Hannah More and her kind were presented to the Welsh women readers of *Y Frythones* as paradigms of a virtue and good breeding that needed to be emulated. But this late introduction of an ideology not indigenous to Welsh ways of life does suggest that prior to this time there may well have been significant cultural differences between Welsh and English attitudes toward women.

Hannah More was a devout Anglican, a member of a group of Evangelical Anglicans who strenuously sought to rectify the morality of the English masses during the last years of the eighteenth century. In the 1847 *Report,* the blame for Welsh women's alleged want of chastity, as for the deplorable state of affairs in Welsh education generally, was laid not only on the effect of the Welsh language in distancing the nation from civilizing English influences, but also on the marked prevalence of nonconformist religious practices in nineteenth-century Wales. Dissent was seen as presenting a major obstacle to the adoption of English and Anglican ideals. Ieuan Gwynedd — himself a nonconformist minister — argued strongly that it was on the contrary social and economic reasons, rather than linguistic or religious ones, that accounted for the apparent disadvantages of Welsh men and women. The relatively late onset of the Industrial Revolution in Wales, and the fact that when it came its management was largely in the hands of English capitalists, meant that there was virtually no middle-class grouping in indigenous Welsh society. Because the "Angel in the House" ideal was middle class in origin, although it was always presented by the reformers as a model for working-class women also, the relevance of Ieuan Gwynedd's argument to the woman question cannot be gainsaid, but I would like to suggest that there may indeed be some truth in the proposition that nonconformity also played its part in Welsh and English differences with regard to gender. Among the nonconformist denominations active in Wales

at this time, only one can be considered fully indigenous to Welsh society, but that one is generally held to have exerted the strongest influence of them all over the religious and cultural life of modern — that is, post-Reformation — Wales. Welsh Methodism, although it originated in the same historical epoch as Wesleyan Methodism, was always independent of, and different from, its English counterpart. Wesleyan Methodism was Arminian; the sect established in Wales by Howell Harris and Daniel Rowland in the first half of the eighteenth century was Calvinist. By analyzing the representation of women in Calvinist texts and by comparing Welsh Methodist and Anglo-Welsh non-Methodist women's writings, this paper aims to explore the contribution of Calvinist influences to concepts of gender in Welsh culture.

II

When William Williams, Pantycelyn, sought to embody in prose the spirit of the Welsh Methodist revival, he gave it a female voice: in his fictional *Llythyr Martha Philophur* of 1762, Martha Philophur tells the story of her conversion in a letter to her religious mentor Philo-Evangelius. The choice of a woman to represent the Calvinist Methodist experience in eighteenth-century Wales fits the historical facts: the sect's records reveal that the majority of its converts were indeed female. What women had to gain from the experience is made abundantly clear in Martha's narrative. Before her conversion, she tells Evangelius, she was a confused and conflicted creature, timid in company, fearful and ashamed, and yet full of frustrated pride and aimless passions. After it, convinced according to Calvinist theology of the pre-election of her individual soul through grace as a "brand plucked out of the burning," as one chosen in particular from the myriad hosts of the damned to have "a share," she says "yes, an eternal share in the living God," she is transformed. No longer timid, she fearlessly shouts out his praises "before the large congregation" and blesses his name "under the gaze of the multitudes"; no longer conflicted, her mind and body now know their place and purpose, she says, and unite in a demonstrative ecstasy of worship, leaping, jumping, dancing, and singing, in the face of the derision, and persecution, of the non-elect (*Gweithiau William Williams* 2: 2–3; my translation).

Much of Martha's letter is made up of justifications of the physical abandonment of early Methodist worship, through reference to a series of

Biblical texts illustrating how the children of Israel were exhorted to leap and dance before the Lord of Hosts. But at one point she also feels compelled to defend in particular, through scriptural endorsement, the public expression of faith by women as opposed to men. At this point her exegesis becomes more uncertain and more devious. She was confirmed, she says, in her belief that it was acceptable for women to address God publicly by the eleventh chapter of the "First Book of the Corinthians," in which St. Paul says "every woman that prayeth or prophesieth with *her* head uncovered dishonoureth her head. . . . For a man indeed ought not to cover *his* head, forasmuch as he is the image and glory of God: but the woman is the glory of man. . . . Neither was the man created for the woman but the woman for the man" (1 Cor. 11: 4–10, AV). This would not seem, on the face of it, an encouraging text from the female point of view, but Martha leaps on the fact that at least the verses do speak of women as praying and prophesying, albeit covered up, as a justification of her practice (2: 11). The deviousness of her argument lies in the fact that she is choosing to overlook a further text, in the fourteenth chapter of the same book, in which the apostle unequivocally declares "Let your women keep silence in the churches; for it is not permitted unto them to speak, but they are commanded to be under obedience. . . . And if they will learn anything let them ask their husbands at home: for it is a shame for women to speak in church" (1 Cor. 14: 33–35).

This second text, and others like it in St. Paul's epistles, proved something of a stumbling block for John Wesley, who, as leader of the English Methodist movement, seems to have been personally favourably inclined toward the ordination of women. Eventually, a few women were granted permission to serve as meeting leaders and itinerant preachers within the English Methodist sect, on the grounds of their having received an "extraordinary call"; Dinah Morris in George Eliot's novel *Adam Bede* is a fictional portrayal of one such votary. Wesley argued, somewhat tenuously, that as early Methodist gatherings generally took place in the open air, or in private homes, the bar against females speaking in church did not apply (see Field-Bibb, *Women Towards Priesthood* 11). But the Welsh Methodist movement never named women as preachers or leaders of meetings, though its records show that without the contribution of female converts, as assistants and hostesses to preachers, and as enthusiasts who walked hundreds of miles to secure the services of preachers for their local gatherings and who were often the first to invite them into new parishes, the revival could hardly have succeeded as it did (Morgan, *The Great Awaken-*

ing in Wales 56–60). Nor are there records of Welsh female converts requesting leadership roles. Martha, in her letter, only seeks justification for speaking out in meetings as a member of the congregation, and accepts without demur women's subordinate status in the hierarchical ranks of creation, reminding herself that, as "weaker vessels," women, through Eve, were the first to "fall."

This greater resistance on the part of Welsh Methodism to sex equality among the "elect" may perhaps be attributed to the theological differences between Welsh and English Methodism rather than to a stronger sexist bias among the Welsh. The Welsh Calvinists saw themselves as adhering more strictly than the Wesleyan Arminians to Biblical tenets, particularly to those of the Pauline texts, in which the doctrine of pre-election features large. What is more, had the movement ever gone so far as to recognize the social situation of women as unjustifiably oppressive, it still would not have deemed it fitting to attempt to do anything to redress the gender balance. According to Methodist ideology, all difficulties encountered in the mortal Vale of Tears were but stepping stones to a more rewarding existence in the hereafter: to wear the crown of thorns of secular opprobrium gladly was to gain spiritual grace. In the nineteenth century, its members were actively discouraged from joining class protest movements; any man wearing a Friendly Society badge, for example, was banned from the Methodist Seiat, or Association (Davies, *Religion in the Industrial Revolution in South Wales* 54). Similarly, when the Welsh Women's Temperance Reform Movement, largely a Methodist organization, was asked to give its support to the burgeoning suffragette campaign in the last years of the century, it refused to do so on the grounds that the issue of the vote was irrelevant: their mission was to save souls from Satan, not to gain for themselves or for other women any secular advancement or redress of wrongs (Lloyd-Morgan, "From Temperance to Suffrage" 152).

But if Calvinism did not take up the opportunity to deviate in this respect from the patterns of sex discrimination characteristic of eighteenth- and nineteenth-century society, in other ways its beliefs and practices did much, paradoxically, to alleviate the psychological effects of female subordination. Great stress was laid in the sect's doctrines on the necessity for conversion to be an experience of the "heart" rather than the "head" (Morgan, *The Great Awakening* 122). Humanity being in all its parts essentially sinful, and saved only by virtue of Christ's sacrifice of himself, such human attributes as knowledge, rationality, or the performance of good works, could have no share in redemption. Conversion entailed,

rather, a shattering of the human ego, a passivity in the face of the divine will, and an opening up of the "heart" to receive lightning flashes of grace. The whole apparatus of logical and conceptual thinking, including language itself, was overthrown in the process; as we have seen the experience was more likely to find expression through groans, cries, and physical demonstrations than through conceptual utterance. According to the conventional division of experience into gendered categories, the capacity to reason, to act, and to maintain a strong and assertive will are attributes more associated with the male of the species than the female, whereas feeling, the body, passivity, and a more permeable ego are seen as more essentially female. It would appear, therefore, given this polarization, that conversion requires and values stereotypically "female" modes of response. Christ is the bridegroom and the convert the bride, whatever the sex of the sinner. As Luce Irigaray puts it in a recent essay on mystical spiritual experience, a mortal "he" becomes a "she" at the point of penetration by the immortal, and follows "her" lead toward the "source of light that has been logically repressed" ("La mystérique," *Speculum* 111). It was men rather than women who had traditionally functioned as the constructors and primary users of rationalist systems of thought, but these organizing human structures only featured in conversion as arrogant and wrong-headed obstacles to truth, to be incinerated in the incandescant moment of revelation. As women had historically been excluded from "head" knowledge, and were thus less likely to be entrammeled by its conceits, the "weaker vessel" was the more prone to catch mystical fire. "This is the only place in the history of the West in which woman speaks and acts so publicly," Irigaray comments in her essay.

It should come as no surprise, therefore, that one of the foremost poets of the Welsh Calvinist movement — and, indeed, of Welsh literature generally — was a woman, Ann Griffiths (1776–1805).[1] In other respects, however, her sex is a great surprise, for Ann Griffiths is the only woman who is given any kind of stature in the traditional canon of Welsh poetry — no general anthology would be considered complete without her inclusion, but it would be unlikely to contain any other work from a female pen, apart, perhaps, from a few poems by one or two contemporary women, scattered about on its final pages in a last minute crisis of conscience. In the many critical tomes devoted to analysis of Ann Griffiths's work, the over-riding note is one of bafflement as to how a young woman with very little formal education, who rarely left her native farm in rural Montgomeryshire, could possibly have expressed herself so powerfully. Her strength is commonly

attributed to the influence of divine inspiration, and, at times, to the profundity of the theological teaching she received from her (male) religious mentors. Of course this is true, in the sense that *she* would certainly have said it was true, but one cannot but suspect that it is to some degree a consequence of the critics' response to her gender: divine inspiration does not feature as a reason for poetic excellence to anything like as great an extent in these critics' comments on male religious poets. But rather than commenting on her commentators, I shall concentrate here on describing those aspects of her poetry which seem to me to exemplify the "female" nature of the conversion experience.

Her method of composition, to begin with, highlights the inward and individualistic nature of that experience, an inwardness that must have been intensified for women converts by nature of the fact that, debarred as they were from preaching or teaching roles, they were not publicly called on to evangelize and spread the faith to the same degree as men. Ann Griffiths must have composed her verses during the years between her conversion to Methodism in 1796, in her twentieth year, and her early death after childbirth in 1805. But they cannot be dated more exactly because she chose never to write them down. They have survived only by virtue of the fact that she recited them to her maid, Ruth Evans, who, though herself illiterate, was fortunately blessed with a particularly retentive memory. Ruth Evans later repeated the verses to her husband, the Methodist preacher John Hughes, who finally put them down on paper. For Ann Griffiths herself, then, the poems served but as a private oral record that gave the relief of expressive form to the pressure of intense inward experience. To conceive of herself as a poet, in any public sense, would no doubt have been as alien to her as it was to most women in her society, poetry being traditionally, because of its high cultural status and the degree of training and self-confidence it required, even more an exclusive male stronghold than the other literary genres. From their first publication in 1806, her poems have been categorized as hymns, and have been highly acclaimed and much used as such by all Welsh nonconformist denominations, but when she composed them she had no such audience or purposes in mind, and was therefore free not only to ignore any possible response to her gender as a poet, but also to take considerable risks with her mode of self-expression.

Her verses frequently become battlefields in which language is pummeled and twisted in the attempt to force it to express experiences that go beyond, and shatter, the linguistic system itself. One of the features in Ann Griffiths's work most frequently remarked on by her commentators is her use of paradox. In the formation of linguistic concepts, meaning is predicated on binary opposition: black is black because it is not white; good is good because it is not bad. But according to Calvinistic theology that which is all bad — man — has to be penetrated by that which is all good — God: the two have been made one in the person of Christ, and the believer has to experience within himself or herself a mirroring equivalent of this eradication of opposites. To express her amazement at this experience, Griffiths constructs lines riddled with conundrums. The crucifixion "puts the author of life to death, and buries the great resurrection" ("Rhoi awdwr bywyd i farwolaeth, / A chladdu'r adgyfodiad mawr"); the believer is "living to see the Unseeable" ("Byw i weld yr Anweledig"); the Christian's path to salvation is a "way" that is "age-old and never ageing, a way without a beginning, which is yet new" ("Ffordd . . . Hen, ac heb heneiddio, yw; / Ffordd heb ddechreu, eto'n newydd") (*Gwaith Ann Griffiths* 27, 43, 303; my translation). In recent feminist theory, this type of both/and, as opposed to either/or, vision is presented as a characteristically feminine way of seeing.[2] The argument does not rely on any essentialist notion of biological difference creating psychological differences, but rather is based on the different patterns of conditioning experienced by male and female children, given the typical family scenario in which women, as opposed to men, are chiefly responsible for the care of infants. According to Nancy Chodorow, a girl's identification with her mother, being more formative and longer-lasting than that of a male child, is not relinquished when the father also becomes important; she is more likely than the boy to retain both as standards of value — both mother and father, as opposed to either mother or father — and thus is not as prone as the male to conceptualize her experience in dichotomized terms (*Reproduction of Mothering* 192–93).

Early patterns of child-rearing also account for the difference in ego strength of men and women, according to Chodorow. Because women mother, girls, identifying with their mothers, and in expectation of fulfilling a similar nurturing role themselves, develop a subjectivity which is more continuous with that of others and more permeable in its ego boundaries than a boy's more detached and separate sense of himself (207). A sense of the self as merging fruitfully with its environment to such a degree that human ego identity is willingly lost is strikingly expressed in one of Ann Griffiths's best-known stanzas:

Gwna fi fel pren planedig, O fy Nuw,
Yn ir ar lan afonydd dyfroedd byw,

Yn gwreiddio ar led, ai ddail heb wywo mwy,
Ond ffrwytho dan gawodydd dwyfol glwy. (*Gwaith Ann Griffiths* 44)

(Make me like a planted tree, O God,
sappy on the bank of the rivers of the waters of life,
rooting widely, its leaves never more to wither,
but fructifying under the showers of a divine wound.)

The blissful physicality of this stanza, particularly its last line, also exemplifies the element of sublimated sexuality in Griffiths's verse. The image of the showers of God's blessing fructifying trees in the landscape of the elect has its Biblical source in the book of Ezekiel, but it can also carry other associations — Zeus impregnated Danae by means of showers of gold. Not that Ann Griffiths would have had any such pagan images in mind, of course: the "divine wound" is a reference to the blood of Christ streaming from his pierced body on the cross. But the "jouissance" of mystical experience does find jubilant expression here. Ann Griffiths in her letters states that she experienced the body as the temple of the Holy Spirit (*Gwaith Ann Griffiths* 23), and, largely through her frequent use of the Song of Solomon as a metaphoric source, she does imbue her poems with an eroticism more characteristic of eastern than of western religious expression. The hands of the living God are upon her; his left hand supports her head while the blessings of his right hand embrace her soul; she lives in expectation of his visitations, ready when he comes "to open to him promptly and enjoy his image fully"; once in Heaven she will "kiss the Son to eternity," without turning her back on him again ("Ei law aswy sy'n fy nghynal, / Dan fy mhen yngwres y dydd, / A bendithion ei ddeheulaw / Yn cofleidio'm henaid sydd"; "Byw dan ddisgwyl am fy Arglwydd, / Bod, pan ddel, yn effro iawn, / I agoryd iddo'n ebrwydd / A mwynhau ei ddelw'n llawn"; "Cusanu'r Mab i dragwyddoldeb / Heb im gefnu arno mwy.") (41, 35, 43).

What I find most surprising, and refreshing, in her poetry is the degree of confidence with which this bride addresses her groom. "Remember, Lord, thy betrothed," she charges him, "leap towards her like the stag." "Awake, Lord, manifest thy strength," she cries ("Cofia, Arglwydd, dy ddyweddi, / Llama ati fel yr hydd"; "Deffro, Arglwydd, gwna rymusder") (35, 36). The critic and dramatist Saunders Lewis, comparing her work to that of William Williams as the other major poet of the Welsh Methodist revival, saw Griffiths as the more masculine poet of the two (Lewis, *Meistri'r Canrifoedd* 312). He was referring to her intellectual strengths, to the way in which she analyzes the paradoxical nature of the conversion experience, but the same contrast might be drawn between the different ways the two poets position themselves emotionally in relation to the object of their devotions. Williams tends to address his Lord with the tentative, pleading voice of the abject lover, begging for his presence, but Griffiths is more likely to command it. At times Christ features as the passive object of her worship:

> Wele'n sefyll rhwng y myrtwydd
> Wrthrych teilwng o fy mryd,
> Er mai o ran yr wy'n adnabod
> Ei fod uwchlaw gwrthrychau'r byd. (37)

> (See, standing between the myrtles,
> an object worthy of my choice,
> although it is but in part I recognize
> his superiority over the world's objects.)

The "Rose of Sharon," "white and blushing, fair of face" becomes the nearly feminized object of her ardent, and — stereotypically — male pursuit. There is also in these lines a tangible sense of relief — "at last! an object worthy of my devotion, after all the human dross": such is her confidence in the worth of her own soul that only a figure of Christ's proportions can measure up to it.

Yet Ann Griffiths's religious experience, unorthodox as it may appear, and for all that she possessed to an unprecedented degree the ability to conceptualize it and give expression to it in verse, may not have been very different in kind from the experience of many of her sisters in the Methodist faith during the second half of the eighteenth century. And they also were provided with a means by which to put their feelings on record: the Methodist Seiat, or Association, was established in order to offer members a regular forum in which to testify to their religious condition and bear witness to that of others in their locality, thus supporting one another in the faith. In some of the extant accounts of these proceedings, it is apparent that women's contribution to the meetings was frequently considered to be of particular value. William Williams, in reporting that the Association at Tan yr Allt, for example, "continues in warmth, in zeal and in love" adds that "the women are more zealous than the men" (Hughes, *Methodistiaeth Gymru* 2: 27; my translation). From the careful listing of the spiritual condition of each individual member in other Seiat records, it becomes clear not only that the women were in practically every gathering more numerous than the men, but that they also tended to express themselves with a greater degree of emotional freedom. Jane John of Dyffryn-Saeth in Cardiganshire is "at peace with God and proceeding beautifully, leaning upon her beloved"; Elizabeth Rhys of Blaenhownant is "full of the certainty of faith, and has experienced much of God's love, in a manner beyond words"; Elinor Evan of Twrgwyn is "longing and thirsting for his presence" (2: 5, 6, 7). As with Ann Griffiths's poems, the language employed by these converts frequently echoes the amorous lyricism of the Song of Solomon: rather than repressing sensuality, Calvinist Methodism made direct use of it, in a sublimated form, as a primary vehicle of the conversion experience. Insofar as it could be sublimated, sensory feeling was valued, and to it women could lay particular claim: their characteristic energy was released rather than repressed within the conversion experience. For all that it was always men who served as counsellors to these meetings, and inscribed their records, there is nothing subservient or passively feminine, in the stereotypically approved manner, about these women's testimonies. A felt conviction of salvation gives to their voices a note of striking self-confidence. Elizabeth Owen is "secure in her belief in the Lamb, and feels at one with him"; Jane Rhys is "in possession of a clear understanding of her condition and proceeding with great freedom" (5).

No doubt it was as a consequence of his personal acquaintance with women such as these that the novelist Daniel Owen, himself a Methodist, portrayed his female characters as generally possessed of greater strength of character than his male ones. When he looked back at Calvinist Wales as it was at the beginning of the nineteenth century in his novel *Gwen Tomos* (1894), he gave to its eponymous heroine an uncomplicated confidence, stemming from her Methodist conversion, which is rarely present in representations of women in English Victorian fiction, whether written by men or women. In one scene from the book, for example, Gwen, in the presence of her brother Harri, not himself a convert, attacks the Anglican parson Mr Jones for his support of fist fighting, which she pronounces to be "contrary to the spirit and teaching of Our Lord." "Good gracious!" replies the parson,

> "What do you know about the spirit and teaching of Our Lord? Are you trying to teach a parson his prayers?"
> "If the parson does not know them, someone must teach him."
> "Gwen!" exclaimed Harri, shocked by her rudeness.
> "What's the matter, Harri?" asked Gwen, perfectly calm. (*Gwen Tomos* 93–94)

The scene ends with the defeated clergyman, as he exits, murmuring "I hope, Gwen, that you'll soon come to your senses. I shall try to pray for you," to which she replies "I shouldn't bother to do so; your prayers will not be answered" (97). Few young unmarried women could hope to address an Anglican clergyman in such a manner in an English novel of the period and get away with it. Her brother is also silenced, knowing "that Gwen was infinitely more courageous and sincere than he." Similarly, in the novel *Rhys Lewis,* Daniel Owen's portrayal of Rhys's mother Mary establishes her as the central moral force in the novel. Hers is not a motherly feminine influence, and she is certainly no anodyne "Angel in the House" figure, but in this novel set in a later Victorian period in which Methodism is presented as in some degree in decline she features as the only effectively evangelizing presence in the text. One of her converts, Thomas Bartley, repeatedly expresses the opinion that had she belonged to the Ranters she would have made an admirable preacher, and the novel is indeed full of her direct and hard-hitting "sermons." At the same time, for all her confidence in the worth of each individual soul, and for all her own hard struggle with poverty, Mary Lewis is vehemently opposed to any form of social protest and quarrels bitterly with her eldest son over his support for a coal-miners' strike. She even faces his death in a pit fire with complete equanimity, once convinced that it has been the means of bringing him "to see the light." Nor had she previously done anything of her own accord to rid herself of her wife-beating villain of a husband, but suffered his blows as her personal cross. Similarly, Gwen Tomos, toward the close of her story, accepts her husband's decision to emigrate to America without complaint, although she considers it misguided, and in the event is proved correct—it brings him little happiness, and kills her.

Against the imbalances of the secular system, such women as Mary Lewis seem proud to be powerless; although fearless in some respects, and apparently untainted psychologically by the trammels of feminine conditioning—indeed, they are not feminine at all according to the definition of femininity in English Victorian culture—they hug to themselves their social subordination. According to the doctrines of their faith, they, like Martha Philophur, had to accept that the female, as a fallen creature, had sunk, through the miserable offices of Eve, to a lower grade of debasement than the male. Once among the elect, however, they experienced themselves spiritually as exalted to yet greater heights in ratio to the depths of their degradation in the fallen sphere. And because spiritual feeling was their all in all, such women cannot, in their ontological understanding of themselves, have suffered that debilitating erosion of self-respect the gender system was inculcating in the majority of their English sisters during their period. That the dogma of gender difference does not appear to have had any rigidly determining psychological effect upon Welsh culture until the second half of the nineteenth century, may, then, paradoxically enough, have been in part the consequence of the influence of Calvinistic Methodism, for all that sect's insistence on the secular subordination of women.

III

The contrasts posited in this argument may become more apparent if we look, for comparative purposes, at the work of two women with Welsh connections who were writing English verse during Ann Griffiths's time, Jane Cave and Felicia Hemans. Of the two, Jane Cave's is perhaps the more interesting case in the present context. Cave, born and reared in Talgarth, Brecon, was the daughter of an English exciseman and glover who had been converted to Calvinist Methodism on hearing Howell Harris preaching. In early adulthood she moved to Winchester, probably to find work, married another exciseman there, and attended the Anglican church. She published a volume of verse in 1783 that went into four editions, with new poems being added to each edition. It is clear from many of these poems, the majority of which are religious in theme, that she felt a great respect for her father's religion, and something of a personal nostalgia for it. The volume includes an elegy on the death of Howell Harris and an attack on Anglican clergymen for not being spirited enough in their preaching: too often, she complains, they treat of "truths which the most exalted mind transcend" with a "cold indifference" that fails to engage their audience. Such "vague address or empty form" is contrasted, in a poem dedicated to her father on his eighty-first birthday, to the fervors of his ardent Methodism:

> yet I hear his hallow'd tongue
> Chant forth the evangelic song.
> . . . .
> My mind retains from infant years
> How oft he kneel'd dissolved in tears,
> And wrestling on his suit preferr'd,
> Till God was present there. (*Poems on Various Subjects* 188, 190)

It is curious here to come across the terminology of Calvinist Methodism employed in the heroic couplet verse form of orthodox eighteenth-century English culture. Yet the characteristic value systems of Augustan poetry are not in fact so alien to Cave as some of her poems would suggest; for all her admiration of her father's religion, reason rather than passion features as her chosen guide, particularly when it comes to assessing the requisite qualities of her sex. The female friend to whom a poem entitled "The Woman's Ornament" is addressed is abjured to resist the distractions of passion:

> Should passion with your better thoughts contend,
> In Reason's empire I've insured a friend. (12)

The "Woman's Ornament" turns out to be reasonableness itself, protected by a most unimpassioned religious principle: those women are described as being "of the pearl possesst" who are

> with a meek and quiet spirit blest,
> Whose soul retains sound judgement, solid sense,
> And virtue, with religion's noble fence . . .
> An heart sincere, sedate — not apt to roam,
> A mind domestic, ever best at home. (14)

Little could be further from Ann Griffiths's unbounded spiritual jouissance than this pragmatic recommendation of religion as a "noble fence." As this poem exemplifies, Cave's acceptance of the values of the Age of Reason also entails a wholesale swallowing of the ideology of sexual difference, with the woman, as potentially the more vulnerable of the sexes to the lure of passion, being safely restrained within the home: here is an "Angel in the House" in the making, with any dangerous feelings strictly supressed.

Yet, at the same time, the rationality Cave prizes also leads her to question the prejudices of her society, when her logic, working on her own experience, reveals them to her as at fault. One of the most arresting poems in the volume was apparently occasioned by a noblewoman's suspicions that she, Cave, as a woman of low social rank, could not have written the poems to which she signs her name. The "Lady" is informed that

> there are beauties of the mind
> Which are not to the great confin'd:

> Wisdom does not erect her seat
> Always in palaces of state:
> This blessing Heav'n dispenses round;
> She's sometimes in a cottage found;
> And though she is a guest majestic,
> May deign to dwell in a domestic ("Poem, Occasioned by a Lady's
>   doubting" 47)

that is, in a servant, a role Cave herself had probably filled at an early stage in her career. From a feminist point of view, the disjunction between the value systems implicit in Cave's and Griffiths's work is a most frustrating one. In Cave's case, male paradigms are accepted wholesale, little is valued except the masculine principles of rationality and control, and yet those terms of reference can sometimes allow her to recognize and criticize social inequities. In Griffiths's case, nothing is of value except feeling, the "heart" and all its associations with the feminine side of gender role polarization; yet because that heart itself is deemed worthless except insofar as its energies are spiritually sublimated, her "way above the world" will never deign to notice in earthly injustices anything but the requisite trials of grace.

But the differences between these two poets cannot be characterized as typical of the discrepancies between the English and Welsh cultures of their period, for Cave is by no means a representative figure of English society. The clarity of her recognition of class prejudice in the "Poem, Occasioned by a Lady's doubting whether the Author composed an elegy, to which her Name is Affixed" owed, perhaps, as much to the democratic influences of her early upbringing in Welsh nonconformist culture as to rationalistic patterns of thought. In the poem to her father she stresses that, though he was of low social rank, "not the most exalted peer" could "boast superior state" (189): hierarchical social divisions are irrelevant in the company of the elected saints.

Much more characteristic of English culture at this time is the poetry of Felicia Hemans. Hemans, the daughter of a well-to-do Anglican merchant, was born in Liverpool, but her family moved to Wales, to Abergele, when she was seven, and she lived there for the next 27 years. The picturesque qualities of Welsh history and folklore appealed strongly to her; the volume entitled *Welsh Melodies,* which she published in 1827, contains numerous lyrics in praise of Welsh warriors of old, though the depth of her commitment to the nationalistic cause can be gauged by the fact that the author of "Owen Glyndwr's War-Song" was also the author of "The

Stately Homes of England." A much-revered poet in England and America throughout the Victorian period, Hemans was particularly praised for her poems of religious devotion, but there is no question of any Methodist influences here. The keynote of her devoutly Anglican verses is a persistent stress on the importance of retaining a childlike attitude in relation to the deity. The poem "The Child Reading the Bible," for example, rhapsodizes over the child's "calm" "power of infant sanctity" and concludes with the poet's request to her heavenly "Father" to

> Teach me, oh! teach me to adore
>   E'en with that pure one's faith —
> A faith, made all of love and light,
> Child-like, and therefore full of might! (1852 *Poems* 583)

The might of this desired faith clearly would not involve any sublimation of adult sensuality. Intensely conscious of her gender, Hemans frequently wrote on women's issues, in a manner which did much to popularize the "Angel in the House" ideal. Like Hannah More, she stressed the need for girls to acquire at an early age a knowledge of their subordinate lot in life. The poem "Evening Prayer, at a Girls' School" tells the girls at their devotions that in their "flute-like voices, mingling low, / Is woman's tenderness — how soon her woe!" For

> Her lot is on you! — silent tears to weep,
> And patient smiles to wear through suffering's hour,
>
> Meekly to bear with wrong, to cheer decay,
> And, oh! to love through all things. Therefore pray! (375)

In this poem the "sweet dew" of a childlike faith is presented as a power which will be the girls' main support in a future womanhood characterized by self-repression and docility.

In 1879 *Y Frythones* presented Hemans to Welsh women readers as the "queen of English poetry," praised her for the "notable brightness" of her religious teachings, and gloried in her Welsh associations. Many of the Welsh poems published in *Y Frythones* show the influence of Hemans and her like, as their titles indicate — "Humility," "The virtuous woman," "I will be an obedient child," "Home," "True Beauty," "The virtuous maiden," and so forth. These verses exist in a different world from that of the impassioned assurance of Ann Griffiths's poetry; their world is a gendered world in which religion aids in the repression of female physicality rather than drawing from it as a source of potentially sublimable energy. But, of course, it was because Calvinism had always supported so strongly the social subordination of women, for all the value it put on feminine psychological attributes, that the discrepancy between these two worlds could be ignored with such apparent ease, and a nervously defensive nation could so readily forgo that freedom from gendered propriety which had so shocked the commissioners of the Blue Books.

Notes

1. For a biographical account in English of Ann Griffiths's life and work, see A. M. Allchin, *Ann Griffiths.*

2. See, for instance, Rachel Blau DuPlessis, "For the Etruscans" 276.

Susan J. Wolfson

"Domestic Affections" and "the spear of Minerva": Felicia Hemans and the Dilemma of Gender

I. Discriminations of Gender

Back in the days of schoolroom and parlor recitations, Hemans's "Casabianca" ("The boy stood on the burning deck") enjoyed a regular place; another poem, "The Landing of the Pilgrim Fathers" ("The breaking waves dashed high / On a stern and rockbound coast"), became a beloved hymn, and "The Stately Homes of England," an anthology standard — their popularity affirming Hemans's place as "the undisputed representative poet of Victorian imperial and domestic ideology."[1] Hemans wrote more than these pieces, volumes in fact. She was one of the most widely read, widely published, and professionally successful poets of the nineteenth century.[2] Yet by its close, she was being written off as a pretty inspirationalist, remembered only by her cherished anthology pieces.[3] Where Wordsworth described the "Poet" as a man speaking to men, Hemans seemed to epitomize the "poetess" as a woman speaking to women — and not for all time, but merely for the passing moment of nineteenth-century sentimental culture. The best that Arthur Symons could manage in his comprehensive retrospect was a summary statement that "it is difficult to say of Mrs. Hemans that her poems are not womanly, and yet it would be more natural to say that they are feminine" (*Romantic Movement* 295).

If this shift from "womanly" to "feminine" seems as opaque as it is discriminating, it is a true register of the role played by Hemans's poetry for readers of her century: the idealizing of female gender roles with the aura, and authority, of "natural" foundation. This ideal was valued in no small part because it was coming to seem merely ideal, an inverse reflection, and reflex, of the contradictory forces of modern life. Although Virgil Nemoianu cites Hemans as a reminder that the "whole field of [now] marginalized literature . . . is replete with acquiescence, formalized harmonies, and translations of obsolete ideologies" and "is *par excellence* the domain of conservatism" (*Hospitable Canon* 240), other readers find Hemans's poetry only tenuously conservative and far from replete. To Jerome McGann, it is consciously "haunted by death and insubstantiality" ("Literary History, Romanticism, and Felicia Hemans," this volume 220). Anne Mellor notes that the celebrations of "the enduring value of the domestic affections, the glory and beauty of maternal love, and the lasting commitment of a woman to her chosen mate" occupy a corpus of work "that constantly reminds us of the fragility of the very domestic ideology it endorses" (*Romanticism and Gender* 124), and Cora Kaplan has suggested that the gloss of "proper sentiments," "normative morality" and "the emerging stereotype of the pure, long-suffering female" are symbolic representations that mask anger turned inward (*Salt and Bitter and Good* 93–95).[4]

Under the power of their imaginary investments, nineteenth-century readers tended to isolate these anomalies as a peculiar "melancholy" and exclude them from its representations of Hemans as quintessentially "female," even a "feminine" ideal. So, too, with the actual, and in some ways "modern," circumstances of her life—her education, wide reading, and considerable help with domestic burdens. "We think the poetry of Mrs Hemans a fine exemplification of Female Poetry," stated Francis Jeffrey in an essay for *Edinburgh Review* (50: 34) later canonized by its reissue in the first edition of her collected works.[5] This social judgment is made to seem a guarantee of nature. Opening with a characteristic bluntness, "Women, we fear cannot do every thing; not even every thing they attempt," Jeffrey explains that they are "disqualified" not only by the "delicacy of their training and habits," but "still more" by the "disabling delicacy which pervades their conceptions and feelings; and . . . they are excluded by their actual inexperience of the realities they might wish to describe"—among these, "the true nature of the agents and impulses that give movement and direction to the stronger currents of ordinary life." Hemans's poetry proves that women's "proper and natural business is the practical regulation of private life, in all its bearings, affections, and concerns" (32).

Half a century later, W. M. Rossetii deploys these genderings with less gallantry. If Hemans's sensibility is "feminine in an intense degree," the weakness of her poetry is that it is "not only 'feminine' . . . but also 'female'": "besides exhibiting the fineness and charm of womanhood, it has the monotone of mere sex" ("Prefatory Notice" 24). Elizabeth Barrett wearied at this monotone, hearing in it not so much "mere sex" as the class and gender formation of being "too ladylike." "I admire her genius—love her memory—respect her piety & high moral tone," she writes to their mutual friend, Mary Russell Mitford, the "but" looming: "But she always does seem to me a lady rather than a woman, & so, much rather than a poetess. . . . She is polished all over to one smoothness & one level, & is monotonous in her best qualities" (23 November 1842; *Letters to Mitford* 1: 88). While Jeffrey is not so disparaging, it is still in a differentiated and diminished realm—distinct from the writing of "the stronger sex" (*Edinburgh* 50: 33)—that he frames his admiration for Hemans's poetry: "It is infinitely sweet, elegant, and tender—touching, perhaps, and contemplative, rather than vehement and overpowering; and not only finished throughout with an exquisite delicacy, and even serenity of execution, but informed with a purity and loftiness of feeling, and a certain sober and humble tone of indulgence and piety" (34). He means to praise "female genius" (34), even "to encourage women to write for publication" (33), but with a propriety of gender. So he concludes urging Hemans to respect that "tenderness and loftiness of feeling, and an ethereal purity of sentiment, which could only emanate from the soul of a woman" and to stick with "occasional verses" rather than "venture again on any thing so long" and awkward as *The Forest Sanctuary* (47)—an epic romance that Hemans herself regarded "as her finest work" (Rossetti, "Prefatory Notice" 17).

As baldly prescriptive as Jeffrey's remarks are, not only for Hemans but for women writers in general, he is tuned to the haunt and mainly "female" region of Hemans's song—home, religion, patriotism, the affections. Although, as we shall see, her poetry often destabilizes, darkens, or even contests the social structures of these values, for nineteenth-century readers the articulation of the value system was enough to contain, even efface any disturbances. Hemans's "delicacy of feeling," crooned the *Quarterly Review* in 1820, is "the fair and valued boast of our countrywomen"—all that is best in "an English lady" (24: 131); "she never ceases to be strictly *feminine* in the whole current of her thought and feeling," chimed *Edinburgh Monthly Review* in the same year; her subjects evince "the delicacy which belongs to the sex, and the tenderness and enthusiasm which form its finest characteristic" (3: 374). "Not because we consider her the best, but because we consider her by far the most feminine writer of the age," George Gilfillan says, he has made her the "first specimen" in his 1847 series in *Tait's Edinburgh Magazine* on "Female Authors": "All the woman in her shines. You could not . . . open a page of her writing without feeling this is written by a lady. Her inspiration always pauses at the feminine point" (NS 14: 360).

Hemans's cultural work in defining the "feminine" locus for ideals of gender, class, and nation is stressed in the first "memorial," by her friend and biographer, Henry Chorley. Referring to Anna Jameson's "rightly" saying that Hemans's poems "could not have been written by a man," he gives his own encomium to their "essentially womanly" character: "Their love is without selfishness — their passion pure from sensual coarseness — their high heroism . . . unsullied by any base alloy of ambition. In their religion, too, she is essentially womanly — fervent, trustful, unquestioning, 'hoping on, hoping ever' — in spite of a painfully acute consciousness of the peculiar trials of her sex" (*Memorials* 1: 138). For elaboration, he cites Maria Jane Jewsbury, a writer who became Hemans's friend: if "other women might be more commanding, more versatile, more acute," no one was "so exquisitely feminine" as she (1: 187).[6] Comparison to Jewsbury herself helps Hemans's sister, Harriett Hughes, to make the same point:

> it was scarcely possible to imagine two individual natures more strikingly contrasted — the one so intensely feminine, so susceptible and imaginative, so devoted to the tender and the beautiful; the other endowed with masculine energies, with a spirit that seemed born for ascendency, with strong powers of reasoning, fathomless profundity of thought. (*Memoir* 158)

Lydia Sigourney's preface to this edition sums up the tenor of this discourse: "critics and casual readers have united in pronouncing her poetry to be essentially feminine. The whole sweet circle of the domestic affections, — the hallowed ministries of woman, at the cradle, the hearth-stone, and the death-bed, were its chosen themes . . . the disinterested, self-sacrificing virtues of her sex" ("Essay," Hughes xv). In an age of recoil from polemics for women's rights, Hemans was summoned to idealize the "essentially feminine" as essentially "domestic" and "self-sacrificing."[7] The conservative advice of arbiters such as Mrs. Sandford that "domestic life is the chief source of [woman's] influence," her "sphere," and the foundation of her happiness (*Woman* 2–5) was echoed by Hemans in many of the letters that Chorley printed: "There is *no* enjoyment to compare with the happiness of gladdening hearth and home for others," she writes to Mitford (another prolific woman of letters); "it is woman's own true sphere" (*Memorials* 1: 224).

The reiteration of these values was crucial to Hemans's reception, especially as a professional writer.[8] The *Quarterly,* with a dig at modern women of letters, pointedly praised Hemans as "a woman in whom talent and learning have not produced the ill effects so often attributed to them;

her faculties seem to sit meekly on her. . . . she is always pure in thought and expression, cheerful, affectionate, and pious. . . . we have not found a line which a delicate woman might blush to have written" (24: 130–31).[9] Gilfillan valued her for giving "the life at once of a woman and a poetess" ("Female Authors" 360), and it mattered that Chorley (also with respect for the gendering of "poetess"[10]) could not only conclude his *Memorials* declaring that "the woman and the poetess were in her too inseparably united to admit of their being considered apart from each other" (2: 355) but also show Hemans measuring other poets by their domestic affections — for instance, Wordsworth:

> This author is the true *Poet of Home,* and of all the lofty feelings which have their root in the soil of home affections. (1: 174, her emphasis)

> his gentle and affectionate playfulness in the intercourse with all the members of his family, would of itself sufficiently refute Moore's theory in the Life of Byron, with regard to the unfitness of genius for domestic happiness. (2: 115)

As far as Chorley was concerned, Hemans had brought feminizing refinements to the national literature: she clothes "the Spirit of romance and chivalry . . . in a female form" and infuses it with deeper affections; in her "female hands," the "homely domestic ballad" is purged of "the grossness, which, of old, stained its strength," while her letters show a "mind in all its *womanliness*" (*Memorials* 1: 137–39). Jeffrey went further, praising Hemans for the happy Englishing of world literature. Taking her themes "from the legends of different nations and the most opposite states of society," Hemans

> retain[s] much of what is interesting and peculiar in each of them, without adopting, along with it, any of the revolting or extravagant excesses which may characterise the taste or manners of the people or the age from which it has been derived. She has thus transfused into her German or Scandinavian legends the imaginative and daring tone of the originals, without the mystical exaggerations of the one, or the painful fierceness and coarseness of the other — she has preserved the clearness and elegance of the French, without their coldness or affectation — and the tenderness and simplicity of the early Italians, without their diffuseness or languor. (*Edinburgh Review* 50: 35)

Hemans's able broadcasting of English standards explains why even the *Quarterly,* for all its cautions about the ill effects of learning in women, could praise her intellect: "Mrs. Hemans . . . is not merely a clever woman, but a woman of very general reading, and of a mind improved by reflection and study" (24: 130).

The *Quarterly*'s admiration on this last point, however, is also a reminder of the atypical material circumstances that produced Hemans as a writer — ones that complicate iconic definitions of the "feminine." With the devotion of her mother and a large domestic library, she became a voracious reader and a precocious student, and quickly developed into a writer, indeed, a capably publishing poet at fourteen. But she was also a romantic. In her teens, she fell in love with Captain Alfred Hemans and married him in 1812, the year of her nineteenth birthday. She had produced two volumes of poems by then, and by 1818 she produced two more to favorable reviews, as well as five sons. Just before the birth of their last, the Captain left for Italy. The reasons are unclear; the explanation was ill health — in any event, she never saw him again.[11] This failed marriage turned out to be productive for her writing — perhaps motivating its compensatory sentimentalities but also a practical advantage. Deciding to support herself and her sons with her writing, Hemans returned to her mother's household in Wales. This situation relieved many of the conflicts usually besetting women writers: with no wifely obligation or husband to obey, with sisters, mother, and brothers to help with the boys and run the home, Hemans had freedom to read, study, write, and publish. The other advantage was ideological, the identification of her as a poetess not only *of* home, but *at* home — a daughter under "the maternal wing" (an image for both Sigourney and Hughes [*Memoir* xi, 52]). At home, Hemans's professional life was immunized against the stigma of "unfeminine" independence.[12] Thus Rossetti, despite his reservations about the real talents of this "admired and popular poetess," warmly describes her in her domestic sphere, a "loving daughter" and an "affectionate, tender, and vigilant mother" ("Notice" 15).

But even so blessed, it is revealing that Hemans, as a writer, has another view of home, one that attenuates its symbolic representation. In 1822, she laments,

> I am actually in the melancholy situation of Lord Byron's 'scorpion girt by fire' — 'Her circle narrowing as she goes,' for I have been pursued by the household troops through every room successively, and begin to think of establishing my *métier* in the cellar; . . . [in] talk of tranquillity and a quiet home, I stare about in wonder, having almost lost the recollection of such things, and the hope that they may probably be regained. . . . when I make my escape about "fall of eve" to some of the green, quiet hay-fields by which we are surrounded, and look back at the house . . . I can hardly conceive how so gentle-looking a dwelling can contrive to send forth such an incessant clatter of obstreperous sound through its honeysuckle-fringed window. (Hughes, *Memoir* 83–84)

Her tone is humorously aggrieved, but her allusion to *The Giaour* (423–38) hints at a torment. Moreover, the need to making a living by writing was always tuned to writing what would make a living. In poor health near the end of her life, she writes to a friend,

> It has ever been one of my regrets that the constant necessity of providing sums of money to meet the exigencies of the boys' education, has obliged me to waste my mind in what I consider mere desultory effusions. . . . My wish ever was to concentrate all my mental energy in the production of some more noble and complete work; something of pure and holy excellence (if there be not too much presumption in the thought), which might permanently take its place as the work of a British poetess. (Hughes, *Memoir* 300)

The restraints that Jeffrey would impose on Hemans's epic ambitions would be realized not so much by proprieties of gender as by material necessity.

The shadow-text in Hemans's story is the "constant necessity" of most women's lives, domestic labor. Sensing this anomaly without identifying it, Chorley wavers in assessing what he calls her "peculiar circumstances," which "by placing her in a household, as a member and not as its head, excused her from many of those small cares of domestic life."[13] Such cares, he realizes, might have compromised her development as a writer: she "might have . . . fretted away her day-dreams, and, by interruption, have made of less avail the search for knowledge to which she bent herself with such eagerness." But they also might have tempered the extreme "feminine" tone of her work, imparting some "masculine health and stamen, at the expense of some of its romance and music" (*Memorials* 1: 43); Hemans seemed too apt a demonstration of how "one of the gentler sex, shielded as she is by her position in society," can become "too exclusive in her devotions" (1: 24). On the verge of analyzing discrepancies in the "feminine" ideal, what Chorley can recognize is one impressive effect: the "often deeply melancholy" cast of Hemans's iconically feminine poetry, its tendency to dwell even "a little too exclusively upon the farewells and regrets of life — upon the finer natures broken in pieces by contact with [the] world" (1: 43–44). The other story he knows is Jewsbury's. Early "seized" with "the ambition of writing a book, being praised publicly, and associating with authors," and having just begun to publish at age eighteen, she found herself after the death of her mother inheriting the management of the household and responsibility for her five younger siblings. Her daily life "became so painfully, laboriously domestic, that it was an absolute duty to crush intellectual tastes. I not only did not know a single author, but I did not know a single person of superior mind, — I did not even know how wretchedly deficient my own cultivation was . . . I could neither read nor write legitimately till the day was over" (Jewsbury, quoted in *Memorials* 1: 165–66).[14]

That Hemans's days were otherwise was crucial to the production of writing that, paradoxically, sustained famous commonplaces of female and domestic virtue.

II. Hemans in the Scales

Chorley's admiration of Hemans and Jewsbury is an unusual sympathy. In the introduction to *Memorials* he presents the dominant attitude, in Jewsbury's voice: if men "still secretly dread and dislike female talent, it is not for the reason generally supposed — because it may tend to obscure their own regal honours; but because it interferes with [men's] implanted and imbibed ideas of domestic life and womanly duty." While Chorley is sure that this "prejudice . . . is fading rapidly away" with "the increase of female authorship" (1: 8), the source of Jewsbury's sentences, *The History of an Enthusiast,* is less certain.

Its heroine is Julia, a young woman who, restless in her "dull, dreary and most virtuous domestic life," reads, dreams, and longs for the "more brilliant sphere" of a fame won by "mental efforts" (*History* 69): "I feel the hope of it, even now, the spirit of my spirit, the breath of my being, the life-blood of my life" (47). She gains this fame as a writer and a London celebrity; but glamor fades into ennui, which she assesses years onward in a letter to her happily married sister. The terms are gender-laden:

> Ah, what is genius to woman, but a splendid misfortune! What is fame to woman, but a dazzling degradation! She is exposed to the pitiless gaze of admiration; but little respect, and no love, blends with it. . . . However much as an individual she may have gained in name, and rank, and fortune, she has suffered as a woman; in the history of letters she may be associated with man, but her own sweet life is lost. (112–13)

The lament is double-edged, however, for in reporting the depletions and negations that beset a female genius, it also expresses frustration at this economy. Representing Julia's internalization of its measures, Jewsbury puts them in a critical perspective, showing their power of seeming unalterable, essential, as enduring as nature itself:

> This is her fate, these are her feelings, if her character predominantly possess the excellence of her sex. If it be otherwise, if that which should be womanly in her is worldly, if she be not so gentle as vain, at heart a creature of ambition rather than of affection, she will be less unhappy; but, alas, she will also be less worthy of happiness! . . . A *man* may erect himself from such a state of despondency; throwing all his energies into some great work, something that shall beget for him "perpetual benediction;" he may live for, and with posterity. But a woman's mind — what is it? — a woman — what can she do? — her head is, after all, only another heart; she reveals her feelings through the medium of her imagination; she tells her dreams and dies. *Her* wreath is not of laurels but of roses, and withers ere it has been worn an hour! (113–15)

In the reflection that Jewsbury writes for Julia, the social fate of "her sex" appears as a guarantee of nature, an inborn tyranny of heart over head. The allusions to Wordsworth's macro-myths of despair — the "despondency" famously "corrected" in *The Excursion* and the amelioration of loss signaled by the phrase quoted from the "Immorality" Ode — are linked by Julia to gender-specific redemptions. Man may enjoy the "perpetual benediction" of mental energy and the fame it may beget. Women's accolades are of a different nature, epitomized for Julia by the wreath: hers is not the poet's laurels but a woman's roses, a headier but transient beauty.

What also begs notice, however, is the italicized language of gender. This double work of Jewsbury's text — its rhetoric of recognition shaded by complaint and protest — carries over into another key scene, a visit from Cecil Percy, whom Julia hoped would be her suitor but who always viewed her ambitions as not "feminine" (100). Not having seen her for six years, he is shocked to find "a sickly verdure, an unnatural bloom, . . . unsound at the core, withered at the root . . . with energies that only kindled their own funeral pile" (118). To him, fame has blighted both her femininity and, in consequence, men's admiration. "I should not like a lioness for a wife," he declares (120), and Jewsbury's narrator paraphrases his recoil: "She who is brilliant in mind, and gifted with the perilous gift of genius, may receive the homage of saloons, may be courted as a companion, and worshipped as a goddess; but for his help-meet, man chooses far otherwise" (127). Then come the sentences that Chorley, resisting their "prejudice," quotes in *Memorials:*

> Man does not secretly dread and dislike high intellect in woman, for the mean
> reason generally supposed—because it may tend to obscure his own regal
> honors; but because it interferes with his implanted and imbibed ideas of
> domestic life and womanly duty. (127)

This is a voice of social judgment that frames rather than simply reports Cecil's prim voice, and in its vibrant irritation at male prejudice Chorley hears a trenchant critique.[15] The phrase, "implanted and imbibed ideas," defines the socioculture that men take as naturally given. Jewsbury in turn discredits the orthodox Cecil. Julia may lose him to a proper English girl, but he never quite escapes the character of a passionless twit, and Jewsbury ends her *History* not with her enthusiast exposed as vain and vacant nor recuperated to domestic happiness, but recovering some of her original spirit. Deciding to leave England as a "second Mary Wolstonecroft [*sic*]" (143) to travel in Europe on her own, Julia draws inspiration from a poem of male rapture, "Ode to the West Wind," whose voice she speaks as her own: "O lift me as a wave, a leaf, a cloud; / I fall upon the thorns of life—I bleed; / A heavy weight of hours has chained and bowed / One too like thee, tameless, and swift, and proud" (160). Although Jewsbury leaves Julia's precise future left untold, what she does expose is the frustration of England in the 1830s to such a woman, and her *History* boldly severs her enthusiast from the constraints of a domestic script.

The regard of Hemans by English men of letters, accolades notwithstanding, has a good dose of Cecil Percy. Wordsworth admits that he "could say much very much in praise of Mrs Hemans" (August 1830; *Letters, Later Years* 2: 311), but he was inclined to regard her success as a clever commercial accomplishment only. "Mrs. Hemans," he writes in the headnote to some tender memorial verses, "was unfortunate as a Poetess in being obliged . . . to write for money, and that so frequently and so much, that she was compelled . . . to write as expeditiously as possible" (*Poetical Works* 4: 461).[16] In his letter, he noted a "draw-back" in this resourcefulness, which he tunes to the genderings of his headnote ("as a Poetess," "as a woman"): "Her conversation, like that of many literary Ladies, is too elaborate and studied—and perhaps the simplicity of her character is impaired by the homage which has been paid her—both for her accomplishments and her Genius" he laments (*Letters, Later Years* 2: 311), though he seemed to have no such worries about the effect of homage paid to his own account.

His difficulty was how to weigh accomplishment and genius in "a woman" whose "education had been [so] unfortunate" as to leave her "totally ignorant of housewifery," as his headnote puts it: this "spoilt child of the world . . . could as easily have managed the spear of Minerva as her needle." His droll distress about Hemans's refusal of "her" needle, the usual instrument of women's "work," may seem to contain as a comedy at her expense his unease with her intellectual power, projected as a spear-bearing deity of wisdom. But even the warrior Minerva had a domestic role as the proud Olympian weaver for the gods.[17] And in Wordsworth's household at least, women's needles not only clothed his family but also stitched his manuscripts.[18] Hemans thus poses a double affront—to notions of proper female labor and to the system of men's dependence on it for their own work. And so he means to remediate. "It was from observing these deficiencies," the headnote continues, "that, one day while she was under my roof, I purposely directed her attention to household economy, and told her I had purchased Scales, which I intended to present to a young lady as a wedding present; pointed out their utility (for her especial benefit). . . . Mrs. Hemans, not in the least suspecting my drift, reported this . . . to a friend . . . as a proof of my simplicity."

Hemans's own report of this scene is amusingly tuned to the ideological contest: the palpable simplicity of Wordsworth's design to point a wayward poetess into a proper female sphere of attention and her deftly polite resistance to his obvious "drift" by recourse to a wittily blinkered aestheticizing of his object of instruction:

> Imagine, . . . a bridal present made by Mr. Wordsworth, to a young lady in whom he is much interested—a poet's daughter, too! You will be thinking of a broach in the shape of a lyre, or a butterfly-shaped aigrette, or a forget-me-not ring, or some such "small gear"—nothing of the sort, but a good, handsome, substantial, useful-looking pair of scales, to hang up in her store-room! "For you must be aware, my dear Mrs. Hemans," said he to me very gravely, "how necessary it is occasionally for every lady to see things weighed herself." "*Poveretta me!*" I looked as *good as I could,* and, happily for me, the poetic eyes are not very clear-sighted, so that I believe no suspicion derogatory to my notability of character, has yet flashed upon the mighty master's mind: indeed I told him that I looked upon scales as particularly graceful things, and had great thoughts of having my picture taken with a pair in my hand. (Chorley, *Memorials* 2: 141–42)

Troping her alienation from Wordsworth's agenda in the voice of an Italianate lament, Hemans answers his discomfort with the pointed instrument that he finds unfeminine, the pen. While her published "To Wordsworth" praises his "gift of soul or eye" (*Records* 232–33), this private report is one of sharpest satires of his vision ever written.

Hemans's tipping the scales against Wordsworth is loaded with the imbalance that women writers imposed on customary male perspectives: not only were they suspected of domestic delinquency, but they made their own claims to authority and competed in the marketplace — often, like Hemans, with notable success. Wordsworth was not alone in wishing her to put down her pen and take up her needle. This was also the point of Byron's nasty puns of gender. To their mutual publisher, John Murray, he tags her "Mrs. Heman," "your feminine *He-Man*," "Mrs. Hewoman's" (*Letters and Journals* 7: 183; 158). The gendered joking is defensively sharpened by Hemans's commercial prowess, an achievement that seemed not only to disdain the female sphere but to challenge the men's: "I do not despise Mrs. Heman — but if [she] knit blue stockings instead of wearing them it would be better," Byron liberally declared (7: 182).

But if Byron and Wordsworth reflect the pressures to which Hemans was subject from without, she was pressured from within by the asymmetry between her fame as the poet of the domestic affections and the depletions of these affections in her actual life — and the inability of her fame to compensate. This pressure reached a crisis when her mother died in 1827, for this was also the end of her status as child, and it felt like her own death: "I have lost the faithful, watchful, patient love, which for years had been devoted to me and mine; and I feel that the void it has left behind, must cause me to bear 'a yearning heart within me to the grave;' . . . I now feel wearied and worn, and longing, as she did, for rest" (Hughes 120). Rossetti rightly suspects that the "affections of daughter and mother were more dominant and vivid in [her] than conjugal love" ("Notice" 14). Hemans was temporarily cushioned by remaining in the family home, now managed by her brother and sister. But when this household was "scattered" by the former's relocation to Ireland and the latter's marriage, the house ceased to be a home. For "the first time in my life, [I am] holding the reins of government, independent, managing a household myself," she tells Mitford, adding, "I never liked anything less than '*ce triste empire de soi-même*'" (10 November 1828; Hughes 170).

In *Records of Woman*, published in 1828, Hemans included "Madeline: A Domestic Tale" (144–49), a fantasy of restoration that sets this sorrow into a cultural register. Madeline's wedding is also a painful parting from her mother, but this figurative death of her life as daughter is revoked by the sudden death of her husband. In one respect, this catastrophe is a symbol to woman of "the part / Which life will teach — to suffer and be still" (147), but it is also a narrative pivot that reverses and ameliorates this lesson, turning the lovelorn wife back into a beloved daughter. Lost in the death-in-life of widowhood, Madeline is rescued by her mother, whom she begs, in the poem's last couplet, to rematriate her to home: "Take back thy wanderer from this fatal shore, / Peace shall be ours beneath our vines once more" (149). This voice echoes many such regressive Romantic longings — ones heard in Shelley, Wordsworth, and Keats, whose texts often involve images of maternal nurture. But Hemans's conception is a more specific fantasy of the actual maternal home, and Madeline's yearning for the "true and perfect love" (149) of its care evokes a gender-specific paradise lost. The counterexample in *Records* is "The Lady of the Castle" (194–99) who runs off to become a king's mistress. She can be spoken of only with shock of gender: "how shall woman tell / Of woman's shame, and not with tears? — She fell! / That mother left that child!" (195). The consequences are radical: in "grief and shame," her husband seeks his death in foreign wars, and her daughter grows up a "blighted spirit" (196). Years later she returns, pale and impoverished, to seek her daughter, who does not recognize her, and instinctively shrinks back. This rejection is fatal to the failed mother, the implied moral judgment on her irrevocable betrayal of home.

Yet these exempla notwithstanding, the sum of Hemans's career — *The Domestic Affections* (1812), *Tales, and Historic Scenes* (1819), *Records of Woman* (1828), and *Songs of the Affections* (1830) — present a diverse, often divided array of female characters and social perspectives. There are women defined by domestic relations (Wife, Bride, Mother, Widow) or subsumed under the sign itself ("A Domestic Tale," "The Domestic Affections"). This sphere is often evoked as a cultural ideal, with its values gendered as feminine: supervised by women, home is a refuge from the world, a place of spiritual and emotional restoration, or even foundation of patriotic love. Yet in other poems Hemans wonders about these relations or pauses over the seemingly inescapable social fate of women to suffer and endure. Sometimes she uses a language of strength and power to infuse women's lives with heroic intensity; but at other times she strains this intensity with records of women in whom affection turns desperate, pathological, and life-destroying. And at still other times she presents women who rupture the domestic sphere with energies that not only betray and destroy its most fundamental codes but also challenge the deepest logic of the masculine world and its politics. These are women who, driven by spiritual honor and domestic fidelity, defy male authority and avenge its treachery with violence, and whose protests may even take their children's lives with their own.

Hemans was more the recorder than the deliberate critic of these divided representations, whose deepest shadows, as we shall see, fall on her accounts of famous women, especially artists. "Fame can only afford *reflected* delight to a woman," she murmurs to Mitford (23 March 1828; Chorley, *Memorials* 1: 159); "How hollow sounds the voice of fame to an orphan!" (10 Nov.; 1: 234). Yet this reading of "woman" by her own sorrow does not dispel her dissatisfaction with the hollow images of women in other poets. She was quite frank about admiring Joanna Baillie, to whom she dedicated *Records,* for representing women who, in their "gentle fortitude, and deep self-devoting affection," are "perfectly different from the pretty '*unidea'd* girls,' who seem to form the *beau ideal* of our whole sex in the works of some modern poets" (ibid 1: 96). A critique of the "beau ideal" stirs remarkably in one of her earliest poems, "The Domestic Affections" (*Domestic Affections* 148–72), in the way that its processes of argument intermittently expose discrepancies of domestic experience and domestic ideal. It begins with standard polarities. Life in the world is prey to perpetual "storms of discord," "war's red lightnings," the desolation of thrones, the destruction of empires, and "rude tumultuous cares." The value of home is thus not just intrinsic —

> Hail sacred home! where soft affection's hand,
> With flow'rs of Eden twines her magic band,
> Where pure and bright, the social ardors rise,
> Concentrating all their holiest energies! (151)

— but accrues by what it contrasts and excludes:

> Nurs'd on the lap of solitude and shade,
> The violet smiles, embosom'd in the glade;
> There sheds her spirit on the lonely gale,
> Gem of seclusion! treasure of the vale!
> Thus, far retir'd from life's tumultuous road,
> Domestic bliss has fix'd her calm abode,
> Where hallow'd innocence and sweet repose
> May strew her shadowy path with many a rose. (149)

Hemans emphatically transfers terms of worldly power into the domestic sphere: "*Her* empire, home! — her throne, affection's breast!" (150).

These celebrations are stretched over some problematic terms, however. As Hemans describes home's "mental peace, o'er ev'ry prospect bright" (150), she also speaks of its shades and shadows, solitude, seclusion, and loneliness, and so fixed a withdrawal from "life's tumutuous road" (149) that the calm abode comes to seem a withdrawal from life itself. In this aspect, what is projected as a refuge from the world turns out to be very worldly, a reflexive ideal premised on female restriction. The only feminine presences in the world are phantasmic nurturers of masculine "Genius": "Fame" ("ev'ry life-pulse vibrates to her voice") and "Freedom" ("her throne of fire!"). Hemans's argument means to bind this feminine pulse and fire to the domestic hearth: with an instructive analogy, she tells us that "th'aspiring eagle" soon and always "descend[s] from his height sublime, / Day's burning fount, and light's empyreal clime . . . speeds to joys more calmly blest, / 'Midst the dear inmates of his lonely nest" (157–58). Yet the syntax marking this descent seems more than a little reluctant, and the word *lonely* in the destination is sufficiently jarring to shade the primary sense of its "inmates" from "cohabitants" into "fellow prisoners." The application of this image to "Genius" further strains the argument, for once again, an equivocal syntax crosses the design to celebrate the "softer pleasures of the social heart" at home:

> Thus Genius, mounting on his bright career,
> Thro' the wide regions of the mental sphere;
> And proudly waving, in his gifted hand,
> O'er Fancy's worlds, Invention's plastic wand;
> Fearless and firm, with lightning-eye surveys
> The clearest heav'n of intellectual rays!
> Yet, on his course tho' loftiest hopes attend,
> And kindling raptures aid him to ascend;
> (While in his mind, with high-born grandeur fraught,
> Dilate the noblest energies of thought;)
> Still, from the bliss, ethereal and refin'd,
> Which crowns the soarings of triumphant mind,
> At length he flies, to that serene retreat,
> Where calm and pure, the mild affections meet;
> Embosom'd there, to feel and to impart,
> The softer pleasures of the social heart! (157–58)

"At length" indeed: with the dilating grammar of *yet, while, still,* the rapturous phase before the syntactic pivot on *retreat* so temporizes that the retreat comes to seem a relinquishment and a reluctant fall. Writing to her aunt of her admiration for the "noble Spaniards" in the Peninsular campaign of 1808 (in which her brother and Captain Hemans served), young Felicia Browne gushes, "my whole heart and soul are interested for the gallant patriots," but not without realizing the social prohibition, that "females are forbidden to interfere in politics" (Chorley, *Memorials* 1: 31).

Not only do such prohibitions erode the poem's high claims for female domestic seclusion, but Hemans's elaborations darken the material rewards of home for women. The idealized map is one where there's no place like home for the "exhausted," "oppress'd," "wearied pilgrim" of life:

> Bower of repose! when torn from all we love,
> Thro' toil we struggle, or thro' distance rove;
> To *thee* we turn, still faithful, from afar,
> Thee, our bright vista! thee, our magnet star! (152)

Hemans's emphatic apostrophe "To *thee*" absorbs the host of apposite, ungendered first-person plurals that involve women as well as men in the trope of exile. By the end of the poem, however, she is concentrating on a gendered inequality of lived experience. With her domestic affection devoted to healing others, a woman must accept her own depletion. Homebound and "whisp'ring peace" to world-battered men, she must "fondly struggl[e] to suppress *her own*" cares, and "conceal, with duteous art, / Her own deep sorrows in her inmost heart" (164, her italics). When Hemans protests, again with plaintive italics, "But who may charm *her* sleepless pang to rest, / Or draw the thorn that rankles in her breast?" (167), the only answer that she can propose is the "Faith" that transcends the phantom Eden of the earthly home to evoke an "Eden, freed from every thorn" (168), namely, the Eden of Heaven. The ideal of home, strained by what it must suppress and exclude, must finally be projected for women "Beyond the sphere of anguish, death, or time" (171) — beyond, that is, the sphere of their social and historical existence.

The language that portrays the "Elysian clime" of the world beyond (171) gains an even more subversive critical force in "The Domestic Affections" in the way it turns out to reflect the sphere of male genius *in* the world. "Genius mounting on *his* bright career, / Thro' the wide regions of the mental sphere" (157) is refigured in the anticipation of woman's death as the moment of *her* "mounting to [the] skies, / . . . releas'd . . . // . . . on exulting flight, / Thro' glory's boundless realms, and worlds of living light!" (168, my italics). Here are "triumphant" smiles and "radiant prospects" where her "mind's bright eye, with renovated fire, / Shall beam on glories — never to expire" (170–71). While "never" projects a transcendence of all worldly limits, it is significant that Hemans casts this scenario in the terms she used to figure earthly glory for men. Only in heaven, it seems, may women devote their affections, "Sublim'd, ennobled" (in the poem's last words), to something other than "assuaging woe" (172).

It is a sign of Felicia Browne's precocious genius that, in attempting to celebrate the domestic affections as a universal foundation of bliss, she winds up exposing a socially specific scheme so inwrought with suppression and denial for women as to evoke a longing for death as their only release. This mournful lesson haunts the scene of instruction in one of Hemans's most anthologized poems in the nineteenth century, "Evening Prayer, at a Girls' School."[19] Contemplating this ritual in a perspective evocative of Gray's on the boys of Eton college, its speaker superimposes the melancholy woman's life that she knows awaits:

> in those flute-like voices, mingling low,
> Is woman's tenderness — how soon her woe!
>
> Her lot is on you — silent tears to weep
>   And patient smiles to wear through suffering's hour
> And sumless riches, from affection's deep,
>   To pour on broken reeds — a wasted shower!
> And to make idols, and to find them clay,
> And to bewail that worship. Therefore pray! (479)

The poem descends into the bitterness of a rueful female (if not feminist) solidarity:

> Her lot is on you — to be found untired,
>   Watching the stars out by the bed of pain,
> With a pale cheek, and yet a brow inspired,
>   And a true heart of hope, though hope be vain;
> Meekly to bear with wrong, to cheer decay,
> And oh! to love through all things. Therefore pray! (479)

The scene of the girls' innocent prayer evolves into a prefigurative image of their only consolation for, and heroic resignation to, all that "Earth will forsake" (479), render vain, and commit to wrong and decay in their lives as women.

These bleak apprehensions inform stories about women such as "young Bianca," literally killed by domestic affection — or rather, disaffection ("The Maremma," *Tales;* rpt. *Poetical Works* [Gall and Inglis] 125–30). Brought with her child by a jealous husband to Maremma to die a slow death by its infamous pollutions, Bianca is betrayed by both nature and domesticity. Here, nature, hailed in "The Domestic Affections" as the type and ally of home values, conspires in the husband's treachery: we are no sooner told of "Italian skies" where "Nature lavishes her warmest hues" than cautioned to "trust not her smile, her balmy breath . . . her charms but the pomp of Death!" The rhyme is a potent pairing; Nature, a false mother, leagues with Death, a treacherous husband who "woos . . . to slumber and to die." Both "charm with seductive wiles": "Where shall we turn, O Nature! if in *thee* / Danger is masked in beauty — death in smiles?" (126). Nature's deceit, personified both in Circe and in the loving husband who conceals "Deep in his soul" the "workings of each darker feeling" ("vengeance, hate remorse") (128), critically contests the naturalized ideals of "The Domestic Affections." Wife and son are utterly and fatally vulnerable to a man's "fancied guilt," with the story of their "Affliction" evolving a sensational contrast to "Affection" (127): the lesson that "It is our task to suffer — and our fate / To learn that mighty lesson soon or late" (130).

III. Domestic Fates

Hemans's ironies of domestic idealism culminate in *Records of Woman*. Even as she exoticizes these "Records" into other cultures and eras (signaling these with historically-researched headnotes), "of Woman" proposes an essential that extends to the social understanding of her English readers. "For is not woman's [patient love] in all climes, the same?" cries Elmina in *The Siege of Valencia* (*Poetical Works* [Warne] 154). *Records* looks two ways, at the cultures it constructs and at Hemans's own. Although Hemans does not reflect critically on such displacements, this double orientation has a critical force in its common and recurring story: the failure of domestic ideals, in whatever cultural variety, to sustain and fulfill women's lives.

What Rossetti disparages as a "monotone of mere sex" sounds in this volume as a reading of the fate of mere sex.

One sign of this fate is the constraint of female heroism to the demands of the affection. On the title-page of *Records* (iii) is a prescriptive epigraph from Wordsworth's "Laodamia" (86–90), the widow's protest to her husband's shade:

> —— Mightier far
> Than strength of nerve or sinew, or the sway
> Of magic potent over sun and star,
> Is love, though oft to agony distrest,
> And though his favourite seat be feeble woman's breast.

Thus the "strength" of Gertrude, the subject of a record subtitled "Fidelity Till Death," sustains her husband in his torture unto death by his enemies with "high words . . . From woman's breaking heart" (*Records* 58). "The Switzer's Wife" takes its epigraph from Jewsbury's "Arria" (*Phantasmagoria* 2: 122), about the heroically suicidal devotion of a Roman matron to her husband and the Roman ideology of honor. Hemans's "Wife" discovers her "power" in fidelity to the domestic and civic relations by which she is named and identified:

> . . . she, that ever thro' her home had mov'd
>   With the meek thoughtfulness and quiet smile
> Of woman, calmly loving and belov'd,
>   And timid in her happiness the while,
> Stood brightly forth, and stedfastly, that hour,
> Her clear glance kindling into sudden power.
>
> Ay, pale she stood, but with an eye of light,
>   And took her fair child to her holy breast,
> And lifted her soft voice, that gathered might
>   As it found language: — "Are we thus oppressed
> Then must we rise upon our mountain-sod,
> A man must arm, and woman call on God!" (*Records* 41)

When Werner (who *is* named) exclaims, "Worthy art thou . . . // My bride, my wife, the mother of my child! / Now shall thy name be armour to my heart," the possessives reflect her roles of service and subordination, heroized by their "armour" to his action (43). What remains undisturbed in this crisis and its female epiphany is the norm of separate spheres and its gendered system of obligations.

An essay on noble and virtuous instances of "The Female Character" published in *Fraser's Magazine* in 1833 reflects the cultural investment in this conservatism. Telling readers that "the exalted heroism of a woman's soul may be excited by love, religion, patriotism, parental affection, gratitude, pity"—the standard inspirations—it also reminds them that even "these qualities are only evinced on extraordinary occasions. . . . it is only in situations requiring the exercise of the most powerful exertions that a female can divest herself of the retiring gentleness of her nature" (594–95). It is as an impulse of "nature," then, that we are to regard "instances of female heroism, of devoted attachment, and of endurance of suffering," especially for "love of offspring." Hemans, who is warmly praised in this essay, represents this last imperative in the maternal devotion of "Pauline," taking it to a fatal extension as she perishes in the fire from which she would save her child. Her "strength" is organic to a mother's "deep love":

> there is no power
> To stay the mother from that rolling grave,
> Tho' fast on high the fiery volumes tower,
>
> . . . .
> Mighty is anguish, with affection twined! (*Records* 120)

Mighty affection is also the fate of "Imelda," who, finding her lover murdered by her brother (their fathers are enemies), determines to die with him:

> . . . love is strong. There came
> Strength upon woman's fragile heart and frame,
> There came swift courage! On the dewy ground
> She knelt, with all her dark hair floating round,
> Like a long silken stole; she knelt and press'd
> Her lips of glowing life to Azzo's breast,
> Drawing the poison forth. (*Records* 67)

Even with the heroic analogue of Juliet's suicide for Romeo, the result is the same for her as it is for passive Bianca: women's affections succumb to the poison of men's undomestic passions. So, too, for the political prisoner in the first poem in *Records,* "Arabella Stuart" (3–20), who gambles with "male attire" (3) to escape to her lover. A series of mishaps returns her to prison, where her fortitude is voiced as an emergence in gender — "Feeling still my woman's spirit strong, / . . . / I bear, I strive, I bow not" (7); "my woman's heart / Shall wake a spirit and a power to bless, / Ev'n in this hour's o'er-shadowing fearfulness" (19). These "natural" resources, infusing affection with faith, feed a heroism only unto death; ultimately the resources that are "woman's" cannot define an alternative or resistance to the power structures of men's politics.

"The Bride of the Greek Isle" (*Records* 21–34) so emphatically constrains its daring heroine to this fate that it verges on social allegory. The issue of gender is keyed by epigraphs from Byron's *Sardanapalus* (21), which involve stark social divisions in the heroics they voice. The first is the Greek slave Myrrha's pledge to die with her lover, the defeated king: "Fear! — I'm a Greek, and how should I fear death? / A slave, and wherefore should I dread my freedom?" (1. 2. 479–80). The second is his pledge, "I will not live degraded" (1. 2. 629). Myrrha speaks from a social situation, slavery, by which a man and king would be "degraded" but from which her death may be idealized as freedom. While Hemans's Greek girl, "Eudora," is not a slave, her name identifies her as a commodity, a "good gift," blazoned and bejeweled, to be passed from father to husband ("She turns to her lover, she leaves her sire" [26]) and entailing in this passage into goods her own paradise lost: "Will earth give love like *yours* again? / Sweet mother!" (25). Hemans does not focus a critical perspective on this gendered economy, but she does tense its representation, both by displaying its operation and by hinting at a mysterious surplus, a potential resistance in the bride: "the glance of her dark resplendent eye" seems "[f]or the aspect of woman at times too high" (28).

This tension is released by a derailment of the patriarchal marriage plot, as pirates murder the groom and abduct the bride (the poem's title is potently ironic misnomer). Shifting her genre from romance to heroic melodrama, Hemans signals the emergent possibilities by staging a new female blazon in the record of the "mother's gaze" (22) that Eudora lamented to lose:

> lo! a brand
> Blazing up high in her lifted hand!
> And her veil flung back, and her free dark hair
> Sway'd by the flames as they rock and flare;

And her fragile form to its loftiest height
Dilated, as if by the spirit's might,
And her eye with an eagle-gladness fraught, —
Oh! could this work be of woman wrought?
Yes, 'twas her deed! — by that haughty smile
It was her's! — She hath kindled her funeral pile! (32–33)

As if kindled by the glances of Eudora's resplendent eye, the fire dilates her meek femininity into heroic female art, a "work . . . of woman wrought." The retaliatory blaze is a self-transformation, too, of the bride from the gift of man to man to an independent, eagle-glad energy. Eudora's bound, bejeweled and braided hair and veiled face are released into the cultural iconography of female revolutionary heroism — an elaboration exceeding the aspect mere revenge. To write "Man may not fetter, nor ocean tame / The might and wrath of the rushing flame!" (32) is to convey not just Eudora's wrath but her self-wrought liberation from the fetters of men.

But if this exclamation congratulates a symbolic escape from commodification of one kind or another — marriage or slavery — Hemans's hesitation about the implied social allegory keeps such freedom a purchase by death, even restricting its transcendence with a simile that recuperates this heroism as a marriage of the suttee: "Proudly she stands, like an Indian bride / On the pyre" (33) — in effect, the pyre to which Myrrha commits herself as she compounds her fate with that of the man she calls both husband and master.[20] And Hemans's narrative further depletes Eudora's blaze with impotence: "The slave and his master alike" escape the ship, while the bride (like young Casabianca) "stands on the [burning] deck alone" (32), in a futile, if impressive heroism.

This self-consuming heroism also haunts the overtly political emergence of female passion in "The Indian City" (*Records* 83–96). When Maimuna's son is murdered for having wandered onto Brahmin sacred grounds, she first "bow[s] down mutely o'er her dead" (89), then, in an epiphany of power, vows revenge:

> She rose
> Like a prophetess from dark repose!
> And proudly flung from her face the veil,
> And shook the hair from her forehead pale,
> And 'midst her wondering handmaids stood,
> With the sudden glance of a dauntless mood.

> Ay, lifting up to the midnight sky
> A brow in its regal passion high,
> With a close and rigid grasp she press'd
> The blood-stain'd robe to her heaving breast,
> And said—"Not yet—not yet I weep,
> Not yet my spirit shall sink or sleep,
> Not till yon city, in ruins rent,
> Be piled for its victim's monument. (90–91)

The kindling gaze, the unveiled face, and unbound hair are Hemans's codes for the eruption of female power from cultural norms—for the rebellion of passion and pride against passivity and meekness. Here, the result is "Moslem war" (91):

> —Oh! deep is a wounded heart, and strong
> A voice that cries against mighty wrong;
> And full of death, as a hot wind's blight,
> Doth the ire of a crush'd affection light. (91–92)

Yet despite the epigraphic alignment of Maimuna with the anguish of Childe Harold (97), the poem always marks her as female. Her strength is not military but muse-like, of voice and body:

> Maimuna from realm to realm had pass'd,
> And her tale had rung like a trumpet's blast.
> . . . words from her pale lips pour'd,
> Each one a spell to unsheath the sword.
> . . . .
> . . . her voice had kindled that lightning flame. (92–93)

Hemans does not regender this warrior woman (cf. Semiramis, the "Man-Queen" of *Sardanapalus*) but projects her into a heightened female power:

> She came in the might of a queenly foe,
> Banner, and javelin, and bended bow;
> But a deeper power on her forehead sate—
> *There* sought the warrior his star of fate;
> Her eye's wild flash through the tented line
> Was hailed as a spirit and a sign,

And the faintest tone from her lip was caught,
As a Sybil's breath of prophetic thought. (93)

And such power, though it shows what Jewsbury praised as Hemans's ability to "combine power and beauty" (*Athenæum* 171: 104), retains the inscription of a female fate: it achieves only a "Vain, bitter glory!" The bereft
mother turns sickening "from her sad renown, / As a king in death might reject his crown" (93), and soon makes good on the analogy by dying herself.
The domestic sphere is symbolically restored and her triumph contained by
her burial with her son in the ruins of the city she destroyed — a tale summed
in the poem's last line as "the work of one deep heart wrung!" (96).

These depletions bind the affectionate patriotism of heroines such as
"Woman on the Field of Battle" (*Songs of the Affections* 123–26). No sooner
are we told that she is there by the "power" of "love" than Hemans exposes
its futility. In the poem's last words, it is a "love, whose trust / Woman's
deep soul too long / Pours on the dust!" (126).[21] While "too long" seems a
call for revaluation, Hemans's sense of a gendered fate is reflected in the way
her starkest tales of women's revenge require the socially derealized genre of
macabre romance and theatrically pathological characters. "The Widow of
Crescentius" (*Tales* 1–49) is an example. Stephania, made thus by the
treachery of Otho III of Germany, is introduced in images that mirror
blazing Eudora: her "rich flow of raven hair / Streams wildly on the
morning air" (11), and her "wild and high expression" is "fraught / With
glances of impassion'd thought," a "fire within" (13). Like Maimuna, she is
impelled into affairs of state by love, but her revenge is more sensational for
its perversion of female codes. Acting with the impulse of a bride whose
heart was "vainly form'd to prove / The pure devotedness of love" (20), she
insinuates herself into Otho's court as a minstrel boy. Hemans then plays
out a patent perversion of domestic affections and its codes of gender.
Stephania-as-Guido "breathes . . . a strain / Of power to lull all earthly
pain" (27), but in an aspect that exudes a dark Byronic passion, legible not
only in iconography but even in diction:

> oft his features and his air
> A shade of troubled mystery wear,
> A glance of hurried wildness, fraught
> With some unfathomable thought.
> Whate'er that thought, still, unexpress'd,
> Dwells the sad secret in his breast;

> The pride his haughty brow reveals,
> All other passion well conceals. (29–30)

Her actual revenge is a poison, an inversion of (female) nurture; and Hemans dwells on the effects in loving detail, launching her narrative with a wickedly tuned sonnet paragraph that begins thus:

> Away, vain dream! — on Otho's brow,
> Still darker lower the shadows now;
> Changed are his features, now o'erspread
> With the cold paleness of the dead;
> Now crimson'd with a hectic dye,
> The burning flush of agony!
> His lip is quivering, and his breast
> Heaves with convulsive pangs oppress'd;
> Now his dim eye seems fix'd and glazed,
> And now to heaven in anguish raised . . . (33–34)

In a gloat of almost sixty lines, Hemans's poetry savors the poisoner's delight:

> And on the sufferer's mien awhile
> Gazing with stern vindictive smile,
> A feverish glow of triumph dyed
> His burning cheek, while thus he cried:
> "Yes! these are death pangs! — on thy brow
> Is set the seal of vengeance now!" (34–35)

She was clearly inspired. But Stephania's triumph is a fatal purchase. The tale ends with her imminent execution and closes in a perspective that effaces her heroism in the pace of men's history: "o'er thy dark and lowly bed / The sons of future days shall tread, / The pangs, the conflicts, of thy lot, / By them unknown, by thee forgot" (39) — an echo of the rueful reverence Pope wrote for Eloisa: "How happy is the blameless Vestal's lot! / The world forgetting, by the world forgot" (*Eloisa to Abelard* 207–8).

In other poems Hemans compounds women's self-sacrifice with infanticide — an act forced by a husband's betrayal or the threat of an invading army, or both — and presents this stark transgression of domestic codes as a radically domestic affection.[22] The singer of "Indian Woman's Death-Song"

(*Records* 102–8) stands in a canoe rushing toward a cataract, "Proudly, and dauntlessly, and all alone, / Save that a babe [a girl] lay sleeping at her breast." This is a fatal heroism profoundly allied to affection:

> upon her Indian brow
> Sat a strange gladness, and her dark hair wav'd
> As if triumphantly. She press'd her child,
> In its bright slumber, to her beating heart,
> And lifted her sweet voice, that rose awhile
> Above the sound of waters, high and clear,
> Wafting a wild proud strain, her song of death. (104–5)

Her song is a heroic Byronic anthem: "Roll swiftly to the Spirit's land, thou mighty stream and free! / Father of ancient waters, roll! and bear our lives with thee! . . . // Father of waves! roll on!" (105–6). But it is also inflected by the specific plight of a woman "driven to despair by her husband's desertion of her for another wife" (so reports the headnote [103]): the father waters thus seem only partly formula, for the name evokes the patriarchy by which this woman has been betrayed. This is the deepest resonance:

> And thou, my babe! tho' born, like me, for woman's weary lot,
> Smile! — to that wasting of the heart, my own! I leave thee not.
> . . . .
> Thy mother bears thee far, young Fawn! from sorrow and decay.
>
> She bears thee to the glorious bowers where none are heard to
>   weep. (107–8)

In a poem for which one of the epigraphs is "Let not my child be a girl, for very sad is the life of a woman" (104), the Indian woman's death-song claims the paternal river for deliverance to a world where the pangs of betrayal are no more.

By making the husband a political traitor in "The Wife of Asdrubal" (*Tales* 189–96), Hemans allies infanticide with national retaliation as well as desperate affection. In exchange for his life, Asdrubal, governor of Carthage, has secretly ceded the city to the invading Roman general. His family and betrayed countrymen hold out in the citadel, torching it when defeat is inevitable. As the flames spread, they retreat to the roof, from which Asdrubal's wife berates him, stabs their sons before his eyes, and throws their bodies from the roof. Infanticide merely accelerates the inevitable, and the mother's charge is against the craven father who "in bondage safe, [shall] yet in them expire" (196). That Carthage itself is feminine politicizes the passion of its "regal" wife as an emblem of cultural destiny. Her "wild courage" signifies a national defiance and radical self-determination in the face of defeat:

> But mark! from yon fair temple's loftiest height
> What towering form bursts wildly on the sight,
> All regal in magnificent attire,
> And sternly beauteous in terrific ire? (194)

Yet Hemans can represent the politicized mother only by displacing her into the supernatural and a discourse of extreme sensationalism:

> She might be deem'd a Pythia in the hour
> Of dread communion and delirious power;
> A being more than earthly, in whose eye
> There dwells a strange and fierce ascendency.
> . . . .
>   a wild courage sits triumphant there,
> The stormy grandeur of a proud despair;
> A daring spirit, in its woes elate,
> Mightier than death, untameable by fate.
> The dark profusion of her locks unbound,
> Waves like a warrior's floating plumage round;
> Flush'd is her cheek, inspired her haughty mien,
> She seems th' avenging goddess of the scene. (194)

The comparison of her unbound locks to a warrior's plumage is a transvestic signal of a crisis in gender, one with domestic as well as political consequences:

> Are those *her* infants, that with suppliant-cry
> Cling round her, shrinking as the flame draws nigh,
> Clasp with their feeble hands her gorgeous vest,
> And fain would rush for shelter to her breast?
> Is that a mother's glance, where stern disdain,
> And passion awfully vindictive, reign? (194–95)

In the spectacle of a mother whose "towering form" has become less (or more) than maternal, domestic affection turns fatal, political, and sensational all at once. "Think'st thou I love them not?" the Wife taunts Asdrubal; "'Tis mine with these to suffer and to die. / Behold their fate! — the arms that cannot save / Have been their cradle, and shall be their grave" (196). The poem closes with a lurid scene of the promised act:

> Bright in her hand the lifted dagger gleams,
> Swift from her children's hearts the life-blood streams;
> With frantic laugh she clasps them to the breast;
> Whose woes and passions soon shall be at rest;
> Lifts one appealing, frenzied glance on high,
> Then deep midst rolling flames is lost to mortal eye. (196)

Here the extremity of politicized rage is localized in one vengeful "Wife," but in "The Suliote Mother" (in *Lays of Many Lands* [1825]; rpt. *Poetical Works* [Warne] 321), Hemans makes it a pervasive social fate. She based this poem on a famous anecdote about Suli women who, seeing the Turkish army advance on their mountain fasthold and with their men already lost to a failed defense, hurled themselves with their children into a chasm to avoid rape and enslavement. No domestic betrayal compels this fatal heroic. The opening image is of the iconic mother standing "upon the loftiest peak, / Amidst the clear blue sky, / A bitter smile was on her cheek, / And a dark flash in her eye" — a flash fulfilled with the suicide chant, "Freedom, young Suliote! for thee and me!" In a world of men at war, the only sure "Freedom" in the domestic world, Hemans suggests, is death.

IV. Women and Fame

In *Literary Women,* Jane Williams cited *History of an Enthusiast* as an exemplum of "a selfish woman of genius, full of worldly ambition" (385), and in her obituary, "Mrs. Fletcher, Late Miss Jewsbury," Mrs. Ellis summoned the passage I quote on p. 135 ("Ah, what is genius to a woman, but a splendid misfortune! What is fame to woman, but a dazzling degradation!") to moralize about Jewsbury herself (39; cf. *History* 112–13). But if, as we have seen, both Jewsbury and her Julia are less precisely contained, Hemans was more susceptible to the instruction. Her assertive women take no joy in their power, and their heroism emerges only inversely to domestic happiness, or to life itself. Cleopatra in "The Last Banquet of Antony and

Cleopatra" (*Tales* 157–69), is addressed only in the aspect of a momentary glory, a heroism on the eve of defeat:

> In all thy sovereignty of charms array'd,
>   To meet the storm with still unconquer'd pride.
> Imperial being! e'en though many a stain
>   Of error be upon thee, there is power
> In thy commanding nature, which shall reign
>   O'er the stern genius of misfortune's hour
> And the dark beauty of thy troubled eye
> E'en now is all illumed with wild sublimity. (164)

Storm, stain, error, trouble, misfortune, balance the scale of power, pride, and charms.

In all her epithets, moreover — "echantress-queen!" "Proud siren of the Nile!" "Daughter of Afric!" (164–65), the missing term is "woman," its absence a sign of hollow glory. It is significant that the story of another woman of national fame, "Joan of Arc, in Rheims" (*Records* 109–15), receives its epigraph from the first stanza of Hemans's "Woman and Fame," a verse that rejects Fame's "charmed cup" to conclude, "Away! to me — a woman — bring / Sweet waters from affection's spring" (110). Staging this poem at the dauphin's coronation and its honors for Joan's "victorious power," Hemans interposes a domestic plot: when Joan recognizes her father and brothers in attendance, "She saw the pomp no more" (114) — a dissolve that Hemans tropes as a revelation of essential womanhood amid the glory of male politics. The evocation of home and family "Winning her back to nature," Joan "unbound / The helm of many battles from her head" (115) — the reverse of the Hemans women whose unbound hair signals their emergence from customary restraints.[23] The verb "Winning" designates the real victory, and its dative, "to nature," essentializes the motive force, summed in the moral apostrophe of the poem's close: "too much of fame / Had shed its radiance on thy peasant-name," Hemans writes, reminding readers that fate gives the "crown of glory unto woman's brow" only in sacrifice of "gifts beyond all price" — namely, the paradise (lost) of home with all its "loves" (115). When Chorley assures his readers that Hemans "wears under all her robes of triumph, the pitying heart of a woman" (*Memorials* 1: 27), it is not just wishful male fantasy, but her deep allegory. "How I look back upon the comparative peace and repose of Bronwylfa and Rhyllon," she wrote of her childhood homes at the height of her fame; "How have these things passed away from me, and how much more was I formed for their quiet happiness, than for the weary part of *femme célèbre* which I am now enacting!" (Hughes, *Memoir* 189). This elegy for her paradise lost is sharpened by a sense of unreality in present celebrity: a weary, stale, and flat, however profitable, glamor, its alienation from domestic norms signaled by the ironic intonation of the French term.

The conflict between this cultural stricture on what is feminine (not *femme*) and Heman's celebrity on both sides of the Atlantic is most acute in her self-mirroring stories of female artists. As "The Sicilian Captive" (*Records* 172–79) sings mournfully of her lost home, the chief force of her art is its fatal effect on her: "She had pour'd out her soul with her song's last tone; / The lyre was broken, the minstrel gone!" (179). One of the deepest impressions on Hemans's imagination was produced by Gibson's "statue of Sappho, representing her at the moment she receives the tidings of Phaon's desertion. . . . There is a sort of *willowy* drooping in the figure which seems to express a weight of unutterable sadness, and one sinking arm holds the lyre so carelessly, that you almost fancy it will drop while you gaze. Altogether, it seems to speak piercingly and sorrowfully of the nothingness of fame, at least to woman" (Chorley, *Memorials* 2: 172–73).[24] This is a common story for Hemans: the lovelorn female poet loses her voice, then her instrument, and then, implicitly, her life. The poet silenced by sorrow is what "seems to speak" so forcefully to Hemans, the sign that woman and fame can never reach a happy coincidence. When she herself writes a voice for Sappho, it is "The Last Song of Sappho" (*Poetical Works* [Warne 591]) at this moment of "desolate grace . . . penetrated with the feeling of utter abandonment" (headnote), just before her suicidal leap into the sea. In the song's last words, the fatal sea is the only recipient of her desire: "*Alone* I come—oh! give me peace, dark sea!" Her leap bears none of the political resistance of the Suli mother nor even the protest against "woman's weary lot" of the desperate Indian woman. Her voice is that of personal pain alone.

The calculus of heart and art is the transparent allegory of "Properzia Rossi" (*Records* 45–54), the monologue of a famous artist who, dying of unrequited love, embodies her desire in one last work of art. In this melancholy, fame is hollow, a "Worthless fame! / That in *his* bosom wins not for my name / Th'abiding place it asked" (52). Hemans's epigraph keynotes Rossi's desperate sense of the incommensurability of woman's desires and the artist's work:

——Tell me no more, no more
Of my soul's lofty gifts! Are they not vain
To quench its haunting thirst for happiness?
Have I not love'd, and striven, and fail'd to bind
One true heart unto me, whereon my own
Might find a resting-place, a home for all
Its burden of affections? I depart,
Unknown, tho' Fame goes with me; I must leave
The earth unknown. Yet it may be that death
Shall give my name a power to win such tears
As would have made life precious. (47)

The division of self between public "Fame" and a solitary "I," a common
trope, is specified in Rossi's voice as a conflict of artist and woman. Her last
gambit is to reconcile the two by making her art serve her desire, as a proxy
to her beloved:

For thee alone, for thee!
May this last work, this farewell triumph be,
Thou, lov'd so vainly! I would leave enshrined
Something immortal of my heart and mind,
That yet may speak to thee when I am gone,
Shaking thine inmost bosom with a tone
Of lost affection; — something that may prove
What she hath been, whose melancholy love
On thee was lavish'd. (48)

Artistic creation bears the frustrated impulses of heart and nature. Hemans
keeps Rossi always aware of the substitution, always expressing her inspiration in the language of what she lacks:

It comes, — the power
Within me born, flows back; my fruitless dower
That could not win me love. Yet once again
I greet it proudly, with its rushing train
Of glorious images: — they throng — they press —
A sudden joy lights up my loneliness, — (49)

The statement of normal "loneliness" blights the momentary rush of glory,
and the rhyme of "power" and "fruitless dower" spells the dominant econ-

omy. Rossi's only and final hope is not for her art, but (in another recurring rhyme pair) to collapse her "fame" into a "name" that may move the Knight to sad thoughts and a final recognition: " 'Twas her's who lov'd me well!" (54).

Records closes with the most overtly self-referential of these allegories of female fame, "The Grave of a Poetess" (160–63). It is striking that Hemans identifies its subject, Mary Tighe, only in a footnote as "the author of Psyche" and that her poem says little of the poetry, beyond eulogizing the "light of song" shrined in "woman's mind" (160–61). This effacement of Tighe is not so much judgmental as self-reflective: "her poetry has always touched me greatly from a similarity which I imagine I discover between her destiny and my own," Hemans remarked (Chorley, *Memorials* 2: 212). Her effort is to cherish Tighe's delivery from the transient beauties and inevitable pains of life on "mortal ground," the repeated themes she reads in her poetry ("Thou has left sorrow in thy song"), and to imagine her redemption: "Now peace the woman's heart hath found, / And joy the poet's eye" (163).[25] In this divorce of "poet" from "woman," Hemans sides with what she takes to be the inevitable determinations of "woman's heart." Visiting Tighe's tomb three years later, she "env[ied] the repose of her who slept there" (*Memorials* 2: 211).

The epitome of this story is "Woman and Fame" (*Poetical Works* [Warne] 523), which Hemans heads with the final lines of her "Corinne at the Capitol" (ibid 503). But "Corinne" itself has an aesthetic effect that resists the moralism of its final lines. Its title is also that of Book II of de Staël's wildly popular novel, *Corinne, ou l'Italie,* where, for the first time, we see the artist Corinne performing in all genius and glory.[26] De Staël elaborates the whole triumph, even transcribing "Corinne's Improvisation at the Capitol" and concluding in a female apotheosis: "No longer a fearful woman, she was an inspired priestess, joyously devoting herself to the cult of genius" (32). As if conceding the prestige of this episode with female readers, Hemans conveys it through a seemingly enthusiastic woman's gaze:

Thou hast gained the summit now!
Music hails thee from below; —
Music, whose rich notes might stir
Ashes of the sepulchre;
Shaking with victorious notes
All the bright air as it floats.
Well may woman's heart beat high
Unto that proud harmony! (523)

But her "well may" indicates a caution, and in her last stanza Hemans shifts this voice into a tone of severe correction implicitly keyed to the melancholy conclusion of de Staël's novel, with Corinne abandoned and fatally despondent:

> Radiant daughter of the sun!
> Now thy living wreath is won.
> Crown'd of Rome! — Oh! art thou not
> Happy in that glorious lot? —
> Happy — happier far than thou,
> With the laurel on thy brow,
> She that makes the humblest hearth
> Lovely but to one on earth! (523)

In this summation, Corinne's crowd-pleasing at the Capitol is no match in happiness for serving "one" at home.[27] It was the sad conclusion of *Corinne*, far more than its energetic opening, that most profoundly impressed Hemans: "its close . . . has a power over me which is quite indescribable; some passages seem to give me back my own thoughts and feelings, my whole inner being" (Chorley, *Memorials* 1: 304). Fame, she insists in "Woman and Fame" itself, is no compensation for a life deprived of "affection" and the "record of one happy hour": "Thou has a voice, whose thrilling tone / Can bid each life-pulse beat . . . / . . . But mine, let mine — a woman's breast, / By words of home-born love be blessed" (523).

Yet this argument for "home-born love" does not mute the "thrilling tone" and "life-pulse beat" of the female artist to which "Corinne" gives over most of its stanzas. In her repeated rehearsals of this ideological dilemma, Hemans never entirely resolves this inconsistency. She continues to indulge the creative energies she means to discredit, even calling into question the controlling assumptions about the greater satisfactions of domestic bliss. This ambivalence keeps the margins, if not the center, of her writing unsettled. She had an uneasy interest in writing the "tale of an enchantress, who, to win and secure the love of a mortal, sacrifices one of her supernatural gifts of power after another" but "is repaid by satiety — neglect — desertion" rather than enduring domestic bliss. The "injurious influence" of contemplating this narrative, Chorley reports, "compelled [Hemans] to abandon" this project (*Memorials* 2: 4–5). But its latent debate about the sacrifice of talent for love returns in Hemans's subtly strained headnote for "Properzia Rossi," a text that first sets forth the pathos of Rossi's celebrity, then obliquely hints at the misguided focus of her affections:

> Properzia Rossi, a celebrated female sculptor of Bologna, possessed also of talents for poetry and music, died in consequence of an unrequited attachment. — A painting by Ducis, represents her showing her last work, a basso-relievo of Ariadne, to a Roman Knight, the object of her affection, who regards it with indifference. (*Records* 45)

The first sentence gives the orthodox economy, but through Ducis, Hemans entertains a discrepant intuition: if Rossi's pathos is the failure of her poignant self-representation in Ariadne to move the Knight, Ducis's point may be the ultimate meagerness of the object of her affection that is exposed by the Knight's indifference to her talents. In one moment of Rossi's lament, Hemans concentrates on the joy of what *is* in Rossi's possession — the uncontaminated, independent gratifications of artistic creation and its emotional intensities:

> The bright work grows
> Beneath my hand, unfolding, as a rose,
> Leaf after leaf, to beauty; line by line,
> I fix my thought, heart, soul, to burn, to shine,
> Thro' the pale marble's veins. It grows — and now
> I give my own life's history to thy brow,
> Forsaken Ariadne! thou shalt wear
> My form, my lineaments; but oh! more fair,
> Touch'd into lovelier being by the glow
>   Which in me dwells, as by the summer-light
> All things are glorified. (49)

This language of creative "power" is proto-critical in the way it appropriates one of the images in masculine poetics for female beauty, the rose, to convey the unfolding of a woman's art. A more specific investment for Hemans is reflected in the way that some of her terms for Rossi's sculpting — the work of the hand, the unfolding of leaf after leaf, the expression of self in form, in line after line — also apply to poetic work, a sign both of Rossi's "talents for poetry" (45) and her own sympathy with them.

The contradictions between these moments of gratification and the normative terms for women's self-esteem were experienced by Hemans and her contemporaries as a necessary restraint on an undeniable energy — but not without critical insight. When she learned of Jewsbury's death by cholera in India (where her husband was a chaplain of the East India Company), Hemans found a curious consolation in imagining her escape from a worse fate for one "so gifted" with unrealized talents:

How much deeper power seemed to lie *coiled up,* as it were, in the recesses of her mind, than was ever manifested to the world in her writings . . . the full and finished harmony never drawn forth! Yet I would rather, a thousand times, that she should have perished thus, in the path of her chosen duties, than have seen her become the merely brilliant creature of London literary life, living upon those poor *succès de société,* which I think utterly ruinous to all that is lofty, and holy, and delicate in the nature of a highly-endowed woman. (28 June 1834, her italics; qtd. in Chorley 2: 312–13; cf. 314–15)

Williams's *Literary Women* quotes these sentences as a caution (378–79), but Hemans's two italicized phrases tell a more complicated story. The patent excess of "a thousand times" not only does not suppress her admiration of the power that she senses coiled up in Jewsbury's mind; it exposes a compelling attraction. The alternative for the fatal "path of her chosen duties" is, in this coil of energy, no mere fame as a *succès de société,* but something Hemans could not, in the blinds of her cultural moment, yet imagine for such a "highly-endowed" woman. What Hemans's own writings stage and restage is a restless debate between domestic affections and the spear of Minerva. It is this unresolved dilemma of gender — of sentimentality versus ambition, of capitulation versus critical pressure — that constitutes the deeper power, and the most potent legacy, of Felicia Hemans's "feminine" poetics.

In developing this essay, I have been grateful for the attentions of Ronald Levao, Peter Manning, Anne Mellor, Terry Kelley, and Carol Barash.

Notes

1. The phrase is from Norma Clarke's *Ambitious Heights* (45). The latest (6th) edition of *The Norton Anthology of English Literature* (Abrams) represents Hemans with these two pieces and another favorite, "England's Dead," whose sentimental-imperial refrain is that wherever you go in this world, "*There* slumber England's dead!"

2. Between 1808 and 1834, Hemans produced nineteen volumes (see Peter Trinder's list in *Mrs Hemans* 67–68), along with several periodical publications.

3. In our century, Alan Hill is not alone in describing her as a "popular versifier" (*Letters of Dorothy Wordsworth,* 175, n. 1). Even Jennifer Breen's recent anthology, *Women Romantic Poets, 1785–1832,* which means to remedy the "long-neglected achievements" of this group (back jacket), is scanting of Hemans. Its introduction mentions her only in passing (xii), and the Notes dismiss her work as "generally . . . chauvinistic, sentimental, and derivative," reporting Wordsworth's

lack of favor, despite her intense admiration of his work (160). She is represented meagerly by two of her least interesting poems — a short dirge of conventional pieties on the death of a child; and a set of reverential verses "To Wordsworth" (147–48).

4. See Mellor's excellent discussion, *Romanticism and Gender* 124–43. Thanks to Tricia Lootens for calling my attention to Nemoianu's remark.

5. This is the Cadell-Blackwood edition organized by Hemans's sister, Harriett Hughes.

6. Chorley is quoting from Jewsbury's portrait of Egeria in *The History of a Nonchalant* (*The Three Histories* 193), popularly thought to have been drawn after Hemans. Rossetti's "Prefatory Notice" quotes lavishly from it for a summary description of Hemans's character (22–23).

7. For the durable view of Hemans's complicity in the cultural project of idealizing women's role in hearth and home, see Clarke, *Ambitious Heights* 55 et passim. Cora Kaplan's headnote in *Salt and Bitter and Good* (93–95) makes a similar point, but reads this complicity as strained.

8. For informative discussions of the cultural stigma on publishing women writers, as well as of the wrenching conflicts felt by women such as Hemans and Jewsbury who internalized these codes, see Clarke's first two chapters in *Ambitious Heights*, "Contrary to Custom" and "The Pride of Literature," and Mary Poovey, *The Proper Lady and the Woman Writer.*

9. As Clarke observes, praise of Hemans serves as "a stick to beat other women writers" (*Ambitious Heights* 33). A blunt example is Gilfillan's declaration that "not a little of [the] charm" of "Mrs. Hemans's poems . . . springs from their unstudied and extempore character . . . in fine keeping with the sex of the writer. You are saved the ludicrous image of double-dyed Blue, in papers and morning wrapper, sweating at some stupendous treatise or tragedy from morn to noon, and from noon to dewy eve" ("Female Authors" 360). The labors of the woman writer earn a mock-heroic allusion to the fall of the Satanically confederate architect, Mulciber: "he fell / From Heav'n, . . . from Morn / To Noon he fell, from Noon to dewy Eve" (*Paradise Lost* 1: 742–43).

10. The term itself was not only diminutive and feminizing, but also discriminating. Rossetti's "Notice," having already suggested "the deficiency which she, merely as a woman, was almost certain to evince" (16), uses its final sentences to accord "Mrs. Hemans . . . a very honorable rank among poetesses" while reserving "he" for the gender of "the poet" (24). But even this domestication as a "poetess," Hemans herself concedes with ironic amusement, strains social propriety: she imagines that in the view of "ladies," she has to contend with "the ideas . . . they entertain of that altogether foreign monster, a *Poetess*" (Chorley, *Memorials* 2: 280, her emphasis).

11. Her sister's *Memoir* insists that the failure of her marriage was painful (Hughes 56), while Chorley suggests that it was "literary pursuits" that "rendered it advisable for [Hemans] not to leave England" (*Memorials* 1: 42). For a discussion of the embarrassment this separation posed to early biographers, see Marlon Ross, *Contours of Masculine Desire* 252. Rossetti spends a full page of his "Notice" (14) speculating about the state of the marriage, the real "motive" of Captain Hemans's

departure, and whether Hemans's fame had anything to do with the permanence of their separation.

12. The depth and durability of this cultural judgment is reflected in Mrs. Sandford's *Woman, in Her Social and Domestic Character* (1832): "There is, indeed, something unfeminine in independence," she cautions; "It is contrary to nature and therefore it offends" (14). Refuting Wollstonecraft's antonymy of weakness and attractiveness, she disdains "a woman . . . acting the amazon. A really sensible woman feels her dependence. . . . her weaknes[s] is an attraction, not a blemish" (14). In "this respect," she adds, "Women . . . are something like children; the more they show their need of support, the more engaging they are" (15). Gilfillan makes the same point by complimenting Hemans, and women in general, "in Wordsworth's language": they lie in "Abraham's bosom all the year, / And God is with them, when they know it not" ("Female Authors" 362). The last line he misremembers, or perhaps deliberately recasts, from the sonnet, "It is a Beauteous Evening," in which, addressing the "Dear Child! dear girl!" walking with him on the beach, Wordsworth wrote "God being with thee when *we* knew it not" (my italics). Gilfillan converts Wordsworth's contemplation of the gap between unknowing adult and blessed child into a contrast of gender, opposing adult men to ignorant, childlike women. But if, as Norma Clarke remarks, Hemans's domestic shelter evoked "the cultural construction of the feminine as essentially childlike" (48), Wordsworth too could be implicated, for his work at home as a writer was greatly enabled by the labor of the (female) adults of his household.

13. Sigourney's "Essay on the Genius of Mrs. Hemans" is an exception in calling attention to her atypical circumstances, noting "her freedom, for many years, from those cares which usually absorb a wife and mother, . . . her prolonged residence under the maternal wing," her "shelter[ing] from the burden of those cares which sometimes press out the life of song"; "the weight of domestic duty fell not heavily upon her, until time had settled the equilibrium of her powers, and poetic composition had become an inwrought habit of her existence" (Hughes, *Memoir* xi–xii).

14. See also Dorothy Wordsworth's sympathy with Jewsbury's lot (*Letters, Later Years* 1: 434–35); though she had similar responsibilities, she at least had the advantage of sharing them with another adult woman (William's wife). Arbiters of conduct such as Mrs. Ellis converted Jewsbury's frustration into an emblem of proper priorities: though "there burned within her soul the unquenchable fire of a genius too powerful to be extinguished by the many cares of her arduous life, so fearful was she of being absorbed by any selfish pursuit, that she made it a point of conscience never to take up a book, until all her little charge had retired to rest for the night" ("Mrs. Fletcher, Late Miss Jewsbury" 34). For a pioneering study of Jewsbury's brief career, and of the importance of her interactions with Hemans and the Wordsworths, see Clarke's *Ambitious Heights*.

15. Clarke's otherwise incisive reading of this tale as an allegory of Jewsbury's conflicts over her own literary fame (*Ambitious Heights* 83–86) mistakes these sentences as Cecil's (84); Jewsbury presents them as a paraphrase of his reasoning. Chorley is more alert to the ironic distance and edginess of these sentences.

16. In the penultimate stanza of the verses in question ("Extempore Effusion

upon the Death of James Hogg"), Wordsworth cites Hemans not for her art, but for her "Holy Spirit, / Sweet as the spring, as ocean deep" (37–38; *Poetical Works* [ed. de Selincourt and Darbishire] 4: 276–78). Of the five writers mourned (also Hogg, Coleridge, Lamb, Crabbe), that only she is unnamed reports the breach of modesty posed by female fame. Wordsworth's stanza was sufficiently noteworthy, however, to become part of the lore on Hemans; Gilfillan closes his essay with it ("Female Authors" 363).

17. I thank Carol Shiner Wilson for pointing this out to me.

18. Hence Dorothy Wordsworth's journal: "still at work at the Pedlar, altering and refitting"; "I stitched up the Pedlar" (13–14 February and 7 March 1802; *Grasmere Journal* 90 and 98).

19. This poem was first published in the 1826 *Forget Me Not* (Leighton, *Victorian Women Poets* 10–11), one of the popular gift-book annuals marketed chiefly to female readers. My text follows *Poetical Works* (Gall and Inglis) 478–79.

20. Hemans's conversion of her Greek bride into "an Indian bride" not only evokes Myrrha but also the marital symbolism of the actual suttee. A poem she would have known, Jewsbury's "Song of the Hindoo Women, while accompanying a widow to the funeral pile of her husband," has an epigraph from "Forbes' Oriental Memoirs" reporting how this "living victim" comes to the funeral pile "dressed in her bridal jewels, surrounded by relations, priests, and musicians" (*Phantasmagoria* 2: 131).

21. Lootens's "Hemans and Home" offers a fine discussion of the role of Hemans's poetry in formulating for Victorians, through an "erratic course among and through mutual contradictions," the links of domesticity to patriotism (241). Mellor's *Romanticism and Gender* provides a sharp reading of how Hemans exposes the futility and fatality of domestic affection when it is tested by the public realm (135–42).

22. Kathleen Hickock remarks that of nineteenth-century English writers, only Hemans gave maternal infanticide "much notice" (*Representations of Women* 26).

23. In emphasizing the way Joan's armor fails to hide the woman within but merely masks an essentially feminine self, Hemans evokes the cultural anxiety aroused by Joan's cross-dressing: she was tried as much for transvestism as for heresy (Marjorie Garber, *Vested Interests* 215–17).

24. This heterosexual, and ultimately suicidal Sappho is the figure of Grillparzer's *Sappho,* published in 1819 in German; an Italian translation, which Byron thought "superb and sublime" (*Letters and Journals* 8: 25), appeared the same year. It is likely that Hemans, who read both German and Italian, knew Grillparzer's tale, as well as Pope's translation of Ovid's 15th epistle, "Sappho to Phaon" (1707).

25. In a letter that she wrote about Tighe (which Clarke quotes in full), Hemans reveals the cultural allegorizing of Tighe's death as caution for ambitious women: "I heard much of her unhappiness was caused by her own excessive love of admiration and desire to shine in society, which quite withdrew her from Hearth and Home and all their holy enjoyments, and that her mother, standing by her deathbed passionately exclaimed [in the sort of voice that Jewsbury gives Cecil Percy] — 'My Mary, my Mary, the pride of literature has destroyed you'" (Clarke,

Ambitious Heights 50–51). Tighe is judged not only by anonymous diagnoses of an unhealthy desire to shine outside the hearth and home, but also, emphatically, by the guardians of the latter: her mother and Hemans, the culturally celebrated poet of hearth and home.

26. *Corinne* was published in France in 1807 and quickly translated into English; it was immensely popular, especially with women, seeing forty editions in the nineteenth century. As "*the* book of the woman of genius," Ellen Moers remarks, its myth operated "as both inspiration and warning" (*Literary Women* 262).

27. Leighton provides a superb reading of this poem's ambivalence in relation to the energetic celebration of de Staël's chapter (30–34).

Felicia Hemans. "Engraved by Edwd Smith from a miniature by M^r. Edwd Robertson." Courtesy New York Public Library.

Mrs. Mary Robinson. Courtesy New York Public Library.

P. Condé sculp.

Oh! Time has Changed me since you saw me last,
And heavy Hours with Time's deforming Hand,
Have written strange Defeatures in my Face.

Published May 15th. 1797. by Cadell and Davies Strand.

Charlotte Smith. Courtesy New York Public Library.

Silhouette of Anna Laetitia Barbauld. Courtesy New York Public Library.

Carol Shiner Wilson

Lost Needles, Tangled Threads: Stitchery, Domesticity, and the Artistic Enterprise in Barbauld, Edgeworth, Taylor, and Lamb

> Every sedentary occupation must be valuable to those who are to lead sedentary lives, and every art, however trifling in itself, which tends to enliven and embellish domestic life, must be advantageous.
> — Richard and Maria Edgeworth, *Practical Education* (1798)

> The conversation of Frenchwomen, who are not so rigidly nailed to their chairs to twist lappets, and knot ribands, is frequently superficial; but, I contend, that it is not half so insipid as that of those English-women whose time is spent in making caps, bonnets, and the whole mischief of trimmings . . . trifling employments have rendered woman a trifler.
> — Mary Wollstonecraft, *A Vindication of the Rights of Woman* (1792)

> Needle-work and intellectual improvement are naturally in a state of warfare.
> — Mary Lamb, under the pseudonym Sempronia,
> *British Lady's Magazine* (1815)

Anna Barbauld, Maria Edgeworth, Jane Taylor, and Mary Lamb learned to sew as soon as they could hold a needle. Mary Lamb, moreover, struggled to support her family for eleven years as a mantua-maker.[1] Needlework was integral to all girls' education, regardless of their social class, and for a girl or woman to be at her "work" meant to be at her *needle*work. Patient and silent, the little girl hunched over samplers on which she stitched mottos of obedience to God and her parents. As adults, the wealthy tended to do *fancywork*, embroidery with expensive threads and fabric, and some *plain-work*, chiefly shirts for male members of the family or inexpensive charity clothing for the poor. Poor women were restricted to plain sewing and

some simple embroidery with cheap materials. In an increasingly indus-
trialized society, indigent women and children also for low wages did
finishing work like dotting and tambouring[2] on manufactured muslin. For
all classes, the needle was an instrument of social control that kept girls and
women sedentary for hours. In *Emile* (1762), Rousseau noted the desirability of keeping little girls in the "habitual restraint" that would produce
"a docility which woman requires all her life long, for she will always be in
subjection to a man, or to man's judgment" (333).

By the 1790s, the needle clearly signified femininity as domesticity
in the new and powerful ideology of what Leonore Davidoff and Catharine Hall call "professional motherhood" (*Family Fortunes* 175). Middle-
class ideology articulated women's domestic roles as vital, not only to the
strength of the family as it was constructed by the increasingly powerful
middle-class and Evangelical culture, but to the moral, economic, and
political strength of a nation that anxiously posited itself as morally superior
to dissolute, anarchical, godless France. The icon of this ideology — reinforced in conduct manuals, children's literature, novels, speeches in Parliament, sermons from the pulpit, clothing and household furnishings — was
the idealized Good Mother, sewing or knitting for her family and home, or
Housewifery, her distaff and sewing basket at her side.[3] She was the model
of virtue, grace, industry, frugality, and religion; her needle was like that of a
compass, guiding family and nation on a steady course. Her selfless needle
put to shame the selfish needle of the vain late eighteenth-century aristocrat,
who, it was presumed, sewed only to adorn herself for a life of parties and
dissipation.[4] The Good Mother's role had already been idealized and celebrated by Cowper's immensely popular *The Task* (1788). In mock heroic
delight, the poetic voice sings the praises of patient "female industry"
whose "threaded steel" stitches intricately detailed flowers and pastoral
figures on the sofa cover in a cozy home: "the needle plies its busy task," the
speaker sighs (Book IV, ll. 165, 150; *Poems* 236). Authors of at least a
hundred nineteenth-century needleworking manuals reverently quoted the
line from Cowper to lend authority to their volumes.[5] The action of
Cowper's poem perfectly captures the simultaneous centrality and marginality of the needleworking icon: the speaker turns from the sofa, the
gendered site of women's work, to the serious business of composing
poetry outdoors among real flowers. In "To Mary" (1793) Cowper reveals
sewing as sign of love for him when he says of his aged protector, Mrs.
Unwin:

Thy needles, once a shining store,
For my sake restless heretofore,
Now rust disused, and shine no more,
   My Mary! (*Poems* 456)

Yet even as the icon of the Good Mother and Housewifery served patriarchal power, it empowered women. Indeed, to female reformers of late eighteenth- and early nineteenth-century England, the Good Mother was more flesh than icon — active, educated, confident in her moral influence, and willing to use it. "Influence" was, in fact, a powerfully coded term in works by Hannah More and others to describe the important, uniquely feminine duty.[6] As Mitzi Myers and others argue, writers as diverse as the conservative More, moderates Anna Barbauld and Maria Edgeworth and radical Mary Wollstonecraft agreed passionately that the maternal mission was central to the strength of post-French Revolution society (Myers, "Reform or Ruin" 201). Paradoxically, in championing the maternal mission with their pens by writing of it — including the immensely popular children's literature[7] that helped little girls become good mothers — many of these women, not biological mothers themselves but with extensive caretaking responsibilities that included teaching, circumvented the needle of domesticity as the primary instrument that defined them.[8] The needle, then — in life and literature of late eighteenth- and early nineteenth-century England — was fraught with tensions, ambiguities, and multiple readings that are particularly compelling to contemporary feminist critics who have engaged in similar readings of women's textile arts: rejection, rediscovery, celebration.[9] For over two centuries, the sewing needle — intersection of class, gender, and race — has been the site of intense debates about women's roles and the potential for artistic and political expression.

If needlework was, as I claim, a site of significant debate in this period, why do we see so little of it in canonical Romantic poetry? Rare in the canonical six (Blake, Wordsworth, Coleridge, Byron, Shelley, and Keats), needlework there signifies the feminine to celebrate simplicity and rustic domesticity (Wordsworth's humble cottagers, the little girl in "We Are Seven," for example) or to depict heterosexual love (Keats's *Isabella: or, the Pot of Basil* and *The Eve of St. Agnes*). It also signifies the feminine when writers like Wordsworth, Byron, and literary reviewers wished to scold women writers for intellectual or political pretensions in their art. For example, an anonymous reviewer for the *Quarterly Review* (June 1812) (probably John Wilson Croker) blasted Anna Barbauld for daring to throw down her knitting needles (appropriate to a writer of stories for the nursery) in order to take up the pen to write *Eighteen Hundred and Eleven*, which boldly criticized the nation.[10] Hemans suffered similar barbs from Wordsworth and Byron. Byron, for example, claimed of Hemans that she ought to "knit blue stockings instead of wearing them" (*Works,* ed. Prothero 5: 81–82).[11] Wordsworth's remarks were similar in trope and tone. Needlework is far more common in novels, conduct manuals, and children's stories because the authors, most of whom were women, lived the reality of the needle and its ideological significance.[12]

What happened, then, when women writers — in this instance, Barbauld, Edgeworth, Taylor, and Lamb — took up the pen to depict the significance of the needle in a girl's education? Needlework in their poems, letters, essays and children's stories confirms, contests, and subtly subverts the domestic ideology that was taking hold in England. Needlework also illuminates issues of class and gender that underlie assumptions about a girl's education, including her imaginative potential with needle or pen. Where, how and from whom should the girl best learn her lessons? What should she know in order to become a wife and mother who would provide stability for the family and the nation? Does her activity with the needle fix limits on her imagination? How are we to rethink hero(in)ism?

When we think of the Child in Romantic literature, we seldom think of girls — let alone sewing girls — as central figures. Rather, we are accustomed to thinking of Wordsworth's idealized self in the "Intimations" ode, the victim chimney sweeper in Blake, or Rousseau's naturally noble Emile. The Child is often figured male and embodies the male Poet's lost innocence and divine wisdom for which he quietly grieves. We do find the Child as little girl sewing in Wordsworth's "We Are Seven." A junior version of the domestic icon, she sews and sings in an eternal present beside the graves of her siblings. Her mathematics — how many are "really" dead — wisely do not match those of the obtuse questioner. Hers is not, however, the powerful wisdom of the child of *The Prelude* or the "Intimations" ode, where the sensitive poetic voice contemplates the loss of his own visionary joy.

Whereas the Child in Wordsworth or Coleridge learns from Nature, often troped female and maternal, girls in children's stories by Barbauld, Edgeworth, Taylor, and Lamb are most often educated indoors by mothers or mother figures.[13] Like Maternal Nature, the ideal mother-teacher is wise in the ways of morality, religion, and feeling. She creates a safe domestic space in which her charge may learn the lesson vital to a life of moral influence: be like your mother—orderly, loving, and strong. Whereas Maternal Nature teaches the Child to love humanity through love of God's natural creation, the mother teaches love of humanity and practical service to humankind (manifest as her family and society) through needlework. Edgeworth's little heroine in "Simple Susan"—a "sweet-tempered, modest, sprightly, industrious lass, who was the pride and delight of the village"—articulates the connection perfectly: "How can I be grateful enough to such a mother as this? . . . She taught me to knit, she taught me every thing that I know . . . and best of all, she taught me to love her, to wish to be like her" (*Parent's Assistant* 2: 50, 78–79).

In women's writing, both child and mother-teacher are socially located, a significant contrast to the Maternal Nature in the canonical male poets. Moreover, we find that the language in many of the children's stories is natural in a different way than the natural language advocated by Wordsworth in the "Preface" to the second edition of *Lyrical Ballads* or the colloquial language of *Don Juan*'s jaunty narrator. Certainly Barbauld, Edgeworth, and Taylor wrote their stories listening to—and reading to—actual children. Barbauld, already a celebrated poetess, became even more celebrated for her children's stories, which she wrote for her nephew and the boys whom she taught at the school she and her husband established. *Lessons for Children* (1778) and *Hymns in Prose for Children* (1781), known to influence Blake's *Songs of Innocence* (1798), established Barbauld as the virtual creator of literature accessible to children: large print, illustrations, situations and settings familiar to the child, and a level of language appropriate for the child's age. Like Barbauld, Edgeworth and Taylor read the tales they had written to children around them, modifying the texts in accordance with their listeners' response. Edgeworth read to a particularly large number of children, the offspring of her father's three marriages subsequent to the death of Maria's mother, his first wife. All three women considered conversation between teacher and learner vital to a child's education.

Although not biological mothers, Barbauld, Edgeworth, and Taylor were trusted as surrogate mother-teachers because of their reputation as writers of moral tales.[14] Parents, then, could feel confident in choosing one of these texts as itself a safe domestic space from which children could learn in the actual domestic spaces of their homes. Mitzi Myers has argued, moreover, that the texts of children's stories were safe spaces for the women writers themselves, since they could construct stories without the complicating marriage plot ("Socializing Rosamond" 52). These writers did not, like Wordsworth or Coleridge, grieve for an idealized past. Rather they constructed an instructional present within the texts that would equip the girls — those in the stories and those who read the stories — for meaningful futures of habits, qualities, and values that would strengthen home and state. As Ann Martin Taylor, author of educational manuals and mother of writers Jane and Ann Taylor, indicated: "The foundation stone of public and private felicity should be laid in the nursery." That nursery, she noted, served as seminary and schoolroom (quoted in Davidoff and Hall, *Family Fortunes* 176).

"Order and Disorder" is illustrative of many children's stories in which needlework is a prominent vehicle of instruction. This moral tale appeared in Aikin's and Barbauld's *Evenings at Home* (1792–96), a volume Maria Edgeworth praised as "the best book for young people from seven to ten years old."[15] The story is representative of the structure, tone, and use of the needle in children's stories and, in fact, influenced a later story by Edgeworth ("The Two Plums") and two works by Taylor ("Careless Mathilda" and "Busy Idleness"). Barbauld's and Aikin's story explores nurturing, sociability, household economy, and female development, including self-discipline and decision making. Its very title suggests the binary opposition explicit in many moral tales. The mother-teacher sets up (or takes advantage of) situations in which the little girl must choose between two opposing qualities, manifest as objects or allegorical figures, or in which two girls, clearly opposite in temperament, are juxtaposed. Through mild consequences of her poor choices, the girl develops the good judgment that will aid her in future decisions. In all tales, Order — inscribed allegorically at times as Housewifery, Charity, or Maternal Love — is valued over Disorder — inscribed as Dissipation and Selfishness.[16]

The action of "Order and Disorder" takes place in a protective domestic space, even though an exasperated mother has sent her daughter, the good-natured, bright, but heedless Juliet, away from home to the country to learn the value of order. In Juliet's needlework, as in other enterprises like her writing and reading, chaos had ruled. She spent more time collecting her things — the housewife,[17] a container for sewing implements, in one place; threadpapers in another; the scissors in yet another; the thimble in yet another — as she did in her work. Her mother's surrogate is the lovely fairy Order, who identifies herself as a good friend of Juliet's mother. Disorder, a bad fairy, looks like an ugly witch, "crooked and squint-eyed, with her hair hanging about her face, and her dress put on all awry, and full of rents and tatters." The extreme external manifestation of Juliet's tendency toward carelessness, the crone is also a warning that the little girl's natural charm and beauty will turn sour should her negligence continue. Disorder presents Juliet with a "workbag full of threads of silk of all sorts of colors mixed and entangled together, and a flower very nicely worked to copy . . . a pansy" with melting hues that required "great accuracy" to bring out its beauty. But Juliet cannot achieve the design since everything is tangled. She bursts into tears and Order appears magically, graceful and neat, to separate the threads. Juliet then completes the pretty design by dinnertime (*Evenings* 43).

On succeeding days, Juliet is tested in straightening out household accounts and copying a poem in ivory letters. Again the good mother substitute assists her, and the wicked fairy, like Milton's Satan, serves Good. At last Juliet renounces her careless habits and is restored to her mother's company. Rehabilitated, she receives presents "to remind her of the beauty and advantage of order," including a cabinet of English coins, a box of watercolors and crayons, and a "very nice Housewife with all the implements belonging to a seamstress, and a good store of the best needles in sizes" (43). Had she not mastered the needle of domesticity, beauty that she could create (the watercolors and crayons) and prosperity (the coins) would have been impossible. Misery rather than happiness would have been her fate. Such gifts as social custom and props in children's literature were familiar throughout the nineteenth century. Edward Austen-Leigh records in his *Memoir of Jane Austen* (1870) that the celebrated author had once worked a small bag with a housewife as a gift for a sister-in-law, Austen-Leigh's mother. He notes: "It is the kind of article that some benevolent fairy might have supposed to give as a reward to a diligent little girl" (quoted in Byrde, *A Frivolous Distinction* 33).

Like Juliet, Rosamond in Edgeworth's "The Two Plums" begins as a charming but disorganized little girl who learns the value of order in a safe domestic space overseen by a nurturing mother. Constantly losing her needles, Rosamond sacrifices pleasant walks, neat clothes, peace of mind, and, most of all, her parents' approval. Through an ongoing dialogue with her mother, she concludes that order is preferable and that a housewife is just what she needs to cure her of what she calls her "little fault." Her literal reward is a beautiful red leather housewife. Her emotional reward is reintegration into family life: the female-signed sewing needle, which she now finds easily, becomes the male-signed instrument in the scientific experiment with magnetism that her father and brother perform. Rosamond watches. Using "Simple Susan" as a model, Mitzi Myers has argued that

Edgeworth's moral tales combine the maternal affective dimension with patriarchal rationality to celebrate female agency ("Romancing" 100–102). Yet Myers also acknowledges that Edgeworth, "fearing disempowerment and displacement . . . woos [her] father with the created ideal little girl" (104). The manner of Rosamond's inclusion in the family at the ending of "The Two Plums" also reveals, consistent with the social reality of Edgeworth's time and her own role as devoted, unmarried daughter, the limits of female agency.

Literal needlework, performed in an orderly manner, manifests all the domestic values the girl must internalize and practice for a strong family and society: shirts for her husband and son; beautiful objects for her home; gifts for her pastor, family, and friends; goods for charity bazaars; clothing for the poor. Moreover, she will perpetuate a stable culture by teaching her daughters to sew and ensure order by supervising her servants' needlework. Her sewing stitches together family and nation, making possible a strong, prosperous, harmonious, and at times beautiful society. As Ann Martin Taylor indicated: "That house is well conducted where there is a strict attention paid to order and regularity. To do everything in its proper time, to keep everything in its right place, and to use everything for its proper use, is the *very essence* of good management" (quoted in Davidoff and Hall 176).

Although fortitude and forbearance, even stoicism, are not directly articulated in Ann Martin Taylor or in stories like "Order and Disorder" and "The Two Plums," they form an important subtext of literature for girls' and women's experience. Women were expected to "suffer and be still" under all difficult circumstances: a bad marriage, children or spouse lost to disease, economic instability, potential infection and death in childbirth. Moreover, they might need to call on their sewing skills to eke out a living, as was increasingly true in the first three decades of the nineteenth century. Learning to be orderly in a literal sense also meant becoming stronger emotionally. Order, then, was more than a quality valuable for politically conservative reasons. Barbauld and Edgeworth conceived of order as essential to a woman's survival — it was both liberating and defensive.

Anna Barbauld's life provides a pointed example of Order learned and lived. While at her husband's school at Palgrave, she kept both the school and family accounts; held classes in composition, literature, and geography; tended to her nephew Charles; supervised domestics' work in her house and the pupils' quarters; did some of the housework herself; and published several pieces for children and adults. She took particular pleasure in the boys' dramatic productions of Molière, Shakespeare, and Milton: directing, writing prologues and epilogues, making masks, and using her needle in imaginative ways to make costumes (*Georgian Chronicle* 77). A sociable woman, she also carried on an extensive correspondence with friends and literary figures and visited literary friends in London. Order was vital to her emotional strength as well. As the years passed, she discreetly endured the increasing strain caused by her husband's deteriorating mental condition, marked by his depression, obsessive washing, and fits of violence. Only after her husband attempted to kill her did Mrs. Barbauld agree to have him cared for in a private institution (*Georgian Chronicle* 136–38).

Learning her place — not just in the home but in the social hierarchy — is another vital lesson of Order that women writers inscribed in their texts for girls. The sewing mother was a middle-class icon who was happiest because she did not aspire to the dissolute ways of the aristocracy and knew her responsibilities toward the deserving poor beneath her. The dangerous figures, always contrasted with the idealized Good Mother, were plentiful in children's and other imaginative literature of the era: Housewifery and Dissipation in John Aikin's "Female Choice"; dutiful Fanny Price and scheming Mary Crawford in Austen's *Mansfield Park*; improvident Charlotte and hard-working Caroline in Taylor's "Busy Idleness." In Edgeworth's "Good French Governess," that noble émigrée teaches the ill-directed biological mother of her charges to turn away from the dissipation of fine clothes and fancy balls to the satisfaction of the hearth and family. Along the way, the wise governess reads her charges Barbauld's books, including *Evenings at Home,* and teaches practical sewing and weaving that is scorned by the social climbing Mrs. Fanshaw, who has bought an elaborate netting box only because a titled lady recommended it (*Moral Tales* 1: 99–100).

In the 1790s, radicals, moderates, and conservatives alike attacked embroidery as a dangerous "accomplishment," cultivated and displayed by upper-class women and those in the middle class mindlessly aping fashionable learning and habits. "Accomplishments" — dancing, drawing, music, French, and embroidery — became a code word for dangerous, idle, upper-class pastimes of women who were self-absorbed and neglectful of their families. Endless hours spent in fancy work, especially embroidering gowns to adorn herself for display at frivolous events like balls, was antithetical to the new moral woman: early rising, tending to the comforts of her husband and children, attending to their moral good, supervising the work of servants, making sure household accounts were in order, and sewing for her family, home and the poor. Although Barbauld aimed much of her criticism at the lavish expense and status anxiety connected with fashion, this "tyrant of our own creation," she also detested the physical pain that women subjected themselves to because of confining garments like corsets (*Legacy* 165–79).

Implicit in much of the criticism of upper-class women's passion for expensive dress was the misogynist assumption—articulated blatantly in Rousseau's critique of embroidery in *Emile*—that *all* women were *by nature* susceptible to the dangers of egotistical self-adornment. "Little girls," he claimed, "always dislike learning to read and write, but they are always ready to learn to sew . . . for their adornment" (*Emile* 331). A little girl desirous to learn to write, first using her needle and then a pen, throws away her writing instrument the moment a mirror reveals that her "cramped attitude was not pretty" (*Emile* 332). Mary Wollstonecraft devoted large sections of *A Vindication of the Rights of Woman* to refuting Rousseau's destructive essentialism. She argued that repressive custom—being taught to adorn themselves as objects to please men—and not female nature kept girls and women at their needles (*Vindication* 170–72, 288).

In her poem "Accomplishment," Jane Taylor brilliantly depicts the shattering results of a girl's upper-class education chosen by her social climbing parents. Taylor first describes a *patchwork* "wrought by the leisurely fair" that violates the beauty and order of Nature, God's handwork, by cramming "every tint of the rainbow," "stars . . . forc'd from their spheres," "magnified tulips," "roses full-blown and red hot" into a "labour of years" that is a "mass unharmonious, unmeaning . . . show . . . void of intelligent grace; / it is not a landscape, it is not a face." Moreover, it is clearly a violation of feminine decorum and innocence: "roses full-blown and red hot" call attention to the young woman and suggest a sexuality of which she should not be aware. Having elicited our antipathy to the worked piece, Taylor then compares the "accomplished" girl to the very *patchwork* the reader has come to disparage. Education, personified not as a mother-teacher but as instructress in a fancy school, "with costly materials, and capital tools," turns out a formulaic sewn jumble of French, Italian, Dancing, Drawing, Geography, and Music:

> Thus Science distorted, and torn into bits,
> Art tortur'd, and frighten'd half out of her wits,
> In portions and patches some light and some shady,
> Are stitch'd up together, and make a young lady. (*Essays* 83)

Stuart Curran's perceptive observation regarding Taylor's poem "Prejudice" applies equally well to "Accomplishment": the writer reveals "the inner life as a thing" through the "accumulation of minute detail" with "a quiet compassion for its costs" (Curran, "'I' Altered" 192–94). Rendered nothing but a nervous confusion of mismatched fabric and design by her education, the girl is unfit to assume the role of the Good Mother who can lovingly educate her children. Moreover, her spiritual death denies her the Heavenly Home, for, as Taylor notes in her poem "The World in the House," worldly pursuits make it as impossible to get into heaven as "the camel passing through the needle's eye" (*Essays* 95). Needlework, the female quotidian, dismissed as "trifling" by popular male conduct manual writers like John Gregory (*A Father's Legacy to his Daughters*, 1774), emerges in Taylor as a powerful and complex challenge to the old order and a disquieting symbol of the new.[18]

Just as the girl must learn her place and avoid the seduction of worldly pursuits, she must learn to condescend to the less fortunate. Dorcas, the maiden aunt in Barbauld's "Live Dolls," is the wise mother figure who rescues her niece Eliza from her negligent, misguided biological mother who has been seduced by the false glamor of the world of money and fashion. Significantly, the story follows "Order and Disorder" in *Evenings at Home* and suggests the practical application of Juliet's lesson of orderly needlework. The primary interest of the story lies in the implicit assumptions about the poor and the related configurations of women's philanthropy, an increasingly important — and acceptable — extension of the domestic into the public sphere. Aunt Dorcas subtly redirects little Eliza's desire to make clothing for her expensive wax doll, a gift from her frivolous mother, toward making clothes for "a real live doll," whom she does not identify but promises to show her niece (*Evenings* 44). Intrigued, the little girl accompanies her to a workroom where several girls "with cheerful and busy looks" are industriously stitching clothing for the poor. A humble woman enters the room to thank "the good young ladies" for sewing the garments that protected her "dear little infant" from death. Aunt Dorcas urges Eliza to step forward and "kiss the lips of this infant, and imbibe that affection which is one of the characteristics of your sex. . . . This is the live doll I promised you" (45). At the end of the story, Eliza eagerly establishes herself at the worktable with the other girls. Because of the loving guidance of her aunt, she has turned away from the empty beauty of a wax doll to meaningful service for suffering humanity with her privileged middle-class sisters.

Aunt Dorcas introduces Eliza to the benevolent sewing society, a philanthropic endeavor deemed appropriate for women as an extension of their moral, caretaking activity in the domestic sphere. Increasingly at the end of the eighteenth century, middle-class women engaged in a variety of philanthropic and reformist activities: visiting the sick and poor, teaching Sunday school classes, making clothing for the poor or worked goods for charity bazaars, working in clothing clubs that bought and sold fabric, contributing to lying-in charities, and instructing poor girls in " 'reading, writing, and arithmetic, sewing, mending, marking and cutting out' " (quoted in Davidoff and Hall 431–34). There is little doubt that a sense of privilege — religious and moral even more than social or economic — drove women's philanthropic urge. Moreover, there is little doubt that the language and manner of condescension in their benevolence must have grated on the nerves of many whom they sought to help. Not all shone "with joy and gratitude" like the woman in "Live Dolls." Rather, this is how the middle-class philanthropist needed to think the poor felt. What the story does not permit us to see is whether Aunt Dorcas — if a poor relation in Eliza's house — feels a similar yoke of condescension.

Needlework in this story sharply defines class boundaries. Eliza would have worked a fine cap, trimmed with lace, for her wax doll or as a gift for another member of her family. She and her fellow needleworkers, however, will work on common fabric — flannel, calico, dimity, and old linen — for clothing for the poor. They may choose, though, to decorate the ordinary fabric with some of their fine embroidery. The poor woman, by praising the superiority of the girls' embroidery, accepts the superiority of their class and seems to confirm that the boundaries of her education are just: "I could not have cut [materials] out and contrived them, and made them up myself: for I was never taught to be handy at my needle as you have been, ladies. I was only set to coarse work" (45). Her countenance "shining with joy and gratitude," she is one of the good poor, acknowledging her place and deserving of charity because her husband is ill and cannot work.

In "The Rich and the Poor," Barbauld contrasts the working poor with paupers, often "the idle, the profligate, and the dissolute, who are maintained upon charity" (*Legacy* 60–61). Barbauld's holding to class boundaries is also a stoic's stance regarding misery in the human condition. In pieces as light as "The Flying Fish" in *Evenings at Home* and as serious as her essay, "Against Inconsistency in Our Expectations" or her poem, "To the Poor," Barbauld articulates her belief that God ordained a system of "laws as determined, fixed and invariable, as any of Newton's Principia" (*Works* 1:

192). We must live moderately, with equanimity and even resignation, for to "vex ourselves with fruitless wishes, or give way to groundless discontent" leads to misery. To the poor she urged: "Child of distress . . . Bear, bear thy wrongs — fulfill thy destined hour" (192). Theirs was to be a divine reward by the heavenly Father of love and light. Although privileged in many ways, Barbauld stoically accepted the trials associated with the "laws and order" of marital duty to a husband who attempted to kill her in his fits of madness.

Jane Taylor appears to celebrate the industry and selflessness of Betsey Bond in her sentimentalized "A Person of Consequence." "Who is it that mends John Bond's shirts so neatly; and that runs his socks at the heel so that they last as long again? Oh, why it is his daughter Betsey." Tending to her father and brothers, nursing her sick mother, and waiting on customers in her father's humble shop, the early-rising Betsey is "always busy at her needle, or washing, or ironing." Cheerful and smiling, Betsey is the heroine of the tale, a dutiful daughter and a mother to her family, who radiates joy and does not question her lot (*Writings* 2: 123).

Taylor's correspondence reveals a profound ambivalence toward domesticity that complicates our reading of her dutiful public celebration of Betsey's industrious needle. After her death, Taylor's brother sought to reassure the public that his sister was "so completely feminine" that she was particularly "fond of the labors of the needle, and of every domestic engagement," shunning the egotism and ambition of authorship (*Writings* 1: viii). Yet Taylor resisted domesticity, including marriage and full participation as a dutiful daughter in household chores. She wrote of herself as two people, different in feelings and sentiments. The first was "an active handy little body, who can make beds or do plain work" and the second, whom she clearly preferred, one who "never troubles her head with these menial affairs; — nothing will suit her but the *pen*" (*Writings* 1: 68–69). Her letters are tortured debates between the two selves — what she thinks and what she feels she ought to think. In one letter, she frankly declares that few men

> . . . encourage the mental cultivation of women . . . [because] they tremble for their dear stomachs, concluding that a woman who could taste the pleasures of poetry or sentiment, would never descend to pay due attention to those exquisite flavors in pudding or pie. (*Writings* 1: 106)

Yet she then claims, feeling compelled to cancel herself and to be kind to sisters who must pay more attention to puddings than poetry, that an educated woman will even better appreciate and engage in domestic chores than a woman without learning (*Writings* 1: 106).

In her letters, Taylor mentions her attic as a precious refuge, secluded from the rest of the house and with a view of the countryside, in which she writes: "a table for my writing-desk, one chair for myself and another for my muse" (*Writings* 1: 85). A married woman — as she saw in her own mother's life and in the life of her sister — had no such refuge. In Betsey Bond, then, Taylor attempts to exorcize her hostility to many inconveniences of the domestic enterprise. Betsey is a dutiful daughter, trapped by the needle of domesticity, without privacy, but cheerfully resigned and radiant in a kind of unaware, selfless martyrdom that Taylor at once admired and detested. More appealing to Taylor were the passionate figures of Corrine and her creator Mme de Staël. Taylor discloses, in her poem responding to *Corinne,* the magic spell of de Staël, who seems like "a new friend," in whose work she sees her own "inmost thoughts unfold" of love, grief, and suffering: "While I condemn, my heart replies / And deeper feelings sympathize" (*Poetical Remains* 14). Taylor felt compelled to cancel her self-revelation and restrain her own enthusiasm by articulating the regret that de Staël, misguided, lacked religious conviction:

> . . . Yes, too much I've felt her talent's magic touch.
> Return my soul, to that retreat
> From sin and woe — Thy Saviour's feet!
> There learn an art she never knew
> All to resign that He denies: —
> To Him in meek submission bend . . . (*Poetical Remains* 14)

Unlike Taylor, little tension between domesticity and artistic creation is evident in Barbauld and Edgeworth. Both subscribed to the doctrine of separate spheres, believing that the educated mother-teacher could best influence the direction of society through her work at home. Both valued the transforming power of education, including an appreciation of the potential of the quotidian. Human art and industry, Barbauld notes in *Evenings at Home,* transform sand and ashes into beautiful and useful glass, or old rags into paper on which learning may be miraculously inscribed (*Evenings* 134, 148). Taste, judgment, and intelligence, cultivated and developed by the mother-teacher, enable the little girl to transform an ordinary pattern into a subtly shaded pansy, as Juliet does, or an ordinary life into one with love and beauty, the goal of all the stories.

Moreover, Barbauld posits the feminine ideal, sounding much like Housewifery, as the poetic ideal in her poem "Characters":

Of gentle manners, and of taste refined,
With all the graces of a polished mind;
Clear sense and truth still shone in all she spoke,
And from her lips no idle sentence broke,
Each nicer elegance of art she knew;
Correctly fair, and regularly true.
Her ready fingers plied with equal skill
The pencil's task, the needle, or the quill;
So poised her feelings, so composed her soul,
So subject all to reason's calm controul, —
One only passion, strong, and unconfined,
Disturbed the balance of her even mind:
One passion ruled despotic in her breast,
In every word, and look, and thought confest: —
But that was love; and love delights to bless
The generous transports of a fond excess. (*Works* 1: 48–49)

Rather than challenging the artistic endeavor of the drawing pencil or writer's pen, the needle appears to rest comfortably between the two artistic instruments, central and equal to them. Barbauld does not articulate the conflict between the needle of domesticity and the pen of artistic desire found in many women writers: Fanny Burney, Charlotte Brontë, Emily Dickinson, Louisa May Alcott, and others.[19] As Marlon Ross notes, the feminine ideal preferred by Barbauld enables a woman, whose behavior is usually enforced by multiple, interconnecting socio-moral strictures, to write poetry that simultaneously transcends and is caught in limitations of gender (*Contours of Masculine Desire* 216–18). Barbauld's brilliant mock-heroic poem "Washing Day," for example, elegantly transforms an ordinary soap bubble from a washing tub into an exuberant air balloon of tech-nological and poetic delight. When a strong moral issue must be addressed, as Barbauld did later in her career in "Epistle to William Wilberforce, Esq." and *Eighteen Hundred and Eleven,* the poetess is still a lady, although at this point particularly earnest, vigorous, and uncompromising.

In "The Rights of Woman," which some have read as a reactionary poem, Barbauld employs military tropes to reinforce the moral domain of the feminine ideal: woman, "too long degraded, scorned, opprest," is to gird herself with grace, her cannons "soft melting tones" and her blushes

"Magazines of war" (*Works* 1: 185). Barbauld's ambivalence toward the feminine ideal is suggested in her discussion of her own girlhood education and what she claimed to be desirable for most girls. A precocious child and daughter of the director of a dissenting academy for boys at Warrington, Anna Aikin received an unusual education for a girl. Overcoming her father's objections, she convinced him to teach her Greek and Latin, considered inappropriate subjects for girls (*Works* 1: vii–viii). Moreover, she found exhilarating the intellectual stimulation of congenial parlor conversation in the presence of scholars, including Joseph Priestley and William Enfield, who taught at Warrington. Barbauld's story places her in the tradition of Miranda, Shakespeare's heroine, whose only access to education is through her father's power. That access, Elaine Showalter argues in an essay about Margaret Fuller, distances the female artist from women and a female tradition (*Sister's Choice* 29).

Calling her own education "peculiar," Barbauld declined Elizabeth Montagu's requests that she establish an academy for young ladies. Barbauld's arguments are evasive: she fears creating *précieuses ridicules* in such a setting; moreover, a girl's mother should help prepare her daughter at this point for the consequences of the "empire of passions" coming on (*Works* 1: xx). A good education should prepare girls to be "good wives" and "agreeable companions" (*Works* 1: xviii). Most telling, however, Barbauld notes the unhappiness that a girl sets herself up for if she receives the education deemed appropriate for boys: "I am full well convinced that to have a too great fondness for books is little favourable to the happiness of a woman" (*Works* 1: xix). Women, she argues in "On Female Studies," need have only enough reading to "give spirit and variety to conversation" and to understand the activity "on the busy stage of life from which they are shut out by their sex" (*Legacy* 44). The posture is protective. Barbauld recommends cunning in academic pursuit and restraint in intellectual self-display: "the thefts of knowledge in our sex are only connived at while carefully concealed and if displayed, punished with disgrace" (*Works* 1: xviii). The grace and charm of a lady are, then, modes of self-protection.

Despite hardships in their lives, Barbauld, Edgeworth, and Taylor wrote from a perspective of middle-class privilege and relative economic stability unknown to Mary Lamb. Barbauld, receiving an excellent education atypical for a girl, was acknowledged as one of the Nine Living Muses in a 1779 painting by Richard Samuel, and her engaging personality made her welcome in literary circles throughout England. Edgeworthstown House — the home of comfortable but not wealthy gentry — was the center of constant activity in a communal situation that encouraged intellectual curiosity. Edgeworth, who composed her stories on a desk in her father's library, constantly surrounded by family, drew much of the emotional nourishment she craved from her father through their collaborative literary projects (Butler, *Maria Edgeworth* 82). Like Barbauld, she was a celebrated writer, although she preferred to remain in the family circle at Edgesworthstown. Taylor was also favored by an innovative education from her parents, including games and flash cards of plants and animals that her father designed. Although Isaac senior's serious illness when Jane was a girl underscored the financial vulnerability of the family, they did grow relatively prosperous through their engraving business and the Family Pen (Davidoff and Hall, *Family Fortunes* 61, 69). Barbauld, Edgeworth, and Taylor held positions of particular advantage as celebrated writers of literature for children at a time when an expanding public eagerly bought up tales, poems, and hymns for their offspring. Marginalized as women, they nonetheless enjoyed importance in some areas.

But what of the sewing icon viewed from less privileged eyes? Mary Lamb, humiliated by having to put her needle to hire, depicts a radically different world of sewing and domesticity in "The Young Mahometan," one of seven stories that she wrote for *Mrs. Leicester's School* (1809). In a setting, reminiscent of the narrative frame in Sarah Fielding's *The Governess, or, Little Female Academy* (1749), a teacher-mother surrogate encourages her charges to tell their stories to one another around a cozy fire. Despite the teacher's desire to make her pupils, all marginalized in one way or another, feel accepted, the powerlessness palpable in "The Little Mahometan" dominates the text. Economic dependence, emotional starvation, social displacement, and denial of the pleasures of the imagination pervade this world. Told from the point of view of little Margaret Green, who does not fully realize or articulate her victimization, the tale forces the reader to negotiate, intellectually and emotionally, the injustice of her situation much as we do in Blake's "The Chimney Sweeper," and resist Margaret's chilling numbness. The little girl is neither the sweetly wise child connected to a loving society in Wordsworth's "We Are Seven" nor the intensely self-aware and anguished child of Mary Robinson's "All Alone" or "Savage of Aveyron." Nor is she the lively, spontaneous girl of "Order and Disorder" and "The Two Plums," whom it is so easy to like. Ignored by her widowed mother, who becomes submissively absorbed in her employer's obsession with needlework, Margaret is denied the nurturing maternal experience that protects Juliet and Rosamond. Identifying with the neglected Margaret and the widowed mother who ignores her, Lamb may be attempting, in this semi-autobiographical work, to make peace with the ghost of her own mother, whom she killed in a fit of insanity in 1796.[20]

In the story, Mrs. Beresford, a wealthy widow and Mrs. Green's benefactress, is blinded both literally and figuratively by years of needle-work, deemed proper for a lady of leisure. Her sole "chronology to reckon by . . . [is] what sofa-cover, what set of chairs, were in the frame at that time" (*Works* 5: 306). Although Margaret's mother dislikes stitchery, she must "oblige her kind patroness" by sitting for hours at the frame to work on a carpet, the colors and design the only topic of conversation. This carpet will, no doubt, be covered up and forgotten like all the other worked pieces in the cold, silent house. Margaret, "very fond of reading" but limited the virtually "forbidden pleasure" because of her poor eyesight, steals moments to read while her mother and Mrs. Beresford are at their needlework.

Because the women are so absorbed in their project, they ignore Margaret and she explores the house — based on Blakesware, where Lamb's maternal grandmother worked as housekeeper — unsupervised, interrogat-ing the objects around her, most of which are dumb and reinforce her isolation. Only one object whispers to her: the sole exposed tapestry of the abandoned Hagar and son Ishmael in a "forlorn state . . . in the wilderness" (307). One day, she is able to loosen a lock that has long denied her entrance to the "large library," the contents forbidden her because of her gender and class, "indeed a precious discovery" (309). For Margaret, "very fond of reading," entering the library is access to the powerful world of learning and ideas, signed male. She discovers one book, *Mahometism Explained,* that convinces her through enchanting stories that she is a true believer, a Mahometan (309). Disturbed that her mother, not a true be-liever, would slip from a bridge "no wider than a silken thread" into a bottomless pit once she died, Margaret falls ill and delirious from the conflict between trying to save her mother and admitting that she has been in forbidden places. The doctor's wife "cures" the little girl of her delirium by taking her to the Harlow fair, where she guides her from the dangerous world of imagination and heresy to the safe — and numbing — world of domesticity, submission, and Christianity by buying her a needle-case, a pincushion, and a work-basket. Margaret returns to a world where women sew and do not think or use their imaginations. Passivity, numbness, and sweetness are — as Lamb manifested in her own life — socially acceptable alternatives to delirium, madness, and anger (Aaron, *A Double Singleness*

111). Sewing will not operate as vividly to show painful suppression of female desire until Christina Rossetti's children's story, "Speaking Likenesses" (1874). In that fantasy a cruel knitting narrator scolds the little girls around her for their lack of diligence in their sewing tasks and tells them a sadistic tale in which protagonist Flora becomes a Pincushion in a nasty little boys' game ("Speaking Likenesses" 325–60).

Orientalism in "The Young Mahometan" evokes the color, passion, adventure, and imagination of the *Arabian Nights*, the touchstone of imaginative tales for Romantics like the Lambs and Coleridge, and temporarily rescues Margaret from the staid, cold world of English domesticity, where her gender and class render her invisible. It is also Lamb's fantasy return to the reading pleasures of her own childhood when she and her brother had free access to the library of their father's employer, Samuel Salt, a barrister and Whig member of Parliament. Yet it is inevitable that Margaret return to a world of deadening submission, just as Salt's death in 1792 deprived the Lambs of status, financial security, and access to privileges like reading in a gentleman's library. The text implicitly challenges the popular claim that English women in a monogamous Christian marriage were far more fortunate, because free, than the sexual slaves of the seraglio. Wollstonecraft, Catharine Macaulay, Byron, Charlotte Brontë, and others exploited the seraglio metaphor to illuminate the abuses of western marriage. As Lamb's tale reveals, however, slavery can be self-imposed by internalized structures of inferiority. As Lamb claimed, in an essay for the *British Lady's Magazine* in 1815, needlework for upper- and middle-class women was a form of "self-imposed slavery."[21] It was, of course, an imposed slavery on the seamstress who, like Mary Lamb, attempted to earn a living by putting her needle out for hire.

In the 1815 essay, published under the pseudonym Sempronia, Lamb addresses issues of women's limited preparation for occupations, women's role in marriage, and the implicit tensions among women across social classes. Establishing her authority as one who struggled for eleven years to earn a living by needlework, Sempronia anticipates another sewing icon in British culture: the distressed seamstress of Thomas Hood's poem "The Song of the Shirt" (1843) and paintings by Richard Redgrave (1844), George F. Watts (1848), and Anna Blunden (1854). The appealing figure of the distressed needlewoman galvanized the public imagination primarily after the economic crises of the 1830s and 1840s. A gentlewoman in reduced circumstances, she was pictured as pale and angelic, half starving, in a solitary garret. Part of the appeal was the public's assumption that, in an oversupply of sewing labor, the genteel seamstress risked slipping from the lower-middle-class status of milliner or mantua-maker to the working-class slop worker to prostitution to earn her living. This masculine fascination was simultaneously a voyeuristic speculation into sexuality, a validation of the vital role patriarchal protection supposedly played, and a condemnation, as reinforced in numerous illustrations in *Punch,* of wealthy women's hunger for fancy dress at the expense of the needlewoman. Working-class women, assumed to be less sensitive and therefore less picturesque, did not enjoy the same sympathy. The pretty icon actually subverted the myth of the male provider — after all, death, disease, desertion, loss of money, and other misfortunes precluded that role, with serious consequences for wives or widows and daughters uneducated to make a living.

Lamb's essay — like the sewing icon — illuminates issues of class as it juxtaposes the distressed needleworker with the middle-class wife and mother. Lamb urges the privileged to give up all but the most ornamental work so that distressed needlewomen can have employment. Moreover, by ceasing to waste hours in sewing useless objects that fill up her house, the affluent matron could spend more time on educating herself and her family: "Needle-work and intellectual improvement are naturally in a state of warfare" (Gilchrist, *Mary Lamb* 186). Along the way, like Mary Wollstonecraft and others, Lamb blasts the crippling effects of a limited education that prepared women only for careers in sewing or teaching, especially given the social reality of the failure of men, for whatever reason, to provide economic protection. The ostensible solidarity, based on gender, cancels itself because class expectations of subordination and superiority override sorority. Regrettably, as often happens, the internalized patriarchal script has controlled the action of the female players on the domestic stage. As Jane Aaron argues, Lamb suddenly withdraws from her radical critique, and a "deferential decorum veils the anger of the piece, and muffles its protesting voice" (Aaron, *A Double Singleness* 69). Her submission to middle-class authority — like that of Margaret Green — emerges from an internalized ideology of service, including habitual deference to rank and acknowledgment of obligation, regardless of individual desire. As the children of domestic servants — and needlewoman and clerk themselves — Mary and Charles Lamb were profoundly ambivalent in their portrayal of privilege, power, and hierarchy (Aaron 16).

In 1808, angered by critical response to "Peter Bell," Wordsworth claimed that he was condemned for the very deed that should have earned him praise: "I have not written down to the level of superficial observers and unthinking minds. . . . — Every great Poet is a Teacher. I wish either to be considered as a Teacher, or as nothing" (*Letters, Middle Years* 195). Wordsworth meant — and valued — something and someone very different from the nurturing mother-teacher familiar in Barbauld or Edgeworth. His Teacher is coded in the canonical assumptions about the Romantic Genius: male, solitary, reflective, sharing his wisdom from a distance. His carefully crafted verse only appears to be the "spontaneous overflow of powerful feelings" by a "man talking to men" — to a public whom he does not really see or talk with. We can, in fact, understand all the canonized poets of the Romantic period as Teachers of this sort, whatever guise they took: Blake's Prophet, Coleridge's Philosopher, Shelley's Legislator to the world, Byron's dark Wanderer or satiric Gadfly, Keats's Physician to humanity. We do not think of these poets teaching the reader by conversation at the domestic hearth. Rather, we envision them alone before Mont Blanc, Italian ruins, the raging sea. Even Coleridge's domestic scenes in "Frost at Midnight" and "The Eolian Harp" are merely starting points for transcendental visions. The dialogue or conversation in works by the canonical poets is often with objects animated by their Imagination — urns, breezes, abbey ruins — or their own high souls rather than with readers within the text or even outside it. Moreover, that Imagination is privileged as male, with its implicit energy and sexuality. Domestic ideology cannot accommodate the beautiful but unstable "fading coal" or phallic "sword of lightning, ever unsheathed" of Shelley (*Poetry and Prose* 490, 504). Yet who would argue that Barbauld's brilliant soap bubble in "Washing Day" is any less the creation of a fine poetic imagination than Byron's shattered, glittering "globe of glass" in *Don Juan*? (*Complete Poetical Works* 5: 11.76.4–5).

In 1777, Anna Barbauld wrote a letter to Miss Dixon, thanking her for an embroidered gift that was accompanied by a story her correspondent had written. Barbauld cites the story of Arachne and Minerva in order to compliment the gift giver. We recall that, proud of her skill as weaver, the mortal Arachne challenged Minerva, spear-bearing goddess of wisdom who was fiercely proud of her embroidery, to a contest. Furious that her competitor had crafted a perfect work and would win, the goddess transformed her into a spider, condemned to spin silk from her body for eternity (Ovid, *Metamorphoses,* trans. Gregory 6: 1–147).

> Arachne, my dear Miss Dixon, — so goes the story, — was unfortunate enough to incur the mortal displeasure of Minerva for too pompous a display of her skill in embroidery; and since that event, very few ladies who have courted the favour of Minerva have chosen to run the hazard of provoking her

by the delicacy of their needle-work. . . . I wonder much at your being so great a favourite with the goddess as I find you are by the story which accompanied [the embroidered flowers], and that she thinks proper to encourage in handling both your pen and your needle in the manner you do. (*Works* 2: 70)

The story of Minerva and Arachne, richly coded for intersections of gender, class, power, and the artistic imagination, provides a fitting final stitch to this essay. Warlike Minerva serves and protects the male privilege in which she participates. As the patriarchy's agent, she excludes mortal sisters from the realm of power, literary production, and recognition of genius, just as she forbids those sisters to surpass her in their needlework. Women are not deemed incapable of artistic accomplishment, but they must be careful not to reveal genius in a way that would displease the male establishment's sense of superiority. If their literary works, especially children's stories, are deceptively coded in support of patriarchal power, these women's letters and journals at times suggest less conviction. For many women writers — including Barbauld, Taylor, Edgeworth, and Lamb — in life and literary production, it was best to conceal the knowledge they had stolen from their fathers' libraries. One could conceal such knowledge in the design worked with the needle of domesticity.

I warmly thank Jane Aaron, Fred Beaty, Stuart Curran, Joel Haefner, Larry Shiner, Daniel Wilson, and Susan Wolfson for their helpful responses to this essay. Special thanks are also due my Feminist Research Group for their support and criticism.

Notes

1. The eighteenth- and early nineteenth-century term for dressmaker. The term owes its origins to the Italian city, where fine silks were produced and exported to England in the 1600s. It also refers to a style of gown popular in England until the early eighteenth century.

2. Needlework technique using a tiny hook to draw loops of thread from beneath the fabric to the surface. Tambouring derived its name from the frame, which resembled a drum, that stretched the material and held it taut.

3. The Good Mother was eventually portrayed in Charles W. Cope's painting "Life Well Spent" (1862), originally contrasted with "Life Ill Spent," now lost. A copy of the former may be seen in Susan P. Casteras, *Images of Victorian Womanhood in English Art* 54. Housewifery was the allegorized figure, juxtaposed with Dissipation, in "Female Choice," one children's story in the popular *Evenings at Home* (1792–96), co-authored by Anna Barbauld and her brother John Aikin.

4. The stereotype of the dissipated upper-class woman often proved false. Mary Delany, friend of Bluestockings, for example, was celebrated for her botanical books as well as her exquisitely detailed embroidery of flowers on dresses. "To flower" at this time meant "to embroider," and women were identified with the flowers they sewed, drew, or painted. See A. Heckle, *The Florist: or, An Extensive and Curious Collection of Flowers for the Imitation of Young Ladies, either in Drawing, or in Needle-work* (1759). See also Judith Pascoe's essay in this volume on female botanists.

5. The other most frequently quoted lines are from the deceptively titled "In Prayse of the Needle" by John Taylor, which appeared in his pattern book, *The Needle's Excellency* (1624). A reading of the entire poem reveals that Taylor valued the needle to keep women silent and out of mischief. Nineteenth-century needlework manual authors probably copied the ostensibly laudatory lines from other manuals rather than seeking the original.

6. See, for example, Hannah More, *Strictures on the Modern System of Female Education* 1: 1–54.

7. For the history of children's literature and the marketplace, see, for example, F. J. Harvey Darton, *Children's Books in England: Five Centuries of Social Life,* and Mary V. Jackson, *Engines of Instruction, Mischief and Magic: Children's Literature from Its Beginnings to 1839.*

8. Of the four authors under consideration, none was a biological mother, and only Barbauld married. She and her husband adopted her nephew Charles when he was two. Mary and Charles Lamb adopted the orphaned Emma Isola when Mary was fifty-nine.

9. See, for example, Elaine Hedges, "The Needle or the Pen: The Literary Rediscovery of Women's Textile Work" and Rozsika Parker, *The Subversive Stitch: Embroidery and the Making of the Feminine.*

10. I thank Stuart Curran for noting Croker's editorship of the *Quarterly Review* in 1812. Betsy Rodgers, *Georgian Chronicle: Mrs. Barbauld and Her Family* 140–42 follows earlier reports in attributing the review to Southey.

11. See Susan Wolfson's essay in this volume for Wordsworth's criticism of Hemans.

12. Selected conduct manuals discussing needlework and domesticity are John Gregory, *A Father's Legacy to his Daughters* (1774); Priscilla Wakefield, *Reflections on the Present Condition of the Female Sex* (1798), and Richard Lovell Edgeworth and Maria Edgeworth, *Practical Education* (1798). Selected essays on needlework in eighteenth-century imaginative literature and culture are Laurie Yager Lieb, "'The Works of Women Are Symbolical': Needlework in the Eighteenth Century"; Kristina Staub, "Women's Pastimes and the Ambiguity of Female Self-Identification in Fanny Burney's *Evelina*"; and Cecilia Macheski, "Penelope's Daughters: Images of Needlework in Eighteenth-Century Literature."

13. Two exceptions are Charlotte Smith's *Rural Walks* (1795) and Barbauld's own *Hymns in Prose for Children* (1781).

14. For economic and ideological reasons, a woman who chose artistic creation over marriage and motherhood was rare at this time. By writing for children, women without children of their own evaded suspicions of unwomanliness. For a

psychoanalytic interpretation of the "motherhood myth" and the implications for creative writing, see Nina Auerbach, "Artists and Mothers: A False Alliance" 9, 14; and Susan Rubin Suleiman, "Writing and Motherhood."

15. Maria Edgeworth in Rodgers, *Georgian Chronicle* 123. Although "Order and Disorder" was later attributed to Barbauld, Lucy Aikin does not include it in her list of stories written by her aunt. I will treat it in this essay as a collaborative piece between Barbauld and John Aikin. It was reprinted into the twentieth century, including a 1901 American volume that attributes the story to Barbauld and includes a story each by Taylor and Edgeworth. The three authors knew one another's works well. Barbauld and Edgeworth carried on a lively correspondence. Taylor and Barbauld had met.

16. Anticipating an argument familiar today, Charles Lamb believed that didactic stories, which dominated sales in children's bookshops, had driven out imagination and the pleasure of fantasy and fairy stories. He wrote to Coleridge: "Damn them. I mean the cursed Barbauld Crew, those Blights & Blasts of all that is Human in man & child." See *Letters of Charles and Mary Anne Lamb* 2: 82. There are fairies in "Order and Disorder." Maria Edgeworth wrote to Barbauld that the *Edinburgh Review* had laughed at her for introducing "some charming wife, sister, mother, or daughter, who acts the part of the good fairy" (*Memoir of Mrs. Barbauld*, ed. Anna Letitia Le Breton 114). Charles and Mary Lamb met Mrs. Barbauld socially and enjoyed her company.

17. For two centuries, "housewife" as object and person bore the same name. According to the OED, the object is "a pocket case for needles, pins, thread, scissors, etc." and was first in print in 1749. An illustration of a housewife appears in Gertrude Whiting, *Old-time Tools and Toys of Needlework*.

18. Although the Edgeworths stressed seeking meaning in "trifles" that we overlook every day, their discussion of needlework as "trifling" in *Practical Education* is, at best, ambivalent.

19. An early feminist critical analysis of the conflict is Sandra Gilbert and Susan Gubar, *Madwoman in the Attic: The Woman Writer and the Nineteenth-Century Literary Imagination*.

20. One day, Lamb seized a kitchen knife and chased the apprentice whom she had engaged to assist her in her sewing enterprise. Lamb's mother was killed in her attempt to stop the attack on the girl. For further details and interpretation of the incident, see Jane Aaron, *A Double Singleness: Gender and the Writings of Charles and Mary Lamb* 115–26.

21. Mrs. [Anne] Gilchrist, *Mary Lamb* 193. The entire essay appears, 186–94.

Re-Visioning Romantic Aesthetics

Judith Pascoe

Female Botanists and the Poetry of Charlotte Smith

If we accept Wordsworth's warning against murdering to dissect as an accurate reflection of Romantic writers' vexed relationship with the scientific, we will neglect a considerable number of female poets who found the rigors of botanical dissection and observation to be entirely compatible with, indeed conducive to, the art of poetry.[1] This was especially true of Charlotte Smith, whose posthumously published volume *Beachy Head, with Other Poems*[2] is an important landmark of what deserves to be recognized as a literary movement, a school of British women's writing merging poetry and science. Smith's poetic descriptions of the natural world possess the exactitude of a naturalist's field notes; hers is a poetry of close observation characterized by an attention to organic process in all its minutiae, as well as by a penchant for cataloging. Smith's late hybrid works—*Rural Walks, Rambles Farther, Minor Morals, Conversations Introducing Poetry: Chiefly on Subjects of Natural History*—taken together set forth a poetic manifesto which, in its insistence on close observation and faithfully rendered detail, challenges the prevailing strictures of the artistic establishment of her day. Smith's earth-bound aesthetic provides an intriguing rejoinder to the more transcendent one that we know as "the" Romantic, the central and normative mode. In addition, the scientific eye she casts over the natural world in her botanical poetry makes these poems intriguing points of reference in the ongoing critical debate over the female gaze.

The poems of Smith's posthumously published *Beachy Head, with Other Poems,* as well as the poems interpolated within *Conversations Introducing Poetry,* are informed and animated by Smith's engagement with botany. The increasingly botanical nature of Smith's poetry at the end of her literary career is noted by the writer of her obituary for the *Annual Register* (1806), who states:

> Mrs. Smith was well versed in the captivating science of Botany; and had she been at ease in her circumstances, and in a situation favourable to such

pursuits, she would doubtless have produced many useful works, as well as beautiful effusions, on those pleasing objects in the vegetable world which afford pure delight to the eye and elegant contemplation to the mind. (*Annual Register* 564)

Smith's reputation as a naturalist/poet is also corroborated by an anthology published a year after her death entitled *Descriptive Poetry: Being a Selection from the Best Modern Authors: Principally Having Reference to Subjects in Natural History*. No other poet whose work was selected for this volume was granted as extensive a representation as Smith: five selections from her published volumes were included.

Smith's late poems owe much to the botanist's habits of close observation and cataloging. Botanical science at the turn of the century was largely a science of description recorded through careful note-taking or sketching and kept for the purpose of identifying specimens. If one contrasts passages in Smith's *Beachy Head* with the botanical texts she consulted — those of William Withering, Thomas Martyn, Colin Milne — one begins to suspect that she composed with these authorities close at hand. Withering, describing wood sorrel, writes:

Acetosella. O. Stalk with 1 flower: leaves 3 together: leafits inversely-heartshaped hairy. (*Arrangement of British Plants* 2: 430)

In *Beachy Head*, Smith describes wood sorrel as having "light thin leaves, / Heart-shaped, and triply folded" (231). Withering's entry on the anemone notes: "*Petals*, the outer row with the deepest tinge of purple underneath" and records its natural habitat as being "woods, hedges, and hollow-ways" (2: 499). Smith writes of

> . . . the copse's pride, anemones,
> With rays like golden studs on ivory laid
> Most delicate: but touch'd with purple clouds,
> Fit crown for April's fair but changeful brow. (*Poems* 232)

Even when Smith poeticizes the more clinical descriptions of the botany handbook, converting a description like Withering's "deepest tinge of purple" to "touch'd with purple clouds," she remains true to the observed characteristics of the flower.

It should be noted that the language of botany in this period was not at all removed from the descriptive lavishness we associate with the language of poetry. In Thomas Martyn's edition of Philip Miller's *The Gardener's and Botanist's Dictionary,* a work frequently cited by Smith, one finds the following description of the plant commonly known as a moonwort:

> Lunaria annua. The seed vessels, when full ripe, become transparent, and of a clear shining white like sattin, whence this plant has acquired the name of *White-sattin.* (Miller, *Gardener's and Botanist's Dictionary* 2: 1)

The dictionary also notes that the plant is called "among our women Honestie." Smith, in "Flora," converts the translucent seed vessels of the botanical description into "Lunaria's pearly circlet, firm and light," and adds in a note that the plant is "usually called Honesty" (281).

While Smith does at times introduce an element of fancy to the botanist's more straightforward, if often extremely delicate and pretty, elaborations, she more often makes use of a highly technical botanical terminology in her poems. In "Flora," she uses terms like "hybernacle," "spatha," "calyx," and "umbels," sometimes providing explanations in the notes to her poems, at other times forcing her readers to make use of botanical glossaries of the sort found in Withering. Additionally, instead of relegating scientific nomenclature to the notes of her poems, she often uses the scientific names in the body of the poem and uses the notes to remind her readers of the names by which they are more likely to know particular plants. In "Flora," she refers to "Anthoxanthum" and "Scandix," which are revealed in notes by the more quotidian names of Vernal Meadow Grass and Shepherd's needle.

The common names of plants, which Smith frequently only resorts to in the notes to her poems — names like "Ladies' cushion," "Venus' comb," "Lords and Ladies," "Small skull-cap," — names that are extraordinarily suggestive, would seem to be more suited to a poet's purposes than the cumbersome Latin terminology Smith so often employs. That she insists on using scientific detail suggests that the poems represent acts of intellectual as well as artistic assertion. Naomi Schor has noted the way the detail participates

> in a larger semantic network, bounded on the one side by the *ornamental,* with its traditional connotations of effeminacy and decadence, and on the other, by the *everyday,* whose "prosiness" is rooted in the domestic sphere of social life presided over by women. (*Reading in Detail* 4)

In terms of the botanical, Schor's two poles might be figured as the realm of the florist and that of the kitchen garden, both associated with the feminine.

Smith distances herself from the first of these two realms in "A walk in the shrubbery," in which she writes:

> The Florists, who have fondly watch'd,
>   Some curious bulb from hour to hour,
> And, to ideal charms attach'd,
>   Derive their glory from a flower;
>
> Or they, who lose in crouded rooms,
>   Spring's tepid suns and balmy air,
> And value Flora's fairest blooms,
>   But in proportion as they're rare;
>
> Feel not the pensive pleasures known
>   To him, who, thro' the morning mist,
> Explores the bowery shrubs new blown,
>   A moralizing Botanist. — (303)

Further distinguishing between the decorative and the scientific appropriations of flora, Smith writes in a note to the subtitle of the poem ("To the cistus or rock rose, a beautiful plant, whose flowers expand, and fall off twice in twenty-four hours"):

> The extravagant fondness for the cultivation of these flowers which the art of the gardener can improve, such as Tulips, Ariculas, and Carnations, has excited laughter and contempt; and was, I think, sometimes confounded with the Science of Botany, with which it has little to do. A Florist, however, has very different pursuits and purposes from a Botanist. (303)

In her disdain for the activities of the florist, Smith echoes the pronouncements of the botanical texts of the period that shudder at the florist's labors. Withering writes, "Many flowers, under the influence of garden culture, become double; but double flowers are monsters, and therefore can only rank in a System of Botany, as varieties" (*Arrangement of British Plants* 1: 7). Smith is intent on establishing herself in a scientific, masculine (note the gender of her "moralizing Botanists") tradition rather than a decorative one, but she does not entirely eschew more feminine realms. Rather, in *Beachy Head,* she establishes the cottage garden as a legitimate site for the "pensive pleasures" of the Botanist, the kind of observation that takes in every detail. She writes of

The cottage garden; most for use design'd,
Yet not of beauty destitute. The vine
Mantles the little casement; yet the briar
Drops fragrant dew among the July flowers;
And pansies rayed, and freak'd and mottled pinks
Grow among balm, and rosemary and rue:
There honesuckles flaunt, and roses blow
Almost uncultured . . . (230)

Although the flowers in this patch are only "almost uncultured" and not in the pure state preferred by the botanist, Smith traces in this feminine locale the origin of her enthusiasm for the science of botany.

Smith is not the first poet to augment her poetry with extensive scientific notation, and it is a poetic practice that is not limited to female poets of the period. Erasmus Darwin, to whom I will return shortly, provides the model of this curious practice for many writers of the period. But the problem of authorizing oneself as a poet is more troublesome for Smith than it is for male poets like Wordsworth, whose first volumes of poetry, *Descriptive Sketches* and *An Evening Walk,* announce on their title pages the fact that they were written by "W. Wordsworth, B.A. of St. John's, Cambridge." Lacking this type of educational seal of approval, Smith calls on the scientific authorities of her day to verify the accuracy of her observations. These experts serve to authorize her assertions, but they also allow her to assert her own authority. In a note purporting to explicate the line "Or night-jar, chasing fern-flies —," Smith elaborates on an observation made by John Aikin in "On the Applications of Natural History to the Purposes of Poetry." Aikin points to the ubiquity of the hum of the Dor Beetle in poetic descriptions of night sounds (*Essay on the Application of Natural History to Poetry*). Smith notes that only one poet has ever conveyed the "more remarkable though by no means uncommon noise of the Fern Owl" — that poet being herself in a previously published sonnet (239). In a remarkable display of assurance, Smith calls attention to (1) her knowledge of Aikin's influential essay, (2) the fact that in *Beachy Head* she has avoided the imitative pitfalls of other nature poets, (3) the rest of her oeuvre, as she points to her own sonnet as another example of highly original description, and (4) her own authority as she ends the note with an aside on folklore attached to the Fern Owl.

Intellectual muscle-flexing of this kind suggests that Smith's poetry is a participant in the debate over the role of botany in women's education being waged around the turn of the century. The material barrier to women's acquisition of scientific knowledge was broken down in the eighteenth century with the increasing availability of books about science written in English rather than Latin, and in a layperson's idiom.[3] As Maria Edgeworth notes in her 1795 *Letters for Literary Ladies*:

> Till of late women were kept in Turkish ignorance; every means of acquiring knowledge was discountenanced by fashion, and impracticable even to those who despised fashion. Our books of science were full of unintelligible jargon . . . but now, writers must offer their discoveries to the public in distinct terms, which everybody may understand; technical language will no longer supply the place of knowledge, and the art of teaching has been carried to great perfection by the demand for learning: all this is in favor of women. (*Letters for Literary Ladies* 64–65)

Nowhere is this new, more hospitable method of teaching more evident than in Withering's oft-cited *Arrangement of British Plants*. Withering's text offers easy to follow instructions for preserving specimens of plants, rules for the pronunciation of Linnaean names, and a dictionary of botanical terms, singled out as being of particular interest to female readers: "The ladies too, who, in spite of the obstacles attendant upon a dead language, often have recourse to Linnaeus in the original Latin, will find their researches facilitated by it" (1: 40).

William Mavor's *The Lady's and Gentleman's Botanical Pocketbook* (1800), designed to complement Withering's less portable opus, acknowledges its female audience in its title and also points to the establishment of botany as a stylish pursuit. But far more important than botany's standing among the *ton* is its position at the center of late eighteenth-century writings on female education. Botany was singled out from the other natural sciences as the scientific pursuit most conducive to female character building. While unified in their advocacy of the science, botany's proponents were divided in their ultimate intents. It is revealing to contrast the tone of Rousseau's *Letters on the Elements of Botany* with that of Priscilla Wakefield's epistolary *An Introduction to Botany,* two works which, although similar in stated objective and format, encourage radically different levels of engagement in their female readers.

Rousseau emphasizes the, to him, necessarily diluted version of botany appropriate to female study, and the triviality of the entire enterprise. Distinguishing between the science of scientists and the "charming study" of "frivolous persons," Rousseau goes on to admonish his female interlocutor, "You must not, my dear friend, give more importance to Botany than it really has." He proceeds to warn her against paying too close attention to a particular class of vegetables, which, he writes, "will probably be uninteresting even to you, unless you have imbibed a greater passion for Botany than I wish you to have," and further warns against pursuing a specimen that "must be searched for in places, and at a season, by no means agreeable to your delicacy" (*Letters on the Elements of Botany* 72, 486–87).

Contrasting sharply with Rousseau's advocacy of botanical dilettantism stands Wakefield's careful instructions on the proper dissection of a pea flower. Her female narrator, Felicia, insists on the correct scientific utensils and advises her sister/reader Constance on the necessary equipment for the serious naturalist. She writes:

> In order to assist you in the examination of the minute parts of small flowers, it will be necessary to provide a magnifying glass, a needle, lancet, and a pair of small scissors, to render the dissecting them easier; for many of the parts are too delicate to be handled, for which reason a pair of small nippers will be a useful addition to the instruments that I have already named. (*Introduction to Botany* 23)

Where Rousseau warns against any exploration of the natural world that requires more than "[g]entle exercise," Wakefield's Felicia warns Constance, "[A]s I intend to select our examples from plants of British growth, you must seek for them growing wild in their native fields; nor confine your walks within the limits of a garden wall" (44).

Adding to botany's interest for women — and inspiring Smith's botanically influenced poetry and that of her peers — was Erasmus Darwin's exotic long poem, *The Botanic Garden,* which popularized the Linnaean notion of botanical analogy. Darwin's poem is a curious hybrid of detailed scientific tract and cheap romance, in which anthropomorphized plants engage in languid scenes of courtship. The poem combines sheer fantasy, in the form of supernatural machinery (Gnomes, Sylphs, Nymphs, and Salamanders), and the strictly scientific, in a compendium of notes, indices, and explanations of Linnaean nomenclature. Although it received great attention from both male and female writers, Darwin's poem became an object of particular fascination for women.[4] Darwin's description of the poem's second half, "The Loves of the Plants," as "diverse little pictures suspended over the chimney of a Lady's dressing-room, connected only by a slight festoon of ribbons" marks his understanding of this fact (quoted in King-Hele, *Eras-*

mus Darwin and the Romantic Poets). Women writers took *The Botanic Garden* far more seriously than Darwin's own diminutive description would suggest the poem merited. They embroidered numerous poetic variations on the work and credited Darwin as a kind of poetic mentor, granting him an honorary membership in a literary sorority of shared influence. Charlotte Smith cites Darwin frequently, expatiating in her *Conversations,* for example, on ocean luminescence, a phenomenon "Dr. Darwin never happened to see" (*Conversations* 64). Mary Shelley, in her introduction to *Frankenstein,* credits a discussion of Darwin's studies with providing the germ of her novel,[5] while Clara Reeve, in her 1809 *The Flowers at Court,* singles out Erasmus Darwin and Mrs. Montolieu (the author of *The Enchanted Plants*) for praise (*Flowers at Court* 10).

It is most certainly the open enthusiasm of these women poets for Darwin's championing of Linnaean principles that caused several of them to be criticized for neglecting the demands of propriety in their pursuit of botanical knowledge. Linnaeus himself came under assault for what were seen as lubricious descriptions; Philip Ritterbush, in *Overtures to Biology,* tells of a lecturer at the University of Edinburgh who refused to quote Linnaeus's description of the pansy because it was "too smutty for British ears." Ritterbush notes, "The female parts had been described as white and elegantly handsome, gaping wantonly before the stamens" (*Overtures to Biology* 119). Linnaean botany, as anthropomorphized by Darwin, was perceived as a threat to female modesty. The Reverend Mr. Richard Polwhele, in his vitriolic assault on those women poets of his time whom he perceived as allied to that great champion of female education, Mary Wollstonecraft, singled out the study of botany as cause for particular alarm. Polwhele writes in a note to his poetic diatribe, "Botany has lately become a fashionable amusement with the ladies. But how the study of the sexual system of plants can accord with female modesty, I am not able to comprehend." For Polwhele, the acquisition of botanical authority for women is a descent into lasciviousness. "I have, several times, seen boys and girls botanizing together," he writes, as if this were akin to sexual experimentation, and he overtly links the kind of dissection so clinically delineated by Priscilla Wakefield with wantonness and sexual desire. He writes of female botanists who

> With bliss botanic as their bosoms heave,
> Still pluck forbidden fruit, with mother Eve,

For puberty in sighing florets pant,
Or point the prostitution of a plant;
Dissect its organ of unhallowed lust,
And fondly gaze the titillating dust. (*The Unsex'd Females* 10)

Even Anna Letitia Barbauld,[6] a serious, religious, and politically committed poet, was sullied in at least one person's eyes by her interest in botany, or, more particularly, in Erasmus Darwin's poetry. Samuel Rogers recalls, "Strangely enough, in spite of her correct taste, Mrs. Barbauld was quite fascinated with Darwin's *Botanic Garden* when it first appeared and talked of it with rapture; for which I scolded her heartily" (*Recollections of the Table-Talk of Samuel Rogers* 182). In fact, the prurient interest with which Rogers impugns Anna Barbauld and which Polwhele associates with feminine interest in botany played a smaller part in women writers' fascination with Darwin's poem than did the professional avenues it opened to them and the validation it provided for a new form of poetry that could accommodate their peculiar gifts and training.

Frances Arabella Rowden specifically sets out to de-emphasize the sexual aspect of Darwin's poem in her *Poetical Introduction to the Study of Botany*. In the advertisement to this work she claims to have planned originally to "select a few passages from Mr. Darwin's elegant Poem of the Botanic Garden, and arrange them according to the system of Linnaeus," but finding Darwin's work incomplete and "the language frequently too luxuriant for the simplicity of female education," she embarks on her own botanical opus, a two-part production, half botanical textbook and half Darwin-inspired poetry (*Poetical Introduction* vii–viii). Alan Bewell, in a suggestive treatment of the politics of botanical literature, writes:

> The increasing importance of female readers combined with the metaphoric and intellectual traditions linking them to flowers make botanical literature a kind of writing that necessarily raised questions about gender and sexuality, even if a writer chose to repress or expurgate them. ("'Jacobin Plants'" 137)[7]

Without disagreeing with Bewell's assertion, I would suggest that for the female practitioners of botanical writing such questions take the overt form of a claim to scientific authority utilized in the service of a poetics of the botanically exact. Certainly the reviews of both Smith's and Rowden's work respond to this kind of intellectual assertion. "Little inaccuracies occur more frequently than we could have supposed," the *Monthly Review* complains of Smith's *Conversations Introducing Poetry: Chiefly on Subjects of Natural History* (82, Jan. 1806). The same journal rather pedantically reminds Rowden, "*Chick-weed,* without its restrictive epithet, is not the proper English of *Trientalis Europaea*; neither does the plant in question delight in fertile vales, but in heathy moors" (98, Jan. 1813).

To understand the attraction of Erasmus Darwin's work for women poets, the most logical place to look might seem to be Anna Seward's *Memoirs* of the poet, since Seward had a more intimate acquaintance with Darwin than any of her female peers. But Seward, whose own poetry owes much less debt to Darwin than does the work of Smith, is a problematic guide to Darwin's appeal for women poets. Seward's account of Darwin's life is vexed by the fact that she was angry at Darwin for using lines from her poetry without attribution. The hostility provoked by this incident reveals itself in her tone as well as in a tendency toward less than flattering descriptions of this "lame and clumsy" man (*Memoirs* 25). Seward faults Darwin for exactly those elements of his work which were most appealing to many of her female contemporaries. She criticizes Darwin's "too exclusive devotion to distinct picture in poetry," and observes of his description of the perforated border of a shroud: "The expression is too minute for the solemnity of the subject. Certainly it cannot be natural for a shocked and agitated mind to observe or to describe with such accuracy" (*Memoirs* 84–85).

But it is Darwin's very "minuteness," his holding a magnifying glass to the tiniest facets of the natural world, that acted as a force of liberation for Charlotte Smith. The wood sorrel that Charlotte Smith describes as having "light thin leaves, / Heart-shaped, and triply folded" (231) is representative of a school of Darwin-inspired botanical writing intent on fashioning a world in which the forest is less important than the trees, or, rather, than the lacework of veins on one particular leaf. That there is something of a poetic revolution implicit in women poets' borrowings and, finally, departures from Darwin is discernible in what amounts to a manifesto by Smith in her innovative hybrid works, *Rural Walks* and *Rambles Farther.* In the preface to the former she announces her plan to

> unite the interest of the novel with the instruction of the school book by throwing the latter into the form of dialogue, mingled with narrative, and by giving some degree of character to the group. (*Rural Walks* iv)

Smith, through the course of both works, dispenses with a distant vantage point in favor of the close-up view. The proponent of this aesthetic is the aptly named Mrs. Woodfield, in dialogue with her daughters and a visiting cousin, Caroline. When Mrs. Woodfield chides Caroline for her inability to appreciate natural detail, Caroline recalls her aunt's disdain for the "affectation of being in raptures at prospects, and of making a parade of taste for *picturesque beauty.*" Thus provoked, Mrs. Woodfield launches into a litany of natural detail only available to the discerning eye, "to those who have learned to look . . . with the eye of a painter or a poet" (43–44). Indeed, Mrs. Woodfield's chief endeavor in these two works is to teach her daughters how to look at the world, and, it becomes clear, the distancing vantage of the painter is inferior to the amplifying awareness of the botanical poet. After describing at great length the minute plant life thriving in the crevices of rock, Mrs. Woodfield comments:

> But these and many other small plants are rather the pursuit of the botanist than the landscape painter, who ought, however, in drawing these rocky scenes, to catch the forms, though he cannot minutely describe the long tangling branches of the blackberry; the festoons of briony woodbine, night shade, or wild hop, that creep or flaunt among the rugged hollows. (*Rambles Farther* 99)

By the end of these companion volumes, the ability to "minutely describe the long tangling branches of the blackberry" — as Smith does in her poetry — is clearly more desirable than the ability merely to "catch the forms" of things. In this advocacy of the realistic detail, Smith places herself in absolute opposition to the dominant aesthetic formulations of her day, to a Royal Academy that considered "mechanical" imitation vulgar and placed value, instead, on the ability to generalize or abstract from the particular.[8] At the close of *Rambles Farther,* Mrs. Woodfield delights in her daughter Henrietta, who has imbibed the lesson of the two volumes and is on her knees in a bed of flowers, exulting in particularity. As Mrs. Woodfield looks on, Henrietta cries:

> Oh! here is the saxafragas which I have in my garden; and here is a distaff hyacinth; and look, mamma, what a number of foldinella's; there are frettilaria's of two or three sorts; anemones too, much finer than we have at home. (*Rambles Farther* 198)

The particularity and inclusiveness of Smith's late poetry points to a different attitude toward nature from what we have come to expect of Romantic poets. Although Smith, like her male contemporaries, turns to nature as an escape from the "crimes and follies of mankind / From hostile menace, and offensive boast," the nature she experiences seems to be much more an intimate acquaintance than an awe-inspiring force (*Conversations*

183). It is a nature she has examined with her eyes two inches from its petals (the better to determine they are "rayed, and freak'd and mottled"), rather than observed mid-stride on a walking tour. Wordsworth, in *The Prelude*, recalls dangling over a raven's nest "But ill sustained, and almost, as it seemed, / Suspended by the blast which blew amain, / Shouldering the naked crag . . ." (1805 *Prelude* 1: 333–35). Smith, in contrast, remembers:

> An early worshipper at Nature's shrine,
> I loved her rudest scenes — warrens, and heaths,
> And yellow commons, and birch-shaded hollows,
> And hedge rows, bordering unfrequented lanes
> Bowered with wild roses, and the clasping woodbine
> Where purple tassels of the tangling vetch
> With bittersweet, and bryony inweave,
> And the dew fills the silver bindweed's cups —
> I loved to trace the brooks whose humid banks
> Nourish the harebell, and the freckled pagil;
> And stroll among o'ershadowing woods of beech,
> Lending in Summer, from the heats of noon
> A whispering shade . . . (231)

The difference in these two poets' remembered experiences of nature is partly attributable to their difference in gender. As Marlon Ross points out, the favored stance of the Romantic poet — poised on a mountain top overlooking the world — is not an easy one for a female poet to assume ("Romantic Quest" 44). Although Smith writes at the opening of *Beachy Head* from the "stupendous summit" of "a rock sublime," she moves quickly from the majestic to the minute, from the sublime to the beautiful, refusing to reinscribe her contemporaries' hierarchization of these terms.[9] It should not surprise us, given the fact that women of the Romantic period could not ramble with the abandon of their male contemporaries, that they should attend more carefully to the minute characteristics of a smaller space.[10] Certainly Smith, by virtue of her gender and her large family, could not travel across Europe encumbered only by a small valise, as Wordsworth was known to do.[11]

Smith's poetry seems in an odd way to break the bonds of containment by celebrating the infiniteness of particularity. The sheer material abundance of *Beachy Head*'s close-up tableaux suggests that the most circumscribed outdoor space — for example, the narrow loop of a lady's daily promenade — can serve as easily to expand as to constrict. By insistently focusing on the minute within even the grandest expanse, Smith suggests the escapist possibilities of the particular. Within the carefully delineated realm of the cottage garden, locus of female work and duty, Smith employs the extreme close-up of the botanist's gaze, creating an explosion of dazzling specificity, so that the limitations of a female vantage point become forces of liberation.

Nowhere is this more true than in Smith's "Flora," a poem that mirrors Darwin's easy accommodation of the botanical and the fanciful. "Flora" is a poetic fairy tale interwoven with botanical detail and extensive scientific and illustrative notes. Smith creates an alternate world from the minutiae of botanical detail, a fairy world in which the specific characteristics of individual plants are fancifully called into service. Describing the entourage of "Flora," the "enchanting goddess of the flowery tribe" (279), Smith writes:

> Nor less assiduous round their lovely queen,
> The lighter forms of female fays are seen;
> Rich was the purple vest Floscella wore,
> Spun of the tufts the Tradescantia bore;
> The Cistus' flowers minute her temple graced
> And threads of Yucca bound her slender waist. (282)

Writing of Emily Watson's 1862 *Fairies of Our Garden,* Susan Stewart observes, "Systematically, each sign of nature is transformed into a sign of culture, just as the domestic arts of the time turned pine cones into picture frames, sea shells into lamps, and enclosed a variety of natural objects 'dried' under glass" (*On Longing* 114). While such a domestication of nature also seems to be occurring in Smith's use of flowers as fairy garments, it is complicated by her insistent interpolation of the scientific. In the passage above, in which Smith transforms the "tufts the Tradescantia bore" into a purple vest for Floscella, she adds the following note:

> Tradescantia. The silk-like tuft within the plant called *Tradescantia* appears to the eye composed of very fine filaments; but on examining one of these small silky threads through a microscope, it looks like a string of amethysts. (282)

Rather than view the scientific and the fantastic as incompatible extremes, Smith actually seems to arrive at the magical by way of the empirical. The scientist's microscope, rather than pronouncing exactly and unquestionably the reality of the natural world, seems to reveal for Smith the possibility of other worlds, each opening to reveal another in an infinite pattern of egress. Scientific observation, rather than negating the musings of the imagination, seems for Smith to initiate them.

This essay has thus far provided a liberationist reading of women poets' engagement with botanical science, a reading that portrays Smith's appropriation of the botanist's gaze as a gesture of empowerment, a strategy that allows her to advance her artistic and professional ambitions. Such a reading is complicated, of course, by the current debate over the female gaze, a debate summarized and advanced in the field of Romanticism by Beth Newman's essay on *Wuthering Heights* ("'The Situation of the Looker-On'"). A less optimistic reading of Smith's botanical poetry might insist that, even if in appropriating the naturalist's gaze Smith moves from the traditional female object position, she only impersonates the masculine position of spectator without dismantling the gender conventions that name man subject and woman object of the gaze. Mary Louise Pratt's analysis in *Imperial Eyes* of the eighteenth-century botanical movement renders the issue of spectatorial power even more worrying in its association of Linnaean categorizing with the advancement of a myth of European superiority. Any attempt to come to terms with botanically inspired writing like Smith's must take Pratt's assertions seriously.

Pratt aligns the discourse of eighteenth-century natural science with that of navigational mapping, both structures of thought that enabled and furthered an imperialistic view of the world, but she finds in botany a transformative power absent from the mapping of newly discovered territories. Pratt writes:

> One by one the planet's life forms were to be drawn out of the tangled threads of their life surroundings and rewoven into European-based patterns of global unity and order. The (lettered, male, European) eye that held the system could familiarize ("naturalize") new sites/sights immediately upon contact, by incorporating them into the language of the system. (*Imperial Eyes* 31)

In Pratt's description of the systematizing of the early naturalists, difference gets factored out: "with respect to mimosas, Greece could be the same as Venezuela, West Africa, or Japan" (31). Facilitating this totalizing new construction of natural life is the deceptively benign figure of the naturalist, who, unlike the explorer or conquistador, his navigational counterparts, goes about his acquisitive mission in unheroic guise, a homely wanderer wielding only a specimen bag (33).

Female botanical writers like Smith fall outside the range of Pratt's study, but an extrapolation from her work might label Smith a "seeing-woman" after Pratt's "seeing-man," a pejorative phrase for one "whose imperial eyes passively look out and possess," and whose propensity for accumulation Pratt allies with "the extractive, transformative character of industrial capitalism" (7, 36). Such a reading would, I think, inadequately account for the extent to which Smith was disenfranchised from the masculine structures of power whose discourse she borrowed (besides being oblivious to the irony inherent in a dismissal of Smith's work based on its failure to escape these structures, a dismissal that is, itself, articulated in the discourse of another such power structure, that of institutional academia). Also, and important, just as in merging poetry with botany Smith creates the possibility of a newly objective poetry premised on accurate description, in merging botany with poetry she suggests (or reveals) a newly subjective science. This is especially true in a poem like "Flora," which in its blending of fantasy and botanical detail calls into question the objectivity of the scientist's gaze and thereby diminishes its power to objectify. In leveling a scientific gaze on the world around them, women writers do not, perhaps, dismantle the systems of power that grant the gaze its totalizing authority, but they do subtly alter the force field in which it operates.

In conclusion, I wish to return to Priscilla Wakefield, one of the many promulgators of scientific knowledge for women. Wakefield's Felicia in *An Introduction to Botany* spends a summer working her way through Linnaean classification and writing her sister Constance of her findings. Having progressed to the sixteenth class, she writes:

> Before you dismiss the Mallowtube, take your microscope, and examine the dust of the anthers; it will afford you entertainment, being curiously toothed like the wheels of a watch. The most minute parts of nature are finished with an elegant nicety, that surpasses the utmost efforts of art. (*Introduction to Botany* 43)

This conception of raw nature as existing on the same continuum with art, one that Smith's most determinedly descriptive verse seems to take as its credo, counters that other nature we find in Romantic poetry, the one that is recollected (and transformed) in tranquility. Smith's poetry forces us to reconsider our assumptions about the relationship between science and poetry in the Romantic period, as well as to question why the female gaze of the period has so little informed our discussions of Romantic vision.[11] A new model of the Romantic poet is in order, one who, confronted with a field of daffodils, would count petals before launching into verse.

Notes

   1. A list of botanical works by women would include Sarah Hoare, *A Poem on the Pleasures and Advantages of Botanical Pursuits;* Lucy Hooper, ed. *The Lady's Book of Flowers and Poetry;* Mary Howitt, *Sketches of Natural History;* Mary Elizabeth Jackson, *Botanical Lectures;* Maria Henrietta Montolieu, *The Enchanted Plants;* Frances Arabella Rowden, *A Poetical Introduction to the Study of Botany;* Charlotte Smith, *Conversations Introducing Poetry: Chiefly on Subjects of Natural History;* Smith, *Minor Morals, Interspersed with Sketches of Natural History;* Smith, *Rural Walks: in Dialogues;* Smith, *Rambles Farther: A Continuation of Rural Walks;* Priscilla Wakefield, *An Introduction to Botany.* See also Elizabeth Moody's "To Dr. Darwin, On Reading his Loves of the Plants" in her *Poetic Trifles,* and Catherine Maria Fanshawe's "Epistle on the Subjects of Botany," in *The Literary Remains of Catherine Maria Fanshawe.* Stuart Curran led me to most of these collections. Paula Feldman also contributed to this listing.
   2. Included in *The Poems of Charlotte Smith,* ed. Stuart Curran. This is the edition cited in the text hereafter.
   3. For a helpful survey of women's historical relationship to the various realms of science, see Margaret Alic's *Hypatia's Heritage: A History of Women in Science from Antiquity to the Late Nineteenth Century.* For a discussion of nineteenth-century female botanical writers, see Ann B. Shteir, "Botany in the Breakfast Room: Women and Early Nineteenth-Century British Plant Study."
   4. The poem received much less positive attention from the more famous male poets. Coleridge in his *Biographia Literaria* compared the work to "the Russian palace of ice, glittering, cold and transitory." He further commented that

> Darwin's *Botanic Garden,* which for some years, was greatly extolled, not only by the *reading* public in general, but even by those, whose genius and natural robustness of understanding enabled them afterwards to act foremost in dissipating these "painted mists" that occasionally rise from the marshes at the foot of Parnassus. (2: 11–12)

Coleridge's comment exactly describes Wordsworth's reaction. Early enamored of the poem, he later renounced it as an injurious influence.
   Evidence of the endurance and ubiquitousness of Darwin's poem is provided by an amusing episode in Sydney Owenson's 1817 *France.* Owenson describes witnessing a performance at the Vaudeville, which she first took to be a dramatization of *Loves of the Plants,* but which was actually a floral panegyric to the French King in which a violet is suspected of disloyalty but then granted amnesty. I am grateful to Jeanne Moskal for bringing this episode to my attention. See *France* 2: 86–88.
   5. Mary Shelley writes:

> They [Byron and Shelley] talked of the experiments of Dr. Darwin (I speak not of what the doctor really did or said that he did, but, as more to my

purpose, of what was then spoken of as having been done by him. (*Franken-stein* xxiv)

6. The spelling "Letitia" here follows the forthcoming edition of Barbauld's works.

7. See also Bewell's interesting work on Keats and floral imagery, "Keats's 'Realm of Flora.'"

8. For a discussion of the complicated variables that determined the valoriza-tion of the general over the particular, see John Barrell, *The Political Theory of Painting from Reynolds to Hazlitt*, especially his discussion of women's disenfran-chisement from the republic of taste (65–68).

9. Edmund Burke wrote that the virtues of the beautiful are "of less immedi-ate and momentous concern to society and of less dignity" than those of the sublime. See *A Philosophical Enquiry into the Origin of Our Ideas of the Sublime and Beautiful* (111).

10. While Wordsworth also wrote poems about flowers from an intimate perspective, he did not share Smith's penchant for botanical exactitude. Rather, Wordsworth's flower poems, such as "To the Daisy" and "To the Small Celandine," emphasize the speaker's observational power or genius for metaphor rather than the plant's morphology.

11. Evidence of this fact is provided by Dorothy Wordsworth, who was chastised by her aunt for "rambling about the country on foot." She responded:

So far from considering this as a matter of condemnation, I rather thought it would have given my friends pleasure to hear that I had courage to make use of the strength with which nature has endowed me, when it not only procured me more pleasure than I should have received from sitting in a post-chaise — but was also the means of saving me at least thirty shillings. ("To Mrs. Christopher Crackanthorpe," 21 April [1794], letter 6 of *Letters of Dorothy Wordsworth* 18.)

12. Stuart Curran first raised this issue in "The 'I' Altered." His work informs and inspires this essay.

Jerome J. McGann

Literary History, Romanticism, and Felicia Hemans

Interlocutors: Anne Mack, J. J. Rome, Georg Mannejc

AM. How agreeably "historical" we've all become in thinking about literature. But have we "returned to history" only to discover its ruins? Traditional historicism was difficult enough with "all those proper names and dates" beneath which "the contemporary mind staggers" (see Hartman, "The Culture of Criticism" 371–72). These new historicisms are worse. The older forms at least prized thoroughness and coherence. But a generation of fierce skepticism has brought historicism, like the rest of literary studies, to scenes of fragmentation — Lovejoy's splendid project turned into the *disintegration* of romanticisms.

JJR. So we are in a crisis? How romantic! How opportune!

Effort, and expectation, and desire,
And something evermore about to be. (quoting Wordsworth's *The Prelude*)

GM. "Endless play", in other words?

JJR. Georg, read some Oscar Wilde for a change. One needs critical distance to think clearly. Don't you think so, Anne?

I mean, if you're interested in exploring the historical shape of romanticism in England, it won't help very much to approach the problem in a romantic attitude. Wasn't it Blake who said you become what you behold? Assume a crisis and you'll get one.

AM. But a crisis does exist. The traditional picture of the Romantic Period has been smashed beyond recognition.

JJR. So what if it has. Let a thousand flowers bloom. Besides, this splintering may have been a fortunate fall, leaving the world all before us. "The prospects for a coherent and all-encompassing history of literature . . .

depend on a new politics of knowledge taking the place of the old bellig-erence of ideologies. Literary historians and critics must be willing to discover the limits as well as the power of their methods and must be open to the possibility of new linkages between their accounts of the literary past and the accounts of others" (Walter Reed, "Commentary" 678).

"There are no master narratives," right? — only stories told at different times, for different purposes. The most traditional story of English roman-ticism centers in *Lyrical Ballads* — that is to say, in a book published after the English reaction to the French Revolution had established itself. But sup-pose one were to emphasize the importance of a sentimentalist project like *The Florence Miscellany* (1785)?[1] What a different picture of English roman-ticism emerges from that vantage.

AM. Suppose that, suppose whatever you like! I suppose anyone could suppose anything!

JJR. It's not an arbitrary choice, after all, just an unfamiliar one. Be-cause we've forgotten some of our history. *The Florence Miscellany* launched a decisive and influential early form of romantic writing. The importance of the Della Cruscans is partly measured by the amount of hostility they drew from conservative circles, and partly by the impact of their work on later romantic writing. Keats is probably the greatest product of the movement, the supreme example of its stylistic inertias.

GM. A charmingly outrageous view that I can't believe you mean seriously. And among its greatest charms is the way it might draw our attention away from your agreeably pluralist ideas about literary history. Your Keats remark exposes the poverty of what you're saying. To construct a literary history — any literary history, even a revisionist one like yours — one must torture poetry with gross instruments of scholarly rationalization. Among the worst of these are the periodic structures that march one through a historical bureaucracy of culture. No true poem will abide the questions that are raised by structures of periodization. Trash will abide such questions — that is to say, writing like Della Cruscan verse — but po-etry will not. Keats will not.

AM. So we should abandon periodic categories altogether? Is Keats not properly a Romantic poet? Are the historical conventions of Romanti-cism not apparent in his works?

GM. Those are just the kinds of questions that literary history wants one to ask, but they are completely *mis*leading questions — *so far as the work of poetry is concerned*. For "Romanticism" as the term has come to be defined is nothing but an abstraction covering — I should even say *creating* — a multitude of critical sins. If Keats is a Romantic poet, so is (we all agree, right?) Byron; and yet their work is utterly different. We have been taught to think of Keats as a great lyric poet and of Byron as a mediocre one at best. But the judgment is incompetent because they write completely different kinds of lyrics. What "To Autumn" has in common with "Fare Thee Well!" — in terms of stylistic procedures — is minimal, yet the commonplace evaluative judgment I just gave is licensed by drawing the two poems into an abstract and prefabricated comparison.[2]

Or ask yourselves: What are the great *topoi* of Romanticism? Subjectivity, Nature, Imagination, Reflexive Consciousness? Take any or all of those rubrics to different writers, or even to different works by the same writer, or even to the same work, and you will end up, if you are reading well, only with a mass of differences.

JJR. And yet the very existence of modern literary history argues that it serves the needs of writers and poets. Or are you arguing that the birth of a modern historical consciousness signaled the twilight of the gods of poetry?

GM. That common nineteenth-century view still seems relevant. Poetry entered its Age of Anxiety as much with Wordsworth and Shelley and Mill — its enthusiasts — as it did with Bentham and Peacock and Macauley — its elegists.

JJR. What a paradox lies there! For the renewal of the arts in the Romantic movement was closely connected to that new historical consciousness. The *philosophes*, the antiquarians, and finally the critical philologists and historians all came to break open the treasure houses of western and eastern cultures.

GM. You mean "to invade, plunder, and exploit." And the rape of the biblical inheritance by the historical imagination is the exemplary tale of what happened. When the bible began to be read in referential terms, when its truth was inquired after by factive and empirical measures, the texts were utterly alienated from themselves. The historicist reconstruction of the past was largely founded in that scientism of the text we call hermeneutics: the editing and interpreting of a vast corpus of classical, biblical, and national scriptures. The ultimate meaning of this project would not be the revelation or the renewal of the texts; on the contrary, it would rather bring a revelation of the "truth" of science, the establishment of science *at the ideological level,* as the fundamental myth of modern consciousness.[3]

Of course men like Bodmer, Lowth, Herder, and Wolf all thought that their hermeneutical projects would rescue poetry and even religion from modern rationalism and skepticism. Their faith, however, was already grounded in the myth they were struggling against. Their explications of the texts and cultures of more primitive worlds often seem anything but rationalist or abstract — so filled can they be with minute particulars and "thick description." Nevertheless, the details emerge through the redeployment of the myth of objectivity, and they only function as signs for various conceptual categories (e.g., "primitive" and "modern," "naive" and "sentimental," or the more complex historical and structural schemas erected by scholars like Eichhorn and Wolf).[4]

This is a cultural world not merely turned upside down, but rent with contradiction. Out of the cooked comes the raw, out of the sentimental appears the naive. The cool light of the scholars creates a superheated literal scene that their own prose works then replicate: not necessarily in a positive extravagance of style — though some, like Herder, were so inclined — as in texts where restraint and methodical pursuit become negative signs of enormous moment.

The eighteenth-century antiquarians, philologues, and orientalists thus supplied only a fragile second order life to the ancient cultures and poetries they so loved. This fragility passed over into the poetry of romanticism, which plundered the philological tradition for many of its key theoretical ideas, generic forms, and tropic resources.[5] Indeed, the new philology was itself nothing more — and nothing less — than the orientalist's dream come true, a mechanism for appropriating alien forms of cultural life. The richness of the poetry of Keats, as Arnold was acute to see, was an ominous symptom of aesthetic disease. Is anyone surprised that the consumptive should have become an emblem of romantic imagination? The famous "pale hectic" is the *figura* of an illusory life, a false image, a death-sign.

AM. Meaning?

GM. I am narrating a cautionary tale.

AM. It sounds like literary history to me.

GM. I'd call it literary anti-history. With the advent of modern philology all the poets, ancient as well as modern, stand in peril of their lives. And in their peril we observe a serious threat to culture at large. Orientalism, like apartheid, is a fate that will not cease until its fruits, for good and for evil, are uniformly distributed.

AM. Meaning?

GM. That we want to unravel as many stories as we can. This is what literary anti-history might do. The poems must be removed to a world elsewhere, alienated from their original homes. Literary anti-history, like the poems themselves, will then tell us equally of origin and of alienation, and of the relations that the two keep with each other.

JJR. Taking that point of reference, what would you say about Roger Lonsdale's recent pair of anthologies of eighteenth-century poetry?[6] Are they models of what literary anti-history might be aspiring toward?

GM. Yes, exactly that. Their very form — which is anti-narrative — shows us that these are anti-histories. Both anthologies urge us to re-imagine a historical shape for eighteenth-century poetry. And by fore-grounding the poetry (rather than stories about the poetry) these books are committed to imagination and to acts of critical reimagination. *Literary* history should seek the truth of imagination, not the truth of science and history (thoroughness, accuracy) or the truth of philosophy (theoretical rigor and completion). The truth of the imagination is reimagination.

JJR. Reimagination of what?

GM. The poetry, of course! What else are we concerned with?

JJR. Well, some of us are at least as concerned with *history*. And Lonsdale's anthologies leave all the historical questions to implication. By keeping our attention on the poems, Lonsdale tends to invisibilize the theatre of their eventualities. In the end those anthologies are committed to an "imagination" that repudiates history for poetry and writing.

I'm not criticizing Lonsdale's work. I'm just suggesting that there are other things to be done — for instance, drawing out what his books leave only to implication. One starts by imagining an impossible object — let us call it "the origins of English romanticism." Every historian knows that even the simplest event is meshed in a complex network of relations that no one could hope to unravel. So the quest for "the origins of English ro-manticism" is an imaginative and hypothetical journey from the start — a romance-quest, which is, in that sense, also a kind of anti-history.

But then why even bother, one might ask? And the answer is that the quest is undertaken not to discover "the origins of English romanticism" but to clarify the various ways this imaginary object might be defined and interpreted. To reimagine "the origins of English romanticism" through a recovery of *The Florence Miscellany* and Della Cruscan poetry in general is, as you were arguing, to suggest a whole new series of related reimaginings. And so the ultimate object of the immediate hypothetical project emerges. We would not only have to read and re-evaluate a considerable body of unfamiliar poetry and cultural materials, we would have to re-read and re-evaluate the cultural deposits that have grown so familiar to us — perhaps, indeed, all too familiar. And we would have to re-read and reimagine the instruments by which our received books of memory and forgetting were made.

GM. What for, a compendious treatment of the varieties of literary experience? Something like the fifteen-volume Cambridge History of English Literature, where we are given the materials to see (for example) "the origins of English romanticism" in a variety of possible perspectives? The Cambridge History's encyclopaedic character—its mass of details and scholarly apparatus—undermine the work's inertia toward coherent explanatory narrative. It is history and anti-history at the same time.

JJR. But its anti-historical potential is too obedient to the (historian's) signs of accuracy and thoroughness. I want a history at once more energetic and imaginative—a history that assumes the past has not yet happened, that it remains to be seen. If a history is to reflect its subject back to us, then the ideal literary history will be a structure of hypothetical worlds.

These will have to be precisely designed. To stay with our possible topic, "the origins of English romanticism," I imagine a critical narrative unwinding from suppositions like this. If we suppose romanticism to be structured on the double helix of the naive and the sentimental, what is the historical place, in English romanticism, of Burns's *Poems, chiefly in the Scottish Dialect* (1786)? Or of Sir William Jones's translations of the Vedic hymns published in the mid-1780s? Or of the Della Cruscans' poetry, Blake's *Songs,* or the *Lyrical Ballads*?

Then one might advance other suppositions altogether. The best history of this kind, to plagiarize Byron, will "suppose this supposition" itself, exposing the hypothetical character of the historical constructions and thereby encouraging other hypotheses. The point is to reveal what can be and has been supposed, what might be imagined and why. It is to reveal, precisely, not the truth of fact or of reason, but the truth of imagination as it operates in history.

AM. This is madness, or lies in the way to madness. It's worse than Georg's "literary history as cautionary tale." He comes in the posture of the critic, warning of the historian's abstractions. But you seem to be arguing for a kind of positive literary anti-history—as if the past were something that could be invented.

JJR. Romanticism, like its many works, *is* an artistic and poetical invention. And because the writers could not stop for death, scholarship came and kindly stopped for them, and escorted them to Beulahland. It is a killing kindness. Scholarship preserves the poetry of the past, but threatens it with a night of the living dead. What I say is, let us reimagine what history can do—at least for those who live by imagination and who carry out its work.

AM. But you can't just *invent* the past according to your desire! History's devotion to accuracy and thoroughness are important exactly because of the limits they set to imagination.

JJR. Exactly, as you say. But what you forget is that the historian's tools are themselves inventions. We have to invent and continually reinvent the limits of imagination, along with the instruments that will define the limits. For we do not desire the unlimited. *Le goût de l'infini* is an emblem for a desire toward new limits, to have the shape of the world redefined. It is a form of desire that is, like all such forms, historically specific. The desire for the infinite is a finite—a human—desire.

GM. This is mere sophistical avoidance of the presence of the past and its eventualities. Of course we are always inventing new ways of seeing; but we don't invent what has been seen, what has been done. These things have an independent existence, and their value to us lies in that independence. If the desire for the infinite is—what did you say?—"an emblem for a desire toward new limits," then a "stubborn fact" is an emblem of everything that lies beyond desire and imagination. It is not a "limit of imagination," it is a stumbling block, the unaccountable. There are powers as great as the imagination—forbidding powers that put a limit on the truths we might want to imagine, for example, about John Keats on one hand and Charlotte Dacre on the other.

AM. Such powers exist and their emblems *are* those stubborn, difficult "facts" you want to celebrate. But they are never "unaccountable," those facts. We always fit them to our stories, if only by writing them out.

I suggest we look—right now—very closely at a few of those unaccountabilities. For instance, do we know (or remember) that Felicia Hemans was the most published English poet of the nineteenth century? Do we know, or even think we know, what that might mean? Do we remember any of her poems? And if we do, are we so certain that the Victorians' admiration for her work was misguided? What would it mean to reimagine a work like "The Homes of England," once so celebrated—or are we to reimagine only the rightful inheritance, the works that come to us sanctioned by what is now taken for established authority? The fate of "The Homes of England" might well serve as a lesson to all literary authorities. Where is the coward that would not dare to fight for such a poem?

THE HOMES OF ENGLAND

Where's the coward that would not dare
To fight for such a land?   Marmion

The stately Homes of England,
  How beautiful they stand!
Amidst their tall ancestral trees,
  O'er all the pleasant land.
The deer across the greensward bound
  Through shade and sunny gleam,
And the swan glides past them with the sound
  Of some rejoicing stream.

The merry Homes of England!
  Around their hearths by night,
What gladsome looks of household love
  Meet, in the ruddy light!
There woman's voice flows forth in song,
  Or childhood's tale is told,
Or lips move tunefully along
  Some glorious page of old.

The blessed Homes of England!
  How softly on their bowers
Is laid the holy quietness
  That breathes from Sabbath-hours!
Solemn, yet sweet, the church-bell's chime
  Floats through their woods at morn;
All other sounds, in that still time,
  Of breeze and leaf are born.

The Cottage Homes of England!
  By thousands on her plains,
They are smiling o'er the silvery brooks,
  And round the hamlet-fanes.
Through glowing orchards forth they peep,
  Each from its nook of leaves,
And fearless there the lowly sleep,
  As the bird beneath their eaves.

The free, fair Homes of England!
  Long, long, in hut and hall,
May hearts of native proof be rear'd
  To guard each hallow'd wall!

> And green for ever be the groves,
>   And bright the flowery sod,
> Where first the child's glad spirit loves
>   Its country and its God! (1827)[7]

Hemans recurs to this fantastic scene again and again, in a rich variety of poetical transformations. Speaking of another of those transformations, Kingsley Amis has described Hemans's once equally famous "The Graves of a Household" as a "superficially superficial piece" (*Faber Popular Reciter* 15). The phrase is apt in either case, for it calls attention to this poetry's deep involvement in the exposition of wealth and power as spectacle, ideology, *superficies*.

GM. Do you seriously mean to offer a troglodyte like Kingsley Amis as a voice of authority?! That spokesman, that *epitome*, of reaction.

AM. All the more reason to listen carefully to what he has to say. As I recall, Trotsky quoted liberally from the Tsar's and Tsarina's papers, and from government police reports, when he constructed his *History of the Russian Revolution*. Every word uttered makes a commitment to the truth — even those which are mistaken or duplicitous, even those which are self-deceived. In Amis's case, his very historical backwardness gives him a privileged view of Hemans's poem.

GM. An interesting theory that would allow you to translate any text into anything you might want it to say. But there are no secret subversive meanings in the intense inanity of Hemans's "The Homes of England," and I hardly think that Amis meant to suggest there were. In any case, Hemans's poem offers no resistance to its own superficialities. The bland verbal surface is the index of the poem's sentimental attachments to its subjects.

AM. Those are the judgments of a mind schooled in twentieth-century critical canons. But perhaps, by invoking them before this poem, you have merely made it impossible to see or read "The Homes of England," which evidently works through conventions not favored by classical modernist styles. Pound, Eliot, Yeats, Stevens, Auden: these are the wrong points of departure for an encounter with Hemans.

If we want to read her, we would do better to start from the expectations and conventions of an early postmodern style like that of John Ashbery or — Ashbery's precursor in these matters — Gertrude Stein.

Hemans's poetry covets an undisturbed appearance: "bland," your word, is a fair description, just as it is a word one sees applied fairly often to Ashbery. Nineteenth-century readers of Hemans repeatedly remark on this quality in her work when they praise its "elegance," its "purity," its "taste" and "harmony." Francis Jeffrey's once famous 1829 review of *Records of Woman* and *The Forest Sanctuary* typifies this now forgotten tradition of reading. Hemans's poetry, he says, is

> regulated and harmonised by the most beautiful taste. It is singularly sweet, elegant, and tender — touching, perhaps, and contemplative, rather than vehement and overpowering; and . . . finished throughout with an exquisite delicacy, and even severity of execution.[8]

With due allowance made for the differences between a Romantic and a Modern dialect, this passage might easily be applied to the work of Gertrude Stein. The critical terms here all carry a double burden, in that they are addressing at once the aesthetic and the moral qualities of the verse. Jeffrey's commentary shows that he refuses to distinguish the two. In this respect the analysis rhymes with its poetical subject. Not only is there to be no apparent divorce between content and form in this work, that wedding is to be celebrated in an equally intimate relation with moral and spiritual values.

"The very essence of poetry," Jeffrey observes (sounding not a little like Coleridge), "consists in the fine perception and vivid expression of that subtle and mysterious Analogy which exists between the physical and the moral world." Because Jeffrey finds this axiom perfectly illustrated in Hemans's work, he praises its harmony, regularity, and delicacy — the latter (its delicacy) because Hemans has managed not only to execute the Analogy, but to convey its "subtle and mysterious" character as well. What Jeffrey calls her "deep moral and pathetic impression" (475) — her elegiac tone, the emotional sign of a condition or experience of inveterate loss — places her work in the center of the romantic tradition, which Hemans of course consciously appropriates.

GM. She sounds to me like a debased Wordsworth: "Accomplishment without genius, and amiability without passion" is how I should characterize her writing. She "expresses with the richest intensity the more superficial and transient elements of Romanticism. She is at the beck and call of whatever is touched with the pathos of the far away, the bygone. . . . Her imagination floats romantically aloof from actuality, but it quite lacks the creative energy of the great Romantics, and her fabrics are neither real substance nor right dreams."[9]

AM. That is not the Hemans Wordsworth elegized in his famous lines about her:

> Mourn rather for that holy Spirit,
> Sweet as the spring, as ocean deep;
> For Her who, ere her summer faded,
> Has sunk into a breathless sleep. ("Extempore Effusion Upon the
>   Death of James Hogg" 37–40)

Besides, a work like "The Homes of England" illustrates the special paradox of a style that seems at once so rich and so empty. The poem is a celebration, but an indirect celebration. A superficial reading will only see it as a piece of sentimental Burkean ideology, a hymn in praise of the values of vertical and horizontal social continuities, and a statement of their perduring strength. But the poem is actually a celebration not of those ideological reference points but of the images and forms the ideology requires for its sustenance.

"The Homes of England," that is to say, operates at two interconnected semiological levels: the linguistic level and the level of an iconic semiology of architecture. This is another of Hemans's superficially superficial poems. It is a poem evoking the superficiality of those apparently substantial things (language and architecture), and the substantiality of those apparently intangible things (ideas and moral attitudes).

To say that "her fabrics are neither real substance nor right dreams" seems to me exactly right, though in my view to say this is also to explain why the work is important rather than why it should be dismissed. Hemans's poetry does not respect the distinction between substance and shadow that is posited in those anomalous Keatsian terms "real substance" and "right dreams." In her poetry what appears as substance is imagined on the brink of its dissolution, just as what comes as shadow continually refuses to evaporate. This is why she says that she has "a heart of home, though no home be for it here" (Harriett Hughes, *Memoir of the Life* 188): like the stately houses reimaged through her poem, Hemans's works understand that they are haunted by death and insubstantialities. And like Tennyson's *Idylls of the King,* her work is a vision of the doom of an order of values which it simultaneously, and paradoxically, celebrates as a solid and ascendant order of things.

Mrs. Hemans herself commented on these paradoxical experiences of substantial apparitions and superficial superficialities in one of her notebooks:

> Our home! — what images are brought before us by that one word! The meeting of cordial smiles, and the gathering round the evening hearth, and the

interchange of thoughts and kindly words, and the glance of eyes to which our hearts lie open as the day; — there is the true "City of Refuge;" — where are we to turn when it is shut from us or changed? Who ever thought his home could change? And yet those calm, and deep, and still delights, over which the world seems to have no breath of power, they too are like the beautiful summer clouds, tranquil as if fixed to sleep for ever in the pure azure of the skies, yet all the while melting from us, though imperceptibly "passing away!" (*Memoir of the Life* 131)

In a letter of 1829 she commented on her "passion for intellectual beauty" as an ambiguous gift and compared it to a "rainbow, made up of light and tears." This evaporating imagination, so close to Shelley's, acquires an entirely different character when it is carried out in the tents of prosperity, in the stately homes of England:

I heard a beautiful remark made by the Chief Justice, when I met him at Kilfane. I think it was with regard to some of Canova's beautiful sculpture in the room, that he said — "Is not *perfection always affecting?*" I thought he was quite right; for the highest degree of beauty in art certainly always excites, if not tears, at least the inward feeling of tears. (*Memoir of the Life* 249)

Hemans's comments help to explain (and expand) the relation Jeffrey and others have noticed between the melancholy of her work and its exquisite surface. Hers is a "finished" poetry, in both senses — an imagining of ultimate loss through the presentation of ultimate forms of gain.

No one ever thinks her home can change until she escapes the imagination of the home's substantiality. In *Brideshead Revisited*, Waugh's hero Charles Ryder loves the "buildings that grew silently with the centuries, catching and keeping the best of each generation." England once "abounded" in such forms of a stable and continuous social fabric, Charles thinks, but now they seem so fragile that he must "salute their achievements at the moment of extinction" (226–27).

Charles dates the period of dissolution in the Edwardian age, but Hemans knows better. Her superior knowledge comes from her understanding that the stately homes and all that we associate with them are only signifying systems. Hemans distances and reimagines the stately home by raising it up again in the form of an ideological network, a system of images and signs. In that condition the home as figure of continuity and substance is already actively "melting from us."

This is the experience set forth in Hemans's poetry, and this is why the stately homes of England are the perfect topic for such an act of reimagination. Although those edifices were always homes, they were also always emblematic forms, part of a non-linguistic and widely dispersed system of social signification. The great English houses "were not originally . . . just large houses in the country in which rich people lived. Essentially they were power houses." In this respect they functioned at two related levels, one administrative, the other ideological. The country house was "the headquarters from which land was administered and power used," of course, but it was also "a show-case" and "an image-maker" through which to display the credentials of power (see Girouard, *Life in the English Country House* 2–3).

From at least as early as the seventeenth century, the discourse of the stately home and the country house was firmly in place. The contemporary tourist is no more than the latest representative of a long tradition of people who would visit such places not as guests but as spectators. Ladies and gentlemen regularly went on trips to celebrated and picturesque country homes, as we know from Pepys and other diarists. Dudley Ryder's diary for 1 June 1817 is the record of a picnic to Dyrham Park in Glouchestershire by himself and a company of his friends (see Lees-Milne, *The Country House* 97).

But even the guests in a stately home behaved as observers, judges, and interpreters. This happened because such places were always on display — indeed, were conceived and constructed, from the very first, as demonstrative and signifying forms. When Henry James describes his experience of Compton Wynyates, in Warwickshire, he says "It is impossible to imagine a more perfect picture" (*Portraits of Places,* quoted in Lees-Milne 9). James is looking at an aesthetic and symbolic object — something that is understood to have been imagined, and hence as a signifying thing.

GM. Are you arguing that Hemans's poetry is valuable because it is clichéd and sentimental?

AM. No, I am arguing that Hemans's is a poetry of quotation, a conscious elevation of various inherited and signifying signs. I do not mean so much her language as the materials and topics she handles. She favors the representation of legendary materials because what is legendary (whether ancient or modern) is already seen to be quoted. Furthermore, to be able to "quote" from what appears to be real — which is what happens not only in a poem like "The Homes of England" but in her many historical texts — is to erode the distinction between what is real and what is mediated, between referent and sign, between acts and texts.

As for Hemans's language as such, it is not in fact clichéd and conventional, it is rather a vision and prophecy of such things, and of the significance of such things. It appears as a poetry asking to be repeated, rewritten, recited. Her poetry is not clichéd and sentimental, as many have charged, it is a prolepsis of the ideas of cliché and sentimentality. In the work's actual achievement, therefore, in its century of success and imitation and repetition, Hemans executes a remarkable critique of the ideology of cultural endurance — a critique all the more stunning for its domesticity and lack of pretension. Modernism and its muscular academic spokesmen would labor to sweep away Hemans's poetry in order to preserve and re-establish the romance of art's power, and of Power's art — that is to say, in order to preserve the illusion of such things. These are not illusions that can endure — in either sense of that word — Hemans's cabinets of perfection and polished surfaces. They are not illusions that can endure her success, or the success which her own work prophecies for them.[10]

Hemans's work is not so elaborate an achievement as Tennyson's, nor so demonic as D. G. Rossetti's. But it is the same order of achievement, and coming at the beginning of the Victorian Age, it announces much of what the poetry of that age had to bring. Idolatries, monuments, and illusions: one of the great missions of Victorian poetry was to expand itself in the service of such things, and to leave, thereby, little room for reimagining them as anything but whited sepulchres.

The poet of all that is admirable, exquisite, and celebrated, Hemans saw deeply into a (textual as well as human) condition governed by attributions and adjectives:

> A moment's transient entertainment — scarcely even that at times, is the utmost effect of things that "come like shadows, so depart." Of all things, never may I become that despicable thing, a woman living upon admiration! (*Memoir of the Life* 188).

And yet this result would be, like that of her age, her fate. As her fame grew during that now forgotten decade, the 1820s, she came to lament "the weary part of *femme célèbre*, which I am now enacting." More and more, like some prescience of Emily Dickinson, she shrank from leaving the narrow confines of her house: "my heart is with those home enjoyments, and there, however tried, excited, and wrung, it will ever remain" (*Memoir of the Life* 189; see also 169–70). That last remark is particularly telling for the way it probes painfully for the truth of her own most cherished fiction, the fiction of the stable and love-founded hearth.

GM. An elegant reading, but also a sublimed and generalized reading — a reading, indeed, after the manner of Francis Jeffrey, or Arnold, or any number of other nineteenth-century critics. In avoiding a close examination of the poem's language you betray the illusion of your reading. "The Homes of England" will not stay for a close critical exploration carried out in the manner of Brooks's and Warren's *Understanding Poetry.*

AM. My commentary was not meant to be exhaustive. I was simply sketching a framework where the poem's more localized and particular details might be able to be reimagined. But a "close" linguistic reading of the kind you want would not be difficult to develop.

One could begin, for instance, with the poem's determined resort to a certain kind of diction: words like "greensward," "gladsome," and "hamletfanes," along with their equivalent syntactical units ("O'er all the pleasant land," "Some glorious page of old"). The text comes before us as a careful reconstruction made from materials that in 1827 are not only "legend laden" but *evidently* legend laden. Unlike Keats, Hemans does not strive after "right dreams" or lament their loss; her poem accepts from the start that these kinds of social dreams are the constructions not of the unconsciousness but of the consciousness, even of the super-ego. Their conscious origin is the source of their extreme fragility.

In that context, lines like "Or lips move tunefully along / Some glorious page of old" begin to float free, like ghosts seeking their local habitations and their names. The "glorious page of old" snatches vainly for a specific referent—in real history (perhaps some act of public service in war); in some book or record of the event itself, perhaps an old ballad; in the text of Hemans's poem, which may be imagining its own recitation, its setting to music by someone in the future. The eternal present imagined by the poem calls out each of these possibilities, but in doing so it pulls itself into its own imagining. "The Homes of England" itself becomes one of the glorious pages of old, and the lips that move along its evanescent surface are the lips of shades. The poem's eternal present is what Keats earlier called a "pleasant death," but in Hemans's case we are left with no room for imagining that death as anything but an unreality. The poem that begins "The stately Homes of England! / How beautiful they stand" does not, as Byron once put it, "c[o]me like truth, and disappear . . . like dreams"; it comes as a dream from the start, and what it announces is the fading of the "truth" of the dream, the emergence of the dream as a construct.

Who, then, is the "God" referred to in the poem's last line? The "country" is named—it is "England"—but that word, by the end of the poem, has acquired the same kind of nominal existence as everything else in the poem. The god of this work, we might want to say, is Felicia Hemans—

a mother-god answering the calls of the children evoked in the poem's penultimate line. That reading works because it is so consonant with Hemans's fundamental myth of domesticity — and, of course, because Hemans is this text's constructor. But in a poem built up through citation and recitation, Hemans can seem no more than a local deity in an odd kind of pantheistic landscape — or I should say, "textscape." The god of "The Homes of England" is one whose center is nowhere and whose circumference is everywhere. Many would see him as a certain set of social relations and social values — a god very like Jehovah, with his chosen people, his favored nation. In our critical age, he is usually called Ideology.

The great tradition of Cynical philosophy held that one did not philosophize in order to learn how to live, one had first to live and then come later to study and reflect upon that condition of our human being. I am reminded of the Cynical view here because I think one cannot begin a close study of Hemans's work, or of the work of any poet for that matter, until one enters into its life. And you cannot even hope for such an event if you come to Hemans forearmed with the knowledge and truth you think you have acquired.

JJR. I applaud you, Anne. What a splendid reading. Not merely inventive but perverse, not merely perverse but utterly resolute in its perversity. What you say is too good to be true. Which makes it, in a certain sense, even better than if it *were* true.

GM. Is Jay right, is this reading of yours just a critical game? If you're serious I simply say this: I have great difficulty imagining Felicia Hemans as essential reading, even in a radically reorganized canon.

AM. It might prove less difficult if we remembered what sort of values the received canon, from which she was expelled, has come to stand for — and perhaps has always stood for.

GM. Fair enough. But then you will have to make more clear, at least for me, what place *your* Felicia Hemans might occupy in a reimagined canon. You may think that I have appropriated too much of the traditional (masculine) framework for reading literary texts, but your own commentary is hardly innocent in this regard. It is in many ways little more than a classic example of Adornian negative dialectics. The sentimentality of Hemans's poem, in this reading, seems devoid of positive values. It serves merely as a stylistic device for critique and deconstruction. Are those the banners under which your feminist program means to march?

AM. One of the most impressive things about Hemans's poetry is the difference it marks off from the conventions of most Modernist styles in art.

Stein, of course, is the great exception — and (of course) Stein is about as far removed from our canonical views of Modernism as Hemans is from our literary histories of 1815–1835. In "The Homes of England" sentiment is revealed as a ghostly presence, like everything else; but if it comes only in apparitional forms, the poem has not, at any rate, abandoned its faith in what its own sentimentality stands for: an imagination of a communal world held together by sympathy.

GM. But in Hemans's poem it is a sympathy without an object — a kind of abstract sympathy.

AM. Yes, but that is not to be taken simply as a critique of the poetry. It comprises, rather, a definition of the world of Hemans's experience. From our vantage this experience may seem threadbare and limited — as if it were unable wholly to resist its own adverse experiences, the way we imagine Dickinson and Stein did. And so we would say of Hemans that she is not, perhaps, so great a writer as Dickinson or Stein, that she became too much of what she beheld. That is certainly my view. But it is also my view that what Hemans has to offer is distinctive and important.

GM. It can be had for the asking in the magazines and annuals of the nineteenth century.

AM. You are wrong. There is a great deal of what has been called "sentimental verse" in those magazines and annuals, but if you read much of it — by the way, *have* you read it? — you may begin to see the work differently. It is by no means so uniform as (y)our literary histories suggest. In any case, the whole question of the sentimental in poetry needs to be rethought and the relevant texts reread.[11]

GM. And then what? I think then we shall see Hemans's poems sink back into their former "breathless sleep."

AM. We shall see.

Notes

1. Printed privately in Florence in 1785, the volume launched what would become the most important literary movement of the 1790s. See Edward E. Bostetter, "The Original Della Cruscans and the *Florence Miscellany*."

2. For a relevant discussion of Byron's "Fare Thee Well!" see Jerome J. McGann, "What Difference Do the Circumstances of Publication Make to the Interpretation of a Literary Work?"

3. This is very clear, for example, in Herbert Butterfield's account of the rise of modern historical scholarship. See his *Man on His Past: The Study of Historical Scholarship*, especially 1–26, 44, 50.

4. For particular discussions, see Emery Neff, *The Poetry of History: The Contribution of Literature and Literary Scholarship to the Writing of History Since Voltaire*; Peter Hans Reill, *The German Enlightenment and the Rise of Historicism*; Max Wehrli, *Johann Jakob Bodmer und die Geschichte der Literatur*; F. A. Wolf, *Prolegomena to Homer: 1795.*

5. See especially Elinor Shaffer, *"Kubla Khan" and The Fall of Jerusalem* and Jerome McGann, "The Ancient Mariner: The Meaning of the Meanings."

6. See Roger Lonsdale, *The New Oxford Book of Eighteenth Century Verse* and *Eighteenth-Century Women Poets: An Oxford Anthology.*

7. The poem was first published in 1827 in *Blackwood's Magazine*; Hemans printed it again the following year as the first of the "Miscellaneous Pieces" in her *Records of Woman: With Other Poems.*

8. From the *Edinburgh Review* 50 (1829), reprinted in *Contributions to the Edinburgh Review by Francis Jeffrey* 474.

9. GM is quoting C. H. Hereford's judgment of Hemans set forth in *The Age of Wordsworth* (1897). See George Benjamin Woods, *English Poetry and Prose of the Romantic Movement* 1271.

10. Noel Coward's wonderful parody of "The Homes of England," in his *Operette* 53–56 is by no means simply a farcical destruction of the original poem. The parody travesties Hemans's work in order to resurrect the central ideas of the poem in another quarter and on new terms. *Operette* is a celebration of the power, and the necessity, of maintaining appearances. In Coward's play, the standard for a saving artificiality is located in the "low" world of the stage and music hall, not in the insignia of the aristocracy. By inverting the apparitional terms of Hemans's poems, this transformation gives an explicit form to ("explicates") what Hemans was doing in more indirect ways.

11. For some efforts in this direction, see Anne K. Mellor, ed., *Romanticism and Feminism*; Marlon B. Ross, *The Contours of Masculine Desire: Romanticism and the Rise of Women's Poetry*; Laura Claridge and Elizabeth Langdon, eds., *Out of Bounds: Male Writers and Gender(ed) Criticism.*

Julie Ellison

The Politics of Fancy in the Age of Sensibility

I. "Sovereigns of the Regions of Fancy"

Given the familiar personae attributed to aesthetic modes in the late eighteenth century — the masculine agonistics of sublime negativity, the restful feminine tint of beauty's curvilinear surfaces, the shaggy and accessible picturesque — what "character" do we attribute to fancy?

By the late eighteenth century, fancy was established in aesthetic writings as an inferior but therapeutic faculty. Definitions of fancy take the form of catalogues of verbs referring to things done to images and ideas: aggregating, associating, collecting, combining, connecting, disposing, embellishing, mixing (Engell, *The Creative Imagination* 172–96). Fancy treats experience as matter that can be manipulated but not transformed. It conforms to the process of intellectual sorting — arrangement, classification, and comparison — that constituted the methodological core of the human sciences. When speeded up, these pleasurable and empowering mental acts give fancy its dynamic structure. The link to play or performance is made possible by the virtuoso quickness of fancy's work; the instantaneousness of fancy's rapid substitutions give it its ephemeral or airy quality. As the motion from one image to another, it has no substance or content of its own, despite the materiality of the particular representations in which it deals.[1] I want to shift away from the implications of fancy in romantic aesthetics, on which I have been drawing so far, to its status in the surrounding culture of sensibility — a culture that begins earlier and extends later than any chronology of romanticism, a culture of which romanticism, I now believe, forms one episode. Sensibility is not simply a taste for pathos but a varied, contested, and ambivalent discourse of emotional action. Authors working in the languages of sensibility not only deploy its conventions, but comment on their conventionality. The poetry of victimage and pity, tears and melancholia, is troubled by the ethics of affect and is sophisticated about the market for literary suffering.

Sensibility, moreover, is almost by definition the culture of a colonial, mercantile empire. It is an international style, both in the sense of being adopted elsewhere than in England, often by creole literati, and also in the sense of being *about* what we would now call multicultural experience. The literature of sensibility is inconceivable without victims and its victims are typically foreign, low, or otherwise alien and estranged.

In light of the imperial economy of victimage, the flourishing of fancy in the poetry of sensibility is somewhat unexpected. For fancy would appear to be exactly the antithesis of pity, the opposite of the melancholia induced by contemplating imperial guilt. But fancy, despite its status as a victimless form of imagination, enters into the texts of sensibility as an event in a narrated or performed sequence of emotional experiences. It operates both as an antidote to melancholy and as a condition allied to pathos. In the process, it retains the vertical, almost sublime associations implied by the phrase, *flight of fancy*.

As imaginative exercise, fancy is bound up with the prospect, the view from mental heights. Fancy flies and finds itself staging "the magnitude of prospect a rising empire displays" and commenting on visions of imperial time in tones ranging from elegy to celebration, from apocalypse to panegyric.[2] John Barrell has shown to what extent the prospect signifies class privilege (*English Literature in History* 54–61, 71–79). In the later eighteenth century, this empowering potential goes beyond landscape poetry to operate in the staging of historical and cultural overviews, and thus enters into visions of empire and imperial time in poetic (and other) genres that share a repertoire of prospective scenarios. In these historical or geographical prospects, fancy meets politics. Situated in retirement but rising to survey international or even cosmic change, the fanciful poet-speaker relies often on the opportunities of the pastoral in order to frame an inclusive perspective. Panoramas of the progress of empire and of poetry, the big pictures of civilization's ebb and flow, bring into fancy's view vignettes of the other. And with the appearance of a stereotypical sufferer, fancy modulates into sensibility.

The generative moments of imperial sensibility are also bound up with the question of gender. Rethinking the history of sensibility means acknowledging that masculine sensibility, with its origins in the late seventeenth century, emerges prior to forms of sensibility later coded as feminine. The tears and sighs of the virtuous man persist, despite anxieties about "feminization," to become a fundamental component of Anglo-American masculine cultural practices. All the constituent factors of sensibility I have outlined above — melancholy, the reflexive imagination, and the representation of the other—operate in works by men throughout the eighteenth century in identifiably masculine ways. If texts by men reveal a wide array of gendered relationships to pathos and literary aspiration, as they certainly do—if, in other words, there is a masculine difference, as in the tonalities of Kenneth Silverman's "Whig Sentimentalism" (*Cultural History* 82–87)[3]— then the task of describing the politics of sensibility in works by women cannot depend on simple gender dichotomies. It becomes a process, rather, of discerning how sensibility can become, under certain circumstances, an idiom of female ambition and citizenship, invested in national success, as well as a means of resistance.

Through the geography of prospect, fancy temporarily fuses imperial and lyric consciousness in key episodes of poems by women. The activities of "fancy," "reflection," "meditation," and "imagination" that structure the reader's progress through a text have different meanings depending on the gender and position of the speaking subject.[4] These choreographies of invention are bound up with the speaker's desire to conceive a world and to move actively within it. The prospect often furthers the female author's quest for a reading audience or for critical respect earned by taking on public matters, including evangelism, abolition, and the early anthropology of Native Americans.[5] Ambition and fancy often come together in authentically self-conscious moments. "Suffer me to ask," writes Judith Sargent Murray in the *Massachusetts Magazine* of March–April 1790, "in what the minds of females are so notoriously deficient, or unequal. . . . The province of imagination hath long since been surrendered up to us, and we have been crowned undoubted sovereigns of the regions of fancy."[6] How does sovereignty become part of how creativity itself is represented in poems by women? How are historical prospects assigned to fancy, pity, and "musing," and what are the affinities between these conventions and specific emotional and political content?

The studies of Anna Barbauld and Phillis Wheatley that follow are meant to introduce the eighteenth-century strategies that connect the aesthetics of sensibility, always gendered, with a self-consciousness of being implicated in national and international systems. Barbauld's first verse collection, *Poems,* and Phillis Wheatley's only volume of poetry, *Poems on Various Subjects,* were both published in London in 1773. Both volumes were fostered or subsidized by sophisticated transatlantic cultural networks: in Barbauld's case by the community of intellectuals centered in English dissenting academies; in Wheatley's by her looser connections, though her Boston owners, to the evangelist George Whitefield, whom she eulogized, and to the Countess of Huntingdon, the Methodist sponsor she never met. The idioms common to the poetry of Barbauld and Wheatley—common to a surprising degree, though exaggerated by my emphasis on their resemblances—point to a broadly disseminated literary vocabulary that connects the history of feminine authorship to racial politics.

II. Barbauld: "The Intervention of a Lady-Author"

Barbauld's poetry demonstrates the way the motions of fancy can lead both to and away from questions of public policy. In many instances her sensibility is reflexive, not social. What is other to the self takes the form of transcendental or descendental motion, an altered state of consciousness, the spirit's own spatial or temporal prospects. In "A Summer Evening's Meditation" (1773; see full text below), the relationship between fancy and sympathy is narrated by a contemplative female speaker. Impelled by fancy's vertical activity, the speaker rises from the "green borders of the peopled Earth" past Jupiter's "huge gigantic bulk," and beyond to "the dim verge, the suburbs of the system," where Saturn presides "like an exiled monarch" (*Works* 1: 122–29, ll. 73–78). The structure of meditative action in the cosmic system matches the drama of historical vision in other poems by Barbauld in which fancy brings before the reader vignettes of earthly systems: slavery, trade, and cultural transmission. In "A Summer Evening's Meditation," however, fancy leads lyric subjectivity, or intersubjectivity, through the cosmos in search of its own powers and limits. Here fancy finds vistas that connect it to epic aspiration through resemblances to Milton's tours of space, and link it to the history of Europe's geopolitical prospects, as well. There is a clear correlation between cosmic place and power relations: Jupiter is central and dominant; Saturn is dethroned and suburban, in the long-standing negative sense of "the suburbs."

Even more striking than the political geography of center and suburb are the implications of another term, "the system." For sensibility is bound up with notions of interdependent structures and economies, the circulatory systems that no liberal author feels able to escape. The culture of vicariousness includes experiences of desire, projection, and substitution that complicate the whole spectrum of subject positions. We are tempted to think of a writer like Barbauld as being within the system, and a writer like Wheatley as being marginal to it. But, as R. Radhakrishnan has observed with reference to postcolonial studies, both "mobilizing the inner/outer distinction" and rejecting "the politics of location" (Adrienne Rich's term) in favor of "radical relationality" pose "serious representational problems" for the scholar ("Nationalism, Gender, and the Narrative of Identity" 81–84). If I cannot resolve this conundrum here, I can at least extend it backward and use Radhakrishnan's dilemma in exploring both the critical status of female poets and the positions of the speaking subject in their works. The dynamics of eighteenth-century sensibility, like the strategies of twentieth-century cultural criticism, rely on the logic of center and margin while simultaneously incorporating both positions into a relational field.

The action of "A Summer Evening's Meditation" centers on the figure of Contemplation. Emerging from her grotto, Contemplation directs the poet/speaker to gaze on the night sky: "with radiant finger points / To yon blue concave swelled by breath divine" (ll. 24–25). When her "unsteady eye . . . wanders unconfined / O'er all this field of glories," the speaker characterizes the "spacious field" of starry "hieroglyphics" as a "tablet" that has been "hung on high / To public gaze." Human viewers are characterized collectively as the "public" that looks upon "the Master." His message is, "Adore, O man! / The finger of thy God" (ll. 28–35). The public, then, including the speaker, is defined by its relationship to elevated power. Contemplation needs the authority of the celestial text in order to create a spatial arena vast enough for the subjective expansion that follows. The upward wanderings of the "Restless and dazzled" eye require the "blue concave swelled by breath divine" (ll. 29, 24).

But this vertical thought sets in motion the process of interiorization that typically complicates fancy's prospective strategy. Elevated perspectives make possible the downward gaze of maternal stars, "pure wells / Of milky light," "friendly lamps" that "light us to our home" (ll. 35–39). The speaker has almost circled back where she began, in Contemplation's "lonely depth / Of unpierc'd woods" (ll. 18–19). Down here in Nature's "thick-wove foliage," the proper language is not the hieroglyphic text spread before the public eye (l. 44). The speaker, instead of intensely looking, is "[i]ntensely listening": "the raised ear . . . drinks in every breath" and hears nature praised by the voice of silence itself and by a "tongue in every star that talks with man" (ll. 45–46, 50). The reader anticipates more gazing at the sky; "Wisdom mounts her zenith with the stars" and we expect the speaker to ride right along (l. 52). She does end up on another vertical trajectory, but the movement is circuitous. Deep space and deep time are now interior to the subject, or, in Barbauld's phrase, to "the self-collected soul":

At this still hour the self-collected soul
Turns inward, and beholds a stranger there
Of high descent, and more than mortal rank;
An embryo God; a spark of fire divine,
Which must burn on for ages, when the sun

. . . .

Has closed his golden eye (ll. 53–59)

This passage characterizes the meditative faculty as turning inward to behold an alienated self-image. The soul is pregnant with itself. But this fiery selfhood has to be a "stranger" of "high descent" in order to give the speaker genealogical access to the "ages." This strange son, the soul's soul, enables a passionately speculative episode.

Looking in, or down, at herself provides a second opportunity for vertical recoil, one that reveals how closely related ambition and tenderness toward the self can be. The speaker links herself temporally and spatially to the "citadels of light" once more, imagining herself at home not in the starlit plane of earthly nature, but up there, in "my *future* home, from whence the soul, / Revolving periods past, may oft look back" (emphasis added; ll. 61–63). Picturing herself at this heavenly remove again provokes gratitude for motherly care, this time extended by the speaker to her own mortal experience, which she will someday regard tenderly "As . . . some fond and doting tale that soothed / Her infant hours" (ll. 67–68). But this hypothetical vista is inadequate to the soul's ambitions, and Barbauld collapses the time frame from the "future" to "now" in the next phrase: "O be it lawful *now* / To tread the hallowed circle of your courts" (emphasis added; ll. 68–69). The speaker gives herself over to fancy's most grandiose possibilities:

Seiz'd in thought,
On Fancy's wild and roving wing I sail,
From the green borders of the peopled Earth,
And the pale Moon, her duteous fair attendant;
From solitary Mars; from the vast orb
Of Jupiter, whose huge gigantic bulk
Dances in ether like the lightest leaf;
To the dim verge, the suburbs of the system[.] (ll. 71–78)

We know this is still the aesthetic of fancy rather than that of the sublime because Jupiter's "huge gigantic bulk" is perspectively transformed into familiar diminutives. Here, as in so many other fanciful poems of the period, "wild and roving" fancy generates figures of motion and ethereality, with both of these compressed into the image of the almost weightless, wind-driven leaf.

But Barbauld's fancy requires a "gigantic" cosmos in which to enact the tension between "beyonding" and diminution. In her tour of the "system," she passes one patriarchal form after another, from "solitary Mars" to Jupiter and finally "cheerless Saturn" (l. 79). Having gone beyond these depressing hulks, the contemplative soul is further exhilarated: "fearless thence / I launch into the trackless deeps of space" (ll. 81–82). Among "ten thousand suns," she reaches the first of two crises of confidence (l. 83). "Here must I stop," she thinks, then asks, "Or is there aught beyond?" To ask about "aught beyond" is already to be in the grip of a "hand unseen" (ll. 89–90). And here the speaker encounters the embryo god again. The soul finds itself in a version of the womblike space that had represented subjective coherence at the beginning of fancy's galactic voyage. She is impelled onward

> To solitudes of vast unpeopled space,
> The desarts of creation, wide and wild;
> Where embryo systems and unkindled suns
> Sleep in the womb of chaos (ll. 94–97)

Fancy travels through its own reproductive zone, its chaotic womb, where the systems that consciousness will continue to explore take shape. Passages like this make it difficult to decide what is internal and what external, what psychological and what public in this poem. And it is difficult not just for the twentieth-century reader, but also for Barbauld. Confronted with its own inside as the ultimate outside, or vice versa, the soul reaches its second, and decisive, crisis of confidence: "fancy droops, / And thought astonished stops her bold career" (ll. 97–98).

In fact, fancy does not just "droop"; it all at once abases itself. The speaker recoils from fertile chaos to the more definite intimidations of Jehovah. Shifting to prayerful address, she apostrophizes the creator's "mighty mind": "Where shall I seek thy presence," she queries, still disoriented, then wonders how, "unblamed," she is going to "[i]nvoke thy dread perfection?" (ll. 99–102). The only thing the soul can be blamed for is its vertical path, a conclusion verified by the rapidity with which the meditative speaker now locates herself distinctly below divinity:

> O look with pity down
> On erring, guilty man! not in thy names
> Of terror clad; not with those thunders armed
> That conscious Sinai felt, when fear appalled
> The scattered tribes; — thou hast a gentler voice,
> That whispers comfort to the swelling heart,
> Abash'd, yet longing to behold her Maker. (ll. 105–11)

The "bold career" of fancy reaches its limits when "thought" cannot go further back than the generative "desarts of creation." This limit is called transgressive, and the chaotic womb is superseded by a single origin, "Thou mighty mind." The speaker collapses "appalled" before the deity's "names / Of terror," then renames divinity for its "gentler," internal voice, that heart-intuited whisper not unlike the stars' tongues that wooed her earlier. The poem concludes rapidly in a chastened and not much comforted key. The "soul, unused to stretch her powers / In flight so daring, drops her weary wing." She plants herself firmly in "the known accustomed spot" that sheltered the figure of Contemplation at the beginning of the poem, the landscape of "sun, and shade, and lawns, . . . streams," and "mansion" (ll. 112–16). Here she will wait for vision to come to her, "When all these splendours bursting on my sight / Shall stand unveiled, and to my ravished sense / Unlock the . . . world unknown" (ll. 120–22).

"A Summer Evening's Meditation" dramatizes an encounter between the poetry of contemplation and the poetry of prospects. Fancy emerges from a fostering nocturnal environment to undertake a prospective mission. Such endeavors derive in part from the poetry of British prospects and polite indolence described by Barrell; they also descend from *Paradise Lost,* where elevated surveys are prophetic or satanic. Barbauld entertains the class-inflected perspective for which the view from on high, an expanded subjectivity, is the goal of leisure thought. She also makes it look as though this expansive mind is alternately bullied and lured into humility by the combined voices of Old and New Testament deities. But the initial shock comes a few lines earlier, when fancy encounters deep space. It is unclear whether it is the cosmic vacuum — "solitudes of vast unpeopled space" — or the cosmic "womb" and its plenitude of "embryo systems" that "stops" fancy cold. Since the "fearless" speaker has already braved "the trackless deeps of space," emptiness does not seem to be the problem. Rather, having traveled across the whole cosmic system, the speaker confronts the source of future worlds in a kind of infinite regress, systems within systems. That

abstract term, "systems," marks a conceptual limit of prospective meditation experienced as panic or extreme alienation. The fertile womb of deep
space is feminine and nocturnal, like the groves from which fancy departed
at the beginning of the poem. But the horizon of unfolding systems calls up
the patriarchal "mind" and "word" that shut off further speculation: "Thus
let all things be, and thus they were" (l. 100). The tensions among masculine authority, feminine ambition, and an interior space of aesthetic
productivity are played out in the field of cosmic perspectives. The idea of
the system provides an opportunity for the woman writer to expand her
scope, then turns into a conceptual frame she cannot escape.

Before taking up Barbauld's *Eighteen Hundred and Eleven,* in which
fancy's prospect is decisively political, I want to look at another poem in
which she imagines the future of the British system. Barbauld's doubts
about the moral efficacy of the literature of sensibility, expressed in her 1773
essay, "An Enquiry into those kinds of Distress which excite Agreeable
Sensations," recur later in an altered tone (*Miscellaneous Pieces* 190–214). In
"Epistle to William Wilberforce, Esq. on the rejection of the bill for abolish-
ing the slave trade" (1791; *Works* 1: 173–79), she insists that sentimental
portrayals of the victim have failed and replaces them with the systematic
logic of moral economy. But although the conventions of abolitionist
sensibility are declared obsolete, they persist in Barbauld's revisionist alternative. The "Epistle" opens with an exasperated catalogue of speakers
who have used the bodily rhetoric of sensibility on British audiences to
no avail:

> The Preacher, poet, Senator, in vain
> Has rattled in [Britain's] sight the Negro's chain;
> With his deep groans assail'd her startled ear,
> And rent the veil that hid his constant tear;
> Forc'd her averted eyes his stripes to scan,
> Beneath the bloody scourge laid bare the man,
> Claim'd Pity's tear, urged Conscience' strong controul
> And flash'd conviction on her shrinking soul.
> The Muse, too soon awaked, with ready tongue
> At Mercy's shrine applausive peans rung;
> And Freedom's eager sons, in vain foretold
> A new Astrean reign, an age of gold:
> She knows and she persists — Still Afric bleeds,
> Unchecked, the human traffic still proceeds (ll. 3–16)

Barbauld's account of abolitionist writing makes clear the link between vicarious suffering and political criticism. The indignation that causes abolitionists to dwell on "the Negro's" tormented flesh carries over to textual reception. The "scene of distress" "forces" the reader to gaze on the beaten slave and "assails" the audience with his groans. Barbauld characterizes the rhetoric of sensibility as itself a scourge that, like the whip, "lays bare" the suffering body of the reader. Barbauld values the language of Wilberforce and his allies insofar as it amplifies the groans and tears of slaves for the resistant British public. She proclaims the shortcomings of rhetorical flagellation while praising the attempt to make the guilty suffer.

Barbauld attributes the failure of sensibility to inspire legislative action to the systematic effects of slavery itself. "Wit, Worth, and Parts and Eloquence" — a rhetoricians' party — have rallied to Wilberforce's cause: "All, from conflicting ranks, of power possest / To rouse, to melt, or to inform the breast" (ll. 20, 23–24). But against the language of "Avarice," the "Nation's eloquence" fails, and "th'unfeeling sneer / . . . turns to stone the falling tear" (ll. 25, 26, 31–32). Wilberforce's cause is hopeless in the face of the country's immunity to feeling guilty: "In Britain's senate, Misery's pangs give birth / To jests unseemly, and to horrid mirth" (ll. 39–40). Sentimental representations of pain duel with conscious cynicism and lose. Barbauld concludes by urging Wilberforce and his allies to give up: "seek no more to break a Nation's fall, / For ye have sav'd yourselves — and that is all" (ll. 116–17). Britain has accepted itself as a profit-driven society, and against this self-knowledge, or "[t]h'acknowledged thirst of gain," the appeal for vicarious suffering is useless (l. 30).

In the face of the defeated campaign of sensibility, Barbauld prophesies Africa's revenge on Britain through the systematic but internalized operations of empire:

> injur'd Afric, by herself redrest,
> Darts her own serpents at her Tyrant's breast.
> Each vice, to minds depraved by bondage known,
> With sure contagion fastens on his own; (ll. 45–48)

The suburbs of this system poison the capital reflexively, through the numbed emotions and degraded appetites of the slave economy.[7] The East India trade, meanwhile, evicts the figures of "Simplicity," "Stern Independence," and "Freedom" from rural England: "By foreign wealth are British morals chang'd, / And Afric's sons, and India's, smile avenged" (ll. 100–

105; Ross, *The Contours of Masculine Desire*, 221–24). Barbauld blends the conventions of sensibility, which rely on vicarious emotion to induce pity, with the threat of contagious corruption. African slaves and colonized Indians become spectators, as England's free population sinks to the condition of slaves: "Shrieks and yells disturb the balmy air, / Dumb sullen looks of wo announce despair, / And angry eyes thro' dusky features glare" (ll. 81–83). This process of role reversal or poetic justice seems to abandon moral judgment to the impersonal reflexes of economic logic. The shift makes possible a change of tone from pity, directed at generic victims, to prophetic, almost Blakean, exasperation. The "angry eyes" glaring out of the sullen faces of degraded British citizens mark the aggressive potential of sensibility. The victim's body houses rage, not the slave's "constant tear" (l. 6).

Two decades later, Barbauld combined the tension between sensibility and system in the "Epistle to Wilberforce" with the power of fancy in "A Summer Evening's Meditation." In *Eighteen Hundred and Eleven* (*Works* 1: 232–50), the logic of systematic moral correction again prevails in declarations that outraged Barbauld's original readers: "Britain, know, / Thou who has shared the guilt must share the woe" (ll. 45–46). The speaker surveys the empire from India to "the Apalachian hills," evoking the spread of British culture "o'er transatlantic realms" (ll. 83, 111). When the visionary tour speeds up and shifts into an apocalyptic tone, Fancy materializes both to suffer and to stage the show, and finally to offer commentary on it. Weeping Fancy represents the fusion of sensibility and mental voyaging. Fancy, a sentimental reader or, perhaps, theater-goer, travels through time, which takes the form of "imaged" events.

> Where wanders Fancy down the lapse of years,
> Shedding o'er imaged woes untimely tears?
> Fond, moody power! as hopes — as fears prevail,
> She longs, or dreads, to lift the awful veil,
> On visions of delight now loves to dwell,
> Now hears the shriek of woe or Freedom's knell:
> Perhaps she says, long ages past (sic) away,
> And set in western wave our closing day,
> Night, Gothic night, again may shade the plains
> Where Power is seated, and where Science reigns;
> England, the seat of arts, be only known
> by the gray ruin and the mouldering stone;

That Time may tear the garland from her brow,
And Europe sit in dust, as Asia now. (ll. 113–26)

The poem begins with the present Napoleonic wars and details their
human cost abroad and to British families at home. With the accusation
of Britain's guilt, Barbauld starts to prophesy the future doom of the empire, moving between tones of rebuke, "moody" fantasy, and elegiac regret.[8] The nation's literary prestige in its "transatlantic realms" assures its
post-imperial fame even "if't is thy fate / To rank amongst the names that
once were great" (ll. 71–72). With the long passage quoted above, however, more agitated emotions than those already expressed by the speaker
find a vehicle in Fancy. Fancy's emotional volatility transforms prophecy
into a series of competing fictions. Oscillating between "fond" or "moody"
feelings depending on whether hope or fear, longing or dread, delight or
woe, is "imaged" in the scene behind the veil, the figure of Fancy abandons
the narrator's dignified tonalities and overreacts. Her "untimely" passion
over unrealized events climaxes in the vision of a new dark age, a "Gothic
night." The trope refers both to the suspenseful genre of Fancy's sentimental
trepidation and to the historical return of the feudal past. Fancy utters a
vision of the orientalization of the West, which combines the myth of the
stagnant or ahistorical East with the topos of the progressive westering of
empire that leaves lands further east in ruins: "Perhaps, she says, long ages
past away," Europe may "sit in dust, as Asia now."

After speaking as passionate historian in the British present, fancy becomes the agent of American inspiration through Britain's arts. Ages hence,
fanciful young Americans will tour the ruins of empire "just as our young
noblemen go to Greece" (*Quarterly Review* [June 1812]: 311). With "throb-
bing bosoms" and "musing mind[s]" but most of all with fancy's "mingled
feelings," these "wanderers" will visit the remnants of London (ll. 177, 187,
157, 169). Reanimated in the fantasies of tourists, a multiracial capital will
stand for the lost empire. The mixed population of the city and the mingled
feelings of the travelers exemplify fancy's heterogeneous aesthetic:

The mighty city, which by every road,
In floods of people poured itself abroad
Ungirt by walls, irregularly great,
No jealous drawbridge, and no closing gate;
Whose merchants (such the state that commerce brings)
Sent forth their mandates to dependent kings;

> Streets, where the turbaned Moslem, bearded Jew,
> And woolly Afric, met the brown Hindu;
> Where through each vein spontaneous plenty flowed,
> Where Wealth enjoyed, and Charity bestowed. (ll. 159–68)

As Barbauld's retrospective, then prospective narrative continues to unfold, the "Spirit" that roams the earth, "Moody and viewless as the changing wind," governs the progress of empire in its passage through Babel, Egypt, and Troy (ll. 215, 217). In the hands of this "vagrant Power," history appears to be the random consequence of "his changeful fancy": "as some playful child the mirror turns, / Now here, now there, the moving lustre burns" (ll. 259, 263–65). In a fine example of how historical prospects convert heterogeneity to unity, a long passage surveying the complicated mix of cultures from Syria to Scandinavia climaxes in praise of modern British refinement.

At this juncture, Barbauld's "Spirit" acts, not in a "vagrant" manner but in accord with the teleological westerly movement that has character-ized it all along. As "the Genius soars" toward South America — executing a striking swerve away from the devotées of British culture to the North — the systematic justice of imperial decay sets in: "Arts, arms, and wealth destroy the fruits they bring. . . . With grandeur's growth the mass of misery grows" (ll. 321, 315, 320). The Genius of history, in the end, consistently exhibits only one of fancy's attributes, the commitment to a mixed or heterogeneous aesthetic. As this figure "pours through feeble souls a higher life," shedding its transcendental influence on "Andes' heights," "Chim-borazo's summits," and La Plata's "roar," it seems to promise both multi-plicity and manifest destiny (ll. 332, 324, 325, 329). The Genius "Shouts to the mingled tribes from sea to sea / And swears — Thy world, Columbus, shall be free" (ll. 333–34). What kind of resolution, and in what tone, is effected by these paradoxical lines? The Genius lumps "mingled tribes" under the imperial singular ("Thy world, Columbus"), but the energetic new-world mix is never wholly homogenized.

The personified Spirit of historical change, then, has multiple relation-ships with the poetics of fancy. The personification itself is invented by Barbauld's fancy. The vistas of past empire created by fancy turn the faculty into a spectator, and fancy crystallizes briefly as the temporally fluid and over-emotional audience of projected historical scenes. Britain's cultural heirs in North America exhibit a more temperate but still fanciful connois-seurship as they reimagine, among London's future ruins, its present flawed glories. History itself, finally, is an artist in fancy's mode, insofar as it repeatedly creates empires out of "mingled tribes." Racial heterogeneity is a sign of health and energy for Barbauld, but she channels the diverse, lively origins of great cultures into a single historical meaning. "Mingled tribes" are infused with the "higher life" of cultural purpose, with its built-in self-destructive feedback loop.

Barbauld uses the language of fancy to engage the pathos of public time.[9] This strategy characterizes authors of both sexes who mourn the violence of the systems they analyze, who cannot think systematically without pity, or mourn without analysis. Yet when women relied on the politics of fancy, criticism of their positions collapsed into attacks on their sex. Reactions to *Eighteen Hundred and Eleven* conform to party lines. The reviewer for the *Anti-Jacobin* argued that the *Monthly Review* praised the poem only because Barbauld expressed dissenting views. Similarly, Croker's article in the *Quarterly Review* lumped Barbauld with "her renowned compatriot," William Roscoe, whose two pamphlets on Parliamentary reform are critically though affectionately reviewed in the same issue. But while the *Anti-Jacobin* categorized the poem's genre as prophecy and dismissed it as dissenting propaganda, the *Quarterly* called it satire and attacked on grounds of gender: "Our old acquaintance Mrs. Barbauld turned satirist! . . . We had hoped, indeed, that the empire might have been saved without the intervention of a lady-author." And Croker goes on to deplore the "irresistible impulse of public duty — a confident sense of commanding talents" that "induced her to dash down her shagreen spectacles and her knitting needles, and to sally forth . . . in the magnanimous resolution of saving a sinking state, by the instrumentality of . . . a pamphlet in verse."[10] In order to oppose the dissenter, Croker excoriates the woman; in order to turn a poem into a "pamphlet," he calls fancy "satire," a masculine — or rather an unfeminine — literary type. Fancy is deflated so that Croker may claim that *Eighteen Hundred and Eleven* fails because of a mismatch of gender and genre.

III. Wheatley's "Mental Optics"

Phillis Wheatley's *Poems on Various Subjects* was published in the same place (London) and year (1773) as Barbauld's first collection of poems. Her career predates the outpouring of sentimental abolitionist poems by women in the late 1780s, and some of the differences between her stance and those of other poets of the eighties and nineties, including Barbauld's "Epistle," stem from the altered rhetoric of those decades (Moira Ferguson, *Subject to Others* 145–64). Nonetheless her poems, too, are structured by the adventures of self-conscious artistry at work in dilated arenas of space and time. Wheatley's status as emblem of slavery and commentator on tyranny puts her in a charged relation to liberal sensibility. She works with and against British and North American texts in which emotion, art, and otherness go together. She accepts the historical identity of slave while refusing that of victim.

A grasp of the "system" can provide an alternative to victimage as well as being one of the cultural prerequisites for late eighteenth-century scenarios of victimage and sympathy. And so Wheatley typically refuses to read her own captivity as a tragedy and elects as her subject matter the collective pathos of the Atlantic theater, especially that aspect of it which Paul Gilroy has called "the black Atlantic." This set of "stereophonic, bilingual, or bifocal cultural forms," "structures of feeling, producing, communicating and remembering," constitutes, Gilroy argues, the "intercultural positionality of black intellectuals" (*Black Atlantic* 3, 6). Wheatley's understanding of an Atlantic system illuminates, in Gilroy's terms, the "inner dialectics of diaspora identification" (23). With her typical preference for collective over private suffering, Wheatley draws on the available rhetoric of protest to characterize America as the weeping child of Britannia, the colonies' "dear mama" (*Collected Works* 134; "America" 1. 21). In the few passages that do present Wheatley's memories of her enslavement, fancy is momentarily the route to recollected pain. But fancy is also a form of ambitious address. And while the language of this ambition mimes the culture of Wheatley's captors and owners, it also uses Wheatley's own forced transatlantic exposure to justify her historical and spatial reach. Her poetry shifts between optative pressure in its public moments and a severe view of personal sin. It thus avoids the mood of collective imperial guilt that emerges in Barbauld. Or rather, Britain's "tyrannic sway" is exposed, but without Wheatley feeling corrupted by it (*Collected Works:* 74; "To . . . Dartmouth," 1. 31).

To locate sin in the individual spirit rather than in the institution of slavery may be a necessary indirection, marking the limit of the African-American writer's investment in complaint and accusation. Wheatley's principal tonal difference from the gloomier British poets of historical fancy, such as Oliver Goldsmith (*The Deserted Village* had appeared in 1770) or Barbauld, and from North American poets, such as Hugh Henry Brackenridge and Philip Freneau in the first version of *The Rising Glory of*

America (1771) or Freneau alone in "The Power of Fancy" (1770, 1786), lies in the optative pressure of her work. She represents her own poetry as pleasure, adventure, and moral opportunity; she experiences as pure gain the writing of poetry and the transatlantic vision it permits. Donna Landry suggests that Wheatley's mimicry of British styles, her acquiescence to the expectations of white readers, causes her to suppress direct references to the catastrophes she herself has suffered.[11] I propose a somewhat different, though, I think, complementary reading. Refusing to testify to her own victimage makes it possible for Wheatley to address the public preoccupations of the British North Atlantic. Sentimental conventions invite her to display the history of her pain, to stage herself as sufferer. Her resistance is apparent precisely in her reluctance to do so.

A few years after Wheatley's death, and fifteen years after the publication of *Poems on Various Subjects,* Hannah More made the connection between fancy and guilt explicit in her influential *Slavery: A Poem* (1788). More sees into Africa by the power of "more than Fancy" here, meaning that fancy's images have been verified or confirmed, not invalidated:

> Whene'er to Afric's shores I turn my eyes,
> Horrors of deepest, deadliest guilt arise;
> I see, by more than Fancy's mirror shown,
> The burning village and the blazing town:
> See the dire victim torn from social life,
> The shrieking babe, the agonizing wife!
> She, wretch forlorn! is dragg'd by hostile hands,
> To distant tyrants sold, in distant lands!
> Transmitted miseries, and successive chains,
> The sole, sad heritage her child obtains! (*Works of Hannah More* 28;
>   ll. 110–19)

Fancy provides More with vignettes that prove England's guilt, and the "dire victim torn from social life" is the focal point of these evidential scenes. If Wheatley had represented herself as a "wretch forlorn" she would have participated in the rhetoric of vicarious relations. Wheatley avoids mounting such a protest, in which she would have to play the role of both victim and witness. But she does use the available conventions of fancy to link active poetic subjectivity to North Atlantic historical life; indeed, while she makes no effort to hide her slave status, she vigorously embraces the "social life" of Anglo-American culture. She downplays the emotions of and for slavery's victims while exploiting the brief pleasures of fancy's upward rush and of her own entry into public address.[12]

"On Recollection" and "On Imagination," which appear sequentially in *Poems on Various Subjects,* comprise flights of fancy similar to those narrated in Barbauld's "A Summer Evening's Meditation" of the same year. Both of Wheatley's poems link the mind's motion with Fancy's capacity for moral critique. Wheatley's "mental optics" combine inspirational ascent with prospective authority. The poet/speaker of "On Recollection" refers to the "eighteen years" of her own life as an instance of memory's Christian power to expose and judge (*Collected Works* 63, l. 31). Wheatley volunteers this span of time as the object of retrospective scrutiny: "In Recollection see them fresh return, / And sure 'tis mine to be asham'd, and mourn" (ll. 35–36). But aside from her testimony to recollection's power to unveil forgotten things and to inspire penitence, the author's past — the narrative of her enslavement, transportation, purchase, conversion, education, and labor — is suppressed. She announces her race and place of origin when she names herself as the "vent'rous *Afric*" (l. 2). She then goes on to describe recollection's acts of vision without describing the content of what it sees.

Recollection, fancy, and the speaker interact as closely related agents of poetic action. The poet establishes a symbiotic relation to Mneme, the muse of recollection: "Assist my strains," she prays, "while I thy glories sing." Mneme, in turn, recuperates "the acts of long departed years" and sets them "in due order rang'd" before fancy, who presides over the domain of the visible: "the long-forgotten . . . sweetly plays before the *fancy's* sight" (ll. 4–8). Mneme shares fancy's wandering habits and its vertical expansiveness:

> Swift from above she wings her silent flight
> Through *Phoebe's* realms, fair regent of the night;
> And, in her pomp of images display'd,
> To the high-raptur'd poet gives her aid,
> Through the unbounded regions of the mind,
> Diffusing light celestial and refin'd. (ll. 11–16)

By referring to herself in the second line of the poem as the "vent'rous *Afric*" who undertakes a "great design," Wheatley has defined the educated slave's literary venture as the desire for both extension ("great") and coherence ("design"). It is hard to tell the poet from the poet's fancy, and to tell either from recollection. The net effect is of redundant aspiration. If recollection offers the "pomp of images," the "high-raptur'd poet" seems majestic enough already. If recollection diffuses the "celestial" light that turns the mind into deep space, that mind already possesses "unbounded regions" (ll. 13–16).

Design and the view from on high go together. The chief power of recollection turns out to lie in its ability to see the simultaneous operation of different peoples from above: "The heav'nly *phantom* [Mneme] paints the actions done / By ev'ry tribe beneath the rolling sun" (ll. 17–18). And here the pleasurable dilation of fancy's perspectival power changes to judgmental scrutiny that turns the "high-raptur'd poet" into a self-tormented, if representative, sinner. Mneme combines the prospective energy of fancy and the internalized, monitory voice of Christian conscience:

> *Mneme*, enthron'd within the human breast,
> Has vice condemn'd, and ev'ry virtue blest
>
> . . . how is *Mneme* dreaded by the race,
> Who scorn her warnings, and despise her grace?
> By her unveil'd each horrid crime appears,
> Her awful hand a cup of wormwood bears.
> Days, years mispent, O what a hell of woe!
> Hers the worst tortures that our souls can know. (ll. 19–20, 25–30)

When the poet's delighted imagination is grounded, its prospective advantage is converted to discipline. The references to "ev'ry tribe beneath the . . . sun" and to "the race" that ignores its own memories of "crime" suggest that Wheatley has aimed recollection's judgmental force against the internal violence of the culture of slavery. But at precisely this juncture Wheatley offers herself as an example of the mourning induced by "follies . . . / Unnotic'd, but . . . writ in bras!" (l. 34). Just when we think the poet/speaker is forcing onto the white "race" its own repressed memory of the violence done to herself and her "tribe," she refuses this option and turns the force of recollection religiously against herself.

Seeming to veer away from political implication, the poem concludes with a prayer for virtue's revisionary effects: "O *Virtue*," Wheatley prays, "Do thou exert thy pow'r, and change the scene" (ll. 37–38). Virtue becomes the recollective "pow'r enthron'd / In ev'ry breast" and directs "the vengeance of the skies" to the wicked while sheltering the good from heavenly "wrath" (ll. 41–43, 50). Is this a self-wounding swerve away from the collective memory of slavery performed by Christian rationalization, which might hold that the converted (and hence penitent) slave is better off than the free African? Is it a variant of the collapse experienced by Barbauld's fancy, the feminine imagination traumatized by its own "vent'rous" dilations? Or is it a shift away from the historical circumstances that separate Wheatley from her white reading audience by virtue of their transgressions and her victimage, and toward the Christian community of "our souls," of all sinners? Wheatley's performances of the risks and pay-offs of fanciful prospects suggest that she will only articulate resistance or negativity from a perspective of inclusion.

In the next poem in the 1773 volume, "On Imagination," Wheatley gives imagination an empire. She empowers the poet through the aerial adventures of fancy and subjects the speaker, finally, to poetry's antithesis, the inhibition of the wintry north. Wheatley addresses imagination as a faintly orientalized "imperial queen," the queen of prospects, whose "forms" and "acts in beauteous order stand" (*Collected Works* 65; ll. 1–3). Fancy enters both as the means of transport through imagination's empire and as the drama of falling in love with the aesthetic "object":

> Now here, now there, the roving Fancy flies,
> Till some lov'd object strikes her wand'ring eyes,
> Whose silken fetters all the senses bind,
> And soft captivity involves the mind. (ll. 9–12)

Imagination, like Barbauld's "self-collected soul," seeks and finds celestial perspectives. Unintimidated by the "thund'ring God" (l. 13) who serves as an ostensible destination, the poet and her inspirational faculties take charge of space ("surpass," "Measure," "range," "grasp"). Imagination is tantamount to the relationship between vertical motion, organizing vision or "mental optics," and the variegated plane of "the mighty whole" thus perceived. Poetry emerges, by implication, from "new worlds," the momentary revelation of an ordered strangeness:

> Soaring through air to find the bright abode,
> Th'empyreal palace of the thund'ring God,
> We on thy pinions can surpass the wind,
> And leave the rolling universe behind:
> From star to star the mental optics rove,
> Measure the skies, and range the realms above.
> There in one view we grasp the mighty whole,
> Or with new worlds amaze th'unbounded soul. (ll. 15–22)

Wheatley claims elsewhere that "an intrinsic ardor prompts to write" (*Collected Works* 15; "To the University of Cambridge, in New-England," l. 1). In "On Imagination," Fancy and Imagination divide up emotional labor in ways that suggest some tension between affection and power, the two aspects of "ardor." The fond gaze of fancy bestows spring on the landscape, creating the "gay scenes" that captivate it (l. 24). Fancy, the lover, is subordinate to the more glamorous Imagination. Imagination wields "the sceptre o'er the realms" of emotion: "Before thy throne the subject-passions bow, / Of subject-passions sov'reign ruler Thou" (ll. 36–38). When Imagination commands, "joy rushes on the heart" and spirits hurry "through the glowing veins" (ll. 39–40). The "passions" are Imagination's slaves, and Wheatley seems to glory in the rush from feeling to writing. But Imagination is subject to austerity's weather. Immediately after these lines, Wheatley shifts into the subjunctive: "Fancy might . . . her silken pinions try"; Aurora "might . . . rise"; "I"—the poet/speaker—"might behold" the sun, "monarch of the day" (ll. 41, 43, 46). The subjunctive mood bodes ill for "th'unbounded soul." Winter pulls the speaker down and away from Imagination's peaks. In the competition between a hot queen and a cold climate, the queen loses:

> But I reluctant leave the pleasing views,
> Which *Fancy* dresses to delight the *Muse*;
> *Winter* austere forbids me to aspire,
> And northern tempests damp the rising fire;
> They chill the tides of *Fancy's* flowing sea,
> Cease then, my son, cease the unequal lay. (ll. 48–53)

If winter is a trope for the North Atlantic zone of Wheatley's adult life, then the locale of her slavery "forbids" the tropical imagination "to aspire." But since New England is also the site of authorship, its chilly dampness may induce as well as discourage warm aspiration. Wheatley, unlike Barbauld in "A Summer Evening's Meditation," attributes the "inequality" of her song to its earthly circumstances, not to fancy's anxiety attack in the face of a patriarchal heaven. Winter, if clearly masculine and frowning, snags the poet from below instead of bullying her from above. And a seasonal cause of poetry's cessation is both more temporary and less transcendent than a celestial one. She concedes much less. Power is less absolute, in Wheatley's poetry, and aspiration is less self-wounding.

In the genre of political panegyric, Wheatley identifies the northern zone with Liberty's kindling effects. In the public sector, as it were, Wheatley is finally free to refer to herself. Wheatley's poem, "To the Right Honourable WILLIAM, Earl of Dartmouth, His Majesty's Principal Secretary of State for North America, &c.," recalls a collective experience of colonial mourning. New England's "race no longer mourns" since the presumably sympathetic Dartmouth, a friend of the Countess of Huntingdon, has been appointed Secretary of State for the American colonies and president of the Board of Trade and Foreign Plantations (*Collected Works* 73; l. 5, 287n.). But Wheatley's contrast between the present rejoicing of the "northern clime" and its previous lamentations keep those complaints alive as a reminder to Dartmouth of the need for revised policies:

> No more, *America,* in mournful strain
> Of wrongs, and grievance unredress'd complain,
> No longer shall thou dread the iron chain,
> Which wanton *Tyranny* with lawless hand
> Had made, and with it meant t'enslave the land. (ll. 3, 15–19)

In this verse paragraph, which had been edited a few months after its publication in *The New York Journal* for *Poems on Various Subjects,* and for the volume's English audience, Wheatley retains the by-now generic connection among tyranny, slavery, mourning, and the rhetoric of complaint (*Collected Works* 321–322n.). In an earlier draft of 1772, however, Wheatley used this passage to vent colonial impatience in the name of Liberty:

>   No more, of Grievance unredress'd complain,
> Or injur'd Rights, or groan beneath the Chain,
> Which wanton Tyranny, with lawless Hand,
> Made to enslave, O *Liberty!,* thy Land. —
> My Soul rekindles, at thy glorious Name,
> Thy Beams, essential to the vital Flame. —
> The Patriot's Breast, what Heavenly Virtue warms,
> And adds new Lustre to his mental Charms!
> While in thy Speech, the Graces all combine,
> Apollo's too, with Sons of Thunder join.
> Then shall the Race of injur'd Freedom bless,
> The Sire, the Friend, and Messenger of Peace.[13] (*Collected Works* 218,
>   ll. 12–24)

Here Dartmouth is assimilated, through the ambiguous repetition of "thy," to the allegorical figure of Liberty, which binds him rhetorically to a program of justice for the colonies. Wheatley is less flattering here, hedging her bet on Dartmouth's commitment to New England's interests.

In both versions, however, New England's identity as "the Race of injur'd Freedom," as the earlier text puts it, leads directly and quite unexpectedly to Wheatley's personal testimony to the links among suffering, slavery, and the poetry of freedom (l. 23). In the collective experience of enslavement, tyranny, and mourning, she finds a public purpose for her own traumatic past. She dramatizes herself as writer and Dartmouth as reader of this poem. Having led him to question the origins of her "love of Freedom" — "Should you, my lord, while you peruse my song, / Wonder from whence my love of *Freedom* sprung" — she restates that question in less individual terms: "Whence flow these wishes for the common good, / by feeling hearts alone best understood" (ll. 20–23). The love of freedom manifests itself in the community brought about by sensibility, the "common good" of "feeling hearts" which Dartmouth is invited to share. Wheatley creates an audience for her own suffering in the projected understanding of the sensitive reader. The story of her own enslavement becomes the motive for her literary participation in the sentimental community. And she justifies her use of the personal by giving it public value. The same "feeling hearts" in New England that lamented their subjection to Britain's tyranny will, along with Dartmouth himself, be sympathetic readers of her own experience of "tyrannic sway" (l. 31).

The poetic representation of enslavement is split by the conflict between Wheatley's need to depict her own authentic suffering and thus to justify her empathy with New England's cause, on the one hand, and on the other, her desire to acknowledge the fortunate teleology of her enslavement and conversion, the conditions for her public voice:

> I, young in life, by seeming cruel fate
> Was snatch'd from Afric's fancy'd happy seat:
> What pangs excruciating must molest,
> What sorrows labour in my parent's breast?
> Steel'd was that soul and by no misery mov'd
> That from a father seiz'd his babe belov'd:
> Such, such my case. And can I then but pray
> Others may never feel tyrannic sway? (ll. 24–31)

The key phrases, "seeming cruel fate" and "fancy'd happy seat," introduce Wheatley's reading of slavery both as a familial catastrophe and as a historical reality subject to recuperation. Imputing "pangs," "sorrows," and "misery" to her father, she makes him the suffering subject whose pain is sympathetically but vicariously experienced by Wheatley. The violence of the verb "snatch'd" exceeds the ambiguous phrase, "seeming cruel." Still, this swerve away from personal sensation, just when we have been led to expect confessional evidence, seems to confirm Landry's opinion of Wheatley's inability to remember. But there are other possible significances.

Instead of remembering her own pains, she speculates about her father's: "What pangs . . . What sorrows?" Not unlike the abolitionist poets, she becomes the artist of long-distance sympathy who has to imagine the pain that others feel. At the same time, however, this is her father, or, as she puts it, "my case," with the claim of personal immediacy. From whose point of view, then, is her fate "cruel"? From whose perspective was Africa "happy"? Clearly from the father's. His experience is one of a stark difference between before (his daughter's presence) and after (her subsequent captivity). The Christian apologist, however, could understand "seeming" and "fancy'd" as code words meaning "not really." He or she might read Africa's happiness as illusory and enslavement as a not-entirely-cruel means to the sacred end of conversion. But here the speaker, while validating both the familial and the apologetic interpretations, also insists on her representative status as one of many victims of "tyrannic sway." She treats her own capture as part of a larger narrative by which the victim protests but also recuperates her suffering by authoring the poetry of Anglo-American public life.

In looking at Barbauld and Wheatley together, I have stressed, first, sensibility, the language that links politics with psychodrama, and second, as one of the elements of sensibility, the celebration of fancy as an allegory of women's literary ambition. The feminist effect of fancy depends on the politics of imperial sensibility. The politics of sensibility—including debates on slavery, national independence, and industrial degradation—become matters of public dispute through the claim to suffering. But sensibility's appeal to women writers is not through suffering per se, since pathos was a hallmark of a wide variety of masculine reactions in this period as well. Otherness elicits representations of distance that invite the adventures of fancy and call forth prospective scenes of warning, hope, and prophecy. These excursions allow the fanciful subject to be mobile and self-pleasing, if often only briefly so. Fancy's visionary excursions are pleasurable only until fancy suffers its characteristic crisis of confidence. It is because fanciful trajectories dramatize the issue of confidence, finally, that fancy takes on meanings specific to women's poetry. Fancy-driven prospects demand and signify confidence, and then, for a time, exhaust it.

A Summer Evening's Meditation.

'Tis past! The sultry tyrant of the south
Has spent his short-lived rage; more grateful hours
Move silent on; the skies no more repell
The dazzled sight, but with mild maiden beams
Of tempered lustre court the cherished eye
To wander o'er their sphere; where hung aloft
Dian's bright crescent, like a silver bow
New strung in heaven, lifts high its beamy horns
Impatient for the night, and seems to push
Her brother down the sky. Fair Venus shines
Even in the eye of day; with sweetest beam
Propitious shines, and shakes a trembling flood
Of softened radiance from her dewy locks.
The shadows spread apace; while meekened Eve,
Her cheek yet warm with blushes, slow retires
Through the Hesperian gardens of the west,
And shuts the gates of day. 'Tis now the hour
When Contemplation from her sunless haunts,
The cool damp grotto, or the lonely depth
Of unpierced woods, where wrapt in solid shade
She mused away the gaudy hours of noon,
And fed on thoughts unripened by the sun,
Moves forward; and with radiant finger points
To yon blue concave swelled by breath divine,
Where, one by one, the living eyes of heaven
Awake, quick kindling o'er the face of ether
One boundless blaze; ten thousand trembling fires,
And dancing lustres, where the unsteady eye,
Restless and dazzled, wanders unconfined
O'er all this field of glories; spacious field,
And worthy of the Master: he, whose hand
With hieroglyphics elder than the Nile
Inscribed the mystic tablet, hung on high
To public gaze, and said, "Adore, O man!
The finger of thy God." From what pure wells
Of milky light, what soft o'erflowing urn,
Are all these lamps so fill'd? these friendly lamps,
For ever streaming o'er the azure deep
To point our path, and light us to our home.
How soft they slide along their lucid spheres!
And silent as the foot of Time, fulfill
Their destined courses: Nature's self is hushed,
And, but a scattered leaf, which rustles through
The thick-wove foliage, not a sound is heard
To break the midnight air; though the raised ear,

Intensely listening, drinks in every breath.
How deep the silence, yet how loud the praise!
But are they silent all? or is there not
A tongue in every star, that talks with man,
And woos him to be wise? nor woos in vain:
This dead of midnight is the noon of thought,
And Wisdom mounts her zenith with the stars.
At this still hour the self-collected soul
Turns inward, and beholds a stranger there
Of high descent, and more than mortal rank;
An embryo God; a spark of fire divine,
Which must burn on for ages, when the sun, —
Fair transitory creature of a day! —
Has closed his golden eye, and wrapt in shades
Forgets his wonted journey through the east.

Ye citadels of light, and seats of God!
Perhaps my future home, from whence the soul,
Revolving periods past, may oft look back
With recollected tenderness on all
The various busy scenes she left below,
Its deep-laid projects and its strange events,
As on some fond and doting tale that soothed
Her infant hours — O be it lawful now
To tread the hallowed circle of your courts,
And with mute wonder and delighted awe
Approach your burning confines. Seized in thought,
On Fancy's wild and roving wing I sail,
From the green borders of the peopled Earth,
And the pale Moon, her duteous fair attendant;
From solitary Mars; from the vast orb
Of Jupiter, whose huge gigantic bulk
Dances in ether like the lightest leaf;
To the dim verge, the suburbs of the system,
Where cheerless Saturn 'midst his watery moons
Girt with a lucid zone, in gloomy pomp,
Sits like an exiled monarch: fearless thence
I launch into the trackless deeps of space,
Where, burning round, ten thousand suns appear,
Of elder beam, which ask no leave to shine
Of our terrestrial star, nor borrow light
From the proud regent of our scanty day;
Sons of the morning, first-born of creation,
And only less than Him who marks their track,
And guides their fiery wheels. Here must I stop,
Or is there aught beyond? What hand unseen

Impells me onward through the glowing orbs
Of habitable nature, far remote,
To the dread confines of eternal night,
To solitudes of vast unpeopled space,
The desarts of creation, wide and wild;
Where embryo systems and unkindled suns
Sleep in the womb of chaos? fancy droops,
And thought astonished stops her bold career.
But O thou mighty mind! whose powerful word
Said, thus let all things be, and thus they were,
Where shall I seek thy presence? how unblamed
Invoke thy dread perfection?
Have the broad eyelids of the morn beheld thee?
Or does the beamy shoulder of Orion
Support thy throne? O look with pity down
On erring, guilty man! not in thy names
Of terror clad; not with those thunders armed
That conscious Sinai felt, when fear appalled
The scattered tribes; — thou hast a gentler voice,
That whispers comfort to the swelling heart,
Abashed, yet longing to behold her Maker.
But now my soul, unused to stretch her powers
In flight so daring, drops her weary wing,
And seeks again the known accustomed spot,
Drest up with sun, and shade, and lawns, and streams,
A mansion fair, and spacious for its guest,
And full replete with wonders. Let me here,
Content and grateful, wait the appointed time,
And ripen for the skies: the hour will come
When all these splendours bursting on my sight
Shall stand unveiled, and to my ravished sense
Unlock the glories of the world unknown.

This essay has benefited from the generous scrutiny of friends. I particularly wish to thank Chris Flint, Donna Landry, Sarah Robbins, and Nan Sweet for their help.

Notes

1. Here I paraphrase my own characterization of fancy and the lengthier survey of romantic debates on fancy in " 'Nice Arts' and 'Potent Enginery': The Gendered Economy of Wordsworth's Fancy." See also Alan Liu on "The Politics of the Picturesque" in his *Wordsworth: The Sense of History,* ch. 3 and Nanora Sweet's

"History, Imperialism, and the Aesthetics of the Beautiful: Hemans and the post-Napoleonic Moment."

2. The passage cited is taken from Mercy Otis Warren's "To a Young Gentleman in Europe," Warren's prefatory letter to *The Ladies of Castile*, which appeared in *Poems, Dramatic and Miscellaneous* (1790). It is reprinted in *Plays and Poems of Mercy Otis Warren* 100.

3. "Whig sentimentalism" is Silverman's phrase for the curiously overwrought tone of the writings, first, of English Opposition Whigs and, later, of colonial pamphleteers. See also Bernard Bailyn's *Ideological Origins of the American Revolution* and Jay Fliegelman's *Prodigals and Pilgrims*.

4. The most useful recent approaches to literary works that stand in this ambivalent relation to colonial systems are those that acknowledge the simultaneously guilty and critical posture of Anglo-American sensibility. I am indebted to Homi Bhabha's notion of mimicry, as applied by Donna Landry to female poets of the late eighteenth century, and to Ross Chambers's argument that melancholia is tantamount to the consciousness of one's own mimic (or hybrid) discourse. Chambers's theory of minorities and melancholia resonates with other treatments of split or multiple subjectivity in cultural studies while addressing the question of affect more pointedly; see *Room for Maneuver* ch. 3. In her discussion of Phillis Wheatley, Donna Landry draws on Homi Bhabha and Gayatri Spivak in describing the "fractured semiotic field" of "other others," non-English women writers marginalized not only by class and gender but also by their distance from the English nationality, which renders their writing "curious, exotic, and ephemeral" (*Muses of Resistance* 240, 217).

5. I use the term "public," not as the opposite of some notion of the "private," but to refer to what signifies the nation in its multiple dimensions, or systems and relationships such as the market, the economy, the empire, or, following Paul Gilroy, "the black Atlantic."

6. Murray's transvaluation of fancy continues:

Invention is perhaps the most arduous effort of the mind; this branch of imagination hath been particularly ceded to us, and we have been time out of mind invested with that creative faculty. Observe the variety of fashions (here I bar the contemptuous smile) which distinguish and adorn the female world; how continually are they changing, insomuch that they almost render the wise man's assertion problematical, and we are ready to say, there is something new under the sun. Now what a playfulness, what an exuberance of fancy, what strength of inventive imagination, doth this continual variation discover? . . . what a formidable story can we in a moment fabricate merely from the force of a prolifick imagination? how many reputations, in the fertile brain of a female, have been utterly despoiled? how industrious are we at improving a hint? suspicion how easily do we convert into conviction, and conviction, embellished by the power of eloquence, stalks abroad to the surprise and confusion of unsuspecting innocence. Perhaps it will be asked if I furnish these facts as instances of excellency in our sex. Certainly not; but as proofs of a creative faculty, of a lively imagination. Assuredly great activity of mind is thereby discovered, and was this activity properly directed, what beneficial effects would follow. Is the needle and kitchen sufficient to employ the operations of a soul thus organized? I should conceive not. ("On the Equality of the Sexes" 1133–34)

7. Moira Ferguson points out that the character of the corrupted mistress of a slave-owning family would have been familiar from Sarah Scott's novel, *Sir George Ellison* (1766), set in Jamaica (*Subject to Others* 102).

8. The attack on *Eighteen Hundred and Eleven* in the *Anti-Jacobin* of June 1812 counters the favorable notice of the *Monthly Review*. Quoting the *Monthly's* approving claim that "poets are prophets as well as satirists," the *Anti-Jacobin* expressed its "sovereign contempt for the prophetic powers of Mrs. Barbauld," especially since those powers depicted "the ruins of England with so much more spirit than . . . her beauties" (209).

9. Commenting on *Eighteen Hundred and Eleven*, Marlon Ross notes, "In a sure, strong voice, Barbauld predicts England's fate as irreversible. How ironic that this tour de force should be executed by a woman who believes that women should not become authors and should refrain from entering the masculine world of politics and knowledge" (*Contours of Masculine Desire* 226).

10. While Barbauld's fantasy of London in ruins is ridiculed in the *Quarterly Review,* a few pages earlier William Roscoe is urged to abandon the mode of rational argument and to speak sentimentally on behalf of slaves: "Whence is it, that an amiable and benevolent man, expressly writing on political affairs, can count over . . . from bead to bead, the miserable round of mewling complaints about peace, taxes, and corruption, without stealing, from the monotony of ave's to Reform, a single thought for the suffering and struggles of the most interesting people in Europe; without stopping to shed 'one human tear,' either of indignation over the record of their cruel wrongs, or of sympathy, hope, and solicitude, over the yet unfinished history of their glorious efforts for deliverance?" *Quarterly Review* June 1812, 281. The pamphlets under review were *A Letter to Henry Brougham . . . on the Subject of Reform in the Representation of the People in Parliament* and *An Answer to a letter from Mr. John Merritt on the Subject of Parliamentary Reform.*

11. Landry finds "a buried idiom of subversion . . . an awareness of revolutionary and abolitionist consciousness that Wheatley can only intimate but not openly embrace" (*Muses of Resistance* 219). John Shields's observations on the gist of Wheatley's revisions from broadside to book, which show that on the subject of slavery she is being careful "not to ruffle the feathers of her overwhelmingly white, and at first, often British audience," support Landry's reading. *The Collected Works of Phillis Wheatley* 195–96.

12. For the details of Wheatley's English journey and the publication and reception of her poems there, see Ali Isani, "The British Reception of Wheatley's Poems," Rawley, "The World of Phillis Wheatley," and William Robinson, "Phillis Wheatley in London."

13. The earlier draft is lustier, with its link between Dartmouth's "paternal Sway" regarded exultantly by a New England "big with Hopes" (ll. 4–5).

Joel Haefner

The Romantic Scene(s) of Writing

> Wir können nur aus dem Standpunkte eines Menschen vom Raum, von ausgedenkten Wesen zu reden. . . . Die beständige Form dieses Receptivität, welche wir Sinnlichkeit nennen, ist eine notwendige Bedingung aller Verhältnisse, . . . eine reine Anschauung, welche den Namen Raum führt.
>
> — Kant, *Kritik der Reinen Vernunft*
>
> (We can only speak of space, of conceptual modes, from the viewpoint of a human being. . . . The constant form of this receptivity, which we call sensation, is a necessary condition for all relationships, . . . a pure concept, which is named space.)

> . . . space reflects social organization, but, of course, once space has been bounded and shaped it is no longer merely a neutral background: it exerts its own influence. . . . So: behavior and space are mutually dependent.
>
> — Shirley Ardener, *Women and Space*

Start with the cover illustration to M. H. Abrams's 1971 magnum opus *Natural Supernaturalism*: John Martin's magnificent painting, "The Bard," now in the Yale Center for British Art. The Scottish bard plays his lyre on a cliff in defiance of an army below; a ruined castle and black peaks loom out of the murky background; river and clouds contend in "Tumult and peace," as Wordsworth writes of the Simplon pass. The painting exemplifies Abrams's "high argument": that self and culture were unified during the Romantic era, and that the unifying thread is secularized theology. The bard on the precipice represents a traditional, spiritual, and poetic voice, a revolutionary in a turbulent natural world. The scene is Romantic *in radix*.

Or is it? Certainly it represents one version of the poetic environment, a version that has been traced in hundreds of canonical works. Although we have been persuaded that this is *the* scene of Romantic writing, there may be alternative scenes, alternative sites for poetic creation. As we look at some of these other creative scenes — the Bluestocking salon and Sappho's agora — we will find at least one tradition that has been obscured by Romanticists over the last fifty years. Imagine the bard's redoubt as one point on the map of "psyche, writing, and spacing," as Derrida calls it in "Freud and the Scene of Writing." There are other scenes of creativity to chart.

The opening epigraph from Kant's *Critique of Pure Reason* highlights a shift in philosophical conceptions of space, a shift that coincides with what Naomi Schor calls "a moment of aesthetic crisis, on the cusp between neo-classicism and romanticism" (*Reading in Detail* 24). Kant alters the argument about space dramatically: space and time are not external, objective realities that we passively apprehend. Instead, Kant claims, space is "something in us," a "pure perception" that is "the form of our outer sense" (Palmer, *Kant's Critique of Pure Reason* 15; Kant, *Kritik*, 3: 41). This radical reformulation of the idea of space, an essential element in Kant's transcendental aesthetics, was assimilated by many of the English High Romantics, notably Coleridge and Hazlitt. Kant presented a subjective perspective on the concept of space that granted to the human mind the active power of shaping external sensation, a perspective shared by phenomenologists like Gaston Bachelard in *The Poetics of Space* and by many modern Romanticists.

There are other ways of constructing the idea of space, beyond a simplistic polarity between objectivity and subjectivity, as my second epigraph suggests. We can think of space as a cultural and behavioral phenomenon. From this perspective, space is not something "out there" that we passively perceive, nor is it a mental construct that the individual human mind imposes on the external world. Instead, space is controlled by cultural factors and by the behavioral patterns of society. Recent theorists have begun to explore this perspective in a field they call behavioral geography.[1] Even these theorists suggest that the "significance of space in art lies in its connection to feeling" (Sack, *Conceptions of Space* 26; see also Tuan, *Space and Place* 135–48).

But fictionalized space does not simply convey emotion, of course; it conveys cultural ideologies as well. Race, class, and gender are embedded in our cultural scenes, intertwined with feelings about, conceptions of, those places and ideologies. Anthropologist Shirley Ardener finds that "space defines the people in it" and conversely that "people define space" (*Women and Space* 12–13). Hence when poets "find a space" for their art, when they fictionalize their aesthetics into a particular scene, they are recreating to some degree the historical dynamics of gender, race, and class that is part of the "cults" (an ideologically charged word) of both domesticity and Sensibility, or the Age (also ideologically laden) of Reason or the aesthetics of the sublime. But only by surveying one of these scenes can we begin to unravel the aesthetics and semiotics of creative space.

Revisit, for a moment, "Tintern Abbey." The quotation marks are significant: you understand that I mean a text, not the actual physical ruins. In fact what I mean here is a conflation of the two: the textual representation of the real space. "Tintern Abbey" is significant space — important not only to Wordsworth in terms of aesthetic self-creation but also to critics in terms of critical fictionalization. The locus of the poem remains for modern critics "his own tangled and inward self" (Foster, "'Tintern Abbey' and Wordsworth's Scene of Writing" 81), the topography of the self as reflected in the natural scene Wordsworth depicts. Geoffrey Hartman targets Wordsworth's "shadowy self-exploration" in the poem (*The Unremarkable Wordsworth* 178), and M. H. Abrams links "Tintern Abbey," "Frost at Midnight," and *The Prelude* in their premise that

> an individual confronts a natural scene and makes it abide his question, and the interchange between his mind and nature constitutes the entire poem, which usually poses and resolves a spiritual crisis. (Abrams, *Natural Supernaturalism* 92)

Several features of the accepted response to "Tintern Abbey" stand out: the solitariness of the poet, his singularity; the drama of confronting loss and change; the connection between text and mind; the spiritual dimension of the poem and of the poet's experience.[2]

Vision and revision both take place at Tintern Abbey: the actual drafting occurs elsewhere, but the real "work" of the writing is done within the parameters of Wordsworth's Tintern Abbey.

> Once again
> Do I behold these steep and lofty cliffs,
> Which on a wild secluded scene impress
> Thoughts of more deep seclusion; and connect
> The landscape with the quiet of the sky. (4–8; *Lyrical Ballads* 112)

That Wordsworth internalized the natural scene of Tintern Abbey, that he "projected" (Abrams, *The Mirror and the Lamp* 66–69) self into nature or "appropriated" nature (Levin, "Romantic Prose and Feminine Romanticism") is not really remarkable. But the fact that he self-consciously made Tintern Abbey a scene of singular, internalized writing is a radically new development. "While here I stand," Wordsworth writes mid-way through the poem, "not only with the sense / Of present pleasure, but with pleasing thoughts / That in this moment there is life and food / For future years" (63–66; *Lyrical Ballads* 114).

"Tintern Abbey" is a scene about writing and a scene that writes writing, but it is a borrowed vantage point: it correlates with the mythos of the bard Ossian declaiming from his cave and the young genius Thomas Chatterton dying, neglected and abused, in his garret.

We could multiply examples of this poetic space from the conventional canon — Blake's Milton surveying the Vortexes of infinity, Coleridge's panoramic view in "Dejection," Byron's metaphor of "lone caves" to describe the poet's alienation in *Childe Harold,* and, most tellingly, the "grey precipice" and "silent nook" where Shelley's Alastor dies. In all these versions the topography of the place reflects the elements of a traditional Romantic aesthetic: the author writes alone; composition is immediate, spontaneous, and fleeting; the text "expresses" the innermost soul/being of the poet; creation consumes the poet in a kind of Romantic agony; the environment of the textual act is Nature, not society. A number of traditions participate in the fictionalization of this aesthetic, including gothic sublimity, Rousseauesque stages of human development, associationism, confessional autobiography, pastoral poetry, landscape painting, epic, the Grand Tour, and Sensibility, but Ossian's cave and its connotations had an immense impact on writers of the late eighteenth and early nineteenth centuries.[3]

While Ossian's cave provided writers with an allegedly epic scene in which to compose, they did not have to look far to find a contemporary scene that carried much of the same meaning: Chatterton's garret. Chatterton in fact modeled his own poet-hero, Rowley, on Macpherson's fictional bard (Taylor, *Thomas Chatterton's Art* 273–84; Kelly, *The Marvellous Boy* 17).

Again, like Ossian's cave, the scene of Chatterton's garret had been deeply inscribed into cultural consciousness. Edward Orme's 1794 engraving on "The Death of Chatterton" and John Flaxman's "Chatterton receives the Cup of Poison from the Spirit of Despair" (circa 1790) were two of many popular images, which also included handkerchiefs printed with Chatterton's garret deathbed (Kelly 60). For male writers, Chatterton's garret was emblematic of the martyrdom a sensitive poet suffers, and the idea of Chatterton became pivotal in Romantic self-representations and aesthetics. As Donald Reiman notes, Chatterton was important to a host of canonized writers: Wordsworth used Chatterton as an illustration of despair in "Resolution and Independence"; Keats acknowledged his debt to

Chatterton in his early poetry; and Coleridge worked on his "Monody on the Death of Chatterton" throughout his writing career (Reiman, *Shelley and His Circle* 7: 127).

As with Ossian's cave, we could find many versions of this creative space: Coleridge's lime-tree bower; Wordsworth's "narrow room" that stands for the rigor and limits of the sonnet; Keats's Chambers of the mind that are so integral to his vision of the poet and poetry. One of the most direct versions of the poet's garret comes from the proletarian poet, Henry Kirke White. White's humorous poem, "My Study," describes "A closet just six feet by four" in the attic, filled with a broken chair and table, "oddities upon the floor," books "on rotten shelves," chipped busts, and portraits "Of mighty men and eke of women, / Who are no whit inferior to men." White concludes:

> With these fair dames, and heroes round,
> I call my garret classic ground.
> For though confined, 't will well contain
> The ideal flights of Madam Brain.
> No dungeon's walls, no cell confined
> Can cramp the energies of mind! (*Poetical Works* 78)

White's poem raises several issues. First, like Wordsworth's "narrow room," the confined space of a garret provides the catalyst the imagination needs. I am reminded of the "usurpation" that seems essential to the "awful Power" of imagination as Wordsworth crosses the Alps in the sixth book of *The Prelude*. A common aesthetics links the poet's garret and the sublime cave or precipice: imagination is projective, art is internalized and expressive, the poet is sensitive, appropriative, and, most important, alone. Second, White's "Study" bears, in the chips, cracks, and second-hand bric-a-brac of its furnishings, the signs of class. Like the physical confines of the garret, poverty itself created restrictions that intensified genius — a significant element in the Chatterton iconography. When canonical Romantic writers adopted Chatterton and his garret as part of their poetics, the economic limitations of class became translated into general social ostracization: even aristocratic poets like Byron and Shelley could thus identify with a "common" poet like Chatterton (see Reiman, *Shelley and His Circle* 7: 127). Third, White at least generally acknowledges the contributions of women, though only men are actually named in the poem. White casts his brain as female, as he and other poets gendered the Muse, the heart, and the soul as woman. There is a process of assimilation at work here, probably analogous to the appropriation of Sensibility that Marlon Ross identifies with mainstream Romantic poets. In short, embedded in conventional Romantic aesthetics are traces (here carried by spatial signs) of class and gender: the singular imagination thrives under the pressures of penury; the text must be "midwived" by an internalized, female faculty. There is no sense of a collective or collaborative creative process, there is only the writer who writes alone.[4]

But these premises alter radically when we change scenes, for example, to the Bluestocking salon of the late eighteenth century. The Bluestockings were originally an informal group of men and women who gathered to discuss literature, philosophy, politics, and other intellectual topics, roughly between the early 1760s and 1790. Although the term bluestocking originated in the lower-class blue worsted hose that one man wore to some of the gatherings, it quickly came to designate thinking women with literary abilities. Later — particularly in response to the feminism of the 1790s — the term became pejorative.

The Bluestockings included men like Samuel Johnson, David Garrick, Horace Walpole, Sir Joshua Reynolds, and Dr. Burney. But its locus, the image that arose in most people's minds when the word was used, is the intellectual woman conversing in a circle of friends. "For the bluestockings themselves," writes Sylvia Myers,

> learning, virtue, and friendship *were* inextricably linked. In their own eyes to be a bluestocking meant to be an impeccable member of an intellectual community which included both men and women. (*The Bluestocking Circle* 11)

The Bluestockings, or "Blues," as they were sometimes called, fell into two periods: the first group of bluestockings, roughly 1758–1775, and the second wave of blues, roughly 1775–1790. The first group included women like Elizabeth Carter, Elizabeth Montagu, Catherine Talbot, and Hester Chapone; the second group included Hannah More, Fanny Burney, Hester Thrale, Anna Laetitia Barbauld, and many others.

Hannah More's poem, "Bas-Bleu: or, Conversation," became the "signature" text for this well-known salon. The poem opens with a tongue-in-cheek comparison of the Bluestocking gathering to Socrates's symposium and Lucullus's salon. While establishing her mock-epic, More indulges in gentle self-deprecation that implicitly challenges the use of authority in argument and the common perception that women could not know learned tongues like Greek:

I shall not stop to dwell on these,
But be as epic as I please,
And plunge at once *in media res.*
To prove the privilege I plead,
I'll quote some Greek I cannot read;
Stunn'd by Authority you yield,
And I, not reason, keep the field. (1835 *Complete Works* 1: 292)

More disparages the mindless, superficial social gatherings of her era, and lauds the depth of the Bluestocking conversation.

Long did Quadrille despotic sit,
That Vandal of colloquial wit;
And Conversation's setting light
Lay half-obscur'd in Gothic night.
At length the mental shades decline,
Colloquial wit begins to shine;
Genius prevails, and Conversation
Emerges into *Reformation.* (292)

She names some of the women and men who joined the group: Frances Boscawen, Elizabeth Montagu, Sir George Lyttleton, William Pulteney, and Horace Walpole. She also depicts the scene by emphatically showing what it is not: not the frivolous French salon of Rambouillet and Voltaire where "Each common phrase is an oration," where "Cold Ceremony's leaden hand / Waves o'er the room her poppy wand" (294–95).

By contrast, the Bluestocking salon unites disparate talkers who actually know what they are talking about:

Here sober Duchesses are seen,
Chaste Wits, and Critics void of spleen;
Physicians, fraught with real science,
And Whigs and Tories in alliance;
Poets, fulfilling Christian duties,
Just Lawyers, reasonable Beauties;
Bishops who preach, and Peers who pay,
And Countesses who seldom play;
Learn'd Antiquaries, who, from college,
Reject the rust, and bring the knowledge;

And, hear it, *age,* believe it, *youth,* —
Polemics, really seeking truth. (298)

More's ironic portrait celebrates the mix of people who attend the Blue-stocking salons: men and women who possess real knowledge, who seek real truth, who evince qualities the opposite of those usually found among their peers. This is a dynamic, fertile, crowded scene that is at the heart of intellectual creativity. More develops (probably in reference to Swift) an analogy between conversation and commerce.

Our intellectual ore must shine,
Nor slumber idly in the mine.
Let education's moral mint
The noblest images imprint;
Let taste her curious touchstone hold,
To try if standard be the gold;
But 'tis thy commerce, Conversation,
Must give it use by circulation;
That noblest commerce of mankind,
Whose precious merchandize is MIND! (301)

In fact, More's apostrophe to conversation echoes Milton's apostrophe to holy Light at the beginning of Book III of *Paradise Lost* and adumbrates Wordsworth's apostrophe to Imagination in the sixth book of *The Prelude.* Like the High Romantic concept of Imagination, Conversation "kindles" knowledge; amalgamates art, science, and ethics; catalyzes morality; secures the stability of society; and is preeminently practical, useful:

Hail, Conversation, heav'nly fair,
Thou bliss of life, and balm of care,
Still may thy gentle reign extend,
And taste with wit and science blend!
Soft polisher of rugged man,
Refiner of the social plan. (300)

Despite the similarities between Conversation and Imagination, however, one crucial difference remained: Conversation was insistently social and collaborative; Imagination was an individual's gift, an individual's experience, that of someone with "a more comprehensive soul" than "supposed to be common among mankind," as Wordsworth wrote in 1802 additions to the Preface to *Lyrical Ballads*. More's Conversation cannot exist (as it were) in the wild, or in the singular. She celebrates "the pure delight / When kindling sympathies unite; / When correspondent tastes impart / Communion sweet from heart to heart" (302–3). A sympathetic exchange is at the core of More's idea of conversation. And while sympathy and "disinterestedness" were central to Hazlitt's (and, by extension, Keats's) construction of the imagination, this is not imaginative sympathy, or a projective sympathy, but an immediate, verbal exchange. We might go so far as to claim that More's Conversation was a kind of practical Sensibility, while traditional Romantic Imagination was a kind of transcendental Sensibility.

And those connections with Sensibility point to the limitations and paradoxes that More, like other Radical and conservative women writers of her time, had to face. To speak out on intellectual issues, on the creative process itself, not only violated gender codes, but also tested the limits of social discourse and the role of the individual writer within society. More was ostracized as a Bluestocking who shunned the usual female trappings of marriage, child-rearing, and housekeeping.[5]

I do not want to suggest here, however, that women alone participated in this conflictive scene of writing—the salon dominated by women—because all the Bluestocking gatherings included men, and More herself insists on that point in "Bas-Bleu." In fact Cowper's *The Task* presents a similar geography of creativity: the drawing room where mixed company meet. The poem itself was solicited by Cowper's patroness Lady Austen, who, partly in jest, asked for a blank verse poem on the sofa. Cowper obliged; the first book is titled "The Sofa." But Cowper does not stay long on the sofa: he is quickly back into his childhood, and into Wordsworth-esque "rural walks." There is a persistent tension throughout "The Sofa" between the social world of the drawing room and the natural world of the countryside, and between Cowper's acknowledgment of how social interaction kindles his art and his urge to locate his art within his own consciousness and experience. Hence the poem opens with Cowper ruefully confessing that his theme was now the Sofa, not "Truth, Hope, and Charity," which were recent poems (*Poems* 165); hence he is attracted to a "peasant's nest" where the poet can "indulge / The dreams of fancy, tranquil and secure" but realizes that life's necessities would be scarce, and concludes "Society for me!" (172). Cowper suffered for his vacillation between a natural, singular scene of writing and a communal scene based on talk: he was branded as effeminate and, finally, crazy.

Cowper remained influential for the canonical or semi-canonical male writers of the period, too, and that influence problematizes the aesthetics of conversation and Romantic creative spaces. Conversation poems by Coleridge, John Thelwall, Southey, and others indicate the impact, perhaps the appropriation, of this composing mode. While a full consideration of the role of conversation poems in this tradition is beyond the scope of this essay, I suspect that the male tradition of conversation remains a formal and psychological manifestation, rather than a creative process. Tilottama Rajan reads Coleridge's conversation poems as reflecting the poet's search for an "alter ego" and his realization that language and poetry bridge and affirm the gap between imagination and reality (*Dark Interpreter* 217–33). Ann Matheson focuses on parallels between Cowper and Coleridge and on the rhetorical style of the latter's conversation poems ("The Influence of Cowper's *The Task*"). As both Matheson and Rajan point out, the form and style of conversation poems are enmeshed in the poets' goal of replicating "natural," "simple," and "manly" language, and hence in the politics of gendered aesthetics.[6]

If gender clearly enters into the meridians of the salon as a scene of writing, so does class. The Bluestocking salon, after all, was aristocratic and bourgeois. That the Blues were writing within the confines of a distinct class ideology became apparent in the clash between More and her protégé, the Milk Woman of Bristol, Ann Yearsley. More arranged printing and subscribers for Yearsley's first volume of poetry, but later refused to relinquish the proceeds to Yearsley. Although More did eventually consign the trust fund to Yearsley, the farrago catalyzed anger and resistance on Yearsley's part. Donna Landry writes that, for Yearsely, "More has ceased to represent a single instance of an insensitive middle-class patron and come to stand for the prejudices of a whole class" (*Muses of Resistance* 157). Economics and class invade the creative space of the genteel salon; hence proletariat writers often rewrite this particular scene of writing.

One of the most vivid rewritings/critiques of the salon is Elizabeth Hands's *The Death of Amnon. A Poem* (1789). A pair of companion poems appear in that volume — "A Poem on the Supposition of an Advertisement appearing in a Morning Paper, of the Publication of a Volume of Poems, by a Servant Maid," and "A Poem, on the Supposition of the Book having been published and read." In both poems, Hands paints the picture of a well-appointed but superfluous drawing room where her book of poems is under fire.

> The tea-kettle bubbled, the tea things were set,
> The candles were lighted, the ladies were met;
> The how d'ye's were over, and entering bustle,
> The company seated, and silks ceas'd to rustle. (*Death of Amnon* 47)

When the advertisement for the book is mentioned, the company break out in derision:

> A servant write verses! says Madam Du Bloom;
> Pray what is the subject? — a Mop, or a Broom?
> He, he, he, — says Miss Flounce; I suppose we shall see
> An Ode on a Dishclout — what else can it be? (47)

The group condemn the author on several levels: for being "out of her sphere," for cheating her employer of her time, for not producing something "useful" like a recipe. One speaker claims it would be better to have a scribbling maid than a promiscuous one. The book has not been read at all, but the class of the author has been very clearly read. This is a very different vision of aesthetics from the one Wordsworth offers. The writer must write and publish in the social context of her class, and the text itself is subject to, in fact becomes, the conversation of a middle-class gathering of women.

In the companion poem, set after publication of the book, the company is mixed, and the evaluation of the poetry becomes grounded in gender as well as class.

> There's one piece, whose subject's a Rape.
> A Rape! interrupted the Captain Bonair,
> A delicate theme for a female I swear;
> Then smirk'd at the ladies, they simper'd all round,
> Touch'd their lips with their fans, — Mrs. Consequence frown'd.
> (50–51)

The domestic, the rural, the sexual are all taboo themes for a woman writer, according to this group. Elizabeth Hands's sphere of writing is separate and limited by both class and gender. In an ironic reference to Pope's "Essay on Man," Hands writes:

Says Sir Timothy Turtle, my daughters ne'er look
In any thing else but a cookery book:
The properest study for women design'd;
Says Mrs. Domestic, I'm quite of your mind. (53)

This is a kind of negative aesthetics, a negative space: Hands is showing us the collective aesthetic she was working against, "her consciousness
of such displacement and maneuvering," as Donna Landry writes (188).
And in this instance class may be a bigger barrier than gender. Some
subjects remain acceptable for women — love, for example, or celebrations
of weddings — but no subjects (except cooking) are proper for working-
class women. Hands is hardly writing alone, in isolation; she imagines (and
may well have endured) the kind of criticism she depicts and on which she
has her own textual revenge (see Landry 189). What these poems do
indicate is that all women, of whatever social class, had to write in a social
context that may have been supporting (as More's "Bas-Blue" suggests) or
may have been burdensome (as Hands's twin verses suggest).

The same ambivalences and aesthetic premises persist in women's
poetry and some men's poetry throughout the first third of the nineteenth
century. While a full historical survey of the permutations of this tradition
of creative space is beyond the scope of this essay, I believe that the backlash
to the feminism of the 1790s led to changes in the aesthetic geography
available for women writers. It was no longer safe to write within a Bluestocking salon of women or (worse yet) the radical circle around Mary
Wollstonecraft; that had become pejorative (see Ross, *Contours of Masculine
Desire* 232–43). One solution was for women to write within a familial
environment, a "safe" place because domesticity could be accommodated
with writing within one sphere. In the "ideal" family circle, women writers
could theoretically discharge their gender duties while being supported in
their writing by parents, brothers, and sisters.[7]

But for many women writers the family circle was incomplete, and
another kind of space — one that perhaps spoke more directly to the contradictions of being a woman and a writer — had to be mapped. Poets like
Felicia Hemans and Letitia Elizabeth Landon (L.E.L.), both of whom
experienced problematic family circles, discovered a new creative site in the
legend of Sappho which was broadened and enriched in the early decades of
the nineteenth century.

Even the devoutly religious Jane Taylor felt attracted to Madame de
Staël's Corinne, "subject to the 'magic' of *Corinne's* pages," as Davidoff and

Hall put it (*Family Fortunes* 161). In fact, Corinne and the space in which she creates denote an alternative aesthetics, an aesthetics linked to women's salons. Joan DeJean's 1989 study *Fictions of Sappho, 1546–1937* details how convoluted the development of the myth of Sappho is, and how Sappho was known as "the female counterpart, and presumably the equal, of 'the poet,' Homer" (1). Sappho — and Madame de Staël's fictionalization of the poet, Corinne — represents an alternative creative mode to the model represented by the High Romantics.

The special creative powers of Corinne/Sappho were improvisational. De Staël had heard Italian improvisatrices during travels, DeJean notes, who

> are geniuses of a more sublime type of fugitive passion, women who can abandon themselves to the transport of their gift so that their poetic voice issues forth in apparent spontaneity. In *Corinne,* improvisation is the Sapphic language. . . . For as the improvisatrice is transported outside of herself, so she also has the power to sway her audience. (*Fictions of Sappho* 179)

De Staël takes pains to fix the scenes of Corinne's performances, which often take place in public and semi-public places: at the Roman Capitol, and in her own home, before friends. In terms of the creative process, there (curiously) seems little difference between the two spaces. En route to the Roman Capitol, Corinne "seemed at once a priestess of Apollo making her way toward the Temple of the Sun, and a woman perfectly simple in the ordinary relationships of life" (21). It is almost as if de Staël, in fictionalizing her own creativity, had to make public the domestic and domesticate the public. While there is clearly an expressive dimension to Corinne's poetics, it is a poetics that is affective, rooted in the response of her audience. Corinne, and her inner feelings, becomes a representative voice for larger groups: friends, Romans, Italians, all who feel strongly. De Staël, like More, grounds her aesthetics in the notion of conversation, because it fuses expressivism and affectivism and because it successfully negotiates the perils of gender and genius: that is, woman's art based on woman's skills (conversational abilities) will slip by cultural censors/critics. "I shall say that for me," Corinne tells her British admirer Oswald early in the novel,

> improvisation is like a lively conversation. I do not let myself be bound to any one subject; I go along with the impression my listeners' interest makes on me, and it is to my friends that I owe most of my talent, particularly in this genre. (*Corinne* 179)

From this brief quote we can begin to see some of the demarcations of Sapphic creativity: an emphasis on spontaneity; a theory firmly rooted in invention; an aesthetics that is obviously expressive but is also clearly audience-centered; a sense of the poet speaking for her audience, becoming almost a collective speaker, like a Greek chorus; an emphasis on the emotional and sympathetic dimension of discourse; and a belief in the importance of conversation and dialogue in the creative process.

The Sappho/Corinne myth was frequently celebrated by Romantic women poets, and indeed they adopted this fiction of the writer as their own, becoming, in a sense, Corinne themselves, just as the High Romantics became their own model of solitary genius — Ossian or Chatterton. As early as 1796 Mary Robinson published her sonnet sequence *Sappho and Phaon.* Constance Grace Garnett published a play entitled *Sappho: A Dramatic Sketch* in 1824, celebrating the martyrdom of the poetess to hopeless love. L.E.L. penned several versions of the Sappho myth, including "The Improvisatrice," "A History of the Lyre," and "Sappho"; Felicia Hemans also wrote variations on the theme, including "The Dying Improvisator," "The Last Song of Sappho," and "Corinne at the Capitol" (the title of the second book of de Staël's novel). All these texts inscribe the fiction of Sappho's unrequited heterosexual love and her suicide, but they also inscribe an impromptu, collaborative, conversational, and audience-centered vision of writing.

L.E.L. opens "Sappho," for example, with a scene of the poet creating in the midst of a crowd of admirers:

> She leant upon her harp, and thousands look'd
> On her in love and wonder — thousands knelt
> And worship'd in her presence — burning tears,
> And words that died in utterance, and a pause
> Of breathless, agitated eagerness
> First gave the full heart's homage: then came forth
> A shout that rose to heaven; and the hills,
> The distant valleys, all rang with the name
> Of the Æolian Sappho — every heart
> Found in itself some echo to her heart. (1841 *Poetical Works* 212)

While the scene has shifted here away from the salon of Hannah More, the most important features of the creative space remain the same: More's "Communion sweet from heart to heart" is transcribed here by L.E.L. as "every heart / Found in itself some echo to her heart." A domesticated natural world is the arena for this aesthetics, not a middle-class drawing room, but nevertheless here we have a poetics that is audience-centered and relies on an emotional union reminiscent of Sensibility.

L.E.L.'s "The Improvisatrice," published in 1824, is one of her finest poems, and perhaps one of the most complete statements of her ideas about poetry. This poem, she writes in the Advertisement,

> is an attempt to illustrate that species of inspiration common in Italy, where the mind is warmed from earliest childhood by all that is beautiful in nature, and glorious in art. The character depicted is entirely Italian, — a young female with all the loveliness, vivid feeling and genius of her own impassioned land. (1841 *Poetical Works* 6)

This would seem to bear close resemblances to *The Prelude,* but as the opening scene unfolds, we discover that the improvisatrice is very conscious of the social context and the cultural tradition in which she writes. "I am a daughter of that land," the poem begins,

> Where the poet's lip and the painter's hand
> Are most divine, — where the earth and sky,
> Are picture both and poetry —
> I am of Florence. (7)

Significantly, the poet must situate herself clearly for the reader, must map her literary location. The artifacts that surround her in this creative space contribute significantly to her art: statues, paintings, music, "language so silvery," "And songs whose wile and passionate line / Suited a soul of romance like mine." The improvisatrice's scene of writing is specifically Florence, a site that unites nature and culture, creation and ruin:

> Florence! . . .
> Where Time had spared each glorious gift
> By Genius unto Memory left!
> . . . In the dim loveliness of night,
> In fountains with their diamond light,
> In aged temple, ruin'd shrine,
> And its green wreath of ivy twine; —
> In very change of earth and sky,
> Breathed the deep soul of poesy. (8)

For L.E.L. as for de Staël and Hemans, the past is one of the most important parameters of the creative scene, and the wreckage of that past becomes part of the emotional texture of the poem and part of the writer's and readers' mutual experience of the text. While we could read this as part of McFarland's "diasparactive triad," "the [fragmented] phenomenology of human awareness" (*Forms of Ruin* 3, 5), it may be that only in the suspension of conventional culture, in the spatial ruins of society, could women writers find the room to create.

This becomes clearer later in "The Improvisatrice" when the narrator locates herself in the domain of gender. At best, this is an ambivalent site for the speaker: she finds herself in a world of tradition and culture, but it is a world that diminishes women's accomplishments. "My power was but a woman's power; / Yet, in that great and glorius dower / Which Genius gives, I had my part . . ." (7). While the improvisatrice does give Petrarch as one of her mentors, it is clearly Sappho with whom the speaker identifies: the woman writer speaks in the poem, while Petrarch does not.

The scene of "The Improvisatrice" is Florence, and I think that is significant. Urban space is not "charter'd," as it was for Blake, not "blank confusion" that "lays the whole creative powers of man asleep," as it was for Wordsworth in the seventh book of *The Prelude*. For L.E.L., More, de Staël, Hemans, and other writers, the scene of creativity — a salon or an intimate and "ruined" public space — denotes and actualizes an aesthetic that is inscribed by class and gender, an art that is representative of, even created with the help of, a whole group of people. The artist creates spontaneously surrounded by her audience, without whom the creative process would be impossible. Her discourse is expressive, but it is expressive of the audience as well as of herself: "every heart / Found in itself some echo to her heart." The symbiosis between writer and audience is even clearer in L.E.L.'s "A History of the Lyre," where Eulalie (the Sappho/Corinne improvisatrice) is "The centre of a group, whose converse light / Made a fit element, in which her wit / Flash'd like the lightning" (1841 *Poetical Works* 116).

The sense here is that the writer composes in a collaborative environment and becomes a representative voice for the group. The production of discourse becomes a collective, not an individual enterprise. Elizabeth Benger's 1791 poem, "*The Female Geniad*," is, tellingly, plural, not singular; and even when (as is true later in the period) greater emphasis is put on the individual writer, that writer is usually construed as "representative," as a distillation of a collective voice, a community. Felicia Hemans, according to an 1853 memoir by her friend and poet Lydia Sigourney, is "the poet of her own sex. The hopes, the affections, the duties of woman, *as woman,* find expression in her highest eloquence of song" (Hemans, 1849–52 *Works* 46).

While I have been arguing for an alternative mapping of the creative process, a different site of composition, I want to emphasize that strict polarities between men and women writers do not exist. Certainly we can find instances of the writer on the precipice or in the garret in texts written by women, such as Charlotte Smith's *Beachy Head.* Conversely we can find texts written by men that locate creativity within a domestic or an intimate public space: Hemans, after all, considered Wordsworth "the true *Poet of Home*" (Chorley, *Memorials* 1: 99; Hemans's emphasis); and we recall some of the celebrated all-male social gatherings of the period, including Benjamin Robert Haydon's famous dinner party. The crux of the argument here is that we have mapped our vision of Romanticism along the meridian of Ossian's cave and Chatterton's garret, the individual genius writing in splendid isolation. In the process we have ignored other sites and poetics, including the salon and Sappho's agora, a collaborative, conversational, and improvisational aesthetics. The task of charting the scenes of Romanticism should go forward, because there remains, in Stuart Curran's words, "a *terra incognita* beneath our very feet" ("The 'I' Altered" 189).

Notes

1. For philosophical approaches to theories of space, see Graham Nerlich, *The Shape of Space* and Bas C. van Fraassen, *An Introduction to the Philosophy of Time and Space.* For analyses of behavioral geography, see Robert D. Sack, *Conceptions of Space in Social Thought: A Geographic Perspective,* Reginald G. Golledge and Gerard Rushton, eds., *Spatial Choice and Spatial Behavior,* and Yi-Fu Tuan, *Space and Place: The Perspective of Experience.* See also Leonard Lutwack, *The Role of Place in Literature.*

2. Abrams, of course, made "the secularization of inherited theological ideas and ways of thinking" the *leitmotif* of *Natural Supernaturalism* and his version of Romanticism (12). But the narrative of crisis and epiphany (and many critics will acknowledge Augustine's *Confessions* as the base text) has been adopted by many Romanticists. Geoffrey Hartman's chapter on "The Poetics of Prophecy" in his *The Unremarkable Wordsworth* analyzes both *The Prelude* and "Tintern Abbey" as prophetic texts, revisions of Psalm 42 and Romans 8 (179).

3. Paul J. deGategno briefly reviews Ossian's influence, and argues that Ossian's successors either directly alluded to James Macpherson's poetry or generally modeled themselves after Ossian (*James Macpherson* 112–34). The most famous contemporary defense of Ossian, Hugh Blair's "A Critical Dissertation on the Poems of Ossian, the Son of Fingal," asserts that Ossian "moves perpetually in the high region of the grand and the pathetic," an epistemology Blair overtly links to the

"wild and romantic" scenery pictured in Ossian's verse. By calling Ossian's writings "the poetry of the heart," and arguing that "Ossian did not write, like modern poets, to please readers and critics," Blair was in essence theorizing Ossian's scene of writing as an aesthetic environment (Macpherson, *Poems of Ossian* 107–8).

4. For an extensive discussion of what Anne K. Mellor calls "masculine Romanticism," see the first chapter of her *Romanticism and Gender* 17–29. The bulk of Mellor's book (31–169) is an attempt to construct a "feminine Romanticism."

5. De Quincey's "Recollections of Hannah More," which appeared in *Tait's Magazine* in December 1833, characterized More as "a clever woman" who "had been pushed forward by feeble-minded women of rank to assume a station of authority which did not naturally belong to her" (*Selected Writings* 553). De Quincey also launches into a vitrolic attack on women intellectuals: "they have their peculiar province," De Quincey allows, "But that province does not extend to *learning*, technically so called" (552). Both Ross and Wolfson (in this volume) have written on Byron's castigation of the "Blues"; see, for example, the famous reference to the Blues "bear[ing] false witness" in stanza 206 of *Don Juan*.

6. Coleridge's most well-known conversation poems are, of course, "The Eolian Harp," "This Lime-Tree Bower my Prison," "Frost at Midnight," "Fears in Solitude," "The Nightingale," and "Dejection." John Thelwall's "Paternal Tears," a series of ten "Effusions," is another good example of conversation poems following Coleridge's earlier productions, printed in his volume, *Poems chiefly written in retirement*. Southey also worked in this genre.

7. Elizabeth Janeway (*Man's World, Woman's Place* 42–43), Ann Oakley (*Woman's Work*), and Leonore Davidoff and Catherine Hall (*Family Fortunes*) all argue that during the early development of industrial society the home remained a site of production, not simply passive consumption. As Oakely suggests, all that changed during the Romantic period, and I would argue that, as the home became separated from the sphere of economic production, it also became the site of its own fictionalization, a symbol for women's creativity. The fact that Jane Austen and Maria Edgeworth wrote in the drawing room reflects the importance and the limitations of the family circle as a creative space. An interesting text in this regard is Isaac Taylor's *The Family Pen*, which celebrates Jane Taylor and her family's literary accomplishments, a family analyzed in Davidoff's and Hall's exhaustive study. For the cultural prelude to the entrenchment of domesticity and the fate of sensibility, see Janet Todd's *Sensibility: An Introduction* and Mitzi Myers's "Reform or Ruin."

Catherine B. Burroughs

English Romantic Women Writers and Theatre Theory: Joanna Baillie's Prefaces to the *Plays on the Passions*

During the past two decades several developments have occurred to set the stage for studies that consider the contributions of women to Romantic theatre: the revisionist readings of early nineteenth-century British drama and theatre that began to appear after 1968;[1] an increase after 1987 in the books published on women writing in the English Romantic period;[2] and the work of feminists who, especially since 1985, have provided women in theatre with a richer context for their reexaminations of dramatic literature and what Jill Dolan calls theatre's "representational apparatus" (46)[3] This essay discusses as theatre theory several of the play prefaces of the Romantic playwright and critic Joanna Baillie and locates them within a tradition of women writing about the stage, a context that has been largely unexplored and, when considered, identified primarily with feminist theatre artists of the past twenty years. Baillie's sensitivity to the potentiality of "the closet" to provide alternative models for the staging of her characters' domestic experiences anticipates the work of women in contemporary theatre — especially lesbian performers and theorists — who have struggled to "clear . . . public spaces for the foregrounding of women's realities" (Lynda Hart, "Introduction," *Making a Spectacle* 13).

A close look at what women in Baillie's era wrote about and for the theatre will reveal that traditional conceptions of theatre theory must undergo reevaluation if one is to appreciate the wealth of theoretical discourse that survives from this period. Anthologies and discussions of theoretical trends in theatre history, such as Marvin Carlson's critical survey published in 1984, have left the impression that the valuable theories of theatre being written throughout the ages were composed for publication by men.[4] While women in Romantic theatre wrote in traditional forums and forms — in the usually anonymous play reviews and theatre commentaries published in magazines, newspapers, and periodicals, as well as prefaces, advertisements, prologues, and epilogues attached to single and collected editions of plays—a less conventional, sometimes more candid, form of theoretical discourse emerges from journals, diaries, letters, and memoirs, some of which were never intended for public perusal. The category of theatre theory can be expanded further to include discourse that blurs the boundaries between theatrical performance and the performance of gender roles in the social arena.

For example, although Mary Wollstonecraft is not commonly associated with Romantic theatre, her *Letters Written During a Short Residence in Sweden, Norway, and Denmark* (1796) — in which she sometimes cites passages from Shakespeare and other dramatists and uses an occasional theatrical metaphor to describe the performance of gender and class roles — can be read as discourse that not only engages theatrical issues but also theorizes a position in both social and theatrical settings for the feminist subject. She never wrote a full-length drama; indeed, William Godwin burned her "sketch of a comedy, which turns," he wrote in his memoirs of her life, "in the serious scenes, upon the incidents of her own story" (*Memoirs* 255), including her tortured relationship with Gilbert Imlay. But Wollstonecraft's references to theatre in the letters she wrote to Imlay suggest her keen interest in the social performances of those like herself who would enact the role of gender maverick. Echoing Shakespeare in her twenty-second letter, she wrote: "All the world is a stage, thought I; and few are there in it who do not play the part they have learnt by rote; and those who do not, seem marks set up to be pelted at by fortune; or rather as sign-posts, which point out the road to others, whilst forced to stand still themselves amidst the mud and dust" (*Memoirs* 186).

Could Romantic theatre provide women with a platform for dramatizing such a position as Wollstonecraft describes above? This is the kind of question constructed by the theatre theory of women writers of the period, even though women had been working in London theatres for well over a century. Sue-Ellen Case and Janelle Reinelt have recently observed that when people view as spectacle the struggle for and against control of social relationships, they are acknowledging their participation in "the performance of power": theatrical metaphor or analogy "accommodates the materialist perception that there is a 'playing out' of power relations, a 'masking' of authority, and a 'scenario' of events" (*Performance of Power* x). Case and other feminist deconstructionists like Judith Butler have worked to demonstrate that the boundaries between social and theatrical performances are more permeable than previous discussions would suggest, especially in reference to women's theatre history.

More than ten years have now passed since Dale Spender wrote the impassioned preface to her book on women intellectuals, *Women of Ideas and What Men Have Done to Them* (1982), but her words still sound urgent. In order to accommodate women's attempts throughout history to "describe and explain the experience of women in a male-dominated society" (23–24), Spender stated emphatically that the terms "theory," "theorist," and "criticism" would need to be redefined. This was the view of Susan Sniader Lanser and Evelyn Torton Beck, who, even earlier than Spender, posed the following question as the title of their essay: "[Why] Are There No Great Women Critics?" Arguing that "not only the conception of criticism, but the critical theories themselves, have been seriously distorted by the omission of women's thought" (87), Lanser and Beck focus in their essay on three neglected women thinkers to show how a reconsideration of their work could cause one to revise "the categories and the terminology of critical discourse" (89). The forthcoming anthology edited by the Folger Collective on Early Women Critics (1660–1820) will surely assist in this goal, but, as Lanser noted at the first Modern Language Association session to concentrate on early women writers and their criticism (December 1991), "there is more at stake in reading early women critics than a revised understanding of women's place in the critical projects of the eighteenth century" ("Women Critics" 5). The feminist reader will now want to raise a number of questions that focus on the issue of how "to go about telling the history of women critics and their work" (8).[5]

For some time I have been interested in how theatre scholars perform the story of women in theatre and how — as Lynda Nead and Tracy Davis have wondered — their narratives "challenge the terms, periodization, and categories of the scholarly tradition" (Davis, "Questions for a Feminist Methodology" 63).[6] In prefaces to their scholarship, Jill Dolan and Sue-Ellen Case, both of whom have produced a body of rich theoretical material about the theatre, try as carefully as possible to confront the ways in which their positionality informs their narratives. A similar impulse seems to be operating in the prefaces and advertisements of women in Romantic theatre. Often documents of their enculturated fears, the prefaces of these theatre artists yield moments "in which social attitudes about gender [can] be made visible" (Diamond "Brechtian Theory/Feminist Theory" 91).

For regardless of the successes of a number of individuals — including Hannah More, Hannah Cowley, Sarah Siddons, Elizabeth Inchbald, and Dorothy Jordan — women artists in the Romantic period still had to wrestle with the central tension structuring the work of every woman involved in theatre since the Restoration. This was the conflict between conforming to social strictures on the performance of femininity and interpreting femininity on a theatrical stage, a conflict alluded to earlier in the mid-eighteenth century in the prologue to Frances Sheridan's play, *The Discovery* (1763):

> A Female culprit at your bar appears,
> Not destitute of hope, nor free
> Her utmost crime she's ready to confess,
> A simple trespass — neither more nor less;
> For truant-like, she rambled out of bounds,
> And dar'd to venture on poetic grounds.

Fear of "rambling out of bounds" caused a number of Romantic women playwrights more often than not to portray themselves in their prefaces as "anxious" and "trembling" at the prospect of public representation.[7] Frequently these artists cast themselves as innocents initiated into the world of experience by a sometimes kindly, often inattentive paternal actor-manager or male friend, who urges them before the public against their modesty or better judgment. In her preface to *The School for Friends* (1806), for instance, Marianne Chambers apologizes for being "[y]oung and unacquainted with that knowledge of the stage, which is only to be acquired by Experience," the same gesture contained in a letter written to a female correspondent by sometime playwright Felicia Hemans on January 26, 1825, concerning a prospective performance of *The Vespers of Palermo* (1823):

> You will find from Mr. — that I am again likely to appear before the public. I cannot help feeling more anxiety than usual on the occasion. I believe it is the ill-nature apparently excited by the "Vespers" which has disagreeably enlarged my knowledge of the world, and given me a timidity to which, at least in its present degree, I was before a stranger. (cited in Chorley, *Memorials* 1: 108)

Mary Russell Mitford's introduction to the edition that contains *Rienzi, Foscari, Julian*, and *Charles the First* (1854) resembles a soliloquy with which she expresses the tensions that women in Romantic (and, by the time these plays were collected, Victorian) theatre performed as they pursued a public career. Mitford writes:

> How he [Francis Bennoch] chanced upon these plays of mine, I hardly know. I think he picked them up in the library of a great country-house where he was visiting. They had fallen into such utter oblivion, that I also might have forgotten them, but for an occasional dream, too vague to be called a hope, that in the brief moment of kindly indulgence, which follows the death of any

one who has contributed, however slightly, to the public amusement, some friend might gather them together in the same spirit that prompts the string-ing verses into an epitaph. To edite these tragedies to myself, seems a kind of anachronism, not unlike engraving the inscription upon my own tombstone. I can only pray that my poor plays may be mercifully dealt with as if they were indeed published by my executor, and the hand that wrote them were laid in peaceful rest. (*Dramatic Works* 1: vi)

While one could certainly read these words playfully — a little later, in fact, Mitford tells her reader that she has "no mind to forfeit so pleasant a privilege" as the tradition of indulging "in the permitted egoism of a rambling preface" (1: vi) — the vocabulary and images Mitford uses suggest a more somber performance of these lines. This preface writer creates a persona clearly conflicted about the desirability of publishing her "poor plays." In one breath she entertains the "dream" of having died so that she might "merit a brief moment of kindly indulgence" from her male friend, Francis Bennoch,[8] who — playing the office of executor — will take all re-sponsibility for publication from her shoulders. Yet she also identifies her discovered plays as residing in a country-house library, rendering them part of the established male literary tradition. By synechdochizing herself as "the hand that wrote [these tragedies]" — which she imagines "laid in peaceful rest" — Mitford creates an image that expresses her desire both to distance herself from and call attention to the fact of her authorship.

Mitford's performance of her uneasy relationship to publication is familiar because representative of "women writing in all periods of literary history" (Levin, "Romantic Prose" 191). But while the prefaces of women in Romantic theatre codify their anxiety, their correspondence frequently reveals an understanding of the importance of providing each other with professional and emotional support.[9] For instance, Maria Edgeworth, who published her *Comic Dramas* in 1817, wrote to Elizabeth Inchbald seeking her advice "because you are one of the very few persons in the world who *can* form a decided opinion, and who *will* have the courage to tell the truth to an author" (cited in Boaden, *Memoirs of Mrs. Inchbald* 2: 208–9). Hemans corresponded about theatre and playwrighting with Mitford and Joanna Baillie. Instances of women either directly or indirectly acknowl-edging the work of their female colleagues include Sarah Siddons, who during her first season in London performed as Emily in Hannah Cowley's first play *The Runaway* (1776) and later acted in More's *The Fatal Falsehood* (1779) and Baillie's *De Montfort* (1798). Dorothy Jordan, the era's great comic, performed in Inchbald's *The Wedding Day* (1794), Mary Robinson's farce called *Nobody* (1794),[10] and Chambers's *The School for Friends* (1806). Harriet Lee wrote both prologue and epilogue to one of her sister Sophia's plays, *Almeyda, Queen of Granada* (1796), which was dedicated to Siddons, who in turn was praised in a poem by Baillie. Baillie framed Mary Berry's *The Fashionable Friends* (1802) with two verse speeches when it was performed as a private theatrical in 1800. These artists among many — Elizabeth Craven, Eglinton Wallace, Frances Burney, Jane West — discussed playwrighting, staging, managing-directing, costuming, acting, and theatre reviewing in the process of creating a support system through which they might more readily develop their confidence in theatrical endeavor and produce what could today be called a gendered theory of theatre derived from the experience of being female in the Romantic period.

Joanna Baillie is among the most significant theatre theorists of her era. I have lately found it a relief to read again Baillie's prefatory remarks, to encounter the vulnerability she performs in front of her reading audience, the resistance she maintains to assuming an authoritative posture that cannot be truthfully enacted. While she follows the convention of affixing prefaces to compositions in which the author "begs" for the reader's "mercy" and "indulgence," her discourse is written in the painstakingly honest and self-reflexive voice of someone unfettered by either false modesty or low self esteem.[11] Throughout her prefaces Baillie qualifies her assertions about her work as well as her criticisms of other dramatists, expressing, on the one hand, her sense that she "is about to bring before the public a work with doubtless, many faults and imperfections on its head" ("Introductory Discourse," *Works* 10)[12] and, on the other, a belief that she has done something wonderfully unusual. Her plays, she writes, are "part of an extensive design: of one which, as far as my information goes, has nothing exactly similar to it in any language" (1); to "trace [the passions] in their rise and progress in the heart, seems but rarely to have been the object of any dramatist" (10); "a complete exhibition of passion, with its varieties and progress in the breast of man, has, I believe, scarcely ever been attempted in Comedy" (14); "I know of no series of plays, in any language, expressly descriptive of the different passions" (17).

Indeed, Baillie's prefaces anticipate "the mode of address of positionality" (Case, *Performing Feminisms* 6) in the prefatory writing of a number of contemporary feminist theatre theorists. Here is Jill Dolan in 1988 in her preface to *The Feminist Spectator as Critic*:

> In publication, it seems equally important to take a stand and to state it at the outset of one's writing. If part of the materialist feminist project is to demystify ideological authority in performance and in dramatic literary texts, it is necessary to guard against reinstituting the materialist feminist critic as the absent, naturalized authority. Demystifying the author and particularizing — instead of idealizing — the reader for whom she writes seems imperative as part of the critical process.
>
> I have tried continually to clarify my stance and my ideological, political, and personal investments in the studies that follow. I write from my own perspective as a white, middle-class woman, with every effort to stay aware of and change my own racism and attitudes about class. As a Jew and a lesbian, I also write from my own awareness of exclusion from dominant ethnic and heterosexual discourse. (x)

Dolan's approach to writing theatre theory resembles Baillie's in her three prefaces to the *Plays on the Passions* (1798–1836), for both writers aim to "demystify their authority, "particularize" their reader-spectators, "clarify" their positionality and perspective, and (in Dolan's case more than Baillie's) "stay aware of" their own attitudes towards race and class. Certainly Baillie is no less self-conscious than Dolan about analyzing the relationship that she seeks to create with her writing between her audience-reader and preface-persona.

For example, early in her introductory discourse Baillie reflects upon people's "intercourse with society" (2) and how their experiences of the world affect their experiences as spectators in the theatre. Wondering why people would be drawn to the spectacle of another's distress, Baillie speculates that "multitudes of people" are attracted to "a public execution" (2) because of the pleasures attendant on reading the gestures of the prisoner's body as clues to his or her emotional state. The same must hold true, she reasons, in the case of the "dreadful custom" among the "savages of America" of "sacrificing their prisoners of war" (2). This could "never have become a permanent national custom, but for this universal desire in the human mind to behold man in every situation, putting forth his strength against the current of adversity" (2). For, Baillie asks,

> What human creature is there who can behold a being like himself under the violent agitation of those passions which all have, in some degree, experienced, without feeling himself most powerfully excited by the sight? (3)

Baillie's theory of drama emphasizes her belief that the capacity of her reader-spectators for "sympathetic curiosity"[13] about "others" will be enlarged if they (like Baillie) can witness "what men are *in the closet* as well as in the field; by the blazing hearth and at the social board" (5, my emphasis); if they and she can gaze upon

> even the smallest indications of an unquiet mind, the restless eye, the muttering lip, the half-checked exclamation and the hasty start, [this circumstance] will set [our] attention as anxiously upon the watch as the first distant flashes of a gathering storm. . . . If invisible, would [we] not follow him [the character] into his lonely haunts, *into his closet,* into the midnight silence of his chamber? (3–4, my emphasis)

But how are spectators interested enough in the kind of character described above to follow him "into his closet," especially since Covent Garden and Drury Lane, the theatres licensed in 1737 to perform the legitimate drama — the British canon of plays — each provided seats for over 3,000 audience members? This question structures Baillie's theory of theatre as she dreams of a theatrical environment that would allow the spectator greater access to actors' expression of their private passions.

By proposing with her plays to "lift up the roof of [a criminal's] dungeon," for example, and "look upon" him "the night before he suffers, in his still hours of privacy" (2), Baillie suggests a more literal meaning for the term "closet drama" than what the phrase would come to mean after the Romantic period. Instead of describing a dramatic text that is unperformed or unperformable, the term "closet drama" as it derives from Baillie's theory refers to a genre that actually dramatizes scenes from a character's closet. This focus was in itself certainly not new; the plays of Shakespeare, the domestic tragedies of George Lillo, and elements of the theatre theory of Denis Diderot, among others, provided a context for Baillie's desire to create plays about private emotions in closeted settings. Baillie's theory of the closet is notable primarily for its recognition of the closet's dramatic potential, for its resistance to antitheatricality. Whether contemplating the behavior of prisoners, "the savages of America" (2–3), children, or "the fall of the feeble stranger who simply expresses the anguish of his soul" (6), Baillie's discourse conveys an intense desire not only to confront intellectually the fact that "many a miserable being . . . is tormented in obscurity" (14) but also to *see represented on stage* the closeted moments of both middle-class[14] and marginalized characters.

It is especially interesting, in this post-Stonewall era, to see the phrase "closet drama" accruing new associations. Today it is likely to be employed to refer to plays that both repress and reveal homosexual experience (see Sky Gilbert, "Closet Plays"; Alan Sinfield, "Closet Dramas"). Certainly the word "closet" has collected connotations that are as yet unchronicled by the *OED*, whose definitions Eve Sedgwick reprints in *Epistemology of the Closet* (66). Sedgwick observes "that the trope of the closet is so close to the heart of some modern preoccupations that it could be, or has been, evacuated of its historical gay specificity" (72). But Sedgwick wants to argue just the reverse in her discussion of closet epistemology:

> I think that a whole cluster of the most crucial sites for the contestation of meaning in twentieth-century Western culture are consequentially and quite indelibly marked with the historical specificity of homosocial/homosexual definition, notably but not exclusively male, from around the turn of the century. Among those sites are ... the pairings secrecy/disclosure and private/ public. Along with and sometimes through these epistemologically charged pairings, condensed in the figures of "the closet" and "coming out," this very specific crisis of definition has then ineffaceably marked other pairings as basic to modern cultural organization as masculine/feminine, majority/minority, innocence/initiation, natural/artificial, new/old, growth/decadence, ur- bane/provincial, health/illness, same/different, cognition/paranoia, art/ kitsch, sincerity/sentimentality, and voluntarity/addiction. (72)

As Sedgwick suggests, it may be difficult in the 1990s for a reader of Baillie's theory to keep at bay contemporary associations with the word "closet," and I question why one would want to, especially since (as I will discuss later) one can see links between the kinds of issues that Baillie raises for women in theatre and the issues with which feminist (i.e., lesbian) theatre theorists engage. In reference to the past century, Sedgwick writes, "So permeative has the suffusing stain of homo/heterosexual crisis been that to discuss any of these indices [above] in any context, in the absence of an antihomo- phobic analysis, must perhaps be to perpetuate unknowingly compulsions implicit in each" (72–73).

Baillie printed her first volume of dramas before they had been per- formed, possessing "no likely channel to the former mode of public intro- duction [the stage]" (16). But even as she admits in this first preface (published anonymously in 1798) that the opportunity to attach a theoret- ical essay to her plays "does more than over-balance the splendour and effect of theatrical representation," she also writes that it should not be supposed "that I have written [the plays] for the closet rather than the stage":

> A play but of small poetical merit, that is suited to strike and interest the spectator, to catch the attention of him who will not, and of him who cannot read, is a more valuable and useful production than one whose elegant and

harmonious pages are admired in the libraries of the tasteful and refined. . . . I should, therefore, have been better pleased to have introduced them to the world from the stage than from the press. (16)

Baillie's desire to see her plays staged suggests that a shift in dramatic focus to the closet does not necessarily have to signal antitheatricality. This is significant, since, as critics have recently noticed, in the Romantic period "the antitheatrical prejudice" (see Jonas Barish, *The Antitheatrical Prejudice*) can be linked to a distrust of what has traditionally been labeled feminine.[15] Because Baillie's theory of play composition values the public performance of dramas that take place in the closet, hers is conducive to emphasizing experiences traditionally performed off stage and behind the curtains. One would surely want to include Baillie's prefaces in discussions that revise traditional views of closet drama from poor imitations of Elizabethan verse plays to innovative playscripts that offer critiques of the Romantic stage and its social context.[16]

Indeed, Baillie's discourse may be contrasted with some of the more familiar criticism of the Romantic age, which portrays the closet as a place to read—rather than to enact—certain kinds of plays (namely Shakespeare's); as a place where one prefers to perform dramatic literature in a "mental theatre" of one's design (see Richardson, *A Mental Theater*) rather than in front of a live audience. Typical of this "closet criticism" was Charles Lamb's famous statement in "On the Tragedies of Shakespeare":

> So to see Lear acted,—to see an old man tottering about the stage with a walking-stick, turned out of doors by his daughters in a rainy night, has nothing in it but what is painful and disgusting. We want to take him into shelter and relieve him. That is all the feeling which the acting of Lear ever produced in me. But the Lear of Shakespeare cannot be acted. . . . The greatness of Lear is not in corporal dimension, but in intellectual: . . . On the stage we see nothing but corporal infirmities and weakness, the impotence of rage; while we read it, we see not Lear, but we are Lear,—we are in his mind. (298)

Here Lamb is not opposed to representation per se, for earlier in this text he writes: "I am not arguing that *Hamlet* should not be acted, but how much *Hamlet* is made another thing by being acted" (293). Rather, Lamb chafes against what he regards as the stage's prioritizing of body over mind: "What we see upon a stage is body and bodily action; what we are conscious of in reading is almost exclusively the mind, and its movements" (300). While for Lamb "the sight actually destroys the faith" (300), for Baillie the act of looking into others' dungeons and closets—and even other cultures—

might arouse one's faith in embodiment as the pathway to "sympathetic curiosity" (3), and thus to higher moral development. Although Baillie believed that there are some subjects (e.g., the "sacred") that should not be represented ("Preface to *The Martyr*," *Works* 512), her vow to write play-scripts that explore the dynamics of passions that occur behind closed doors leads her to consider what kind of theatrical space would be needed to embody such closet dramas. Rather than concluding that theatrical representation inhibits people's imagination or limits their experience of exploring the psychological complexities of human life, in her discourse Baillie turns to the problem of how the London theatre might be changed in order to accommodate her dramatic vision.[17]

From the time of her plays' publication and (in the case of some of them) their subsequent production, writers have criticized Baillie for creating plays that seem to demonstrate little familiarity with stage technique.[18] Reflecting on the 1800 production of *De Montfort* at Drury Lane, which starred Siddons and John Philip Kemble, James Boaden — one of Siddons's biographers — wrote:

> Mrs Siddons did her utmost with the Countess Jane. But the basis of the tragedy was the passion of hatred, and the incidents were all gloomy, and dark, and deadly. On the stage, I believe, no spectator wished it a longer life, and it is to the last degree mortifying to have to exhibit so many proofs, that the talent of dramatic writing in its noblest branch was in fact dead among us. (*Memoirs of Mrs. Siddons* 2: 330)

In recent years P. M. Zall has drawn attention to other critiques of Baillie's stage craft written by her contemporaries. Recalling Siddons's performance of Jane De Montfort in the same production, Thomas Campbell observed that, although Baillie's tragedies "were regarded by the reading world as the sweetest strains that hailed the close of the eighteenth century" (*Life of Mrs. Siddons* 2: 255), she did not know "the stage practically"; if she had, "she would never have attached the importance which she does to the development of single passions in single tragedies" (2: 254). Campbell also shares with readers of his Siddons biography a paraphrase of Edmund Kean's comments about *De Montfort* after a revival of the play in 1821: "though a fine poem, it would never be an acting play" (2: 257). In a letter written in 1800 Inchbald concluded that "De Montford," while a "fine play" is "both dull and highly improbable in the representation; and sure it is, though pity that it is so, its very charm in the reading militates against its power in the acting" (cited in Boaden, 2: 34).[19]

Without at this time entering into the debate about the relationship between "text" and "performance," which closet drama performs beautifully, I would like to suggest in the next few pages that Baillie's observations in her prefaces about Romantic staging comprise a theory of theatre that, if implemented, would more readily allow for the performance of the kinds of experiences that occur in domestic space. For, even though Baillie's discourse focuses primarily on male characters and issues affecting middle-class spectatorship, her "closet theatre theory" shares certain impulses with those who would perform the marginalization of society's less powerful characters; who would enact the offstage, backstage, private experiences of different races, classes, genders, and sexualities that have until recently been revealed primarily through the nontraditional venues of contemporary performance art.

I am less concerned here with the discrepancy between what Campbell calls Baillie's "theory and system" (2: 252) than with exploring Baillie's theoretical vision of a theatrical environment that would show her character studies to best advantage. A thorough discussion of Baillie's plays — including the similarities and discrepancies between her theory and practice — is the subject of a lengthy study, but I will generalize here that one could make a case for some of her plays as practical examples of her theory. Certainly we see a number of Baillie's characters in private moments, in closet performance, if you will. The "introductory discourse" and *De Montfort,* for example, share a vocabulary that underscores Baillie's focus on the closet: "conceal," "small," "secret," "hidden," "unknown." In the second scene of *De Montfort,* Jane goes into her brother's apartments, a move that echoes Baillie's description of female Tragedy following "the great man into his secret closet" in her introductory discourse (*Works* 8). Both *Rayner* (1804) and *Basil* (1798) contain or discuss traditionally marginalized characters: Ohio ("a negro attached to the prison") and northern laborers, the subject of an idealized soliloquy by Gauriecio in II.iii of *Basil.* Yet, these parallels aside, Baillie acknowledges in her earliest preface that "critics do not unfrequently write in contradiction to their own rules" ("Introductory Discourse," *Works* 15).

Midway through her introductory essay, Baillie writes a rhetorical question that serves as the capstone to her detailed characterization of Tragedy as a female person whose responsibility it is "to unveil to us the human mind under the dominion of those strong and fixed passions, which, seemingly unprovoked by outward circumstances, will, from small beginnings, brood within the breast" ("Introductory Discourse," *Works* 8):

> For who hath followed the great man into his *secret closet,* or stood by the side
> of his nightly couch, and heard those exclamations of the soul which heaven
> alone may hear, that the historian should be able to inform us: and *what form of
> story, what mode of rehearsed speech* will communicate to us those feelings, whose
> irregular bursts, abrupt transitions, sudden pauses, and half-uttered sugges-
> tions, scorn all harmony of measured verse, all method and order of relation?
> (8, my emphasis)

With this question, Baillie introduces stage theory to her theory of the
drama by suggesting that the playwright of tragedy will want to consider
not only "what form of story" but also "what mode of rehearsed speech"
might be required to follow "the great man into his secret closet." Here,
and especially in her preface to the 1812 volume of the *Plays on the Passions,* Baillie raises questions about what dramaturgical structure and acting
method would be needed to communicate her special brand of drama. She
also focuses on issues of spectatorship, theatrical lighting, and blocking (or
stage movement) as these elements contribute to or distract from the
staging of her closet scenes.

By the time she wrote her third preface to the third volume of her
"passion plays" (1812), Baillie had already endured the vicissitudes of
public response to the staging of several of her dramas and, like many of her
contemporaries, blamed their mixed reception on the size of the theatres.
For this reason she is less concerned in 1812 with distinctions between the
study and the stage than with arguing for a transformation of the current
theatrical environment that would allow for the representation of a different kind of dramatic fare:

> The Public have now to choose between what we shall suppose are well-
> written and well-acted plays, the words of which are not heard, or heard but
> imperfectly by two-thirds of the audience, while the finer and more pleasing
> traits of the acting are by a still greater proportion lost altogether; and splendid
> pantomime, or pieces whose chief object is to produce striking scenic effect,
> which can be seen and comprehended by the whole. (*Works* 231)

Rather than pantomimic movement, Baillie would like to see the kind of
"natural and genuine" (233) acting style practiced in the "small theatres" in
which Siddons and "the most admired actors of the present time" (232)
were trained, where they "were encouraged to enter thoroughly into the
characters they represented, and to express in their faces that variety of fine
fleeting emotion which nature in moments of agitation assumes . . ." (232).
Because the London theatres were so large, stage acting there was marked,

in Baillie's observation, by falseness and exaggeration of body movement and facial expression, to "say nothing of expression of voice" (232). Her plays, with their emphasis on the discovery of the concealed passions of closeted characters, would inevitably be acted to ill effect in these larger spaces. In this environment, she asks,

> What actor in his senses will then think of giving to the solitary musing of a perturbed mind, that muttered, imperfect articulation, which grows by degrees into words; that heavy, suppressed voice, as one of speaking through sleep; that rapid burst of sounds which often succeeds the slow languid tones of distress; those sudden, untuned exclamations, which, as if frightened at their own discord, are struck again into silence as sudden and abrupt, with all the corresponding variety of countenance that belongs to it; — what actor so situated will attempt to exhibit all this? No; he will be satisfied, after taking a turn or two across the front of the stage, to place himself directly in the middle of it; and there, spreading out his hands, as if he were addressing some person whom it behoved him to treat with great ceremony, to tell himself, in an audible, uniform voice, all the secret thoughts of his own heart. When he has done this, he will think, and he will think rightly, that he has done enough. (232–33)

This passage demonstrates Baillie's sensitivity to acting technique and articulates why she prefers a less "uniform" mode of speech and movement: such a style would allow for "the gradual unfolding of the passions" (232) during an actor's soliloquy, in Baillie's view one of the most important features of her plays. This passage also shows Baillie confidently entering into the Romantic debate about whether "the actor [should] empathize to such a degree that his own personality would be overcome by the role, or, should he distance himself emotionally so as to enliven the role?" (Flaherty, "Empathy and Distance," 126). It is not "enough," in Baillie's view, for actors to plant themselves center stage (as was the custom during soliloquies), to "spread out" their hands, and to speak in the formal tones of someone "addressing [a] person whom it behoved [them] to treat with great ceremony." To make more credible the convention of speaking aloud one's inner thoughts would require a different approach to acting. But first, a change in theatre architecture must occur, a move from "over-sized buildings" that dwarf "the appearance of individual figures" and work against what Baillie calls "the proper effect" (233) of stage pictures. In current productions, Baillie complains,

> when many people are assembled on the front of the stage to give splendour and importance to some particular scene, or to the conclusion of a piece, the

general effect is often injured by great width of stage: for the crowd is supposed to be attracted to the spot by something which engages their attention; and, as they must not surround this object of attention (which would be their natural arrangement), lest they should conceal it from the audience, they are obliged to spread themselves out in a long straight line on each side of it: now the less those lines or wings are spread out from the centre figures, the less do they offend against natural arrangement, and the less artificial and formal does the whole scene appear. (234)

The idea of a smaller stage attracts Baillie because she imagines it would allow audiences to appreciate her dramatization of "the progress of the higher passions in the human breast" (11) in scenes that should elicit "less artificial and formal" acting and blocking. Certainly in the area of stage lighting the smaller stage would allow for technical subtleties that could reveal and emphasize nuances of character.

The then construction of the London stages makes it "more difficult" she writes, "to produce variety of light and shadow," particularly the technique of "throw[ing] down light upon . . . objects," which she explains in a footnote will "present . . . a varied harmonious mass of figures to the eye, deep, mellow, and brilliant" (234). While Baillie hastens to tell her readers that she does not know "to what perfection machinery for the management of light may be brought in a large theatre," she uses her observations of theatre practice as well as her imagination to conclude that

a great variety of pleasing effects from light and shadow might be more easily produced on *a smaller stage,* that would give change and even interest to pieces otherwise monotonous and heavy; and would often be very useful in relieving the exhausted strength of the chief actors, while want of skill in the inferior could be craftily concealed. (234, my emphasis)

At this point in her third preface Baillie attaches a lengthy footnote on stage lighting, which not only attests to her sophisticated knowledge of Romantic theatrical production but also portrays her as a theatre theorist compelled by her own dramatic vision to search for alternative modes of stage practice. Presently, she writes, the "strong light cast up from lamps on the front of the stage . . . is certainly very unfavourable to the appearance and expression of individual actors" (234). Baillie envisions the following solution to this problem, even while, like a refrain, she states that she is "not at all competent" to address this issue (234):

I should suppose, that by bringing forward the roof of the stage as far as its boards or floor, and placing a row of lamps with reflectors along the inside of the wooden front-piece, such a light as is wanted might be procured. The green curtain in this case ought not to be let down, as it now is, from the front-piece, but some feet within it; and great care taken that nothing should be placed near the lamps capable of catching fire. If this were done, no boxes, I suppose, could be made upon the stage; but the removal of stage-boxes itself would be a great advantage. The front-piece at the top; the boundary of the stage from the orchestra at the bottom; and the pilasters on each side, would then represent the frame of a great moving picture, entirely separated and distinct from the rest of the theatre: whereas, at present, an unnatural mixture of audience and actors, of house and stage, takes place near the front of the stage, which destroys the general effect to a very great degree. (235n)

This detailed passage provides readers with insight not only into London theatre in the early nineteenth century but also into Baillie's theatrical mind. She carefully balances her observations of the specifics of Romantic theatre practice with pragmatic and imaginative suggestions for how to represent what her theory has defined as closet drama. When, at the end of this preface, she apologizes for being "impertinent" (235), she offers as an "excuse" an "almost irresistable desire to express my thoughts . . . upon what has occupied them considerably; and a strong persuasion that I ought not, how unimportant soever they might be, entirely conceal them" (235). With these words she paints herself as the impassioned soliloquizing character her dramatic theory purports to discover for spectators: since she cannot any longer "conceal" her thoughts, the process of producing prefaces to her projected dramatic oeuvre allows her to perform a heroine's soliloquy.

Like Baillie's, Hannah More's concern with the dramatic content of her own plays arose from her belief that the stage is "no *indifferent* thing"; the "impressions it makes on the mind are deep and strong; deeper and stronger, perhaps, than are made by any other amusement" (1830 *Works* 2: 157). But unlike Baillie (who was herself a devoted Christian), More shapes her discourse with the overriding question, "Should a Christian frequent it?" (2: 157).[20] In her "Preface to the Tragedies" that appears in the second volume of her collected works (1830), More refuses to imagine an alternative theatrical space to the large auditoria of the licensed London theatres. "What the stage might be under another and an imaginary state of things," she writes, "it is not very easy for us to know, and therefore not very important to inquire. . . . Would it not be more safe and simple to determine our judgment as to the character of the thing in question on the more *visible,* and therefore more *rational* grounds of its *actual* state, and from the effects which it is known to produce in that state?" (2: 128, my emphasis).

More therefore concentrates on describing the current theatrical offerings of the London stage from concern that they threaten to corrupt the behavior of young female spectators, as they head home inevitably to replay these dramas in their closets (2: 147–48).

Concern for the moral development of her theatre audiences structures many of Baillie's remarks, especially in the prefaces to her later plays such as *The Martyr* (1826). But she does not write from nostalgia for the seventeenth-century tradition that linked private domestic space to upper-class religiosity (Hunter, "The World as Stage and Closet" 282). Instead, Baillie pays attention to "the phenomenology of the English closet" (282) in order to determine how to provide theatregoers with the model for a new approach to representation. While Baillie's Christianity informed much of what she did and wrote — she would never have rested easy if accused of sacrilege — her willingness to compare the current theatrical fare with her speculations about the kind of theatre necessary to dramatize her closet plays makes her discourse seem especially far-sighted and significant in the context of female-authored theatre theory.

The theatrical innovations implied by Baillie's closet theatre theory — a smaller stage that permits the more subtle dramatization of public and private realms, a more naturalistic acting style, a lighting design that would allow audiences to read psychological shifts — are among the legacies for modern and contemporary theatre created by the Romantic stage. These innovations also find their place in a tradition of women experimenting with "language, space, and the body" (Hart, "Introduction" to *Making a Spectacle* 13) in order to dramatize more readily their particular experiences as an oppressed class. Baillie's interest in representing the traditionally unseen and unheard by peering into the closet forecasts Sue-Ellen Case's recent discussion of what she labels "personal theatre" (46) in her landmark polemic, *Feminism and Theatre* (1988). According to Case, personal theatre is another name for women's performances of domestic life, the staging of gender roles in spaces to which they have been confined, or "bastilled" (155) to use Wollstonecraft's word in *The Wrongs of Woman* (1798). Case's extension of the label "theatre" to women's offstage performances in settings such as the salon or garden (46–47) explodes conventional categories in theatre history that would pit the "theatrical" and "dramatic" against the unperformable or the privately "mundane." Case revises the term "theatre" to suggest that women throughout history have created closeted performances that chronicle the experience of those who live behind closed doors, a theatre previously unacknowledged by historians because hidden away from public view. In her plays Baillie does not by any means eschew the public realm — in fact, she is fond of including processions and moments of spectacle in a number of her plays — but she does argue for a smaller theatre space in which life in the closet might be more realistically represented. In theory, she seems to yearn for a theatrical environment conducive to representing the "personal theatre" that Case identifies as among women's contributions to western theatre history.

Might Baillie's closet theatre theory resonate with contemporary lesbian theatre artists for whom the word "closet" perhaps has special significance? I acknowledge the transhistorical and heterosexist dangers of suggesting affinities between the discourse of a nineteenth-century middle-class Scottish woman in Romantic theatre and contemporary lesbians in theatre, even as I am struck by the similarities between Baillie's theoretical implications and lesbian theorists who have written about the stage. Certainly I am reminded that lesbian theatre artists have sometimes found it necessary and desirable to explore their closet revelations in front of audiences restricted to lesbians, in spaces not easily accessible to heterosexual spectators who may be alternately curious, empathetic, or even openly hostile to the works at hand (Case, *Feminism and Theatre* 76). The result has been the creation of a kind of closet theatre that has led to some of the most innovative and influential theories of theatre and performance being written today.

It would be difficult to dispute that Case and Dolan, two of the most prominent critics in academic theatre, have transformed the field of feminist theatre theory by writing about the performances of groups like Split Britches and Red Dyke Theatre, the plays of Jane Chambers and Monique Wittig, and the performance art of Karen Finley, Alina Troyano, and Rachel Rosenthal. In a now classic essay Case proposed that, in order for theatre to present a feminist subject "endowed with the agency for political change," theatre artists might want to consider that "the lesbian roles of butch and femme, as a dynamic duo, offer precisely the strong subject position the movement requires" ("Butch-Femme" 283). First, however,

> the lesbian subject of feminist theory would have to come out of the closet, the basic discourse or style of camp for the lesbian butch-femme positions would have to be clarified, and an understanding of the function of the roles in the homosexual lifestyle would need to be developed, particularly in relation to the historical class and racial relations embedded in such a project. (283)

Certainly Case, Dolan, and other feminist critics are busily engaged in bringing this subject into more public view at the same time that they recognize the value of closeting. Like Case, Judith Butler has concentrated on how "the cultural practices of drag, cross-dressing, and the sexual stylization of butch/femme identities" ("Gender Trouble" 337) underscore the idea that gender is performative and that the disclosure of gender also contains "a certain radical *concealment*" ("Imitation" 15). "If I claim to be a lesbian," Butler writes, "I 'come out' only to produce a new and different 'closet'" (15), a situation less to overcome than to value:

> Conventionally, one comes out *of* the closet (and yet, how often is it the case that we are "outted" when we are young and without resources?); so we are out of the closet, but into what? what new unbounded spatiality? the room, the den, the attic, the basement, the house, the bar, the university, some new enclosure whose door, like Kafka's door, produces the expectation of a fresh air and a light of illumination that never arrives. Curiously, it is the figure of the closet that produces this expectation, and which guarantees its dissatisfaction. For being "out" always depends to some extent on being "in"; it gains its meaning only within that polarity. Hence, being "out" must produce the closet again and again in order to maintain itself as "out." In this sense, *outness* can only produce a new opacity; and *the closet* produces the promise of a disclosure that can, by definition, never come. (16)

In light of Butler's discourse on the dramatic movement that operates when one recognizes her participation in the act of "closeting" as both an unmasking and a veiling, might it be helpful to read — and even perform — Baillie's numerous plays as discussions of this process? And might Butler's comments on the performative aspect of identifying gender and sexuality be enriched by an "intertextual reading" (Diamond, "Brechtian Theory/Feminist Theory" 83) that splices Butler with Baillie's closet theory?

By providing those of us who write about theatre with new tools for rereading theatre history, contemporary gay and lesbian critics sensitize readers to subjects like closet drama and perhaps inadvertently establish links between the contributions of those who perform a homosexual identity and those who identify themselves as "straight" actors. After reading Baillie's critical discourse through the filter of (primarily) lesbian theatre theory, it is easier to assert that her criticism cannot, in her own words, "be seen with indifference," especially by "those who have played at hide and seek, who have crouched down with beating heart in a dark corner, whilst the enemy groped near the spot" ("Introductory Discourse," *Works* 12). Yet it hardly needs reiterating that after the early Romantic period Baillie's popularity waned to the point where almost two hundred years had to pass before her words began to garner the attention they deserve, or even became more readily available for study.[21]

In *De Montfort* (1798), one of the first three plays in Baillie's "passion" series and her best-known drama, Jane De Montfort speaks several lines to her brother that might easily serve as the epigraph to Baillie's closet theory and a directive for reading her work:

Come to my closet; free from all instrusion,
I'll school thee there; and thou again shalt be
My willing pupil (II.ii).

(Re)reading Baillie's prefaces can indeed "school" us in how her closet theatre theory contributes to and helps to create a tradition of female-authored theatre criticism. This process can also help give women in theatre a better sense of the tradition that informs our current inquiry into representation, spectatorship, mimesis, and performance.

Funding for the research for portions of this article was provided by the William Andrews Clark Memorial Library, the Midwest Faculty Seminar Occasional Fellowship Program at the University of Chicago, and Cornell College. I am also grateful to staff members at the Newberry Library for their assistance in procuring some of the materials for this research. Sections of this article were first presented at the session on Women's Voices and the Theatre chaired by Heidi Hutner at the Western Society for Eighteenth-Century Studies (February 1991); the session on Women Dramatists chaired by Carol K. Cyganowski at the Midwestern Modern Language Association (November 1991); and the session on Early Women Critics (1660–1820) chaired by Susan Green at the Modern Language Association (December 1991). I would also like to thank Theresa Kelley for her helpful commentary on an earlier draft of this essay.

Notes

1. Although a number of articles and books on Romantic theatre and drama have been written between 1968 and the present, as of this essay's completion the lone book on women in Romantic theatre is the 1991 publication of Mary Anne Schofield and Cecilia Macheski, eds., *Curtain Calls: British and American Women and the Theater, 1660–1820.*

2. The most significant of these recent books on women in Romanticism are by Anne K. Mellor: see *Romanticism and Gender* (1993) and the edited volume, *Romanticism and Feminism* (1988).

3. For an indication of the range and number of publications on feminist theatre see Susan Steadman's *Dramatic Re-Visions: An Annotated Bibliography of Feminism and Theatre 1972–1988* (1991). Since 1988, the publications in feminist theatre have proliferated.

4. Since the completion of this essay, Carlson has published an expanded edition of the book, *Theories of the Theatre,* which includes contemporary feminist theatre theory (1993).

5. I am grateful to Susan Lanser for her permission to cite here the remarks she made at the MLA session on early women critics (December 1991).

6. See the collection of essays — containing Davis's article — that theorizes about the position of the historian in relation to his/her material: *Interpreting the Theatrical Past,* edited by Thomas Postlewait and Bruce McConachie (1989). See also Susan Bassnett's article on how feminist theater historians can approach the telling of women's theatre history so that they do not privilege "text-based theatre in light of the role of women in the alternative theatre" ("Struggling with the Past" 112).

7. A vivid exception to this tendency occurs in the preface that Eglinton Wallace wrote to *The Whim* (1795), in which she angrily tells her public readers that the Licenser of plays had "disapproved of the Piece" (4) and had therefore caused its withdrawal from the stage.

8. Although Mitford does not identify Bennoch by name in her introduction, she makes it clear that she is speaking of him when she writes: "For the publication of these volumes, the excellent friend *to whom they are inscribed* is solely accountable" (1: v, my emphasis).

9. The conflict in 1779 between Hannah More and Hannah Cowley concerning which one had plagiarized the other seems to have been an exceptional event, largely fueled, according to Ellen Donkin, by a public eager to see women "go at it" ("The Paper War" 153). Also unusual is the document called *Mrs. Galindo's Letter to Mrs. Siddons* (1809) in which Catherine (Gough) Galindo accuses Siddons of having an affair with her husband.

10. For further information about this farce, as well as the fascinating life of its author, see the *Memoirs of the Late Mrs. Robinson, Written by Herself* (1801).

11. For a comparison of the tone of Baillie's introductory discourse with William Wordsworth's in his Preface of 1800, see Judith Page's *Wordsworth and the Cultivation of Women* (forthcoming). Her observations about Baillie's first preface are relevant here: "In feminist terms, Baillie sees herself as a collaborator, not as a solitary genius. She is not so much interested in founding a career or attaining fame in posterity as she is in teaching the people of her own time" (Chapter Two). I am grateful to Judith for her permission to cite this manuscript here.

12. All further references to Baillie's prefaces are quoted from the 1976 reprinting of the 1851 edition of her collected works.

13. Marlon Ross has written about what he identifies as Baillie's "concept of 'sympathetic curiosity'" (*Contours of Masculine Desire* 285). He has also provided a context for Baillie's *Plays on the Passions* in his extensive analysis of women Romantic poets, calling this series of plays "perhaps the most ambitious poetic project taken on by a woman in the early nineteenth century" (258). See also Stuart Curran ("The

'I' Altered"), who has observed that Baillie's plays "exerted the most direct practical and theoretical force on serious drama written in the Romantic period" (186). Other recent discussions of Baillie include P. M. Zall, "The Cool World of Samuel Taylor Coleridge"; Mary McKerrow, "Joanna Baillie and Mary Brunton"; Daniel P. Watkins, "Gender, Class, and Social Motion"; and Jeffrey Cox, *Seven Gothic Dramas*.

14. Note that Baillie does not consider the audience of "the drama" to be "the lowest classes of the labouring people, who are the broad foundation of society, which can never be generally moved without endangering every thing that is constructed upon it, and who are our potent and formidable ballad-readers." Instead, her plays "reach to the classes next in order to them, and who will always have over them no inconsiderable influence" (14).

15. See Terry Castle, *Masquerade and Civilization*; Nina Auerbach, *Private Theatricals*; Catherine Burroughs, "Acting in the Closet"; Julie Carlson, "Impositions of Form."

16. Studies that reevaluate closet drama, and sometimes "the dialectic between 'text' and 'performance'" (Thomas Whitaker, "Review Essay" 144), include Mary Jacobus, "That Great Stage Where Senators Perform"; John Gatton, "'Put into Scenery'"; Julie Carlson, "An Active Imagination"; Issacharoff and Jones, eds., *Performing Texts*; the fall 1988 and fall 1992 issues of *Studies in Romanticism*; Alan Richardson, *A Mental Theater*; Thomas Whitaker, "Review Essay"; Greg Kucich, "'A Haunted Ruin'"; and the spring 1992 edition of *The Wordsworth Circle*. See also Michael Evenden's discussion of how the performance of closet plays by Seneca, Roswitha, Byron, Stein, and Brecht can provide theatricians with models of performance in which the actor's body becomes the stage for theorizing the relationship between actor and character, self and "other" ("Inter-Mediate Stages").

17. It is a subject of debate whether Romantic dramatic criticism is antagonistic toward the stage or whether the "closet criticism" of Hazlitt, Coleridge, Lamb (and sometimes Leigh Hunt) should be regarded as sophisticated reconsiderations of the activity of playreading. For both sides of this issue see Jonas Barish's *The Antitheatrical Prejudice* and Janet Ruth Heller's recent study in which she argues for "a reevaluation of romantic drama criticism that puts [the writings of Coleridge, Lamb, and Hazlitt] in the context of literary history of ideas" (*Coleridge, Lamb, Hazlitt* 1).

18. Margaret Carhart discusses Baillie's remarks on the theatre in her 1923 literary biography, still the best source on Baillie's life. She also includes a helpful section on the performance history of Baillie's dramas.

19. This letter by Inchbald quoted in Boaden is to "Mrs. Phillips" and dated 8 May 1800.

20. More seems to be responding directly to the project Baillie undertook in her series of plays — to write dramas that would each delineate the effect of a single passion on a character — when she writes in her "Preface to the Tragedies": "Love, jealousy, hatred, ambition, pride, revenge, are too often elevated into the rank of splendid virtues, and form a dazzling system of morality, in direct contradiction to the spirit of that religion whose characteristics are 'charity, meekness, peaceableness, long-suffering, gentleness, forgiveness'" (2: 135). Baillie, whose Christianity informs much of her work — and who wrote *A View of the General Tenour of the New*

Testament Regarding the Nature and Dignity of Jesus Christ (1831) — was certainly concerned with the question of what aspects of human existence were appropriate to dramatize (see her prefaces to *The Martyr* and *The Bride* and to the second volume of *Dramas*). Evidently she found no conflict between being a Christian and writing the *Plays on the Passions,* especially since she viewed them as capable of reforming and refining rowdy audiences.

21. Studying the play prefaces by women in Romanticism is made a bit easier by the 1990 reprinting of Elizabeth Inchbald's *Remarks for the British Theatre (1806–09)* prepared by Cecilia Macheski, as well as the anthology edited by Robert W. Uphaus and Gretchen M. Foster, *The "Other" Eighteenth Century: English Women of Letters 1660–1800* (1991), in which an edited version of Baillie's "Introductory Discourse" appears. See also the 1976 facsimile edition of Baillie's 1851 collected works as well as the 1977 facsimile edition of the three volumes of *The Plays on the Passions.* Several of Baillie's plays — *Count Basil, The Trial,* and *De Montfort* — and her "introductory discourse" were recently published by Woodstock Books in the "series of facsimile reprints chosen and introduced by Jonathan Wordsworth" (1990). Jeffrey Cox's collection of seven gothic dramas includes an edition of *De Montfort* that aims go give "the fullest account of the play's historical life as both a printed work and a performed theatrical piece" (83).

Bibliography

Primary Works

Abrams, M. H. et al., eds. *The Norton Anthology of English Literature.* 5th ed. New York: Norton, 1986.

——. *The Norton Anthology of English Literature.* 6th ed. New York: Norton, 1993.

Aikin, John. *An Essay on the Application of Natural History to Poetry.* London: J. Johnson, 1777.

Aikin, John and Anna Barbauld. *Evenings at Home, or the Juvenile Budget Opened.* 1792–96. 15th ed. New York: 1839.

——. *Miscellaneous Pieces in Prose.* London: J. Johnson, 1773.

Aikin, Lucy. *Epistles on women, exemplifying their character and condition in various ages and nations.* Boston: W. Wells and T. B. Wait, 1810.

Alfieri, Vittorio. *Myrrha. The Tragedies of Vittorio Alfieri.* Ed. Edgar Alfred Bowring. 1876. Westport, CT.: Greenwood Press, 1970. 2: 311–64.

Amis, Kingsley, ed. *The Faber Popular Reciter.* London: Faber and Faber, 1978.

Annual Register, or a View of the History, Politics and Literature, for the Year 1806. London: W. Otridge and Son et al., 1808.

Anti-Jacobin. June 1812: Review of Anna Barbauld's *Eighteen Hundred and Eleven.* 209–10.

Bage, Robert. *Man As He Is: A Novel.* 4 vols. London: William Lane, 1792.

Baillie, Joanna. *The Dramatic and Poetical Works (1851).* Hildesheim and New York: Georg Olms Verlag, 1976.

——. *A Series of Plays: in which it is attempted to delineate the stronger passions of the mind: each passion being the subject of a tragedy and a comedy.* London: T. Cadell and W. Davies, 1798. Oxford: Woodstock Books, 1990.

——. *Series of Plays (1798–1812).* Ed. D. H. Reiman. New York: Garland Press, 1977.

——. *A View of the General Tenour of the New Testament Regarding the Nature and Divinity of Jesus Christ.* London: Longman, 1831.

Barbauld, Anna Laetitia [See also Aikin]. *Hymns in Prose for Children.* 1781. New York: Garland Press, 1977.

——. *A Legacy for Young Ladies.* Ed. Lucy Aikin. London: Longman, 1826.

——. *Lessons for Children.* Edinburgh: T. Nelson, 1845.

——. *Memoir of Mrs. Barbauld.* Ed. Anna Letitia Le Breton. London: G. Bell, 1874.

——. *The Works with a Memoir by Lucy Aikin.* Ed. Lucy Aikin. 2 vols. London: Longman, Hurst, Rees, Orme, Brown and Green, 1825.

Barker, Jane. *Exilius: Or, The Banished Roman. The Entertaining Novels of Mrs. Jane Barker.* 2 vols. in 1. 2nd ed. London: Betteworth and Curll, 1719.

Bennett, Betty T., ed. *British War Poetry in the Age of Romanticism.* New York: Garland Press, 1976.

Berry, Mary. *The Fashionable Friends*. London: J. Ridgway, 1802.

Bloom, Harold and Lionel Trilling, eds. *Romantic Poetry and Prose*. New York: Oxford University Press, 1973.

Boaden, James. *Memoirs of Mrs. Inchbald*. 2 vols. London: Richard Bentley, 1833.

———. *Memoirs of Mrs. Siddons*. 2 vols. London: Henry Colburn, 1827.

Breen, Jennifer, ed. *Women Romantic Poets, 1785–1832*. London: Dent Everyman, 1992.

Browning, Elizabeth Barrett. *The Letters of Elizabeth Barrett Browning to Mary Russell Mitford 1836–1854*. Ed. Meredith B. Raymond and Mary Rose Sullivan. Winfield, KS: Wedgstone Press, 1983.

Burke, Edmund. *A Philosophical Enquiry into the Origin of Our Ideas of the Sublime and Beautiful*. Ed. James T. Boulton. New York: Columbia University Press, 1958.

Byron, George Gordon, Lord. *Byron's Letters and Journals*. Ed. Leslie A. Marchand. 12 vols. Cambridge, MA: Harvard University Press, 1973–82.

———. *Don Juan*. Ed. Jerome J. McGann. Vol. 5 of *The Complete Poetical Works*. 7 Vols. 1980–1992. Oxford: Clarendon Press, 1986.

———. *The Works of Lord Byron: Letters and Journals*. Ed. Rowland E. Prothero. 6 vols. London: John Murray, 1898–1901.

Campbell, Thomas. *Life of Mrs. Siddons*. 2 vols. London: Effingham Wilson, 1834.

Cave, Jane. *Poems on Various Subjects, Entertaining, Elegaic, and Religious*. 4th ed. Bristol: N. Biggs, 1794.

Chambers, Marianne. *The School for Friends*. London: Barker and Son, 1806.

Chorley, Henry F. *Memorials of Mrs. Hemans. With Illustrations of Her Literary Character from Her Private Correspondence*. 2 vols. London: Saunders and Otley, 1836.

Coleridge, Samuel Taylor. *Biographia Literaria*. Ed. J. Shawcross. 2 vols. Oxford: Oxford University Press, 1968.

———. *Collected Letters*. Ed. Earl Leslie Griggs. 6 vols. Oxford: Clarendon Press, 1956.

———. *Essays on His Times*. Ed. David V. Erdman. 3 vols. Princeton, NJ: Princeton University Press, 1978.

Coleridge, Samuel Taylor and William Wordsworth. *Lyrical Ballads, with a Few Other Poems*. Bristol: Longman, 1798.

Cottle, Joseph. *Early Recollections; Chiefly Relating to the Late Samuel Taylor Coleridge, during his long residence in Bristol*. 2 vols. London: Longman, 1837.

———. *The Complete Poetical Works*. Ed. H. S. Milford. London: Frowde, 1907.

Cowper, William. *The Poems of William Cowper, Esq., of the Inner Temple*. Boston: Crosby and Nichols, 1863.

De Quincey, Thomas. *Selected Writings of Thomas De Quincey*. Ed. Philip Van Doren Stern. New York: Random House, 1937.

De Staël, Germaine. *Corinne, or Italy*. 1807. Tr. and ed. Avriel H. Goldberger. New Brunswick, NJ: Rutgers University Press, 1987.

Descriptive Poetry; Being a Selection from the Best Modern Authors: Principally Having Reference to Subjects in Natural History. London: W. Savage, 1807.

D'Israeli, Issac. *The Literary Character; or the History of Men of Genius Drawn from Their Own Feelings and Confessions*. 5th ed. London: Edward Moxon, 1839.

Edgeworth, Maria. *Comic Dramas in Three Acts*. London: R. Hunter, 1817.

——. *Letters for Literary Ladies*. London: J. Johnson, 1795.

——. *Moral Tales for Young People*. 3 Vols. 1802. New York: Garland Press, 1974.

——. *The Parent's Assistant, or Stories for Children*. 2 Vols. 1800. New York: Garland Press, 1976.

Edgeworth, Maria and Richard Lovell Edgeworth. *Practical Education*. 1798. 2 Vols. New York: Garland Press, 1974.

Edgeworth, Richard L. *Essays on Professional Education*. London: J. Johnson, 1809.

Edinburgh Monthly Review 3 (1820): 373–83. Review of Hemans's *The Skeptic*.

Ellis, Mrs. [Sarah]. "Mrs. Fletcher, Late Miss Jewsbury." *The Christian Keepsake, and Missionary Annual*. Ed. Rev. William Ellis. London: Fisher, 1838. 30–42.

Fanshawe, Catherine Maria. *The Literary Remains of Catherine Maria Fanshawe*. London: Basil Montagu Pickering, 1876.

Feldman, Paula R. ed. *British Romantic Poetry by Women, 1770–1840*. Hanover, NH: University Press of New England, forthcoming.

Galindo, Catherine [Gough]. *Mrs. Galindo's Letter to Mrs. Siddons*. London: M. Jones, 1809.

Gilchrist, Mrs. [Anne]. *Mary Lamb*. London: Allen and Co., 1883.

Gilfillan, George. "Female Authors. No. 1 — Mrs. Hemans." *Tait's Edinburgh Magazine* NS 14 (1847): 359–63.

Godwin, William. *Memoirs of the Author of the Rights of Woman*. Ed. Richard Holmes. 1798. New York: Viking Penguin, 1987.

——. *Things as They Are; or, the Adventures of Caleb Williams*. 3 vols. London: Crosby, 1794.

Gregory, John. *A Father's Legacy to his Daughters*. London: Strahan and Codell, 1774.

Griffiths, Ann. *Gwaith Ann Griffiths*. Ed. O. M. Edwards. Conwy: Ab Owen, 1905.

Hands, Elizabeth. *The Death of Amnon. A Poem*. Coventry: N. Rollason, 1789.

Hawkins, Laetitia. *Memoirs, Anecdotes, Facts, and Opinions*. London: Longman, 1824.

Heckle, A. *The Florist: or, An Extensive and Curious Collection of Flowers for the Imitation of Young Ladies, either in Drawing, or in Needle-work*. London: John Bowles & Son, 1759.

Hemans, Felicia [Felicia Dorothea Browne]. *The Domestic Affections, and Other Poems*. London: T. Cadwell and W. Davies, 1812.

——. *Poems of Felicia Hemans*. Edinburgh: Blackwood, 1852.

——. *The Poetical Works of Mrs. Felicia Hemans*. London: Gall and Inglis, 1876.

——. *The Poetical Works of Mrs. Felicia Hemans*. London: Frederick Warne, n.d.

——. *Records of Woman: With Other Poems*. Edinburgh: Blackwood, 1828; London: T. Cadell, 1828.

——. *The Siege of Valencia. A Dramatic Poem. The Last Constantine: with Other Poems*. London: J. Murray, 1823.

——. *Songs of the Affections, with Other Poems*. Edinburgh: Blackwood, 1830; London: T. Cadwell, 1830.

——. *Tales, and Historic Scenes, in Verse*. London: John Murray, 1819.

——. *Works*. Ed. Mrs. Sigourny. 3 vols. New York: C. S. Francis, 1849–52.

——. *The Works of Mrs Hemans; With a Memoir of Her Life, by Her Sister.* 7 vols. Edinburgh: Blackwood & Sons, 1839; London: T. Cadell, 1839; Philadelphia: Lea and Blanchard, 1839.

Hereford, C. H. *The Age of Wordsworth.* London: G. Bell and Sons, 1897.

Hoare, Sarah. *A Poem on the Pleasures and Advantages of Botanical Pursuits.* Bristol: Philip Rose, [1825?].

Hooper, Lucy, ed. *The Lady's Book of Flowers and Poetry.* New York: Derby and Jackson, 1860.

Howitt, Mary. *Sketches of Natural History.* London: Effingham Wilson, 1834.

[Hughes, Harriett Mary (Browne)]. *Memoir of the Life and Writings of Felicia Hemans: By Her Sister; with an Essay on her Genius: By Mrs. Sigourney.* Philadelphia: Lea and Blanchard, 1839; New York: C. S. Francis, 1845.

Hughes, John. *Methodistiaeth Cymru: sef Hanes Blaenorol a Gwedd Bresenol y Methodistiaid Calfinaidd yng Nghymru.* Wrecsam: R. Hughes a'i Fab, 1854.

Inchbald, Elizabeth. *Remarks for the British Theatre (1806–09) By Elizabeth Inchbald.* Facsimile reproductions with an Introduction by Cecilia Macheski. Delmar, NY: Scholars' Facsimiles and Reprints, 1990.

——. *A Simple Story.* 1791. Ed. J. M. S. Tompkins. New York: Oxford University Press, 1988.

——. *The Wedding Day.* London: G. G. and J. Robinson, 1794.

Jackson, Mary Elizabeth. *Botanical Lectures.* London: J. Johnson, 1804.

[Jeffrey, Francis]. Review of *Records of Woman* (2nd ed.) and *The Forest Sanctuary* (2nd ed.). *Edinburgh Review* 50 (Oct. 1829): 32–47. In *Contributions to the Edinburgh Review by Francis Jeffrey.* Boston: Phillips, Sampson, 1854. 473–78.

[Jewsbury, Maria Jane.] "Original Papers. Literary Sketches No. 1. Felicia Hemans." *The Athenaeum* 171 (5 Feb. 1831): 104–5.

——. *The Three Histories: The History of an Enthusiast. The History of a Nonchalant. The History of a Realist.* 1830; Boston: Perkins & Marvin, 1831.

——. *Phantasmagoria; or Sketches of Life and Literature.* 2 vols. London: Hurst, Robinson, 1825.

Jordan, Dorothy. "Epilogue to Hannah Cowley's *The Belle's Stratagem.*" In *The Life of Mrs. Jordan.* 2 vols. London: Edward Bull, 1831. 1: 91–93.

Kant, Immanuel. *Kritik der reinen Vernunft.* In *Kant's gesammelte Schriften.* Vol. III. Berlin: Reimer, 1911.

Lamb, Charles. "On the Tragedies of Shakespeare." In *The Complete Works and Letters of Charles Lamb.* New York: Modern Library, 1935.

Lamb, Charles and Mary Lamb. *The Letters of Charles and Mary Anne Lamb.* Ed. Edwin W. Marrs, Jr. 3 Vols. Ithaca, NY: Cornell University Press, 1975–78.

——. *The Works of Charles and Mary Lamb.* Ed. E. V. Lucas. 7 Vols. London: Methuen, 1903–05.

Landon, Letitia Elizabeth (L.E.L.). *The Poetical Works of Letitia Elizabeth Landon.* Philadelphia: Jas. B. Smith, 1859.

——. *The Poetical Works of Miss Landon.* Philadelphia: E. L. Carey and A. Hart, 1841.

Lee, Sophia. *Almeyda, Queen of Granada.* London: W. Woodfall, 1796.

Lonsdale, Roger, ed. *Eighteenth-Century Women Poets: An Oxford Anthology.* New York: Oxford University Press, 1989.

———. *The New Oxford Book of Eighteenth Century Verse*. Oxford: Oxford University Press, 1984.

Macpherson, James. *The Poems of Ossian*. Boston: Phillips, Sampson, & Co., n.d.

Mahl, Mary R. and Helene Koon, eds. *The Female Spectator: English Women Writers Before 1800*. Bloomington: Indiana University Press, 1977.

Mavor, William. *The Lady's and Gentleman's Botanical Pocketbook*. London: Vernor and Hood, 1800.

Miller, Philip. *The Gardener's and Botanist's Dictionary*, collected and newly arranged by Thomas Martyn. 2 vols. London: F. C. and J. Rivington, 1807.

Mitford, Mary Russell. *The Dramatic Works of Mary Russell Mitford*. 2 vols. London: Hurst and Blackett, 1854.

Monthly Review Jan. 1806: 82. Review of Charlotte Smith's *Conversations Introducing Poetry: Chiefly on Subjects of Natural History*.

———. Jan. 1813: 98. Review of Frances Arabella Rowden's *A Poetical Introduction to the Study of Botany*,

Montolieu, Maria Henrietta. *The Enchanted Plants*. London: T. Bentley, 1800.

Moody, Elizabeth. *Poetic Trifles*. London: n.p., 1798.

More, Hannah. *Coelebs in Search of a Wife*. 1809. New York: Derby and Jackson, 1858.

———. *The Complete Works*. 7 vols. New York: Harper and Brothers, 1835, 1854.

———. *The Fatal Falsehood*. London: T. Cadell, 1779.

———. *The Miscellaneous Works*. 2 vols. London: Thomas Tegg, 1840.

———. *Strictures on the Modern System of Female Education*. 2 vols. London: T. Cadell and W. Davies, 1799. New York: Garland Press, 1974.

———. *Slavery: A Poem*. London: T. Cadell, 1788.

———. *The Works of Hannah More*. 11 vols. London: T. Cadell, 1830.

———. *The Works of Hannah More*. 2 vols. New York: Harper and Brothers, 1835.

Murray, Judith Sargent. "On the Equality of the Sexes." *Massachusetts Magazine* (March–April 1790). In *The Heath Anthology of American Literature*, Vol. 1, ed. Juan David Bruce-Novoa and Paul Lauter, Lexington, MA: D. C. Heath, 1990. 1133–34.

[Nott, John.] *Sappho: After a Greek Romance*. London: Cutbell and Martin, 1803.

Oliphant, Margaret. *The Autobiography and Letters of Mrs. M.O.W. Oliphant*. Ed. Mrs. Harry Coghill. New York: Dodd, Mead, 1899.

"Our Old Actors: 'Perdita.'" *Temple Bar* 51 (1877). 536–48.

Ovid. *The Metamorphoses*. Trans. Horace Gregory. New York: Mentor, 1960.

———. *Metamorphoses*. Trans. Frank J. Miller. 2nd ed. 1916. Cambridge, MA: Harvard University Press, 1984. 2 vols.

Owen, Daniel. *Gwen Tomos*. Trans. T. Ceiriog Williams and E. R. Harries. Wrexham: Hughes and Son, 1963.

———. *Rhys Lewis*. Trans. James Harris. Wrexham: Hughes and Son, 1915.

Owenson, Sydney. *France*. 2 vols. New York: James Eastburn & Co., 1817.

Palmer, Humphrey. *Kant's Critique of Pure Reason: An Introductory Text*. Cardiff: University College Cardiff Press, 1983.

Perkins, David, ed. *English Romantic Writers*. New York: Harcourt, Brace & World, 1967.

Polwhele, Richard. *The Unsex'd Females*. New York: William Cobbett, 1800.

Quarterly Review 24 (Oct. 1820): 130–39. Art. V. Review of several volumes by Hemans.

Quarterly Review 16 (June 1812): 309–13. Review of Anna Barbauld's "Eighteen Hundred and Eleven."

Reeve, Clara. *The Flowers at Court*. London: C. and R. Baldwin, 1809.

Robinson, Mary. *Complete Poetry*. Providence, RI: Brown University/National Endowment for the Humanities Women Writers Project, 1990.

———. *The False Friend: A Domestic Story*. 4 vols. London: T. N. Longman and O. Rees, 1799.

———. *Lyrical Tales*. London: Longman, 1800.

———. *Memoirs of the Late Mrs. Robinson, Written by Herself*. London: Wilks and Taylor, 1801. Reprinted London: Grolier Society, n.d.

———. *Sappho and Phaon. In a Series of Legitimate Sonnets*. London: privately printed, 1796. London: Minerva Press, 1813.

———. *The Widow, or a picture of modern times*. 2 vols. London: Hookham and Carpenter, 1794.

Rogers, Katharine M. and William McCarthy, eds. *The Meridian Anthology of Early Women Writers: British Literary Women from Aphra Behn to Maria Edgeworth, 1660–1800*. New York: New American Library, 1987.

Rogers, Samuel. *Recollections of the Table-Talk of Samuel Rogers*. Ed. Rev. Alexander Dyce. New Southgate: H. A. Rogers, 1887

Rossetti, Christina. "Speaking Likenesses." In *Forbidden Journeys: Fairy Tales and Fantasies by Victorian Women Writers*. Ed. Nina Auerbach and U. C. Knoepflmacher. Chicago: University of Chicago Press, 1992. 325–60.

Rossetti, W[illiam] M[ichael]. "Prefatory Notice." *The Poetical Works of Mrs. Hemans*. Philadelphia: J. B. Lippincott, 1881. 11–24.

Rousseau, Jean Jacques. *Emile*. Trans. Barbara Foxley. New York: Dutton, 1969.

———. *Letters on the Elements of Botany*. Trans. Thomas Martyn. London: B. and J. White, 1794.

Rowden, Frances Arabella. *A Poetical Introduction to the Study of Botany*. 3rd ed. London: G. and W. B. Whittaker, 1818.

Sandford, Mrs. John. *Woman, in Her Social and Domestic Character*. 2nd. ed. London: Longman, Rees, Orme, Brown, Green & Longman, 1832.

Seward, Anna. *Memoirs of the Life of Dr. Darwin*. Philadelphia: W. M. Poyntell, 1804.

Shelley, Mary Wollstonecraft. *Frankenstein*. New York: Bantam, 1981.

———. *Mathilda. The Mary Shelley Reader,* ed. Betty T. Bennett and Charles E. Robinson. New York: Oxford University Press, 1990. 173–246.

Shelley, Percy Bysshe. *Shelley's Poetry and Prose*. Ed. Donald H. Reiman and Sharon B. Powers. New York: Norton, 1977.

Sheridan, Frances. *The Discovery*. London: T. Davies, 1763.

Sigourney, Mrs. [Lydia H.]. "Essay on the Genius of Mrs. Hemans." Harriett Hughes vii–xxiii.

Smith, Charlotte. *The Banished Man*. London: T. Cadell and W. Davies, 1794. 4 vols.

———. *Celestina*. 1791. Ann Arbor: University Microfilms, 1972.

———. *Conversations Introducing Poetry: Chiefly on Subjects of Natural History*. 2 vols. London: Sampson Low, 1799.

——. *Desmond.* 1792. New York: Garland Press, 1974. 3 vols.

——. *Emmeline: The Orphan of the Castle.* 1788. London: Oxford University Press, 1971.

——. *Ethelinde, or The Recluse of the Lake.* London: T. Cadell, 1789. 5 vols.

——. *The Letters of a Solitary Wanderer.* London: Sampson Low, 1800–02. 5 vols.

——. *Marchmont.* 4 vols. 1796. Delmar, NY: Scholars' Facsimiles and Reprints, 1989.

——. *Minor Morals, Interspersed with Sketches of Natural History.* 2nd ed. 2 vols. London: Sampson Low, 1799.

——. *Montalbert.* 1795. Delmar, NY: Scholars' Facsimiles and Reprints, 1989. 3 vols.

——. *The Old Manor House.* 1793. London: Oxford University Press, 1969.

——. *The Poems of Charlotte Smith.* Ed. Stuart Curran. New York: Oxford University Press, 1993.

——. *Rambles Farther: A Continuation of Rural Walks.* Dublin: P. Wogan, 1796.

——. *Rural Walks: in Dialogues.* 2 Vols. Philadelphia: Thomas Stevens, 1795.

——. *The Wanderings of Warwick.* London: J. Bell, 1794.

——. *The Young Philosopher.* 1798. New York: Garland Press, 1974. 4 vols.

Southey, Robert, ed. *Annual Anthology.* 2 vols. London: Longman, 1799, 1800.

——. *The Contributions of Robert Southey to the Morning Post.* Ed. Kenneth Curry. University: University of Alabama Press, 1984.

——. *Metrical Tales and Other Poems.* London: Longman, 1805.

——. *Poems.* Bristol: Cottle; and London: G. G. and J. Robinson, 1797, 1799.

——. *Thalaba the Destroyer.* 2 vols. London: Longman, 1801.

Swift, Jonathan. *Gulliver's Travels and Other Writings.* Ed. Louis A. Landa. Boston: Houghton Mifflin, 1960.

Taylor, Jane. *Essays in Rhime, On Morals and Manners.* Boston: Wells and Lilly, 1816.

——. *Poetical Remains.* Ed. Isaac Taylor. Boston: C. D. Strong, 1842.

——. *Writings.* Intr. Isaac Taylor. 5 Vols. Boston: Perkins & Marrin, 1832.

Taylor, John. *The Needle's Excellency.* 1624. London: 1631.

Taylor, Rev. Isaac. *The Family Pen: Memorials, Biographical and Literary of the Taylor Family of Ongar.* 2 vols. London: Jackson, Walford and Hodder, 1867.

Thelwall, John. *Poems chiefly written in retirement.* 2nd ed. Hereford: W. H. Parker, 1801.

Tonna, Charlotte Elizabeth. *Personal Recollections.* 4th ed. London: Seeleys, 1854.

Wakefield, Priscilla. *An Introduction to Botany.* London: E. Newberry, 1796.

——. *Reflections on the Present Condition of the Female Sex.* London: J. Johnson, 1798.

Wallace, Eglinton. *The Whim.* London: W. Epps, 1795.

Warren, Mercy Otis. *The Plays and Poems of Mercy Otis Warren.* Ed. Franklin V. Benjamin. Delmar, NY: Scholars' Facsimiles and Reprints, 1908.

West, Jane. *A Tale of the Times.* 3 vols. 1799. 2nd ed. Alexandria: Cottom and Stewart, 1801.

Wheatley, Phillis. *The Collected Works of Phillis Wheatley.* Ed. John Shields. The Schomburg Library of Nineteenth-Century Black Women Writers. New York: Oxford University Press, 1988.

White, Henry Kirke. *The Poetical Works of Henry Kirke White*. Boston: Little, Brown, 1856.

Williams, Jane. *The Literary Women of England*. London: Saunders, Otley, 1861.

Williams, William. *Gweithiau William Williams, Pantycelyn*. Ed. Garfield H. Hughes. 2 vols. Caerdydd: Gwasg Prifysgol Cymru, 1967.

Withering, William. *An Arrangement of British Plants*. 3rd ed. 4 vols. Birmingham: n.p., 1796.

Wollstonecraft, Mary. *Mary and the Wrongs of Woman: or, Maria*. 1798. Ed. Gary Kelly. Oxford: Oxford University Press, 1976.

——. *Letters Written during a Short Residence in Sweden, Norway, and Denmark*. 1796. Ed. Richard Holmes. New York: Viking Penguin, 1987.

——. *A Vindication of the Rights of Woman*. 1792. New York: Penguin, 1985.

——. Review of *Emmeline*. *The Analytical Review* (July 1788): 26–27.

Woodring, Carl R., ed. *Prose of the Romantic Period*. Boston: Houghton Mifflin, 1951.

Woods, George Benjamin, ed. *English Poetry and Prose of the Romantic Period*. Chicago: Scott, Foresman, 1916.

Wordsworth, Dorothy. Grasmere Journal. In *Journals of Dorothy Wordsworth*. 2nd ed. Ed. Mary Moorman. Oxford: Oxford University Press, 1971.

——. *Letters of Dorothy Wordsworth, A Selection*. Ed. Alan G. Hill. Oxford: Clarendon Press, 1985.

Wordsworth, William. *Poems, in Two Volumes*. London: Longman, 1807.

——. *The Poems*. Ed. John O. Hayden. 2 vols. 1977. New Haven, CT: Yale University Press, 1981.

——. *The Poetical Works of William Wordsworth*. Ed. Ernest de Selincourt. 2nd ed. rev. Helen Darbishire. 5 vols. Oxford: Clarendon, 1952–59. Cited as *WPW*.

——. *The Prelude 1799, 1805, 1850*. Ed. Jonathan Wordsworth, M. H. Abrams, and Stephen Gill. New York: Norton, 1989.

Wordsworth, William, and Samuel Taylor Coleridge. *Lyrical Ballads 1798*. Ed. W. J. B. Owen. 2nd. ed. London: Oxford University Press, 1969.

Wordsworth, William and Dorothy Wordsworth. *Letters: The Early Years, 1787–1805*. Ed. Ernest de Selincourt, rev. Chester L. Shaver. Oxford: Clarendon Press, 1967.

——. *Letters: The Middle Years, 1806–1820*. Part 1. Rev. Mary Moorman. Oxford: Clarendon, 1969. Ed. Ernest de Selincourt.

——. *Letters: The Later Years, 1821–1853*. Ed. Rev. Alan G. Hill. Oxford: Clarendon Press, 1978–88.

SECONDARY WORKS

Aaron, Jane. *A Double Singleness: Gender and the Writings of Charles and Mary Lamb*. Oxford: Clarendon Press, 1991.

Abrams, M. H. *The Mirror and the Lamp: Romantic Theory and the Critical Tradition*. London: Oxford University Press, 1953; New York: Norton, 1958.

——. *Natural Supernaturalism: Tradition and Revolution in Romantic Literature*. New York: Norton, 1971.

Aikin, Susan Hardy. "Women and the Question of Canonicity." *College English* 48 (1986): 288–301.

Alic, Margaret. *Hypatia's Heritage: A History of Women in Science from Antiquity to the Late Nineteenth Century.* London: Women's Press, 1986.

Allchin, A. M. *Ann Griffiths.* Cardiff: University of Wales Press, 1976.

Ardener, Shirley, ed. *Women and Space: Ground Rules and Social Maps.* London: Croom Helm; New York: St. Martin's Press, 1981.

Auerbach, Nina. "Artists and Mothers: A False Alliance." *Women and Literature* 6 (1978): 3–15.

——. "Incarnations of the Orphan." *ELH* 42 (1975): 395–419.

——. *Private Theatricals: The Lives of the Victorians.* Cambridge, MA: Harvard University Press, 1990.

Bachelard, Gaston. *The Poetics of Space.* Trans. Maria Jolas. Boston: Beacon Press, 1969.

Bailyn, Bernard. *The Ideological Origins of the American Revolution.* Cambridge, MA: Belknap Press, Harvard University Press, 1967; enlarged edition 1992.

——. *The Origins of American Politics.* New York: Vintage, 1970.

Barish, Jonas. *The Antitheatrical Prejudice.* Berkeley: University of California Press, 1981.

Barrell, John. *English Literature in History, 1730–80: An Equal, Wide Survey.* New York: St. Martin's Press, 1983.

——. *The Political Theory of Painting from Reynolds to Hazlitt.* New Haven, CT: Yale University Press, 1986.

Bassnett, Susan. "Struggling with the Past: Women's Theatre in Search of a History." *New Theatre Quarterly* 5 (1989): 107–12.

Bewell, Alan. "'Jacobin Plants': Botany as Social Theory in the 1790s." *Wordsworth Circle* 20 (1989): 132–39.

——. "Keats's 'Realm of Flora.'" *Studies in Romanticism* 31 (1992): 71–98.

Biggs, Murray, ed. Special Issue, Byron's *Sardanapalus. Studies in Romanticism* 31, 3 (1992).

Bloom, Harold. *The Visionary Company: A Reading of English Romantic Poetry.* Ithaca, NY: Cornell University Press, 1961.

Bonham-Carter, Victor. *Authors by Profession.* 2 vols. London: Society of Authors, 1978.

Boose, Lynda E. "The Father's House and the Daughter in It: The Structure of Western Culture's Daughter-Father Relationship." In Boose and Flowers, *Daughters and Fathers.* 19–74.

Boose, Lynda E. and Betty S. Flowers, eds. *Daughters and Fathers.* Baltimore: Johns Hopkins University Press, 1989.

Bostetter, Edward E. "The Original Della Cruscans and the *Florence Miscellany.*" *Huntington Library Quarterly* 19 (May 1956): 177–300.

Bowstead, Diana. "Charlotte Smith's *Desmond*: The Epistolary Novel as Ideological Argument." In Schofield and Macheski, eds., *Fetter'd or Free?*

Brisman, Leslie. "*Maud*: The Feminine as the Crux of Influence." *Studies in Romanticism* 31 (1992): 21–43.

Bromwich, David. *Hazlitt: The Mind of a Critic.* New York: Oxford University Press, 1983.

Brooks, Cleanth. *Modern Poetry and the Tradition.* Chapel Hill: University of North Carolina Press, 1939.

Bruns, Roger. *"Am I Not a Man and a Brother": The Anti-Slavery Crusade of Revolutionary America, 1688–1788.* New York: Chelsea House, 1977.

Burns, Margie. "Oedipus and Apollonius." *International Journal of Moral and Social Studies* 7 (1992): 3–17.

Burroughs, Catherine. "Acting in the Closet: A Feminist Performance of Hazlitt's *Liber Amoris* and Keats's *Otho the Great.*" *European Romantic Review* 2, 2 (1992): 125–44.

Butler, Judith. "Gender Trouble, Feminist Theory, and Psychoanalytic Discourse." In *Feminism/Postmodernism.* Ed. Linda J. Nicholson. New York: Routledge, 1990. 324–40.

——. "Imitation and Gender Insubordination." In *Inside/Out: Lesbian Theories, Gay Theories.* Ed. Diana Fuss. New York: Routledge, 1991. 13–31.

Butler, Marilyn. *Maria Edgeworth: A Literary Biography.* Oxford: Oxford University Press, 1972.

Butterfield, Herbert. *Man of His Past: The Study of the History of Historical Scholarship.* Cambridge: Cambridge University Press, 1969.

Byrde, Penelope. *A Frivolous Distinction: Fashion and Needlework in the Works of Jane Austen.* Bath: Bath City Council, 1979.

Cameron, Kenneth Neill, ed. *Shelley and His Circle.* 2 vols. Cambridge, MA: Harvard University Press, 1961.

Cantor, Paul. "Stoning the Romance: The Ideological Critique of Nineteenth-Century Literature." *South Atlantic Quarterly* 88 (1989): 705–20.

Carhart, Margaret. *The Life and Work of Joanna Baillie.* Ed. Albert S. Cook. Yale Studies in English 64. New Haven, CT: Yale University Press, 1923.

Carlisle, Janice. *John Stuart Mill and the Writing of Character.* Athens: University of Georgia Press, 1992.

Carlson, Julie. "An Active Imagination: Coleridge and the Politics of Dramatic Reform." *Modern Philology* 86, 1 (1988): 22–33.

——. "Impositions of Form: Romantic Antitheatricalism and the Case Against Particular Women." *ELH* 60 (1993): 149–79.

Carlson, Marvin. *Theories of the Theatre: A Historical and Critical Survey from the Greeks to the Present.* Ithaca, NY: Cornell University Press, 1984. Expanded edition 1993.

Case, Sue-Ellen. *Feminism and Theatre.* New York: Methuen, 1988.

——, ed. *Performing Feminisms: Feminist Critical Theory and Theatre.* Baltimore: Johns Hopkins University Press, 1990.

——. "Toward Butch-Femme Aesthetic." In *Making a Spectacle: Feminist Essays on Contemporary Women's Theatre.* Ed. Lynda Hart. Ann Arbor: University of Michigan Press, 189. 282–99.

Case, Sue-Ellen and Janelle Reinelt, eds. *The Performance of Power: Theatrical Discourse and Politics.* Iowa City: University of Iowa Press, 1991.

Casteras, Susan P. *Images of Victorian Womanhood in English Art.* Rutherford, NJ: Fairleigh Dickinson University Press, 1987.

Castle, Terry. *Masquerade and Civilization: The Carnivalesque in Eighteenth-Century English Culture and Fiction.* Stanford, CA: Stanford University Press, 1986.

Chambers, Ross. *Room for Maneuver: Reading (the) Oppositional (in) Narrative.* Chicago: University of Chicago Press, 1991.

Chodorow, Nancy. *The Reproduction of Mothering: Psychoanalysis and the Sociology of Gender.* Berkeley: University of California Press, 1978.

Cixous, Hélène. "Castration or Decapitation?" *Signs* 7 (1982): 41–55.

——. "The Laugh of the Medusa." In *New French Feminisms: An Anthology.* Ed. Elaine Marks and Isabelle de Courtivron. Brighton: Harvester, 1980. 245–64.

Claridge, Laura and Elizabeth Langland, eds. *Out of Bounds: Male Writers and Gender(ed) Criticism.* Amherst: University of Massachusetts Press, 1990.

Clarke, Norma. *Ambitious Heights: Writing, Friendship, Love — The Jewsbury Sisters, Felicia Hemans, and Jane Welsh Carlyle.* London: Routledge, 1990.

Cooke, Michael G. *Acts of Inclusion: Studies Bearing on an Elementary Theory of Romanticism.* New Haven, CT: Yale University Press, 1979.

Cookson, J. E. *The Friends of Peace: Anti-War Liberalism in England, 1793–1815.* Cambridge: Cambridge University Press, 1982.

Copley, Stephen and John Whale, eds. *Beyond Romanticism: New Approaches to Texts and Contexts, 1780–1832.* New York: Routledge, 1992.

Corbett, Mary Jean. "Feminine Authorship and Spiritual Authority in Victorian Women Writers' Autobiographies." *Women's Studies* 18 (1990): 13–29.

——. *Representing Femininity: Middle-Class Subjectivity in Victorian and Edwardian Women's Autobiography.* New York: Oxford University Press, 1992.

Coward, Noel. *Operette.* London: Knopf, 1935.

Cowherd, Raymond G. *The Politics of English Dissent: The Religious Aspects of Liberal and Humanitarian Reform Movements from 1815 to 1848.* New York: New York University Press, 1956.

Cox, Jeffrey N., ed. *Seven Gothic Dramas, 1789–1825.* Athens: Ohio University Press, 1992.

Cross, Nigel. *The Common Writer: Life in Nineteenth-Century Grub Street.* Cambridge: Cambridge University Press, 1985.

Curran, Stuart. *Poetic Form and British Romanticism.* New York: Oxford University Press, 1986. Second edition 1989.

——. "Romantic Poetry: The 'I' Altered." In Mellor, ed., *Romanticism and Feminism.* 185–207.

——. "Romantic Poetry: Why and Wherefore?" In Curran, ed., *Cambridge Companion.* 216–35.

——. "Women Readers, Women Writers." In Curran, ed., *Cambridge Companion.*

——, ed. *The Cambridge Companion to British Romanticism.* Cambridge: Cambridge University Press, 1993.

Darton, F. J. Harvey. *Children's Books in England: Five Centuries of Social Life.* Ed. Brian Anderson. Cambridge: Cambridge University Press, 1982.

Davidoff, Leonore and Catherine Hall. *Family Fortunes: Men and Women of the English Middle Class, 1780–1850.* Chicago: University of Chicago Press, 1987.

Davies, E. T. *Religion in the Industrial Revolution in South Wales.* Cardiff: University of Wales Press, 1965.

Davis, David Brion. *The Problem of Slavery in the Age of Revolution 1770–1823*. Ithaca, NY: Cornell University Press, 1975.

Davis, Robin Reed. "Anglican Evangelicalism and the Feminine Literary Tradition: From Hannah More to Charlotte Brontë." Dissertation Duke University, 1982.

Davis, Tracy. "Questions for a Feminist Methodology in Feminist History." In Postlewait and McConachie, eds., *Interpreting the Theatrical Past: Essays for the Historiography of Performance*. Iowa City: University of Iowa Press, 1991. 59–81.

deGategno, Paul J. *James Macpherson*. Boston: Twayne, 1989.

DeJean, Joan. *Fictions of Sappho, 1546–1937*. Chicago: University of Chicago Press, 1989.

De Man, Paul. *The Rhetoric of Romanticism*. New York: Columbia University Press, 1984.

Derrida, Jacques. "Freud and the Scene of Writing." In *Writing and Difference*. Trans. Alan Bass. Chicago: University of Chicago Press, 1978. 196–231.

Diamond, Elin. "Brechtian Theory/Feminist Theory: Toward a Gestic Feminist Criticism." *Drama Review* 32 (1988): 82–94.

Dolan, Jill. *The Feminist Spectator as Critic*. Ann Arbor, MI: UMI Research Press, 1988.

Donkin, Ellen. "The Paper War of Hannah Cowley and Hannah More." In Schofield and Macheski, eds., *Curtain Calls*. 143–62.

DuPlessis, Rachel Blau. "For the Etruscans." In *The New Feminist Criticism: Essays on Women, Literature, and Theory*. Ed. Elaine Showalter. London: Virago, 1986. 271–91.

Ellison, Julie. "'Nice Arts' and 'Potent Enginery': The Gendered Economy of Wordsworth's Fancy." *Centennial Review* 33 (1989): 441–67.

Engell, James. *The Creative Imagination: Enlightenment to Romanticism*. Cambridge, MA: Harvard University Press, 1981.

Erdman, David V. "Lost Poem Found: The Cooperative Pursuit and Recapture of an Escaped Coleridge Sonnet of 72 Lines." *Bulletin of the New York Public Library* 65 (1961): 249–68.

Evenden, Michael. "Inter-Mediate Stages: Reconsidering the Body in 'Closet Drama.'" In *Reading the Social Body*. Ed. Catherine B. Burroughs and Jeffrey David Ehrenreich. Iowa City: University of Iowa Press, 1993.

Fergus, Jan and Janice Farrar Thaddeus. "Women, Publishers, and Money, 1790–1820." *Studies in Eighteenth-Century Culture* 17 (1987): 191–207.

Ferguson, Moira. *Subject to Others: British Women Writers and Colonial Slavery, 1670–1834*. New York: Routledge, 1992.

Field-Bibb, Jacqueline. *Women Towards Priesthood: Ministerial Politics and Feminist Praxis*. Cambridge: Cambridge University Press, 1991.

Flaherty, Gloria. "Empathy and Distance: Romantic Theories of Acting Reconsidered." *Theatre Research International* 15, 2 (1990): 125–41.

Fliegelman, Jay. *Prodigals and Pilgrims: The American Revolution Against Patriarchal Authority*. New York: Cambridge University Press, 1982.

Foster, Mark. "'Tintern Abbey' and Wordsworth's Scene of Writing." *Studies in Romanticism* 25 (1986): 75–95.

Froula, Christine. "The Daughter's Seduction: Sexual Violence and Literary History." In Boose and Flowers, eds., *Daughters and Fathers*. 111–35.

Garber, Marjorie. *Vested Interests: Cross-Dressing and Cultural Anxiety*. New York: Routledge, 1992.

Garner, Shirley Nelson, Claire Kahane, and Madelon Sprengnether, eds. *The M(o)ther Tongue: Essays in Feminist Psychoanalytic Interpretations*. Ithaca, NY: Cornell University Press, 1985.

Gatton, John Spalding. "'Put into Scenery': Theatrical Space in Byron's Closet Historical Dramas." In *The Theatrical Space*. Ed. James Redmond. Cambridge: Cambridge University Press, 1987. 139–49.

Gilbert, Sandra. "Life's Empty Pack: Notes Toward a Literary Daughteronomy." In Boose and Flowers, eds., *Daughters and Fathers*. 256–77.

Gilbert, Sandra and Susan Gubar. *Madwoman in the Attic: The Woman Writer and the Nineteenth-Century Literary Imagination*. New Haven, CT: Yale University Press, 1979.

Gilbert, Sky. "Closet Plays: An Exclusive Dramaturgy at Work." *Canadian Theatre Review* 59 (1989): 55–58.

Gilroy, Paul. *The Black Atlantic: Modernity and Double Consciousness*. Cambridge, MA: Harvard University Press, 1993.

Girouard, Mark. *Life in the English Country House: A Social and Intellectual History*. New Haven, CT: Yale University Press, 1978.

Golledge, Reginald G. and Gerard Rushton, eds. *Spatial Choice and Spatial Behavior: Geographic Essays on the Analysis of Preferences and Perceptions*. Columbus: Ohio State University Press, 1976.

Gross, John J. *The Rise and Fall of the Man of Letters: A Study of the Idiosyncratic and the Humane in Modern Literature*. New York: Macmillan, 1969.

Hart, Lynda. "Introduction: Performing Feminism." In *Making a Spectacle: Feminist Essays on Contemporary Women's Theatre*. Ed. Lynda Hart. Ann Arbor: University of Michigan Press, 1989. 1–21.

Hartman, Geoffrey H. *Criticism in the Wilderness: The Study of Literature Today*. New Haven, CT: Yale University Press, 1980.

——. "The Culture of Criticism." *PMLA* 99 (1984): 371–97.

——. *The Unremarkable Wordsworth*. Minneapolis: University of Minnesota Press, 1987.

——. *Wordsworth's Poetry: 1787–1814*. New Haven, CT: Yale University Press, 1964.

Hedges, Elaine. "The Needle or the Pen: The Literary Rediscovery of Women's Textile Work." In *Tradition and the Talents of Women*. Ed. Florence Howe. Urbana: University of Illinois Press, 1991. 338–64.

Heller, Janet Ruth. *Coleridge, Lamb, Hazlitt, and the Reader of Drama*. Columbia: University of Missouri Press, 1990.

Henriques, Ursula. *Religious Toleration in England, 1787–1833*. London: Routledge and Kegan Paul, 1961.

Herman, Judith Lewis with Lisa Hirschman. *Father-Daughter Incest*. Cambridge, MA: Harvard University Press, 1981.

Hickock, Kathleen. *Representations of Women: Nineteenth-Century British Women's Poetry*. Westport, CT: Greenwood Press, 1984.

Hirsch, Marianne. *The Mother/Daughter Plot: Narrative, Psychoanalysis, Feminism.* Bloomington: Indiana University Press, 1989.

Homans, Margaret. *Bearing the Word: Language and Female Experience in Nine-teenth-Century Women's Writing.* Chicago: University of Chicago Press, 1986.

——. *Women Writers and Poetic Identity: Dorothy Wordsworth, Emily Brontë, and Emily Dickinson.* Princeton, NJ: Princeton University Press, 1980.

Hopkins, Mary Alden. *Hannah More and Her Circle.* New York: Longmans, Green, 1947.

Hunter, J. Paul. "The World as Stage and Closet." In *British Theatre and the Other Arts, 1660–1800.* Ed. Shirley Strum Kenny. London and Toronto: Associated University Presses, 1984. 271–87.

Ingamells, John. *Mary Robinson and Her Portraits.* London: Wallace Collection, 1978.

Irigaray, Luce. *Speculum of the Other Woman.* Trans. Gillian C. Gill. Ithaca, NY: Cornell University Press, 1974.

Isani, Mikhtar Ali. "The British Reception of Wheatley's Poems on Various Subjects." *Journal of Negro History* 66 (1981): 144–49.

Issacharoff, Michael and Robin F. Jones, eds. *Performing Texts.* Philadelphia: University of Pennsylvania Press, 1988.

Jackson, Mary V. *Engines of Instruction, Mischief and Magic: Children's Literature from Its Beginnings to 1839.* Lincoln: University of Nebraska Press, 1989.

Jacobus, Mary. *Romanticism, Writing, and Sexual Difference: Essays on the Prelude.* New York: Oxford University Press, 1990.

——. "'That Great Stage Where Senators Perform': *Macbeth* and the Politics of Romantic Theatre." *Studies in Romanticism* (1983). Reprinted in *Romanticism, Writing, and Sexual Difference.*

——. *Tradition and Experiment in Wordsworth's Lyrical Ballads (1798).* Oxford: Clarendon Press, 1976.

Janeway, Elizabeth. *Man's World, Woman's Place: A Study in Social Mythology.* New York: William Morrow, 1971.

Johnston, Kenneth R. and Gene W. Ruoff, eds. *The Age of Wordsworth: Critical Essays on the Romantic Tradition.* New Brunswick, NJ: Rutgers University Press, 1987.

Jones, M. G. *Hannah More.* Cambridge: Cambridge University Press, 1952.

Jordan, Frank, ed. *The English Romantic Poets.* 4th ed. New York: MLA, 1985.

Kaplan, Cora. *Salt and Bitter and Good: Three Centuries of English and American Women Poets.* New York: Paddington, 1973.

Kelly, Linda. *The Marvellous Boy: The Life and Myth of Thomas Chatterton.* London: Weidenfeld and Nicolson, 1971.

Kiely, Robert. *The Romantic Novel in England.* Cambridge, MA: Harvard University Press, 1972.

King-Hele, Desmond. *Erasmus Darwin and the Romantic Poets.* London: Macmillan, 1986.

Klancher, Jon. "English Romanticism and Cultural Production." In *The New Historicism.* Ed. H. Aram Veeser. New York: Routledge, 1989. 77–88.

Kucich, Greg. "'A Haunted Ruin': Romantic Drama, Renaissance Tradition, and the Critical Establishment." *Wordsworth Circle* 23 (1992): 64–76.

Landry, Donna. *The Muses of Resistance: Laboring-Class Women's Poetry in Britain, 1739–1796*. Cambridge: Cambridge University Press, 1990.

Lanser, Susan Sniader. "Women Critics — and the Difference They Make: Response to Early Women Critics Session." Paper presented at the MLA Convention, San Francisco, 1991.

Lanser, Susan Sniader and Evelyn Torton Beck. "[Why] Are There No Great Women Critics?: And What Difference Does it Make?" In *The Prism of Sex: Essays in the Sociology of Knowledge*. Ed. Julia A. Sherman and Evelyn Torton Beck. Madison: University of Wisconsin Press, 1979. 79–91.

Larson, Magali Sarfatti. *The Rise of Professionalism: A Sociological Analysis*. Berkeley: University of California Press, 1977.

Lees-Milne, James, comp. *The Country House*. Oxford: Oxford University Press, 1982.

Leighton, Angela. *Victorian Women Poets: Writing Against the Heart*. New York and London: Wheatsheaf/Harvester, 1992.

Levin, Susan. *Dorothy Wordsworth and Romanticism*. New Brunswick, NJ: Rutgers University Press, 1987.

———. "Romantic Prose and Feminine Romanticism." *Prose Studies* 10, 2 (1987): 178–95.

Lévi-Strauss, Claude. *The Elementary Structures of Kinship*. Trans. James Harle Bell, John R. von Sturmer, and Rodney Needham. Ed. Rodney Needham. Rev. ed. Boston: Beacon Press, 1969.

Levy, Martin J. "Coleridge, Mary Robinson, and *Kubla Khan*." *Charles Lamb Bulletin* n.s. 77 (1992): 156–66.

Lewis, Saunders. *Meistri'r Canrifoedd: Ysgrifau ar Hanes Llenyddiaeth Cymraeg*. Ed. R. Geraint Gruffydd. Caerdydd: Gwasg Prifysgol Cymru, 1973.

Lieb, Laurie Yager. " 'The Works of Women Are Symbolical': Needlework in the Eighteenth Century." *Eighteenth-Century Studies* 10 (1986): 28–44.

Linkin, Harriet Kramer. "The Current Canon in British Romantics Studies." *College English* 53 (1991): 548–70.

Lipking, Lawrence. *Abandoned Women and Poetic Tradition*. Chicago: University of Chicago Press, 1988.

Liu, Alan. *Wordsworth: The Sense of History*. Stanford, CA: Stanford University Press, 1989.

Lloyd-Morgan, Ceridwen. "From Temperance to Suffrage?" In *Our Mother's Land: Chapters in Welsh Women's History 1830–1939*. Ed. Angela V. John. Cardiff: University of Wales Press, 1991. 135–58.

Lootens, Tricia. "Hemans and Home: Victorianism, Feminine 'Internal Enemies,' and the Domestication of National Identity." *PMLA* 109 (1994): 238–53.

Lovejoy, Arthur O. "On the Discrimination of Romanticisms." *PMLA* 39 (1924): 229–53. Reprinted in Lovejoy, *Essays in the History of Ideas*. Baltimore: Johns Hopkins University Press, 1948. 228–53.

Lutwack, Leonard. *The Role of Place in Literature*. Syracuse, NY: Syracuse University Press, 1984.

Macheski, Cecilia. "Penelope's Daughters: Images of Needlework in Eighteenth-Century Literature." In Schofield and Macheski, eds., *Fetter'd or Free*.

MacLeod, Duncan J. *Slavery, Race and the American Revolution.* Cambridge: Cambridge University Press, 1974.

Matheson, Ann. "The Influence of Cowper's *The Task* on Coleridge's Conversation Poems." In *New Approaches to Coleridge: Biographical and Critical Essays.* Ed. Donald Sultana. New York: Barnes and Noble, 1981.

Mayo, Robert. "The Contemporaneity of the *Lyrical Ballads.*" *PMLA* 69 (1954): 486–522.

McFarland, Thomas. *Romanticism and the Forms of Ruin: Wordsworth, Coleridge, and Modalities of Fragmentation.* Princeton, NJ: Princeton University Press, 1981.

McGann, Jerome J. "The Ancient Mariner: The Meaning of the Meanings." In McGann, *The Beauty of Inflections: Literary Investigations in Historical Method and Theory.* Oxford: Oxford University Press, 1985. 135–72.

———. *The Romantic Ideology: A Critical Investigation.* Chicago: University of Chicago Press, 1983.

———. "What Difference Do the Circumstances of Publication Make to the Interpretation of a Literary Work?" In *Literary Pragmatics.* Ed. Roger D. Sell. London: Routledge, 1991. 208–24.

McKerrow, Mary. "Joanna Baillie and Mary Brunton: Women of the Manse." In *Living by the Pen: Early British Women Writers.* Ed. Dale Spender. New York: Teachers College Press, 1992. 160–74.

Mellor, Anne K. *English Romantic Irony.* Cambridge, MA: Harvard University Press, 1980.

———. *Mary Shelley: Her Life, Her Fiction, Her Monsters.* New York: Methuen, 1988.

———. "Possessing Nature: The Female in *Frankenstein.*" In Mellor, ed., *Romanticism and Feminism.* 220–32.

———, ed. *Romanticism and Feminism.* Bloomington: Indiana University Press, 1988.

———. *Romanticism and Gender.* New York: Routledge, 1992.

Metzger, Lore. *One Foot in Eden: English Pastoral Poetry.* Chapel Hill: University of North Carolina Press, 1986.

"MLA Survey Casts Light on Canon Debate." *MLA Newsletter* 23 (Winter 1991): 12–15.

Moers, Ellen. *Literary Women.* 1963. New York: Anchor/Doubleday, 1977.

Mooney, Carolyn J. "Study Finds Professors Are Still Teaching the Classics, Sometimes in New Ways." *Chronicle of Higher Education* (6 November 1991): A1, A22.

Morgan, Derec Llwyd. *The Great Awakening in Wales.* Trans. Dyfnallt Morgan. London: Epworth Press, 1988.

Myers, Mitzi. "Reform or Ruin: 'A Revolution in Female Manners.'" *Studies in Eighteenth-Century Culture* 11 (1982): 199–216.

———. "Romancing the Moral Tale: Maria Edgeworth and the Problematics of Pedagogy." In *Romanticism and Children's Literature in Nineteenth-Century England.* Ed. James Holt McGavran, Jr. Athens: University of Georgia Press, 1991.

———. "Socializing Rosamond: Educational Ideology and Fictional Form." *Children's Literature Association Quarterly* 14 (1989): 52–63.

Myers, Sylvia Harcstark. *The Bluestocking Circle: Women, Friendship, and the Life of the Mind of Eighteenth-Century England.* Oxford: Clarendon Press, 1990.

Neff, Emery. *The Poetry of History: The Contribution of Literature and Literary Scholarship to the Writing of History since Voltaire.* New York: Columbia University Press, 1947.

Nemoianu, Virgil. "Literary Canons and Social Value Options." In *The Hospitable Canon: Essays on Literary Play, Scholarly Choice, and Popular Pressures.* Ed. Virgil Nemoianu and Robert Royal. Philadelphia and Amsterdam: John Benjamins, 1991. 215–47.

Nerlich, Graham. *The Shape of Space.* Cambridge: Cambridge University Press, 1976.

Newman, Beth. "'The Situation of the Looker-On': Gender, Narration, and Gaze in *Wuthering Heights.*" *PMLA* 105 (1990): 1029–41.

Oakley, Ann. *Woman's Work: The Housewife, Past and Present.* New York: Pantheon, 1974.

"Our Old Actors: 'Perdita.'" *Temple Bar* 51 (1877): 536–48.

Page, Judith. *Wordsworth and the Cultivation of Women.* Berkeley: University of California Press, forthcoming.

Parker, Rozsika. *The Subversive Stitch: Embroidery and the Making of the Feminine.* New York: Routledge, 1989.

Parrinder, Patrick. *Authors and Authority: A Study of English Literary Criticism and Its Relation to Culture, 1750–1900.* London: Routledge and Kegan Paul, 1977.

Parrish, Steven Maxfield. *The Art of the Lyrical Ballads.* Cambridge, MA: Harvard University Press, 1973.

Peckham, Morse. "Toward a Theory of Romanticism." *PMLA* 66 (1951): 5–23. Reprint in *Romanticism: Points of View.* Ed. Robert F. Gleckner and Herald E. Enscoe. 2nd. ed. Detroit: Wayne State University Press, 1974. 231–57.

Peterson, Linda H. "Female Autobiographer, Narrative Duplicity." *Studies in the Literary Imagination* 23 (1990): 165–76.

Poovey, Mary. *The Proper Lady and the Woman Writer: Ideology as Style in the Works of Mary Wollstonecraft, Mary Shelley, and Jane Austen.* Chicago: University of Chicago Press, 1984.

Postlewait, Thomas and Bruce McConachie, eds. *Interpreting the Theatrical Past: Essays in the Historiography of Performance.* Iowa City: University of Iowa Press, 1989.

Pratt, Mary Louise. *Imperial Eyes: Travel Writing and Transculturation* New York: Routledge, 1992.

Radhakrishnan, R. "Nationalism, Gender, and the Narrative of Identity." In *Nationalisms and Sexualities.* Ed. Andrew Parker, Mary Russo, Doris Sommer, and Patricia Yeager. New York: Routledge, 1992. 78–81.

Rajan, Tilottama. *Dark Interpreter: The Discourse of Romanticism.* Ithaca, NY: Cornell University Press, 1980.

Rawley, James A. "The World of Phillis Wheatley." *New England Quarterly* 50 (1977): 666–77.

Reed, Walter L. "Commentary." *New Literary History* 16 (1985): 671–83.

Reill, Peter Hans. *The German Enlightenment and the Rise of Historicism.* Berkeley: University of California Press, 1975.

Reiman, Donald H. *Shelley and His Circle, 1773–1822*. 8 vols. to date. Cambridge, MA: Harvard University Press, 1961–.

Richardson, Alan. *A Mental Theater: Poetic Drama and Consciousness in the Romantic Age*. University Park: Pennsylvania State University Press, 1988.

Ritterbush, Philip C. *Overtures to Biology: The Speculations of Eighteenth-Century Naturalists*. New Haven, CT: Yale University Press, 1964.

Robinson, Lillian. "Treason Our Text: Feminist Challenges to the Literary Canon." In *The New Feminist Criticism: Essays on Women, Literature, and Theory*. Ed. Elaine Showalter. New York: Pantheon, 1985. 105–20.

Robinson, William H. "Phillis Wheatley in London." *CLA Journal* 21 (1977): 187–201.

Rodgers, Betsy. *Georgian Chronicle: Mrs. Barbauld and Her Family*. London: Methuen, 1958.

Rogers, Katharine M. *Frances Burney: The World of "Female Difficulties."* Hemel Hempstead: Harvester Wheatsheaf, 1990.

Ross, Marlon. *The Contours of Masculine Desire: Romanticism and the Rise of Women's Poetry*. New York: Oxford University Press, 1989.

———. "Romantic Quest and Conquest: Troping Masculine Power in the Crisis of Poetic Identity." In Mellor, ed., *Romanticism and Feminism*. 26–51.

Ruoff, Gene W. "Romantic Lyric and the Problem of Belief." In *The Romantics and Us: Essays on Literature and Culture*. Ed. Gene W. Ruoff. New Brunswick, NJ: Rutgers University Press, 1990. 288–302.

Sack, Robert D. *Conceptions of Space in Social Thought: A Geographic Perspective*. Minneapolis: University of Minnesota Press, 1980.

Sanders, Valerie. "'Absolutely an act of duty': Choice of Profession in Autobiographies by Victorian Women." *Prose Studies* 9 (1986): 54–70.

Saunders, J. W. *The Profession of English Letters*. London: Routledge and Kegan Paul, 1969.

Schofield, Mary Anne and Cecilia Macheski, eds. *Curtain Calls: British and American Women and the Theater, 1660–1800*. Athens: Ohio University Press, 1991.

———. *Fettr'd or Free? British Women Novelists, 1670–1815*. Athens: Ohio University Press, 1986.

Schor, Naomi. *Reading in Detail: Aesthetics and the Feminine*. New York: Routledge, 1989.

Sedgwick, Eve Kofosky. *Epistemology of the Closet*. Berkeley: University of California Press, 1990.

Shaffer, Elinor. *"Kubla Khan" and the Fall of Jerusalem: The Mythological School in Biblical Criticism and Secular Literature, 1770–1880*. Cambridge: Cambridge University Press, 1975.

Showalter, Elaine. *Sister's Choice: Tradition and Change in American Women's Writing*. Oxford: Clarendon Press, 1991.

Shteir, Ann B. "Botany in the Breakfast Room: Women and Early Nineteenth-Century British Plant Study." In *Uneasy Careers and Intimate Lives: Women in Science, 1789–1979*. Ed. Pnina G. Abir-Am and Dorinda Outram. New Brunswick, NJ: Rutgers University Press, 1987. 31–43.

Silverman, Kenneth. *A Cultural History of the American Revolution*. New York: Columbia University Press, 1976.

Simpson, David. "Romanticism, Criticism and Theory." In Curran, ed., *Cambridge Companion.* 1–24.

Sinfield, Alan. "Closet Dramas: Homosexual Representation and Class in Postwar British Theater." *Genders* 9 (1990): 112–31.

Spacks, Patricia Meyer. *Desire and Truth: Functions of Plot in Eighteenth-Century Novels.* Chicago: University of Chicago Press, 1990.

———. " 'Ev'ry Woman is at Heart a Rake.' " *Eighteenth-Century Studies* 8 (1974): 27–46.

Spender, Dale. *Women of Ideas and What Men Have Done to Them.* 1982. Reprint London: Pandora, 1988.

Staub, Kristina. "Women's Pastimes and the Ambiguity of Female Self-Identification in Fanny Burney's *Evelina.*" *Eighteenth-Century Studies* 10 (1986): 58–72.

Steadman, Susan M. *Dramatic Re-Visions: An Annotated Bibliography of Feminism and Theatre, 1972–1988.* Chicago: American Library Association, 1991.

Stewart, Susan. *On Longing: Narratives of the Miniature, the Gigantic, the Souvenir, the Collection.* Baltimore: Johns Hopkins University Press, 1984.

Stone, Lawrence. *The Family, Sex and Marriage in England, 1500–1800.* London: Weidenfeld and Nicolson, 1977.

Suleiman, Susan Rubin. "Writing and Motherhood." In Garner et al., eds., *The M(o)ther Tongue.* 352–77.

Sweet, Nanora. "History, Imperialism, and the Aesthetics of the Beautiful: Hemans and the Post-Napoleonic Moment." In *At the Limits of Romanticism: Essays in Cultural and Materialist Criticism.* Ed. Mary A. Favret and Nicola J. Watson. Bloomington: Indiana University Press, 1994.

Swindells, Julia. *Victorian Writing and Working Women: The Other Side of Silence.* Madison: University of Wisconsin Press, 1985.

Symons, Arthur. *The Romantic Movement in English Poetry.* New York: Dutton, 1909.

Taylor, Donald S. *Thomas Chatterton's Art: Experiments in Imagined History.* Princeton, NJ: Princeton University Press, 1978.

Thorslev, Peter. "Incest as Romantic Symbol." *Comparative Literature Studies* 2 (1965): 41–58.

Todd, Janet. *Sensibility: An Introduction.* London: Methuen, 1986.

Trinder, Peter W. *Mrs. Hemans.* Aberystwyth: University of Wales Press, 1984.

Tuan, Yi-Fu. *Space and Place: The Perspective of Experience.* Minneapolis: University of Minnesota Press, 1977.

Twitchell, James B. *Forbidden Partners: The Incest Taboo in Modern Culture.* New York: Columbia University Press, 1987.

Uphaus, Robert W. and Gretchen M. Foster, eds. *The "Other" Eighteenth Century: English Women of Letters, 1660–1800.* East Lansing, MI: Colleagues Press, 1991.

van Fraassen, Bas C. *An Introduction to the Philosophy of Time and Space.* New York: Random House, 1970.

Watkins, Daniel P. "Class, Gender, and Social Motion in Joanna Baillie's *De Montfort.*" *Wordsworth Circle* 23, 2 (1992): 109–17.

Watson, J. R., ed. *English Poetry of the Romantic Period: 1789–1830.* London: Longman, 1985.

Watts, Michael R. *The Dissenters.* 2 vols. Oxford: Clarendon Press, 1978.

Waugh, Evelyn. *Brideshead Revisited*. Boston: Little, Brown, 1945.

Wehrli, Max. *Johann Jakob Bodmer und die Geschichte der Literatur.* Frauenfeld: Huber, 1936.

Wellek, René. *Concepts of Criticism*. New Haven, CT: Yale University Press, 1963.

——. "The Concept of Romanticism in Literary Scholarship." *Comparative Literature* 1 (1949): 1–23, 147–72. Reprint in Wellek, *Concepts of Criticism*, 128–98.

——. "Romanticism Re-examined." In *Concepts of Criticism*. 199–221.

Whitaker, Thomas R. "Review Essay: Some Reflections on 'Text' and 'Performance.'" *Yale Journal of Criticism* 3 (1989): 143–61.

Whiting, Gertrude. *Old-Time Tools and Toys of Needlework*. 1928. New York: Dover, 1971.

Wolf, F. A. *Prolegomena to Homer.* 1795. Trans. and ed. Anthony Grafton, Glenn W. Most, and James E. G. Zetzel. Princeton, NJ: Princeton University Press, 1985.

Wolfson, Susan. "Individual in Community: Dorothy Wordsworth in Conversation with William." In Mellor, ed., *Romanticism and Feminism*. 139–66.

——. "Questioning 'The Romantic Ideololgy': Wordsworth." *Revue Internationale de Philosophie* 3 (1990): 429–47.

Zall, P. M. "The Cool World of Samuel Taylor Coleridge: The Question of Joanna Baillie." *Wordsworth Circle* 23, 1 (1982): 17–20.

Contributors

JANE AARON, a Senior Lecturer in English at the University of Wales, Aberystwyth, is the author of *A Double Singleness: Gender and the Writings of Charles and Mary Lamb* (1991) and co-editor of the volumes *Out of the Margins: Women's Studies in the Nineties* (1991) and *Our Sisters' Land: The Changing Identity of Women in Wales,* to be published in 1994. She is currently working on a Welsh-language book on nineteenth-century Welsh women's writings.

CATHERINE B. BURROUGHS is Assistant Professor of English and Chair of the Women's Studies Program at Cornell College. She is editor with Jeffrey Ehrenreich of *Reading the Social Body* (1993) and has published articles in *European Romantic Review, CEA Critic, Feminist Teacher, Modern Language Studies,* and *Encyclopedia of Romanticism.* Her research focuses on Joanna Baillie and feminist theatre theory, and she is a member of the Actors' Equity Association.

STUART CURRAN is Professor of English at the University of Pennsylvania and editor of the *Keats-Shelley Journal.* His recent publications include *Poetic Form and British Romanticism* (1986), and two edited volumes, *The Poems of Charlotte Smith* (1993) and *The Cambridge Companion to British Literature* (1992).

JULIE ELLISON is Professor of English at the University of Michigan. Her first two books (*Emerson's Romantic Style,* 1986, and *Delicate Subjects: Romanticism, Gender, and the Ethics of Understanding,* 1990) focused on American and British romanticism. Her current project, "Cato's Tears: Vicarious Relations in Anglo-American Culture," expands received notions of the "Age of Sensibility" in order to rethink the relationships among nationality, subjectivity, gender, race, and sensibility in eighteenth-century writings by "sensitive" intellectuals on both sides of the Atlantic. She is also working on the recent emergence of "emotion theory."

SUSAN ALLEN FORD is Associate Professor of English and Writing Center Coordinator at Delta State University in Cleveland, Mississippi, where she teaches courses in British Romanticism and the English Novel. She has written on a variety of topics related to prose fiction, including Jane Austen, Southern women writers, and women detective novelists, as well as on the expansion of the literary canon and issues of pedagogy in writing centers.

JOEL HAEFNER teaches writing and literature and cajoles computers at Illinois State University. He has published articles in *College English, The Wordsworth Circle, SEL, Prose Studies, Victorian Periodicals Review, College Literature, The Charles Lamb Bulletin,* and other journals. He is currently working on a study of women's theories of writing during the Romantic era.

JEROME MCGANN is John Stewart Bryan Professor of English, University of Virginia. His recent *New Oxford Book of Romantic Period Verse* (1993) offers a major historical revision of the period's poetry.

JUDITH PASCOE, Assistant Professor of English at the University of Iowa, is writing a book on poetry and theatricality in the Romantic period. She is also editing a collection of Mary Robinson's poetry.

LINDA H. PETERSON is Professor of English at Yale University and author of *Victorian Autobiography: The Tradition of Self-Interpretation* (1986). Her recent essays include "Harriet Martineau: Masculine Discourse, Female Sage" in *Victorian Sages and Cultural Discourse* (1990); "Institutionalizing Women's Autobiography: Nineteenth-Century Editors and the Shaping of an Autobiographical Tradition" in *The Culture of Autobiography;* and "Sappho and the Making of Tennysonian Lyric" in *ELH.*

KATHARINE M. ROGERS, Professor Emerita, City University of New York, has co-edited *The Meridian Anthology of Early British Women Writers* and edited *The Meridian Anthology of Early American Women Writers.* Her *Frances Burney: The World of "Female Difficulties"* was published in 1990. Her edition, *The Meridian Anthology of Restoration and Eighteenth-Century Plays by Women,* appeared in 1994.

MARLON B. ROSS is Associate Professor of English and a faculty associate of the Center for Afro-American and African Studies at the University of Michigan in Ann Arbor. He is the author of *The Contours of Masculine Desire: Romanticism and the Rise of Women's Poetry* (1989).

CAROL SHINER WILSON teaches literature and Women's Studies at Muhlenberg and Lafayette Colleges and serves as Coordinator of the Women's Studies Coalition, Lehigh Valley Association of Independent Colleges. Her essays and reviews have appeared in *Mosaic, Annals of Scholarship, Nineteenth-Century Studies, European Romantic Review,* and

Psychohistory Review. She is currently editing two novels by Jane Barker for Oxford University Press and is working on an interdisciplinary book tentatively titled *Pricking Our Conscience: Needlework in Anglo-American Literature and Culture.*

SUSAN J. WOLFSON is Professor of English at Princeton University and the author of several essays and articles on English Romantic writing, as well as *The Questioning Presence: Wordsworth, Keats, and the Interrogative Mode in Romantic Poetry* (1986). Her essay in this volume is related to her book in development about gender and Romantic writing, *Figures on the Margin.*

Index

This book has been set in Linotron Galliard. Galliard was designed for Mergenthaler in 1978 by Matthew Carter. Galliard retains many of the features of a sixteenth-century typeface cut by Robert Granjon but has some modifications that give it a more contemporary look.

Printed on acid-free paper.

PR 457 .R4556 1994

Re-visioning romanticism

DATE DUE			
APR 1 5 2000			